Being Smart about Gifted Children:

A Guidebook For Parents and Educators

Dona J. Matthews, Ph.D.
Joanne F. Foster, Ed.D.

Great Potential Press, Inc.
Scottsdale, Arizona
www.giftedbooks.com

Great Potential Press, Inc.
www.giftedbooks.com

Being Smart about Gifted Children:
A Guidebook for Parents and Educators

Cover design: Mary Velgos Design
Interior design: The Printed Page

Published by Great Potential Press, Inc.
P.O. Box 5057
Scottsdale, AZ 85261

© 2005 by Great Potential Press
08 07 06 05   5 4 3 2

Library of Congress Cataloging-in-Publication Data

Matthews, Dona J., 1951-
    Being smart about gifted children : a guidebook for parents and
educators / Dona J. Matthews, Joanne F. Foster.
        p. cm.
    Includes bibliographical references and index.
    ISBN 0-910707-66-9 (pbk.)
    1. Gifted children—Education—Handbooks, manuals, etc. I. Foster,
Joanne F., 1953- II. Title.
    LC3993.M36 2004
    371.95—dc22

                                                    2004015847

Acknowledgments

We want to thank everyone at Great Potential Press for their confidence in our ability as first-time book authors and for working so hard with us to bring to fruition a manuscript that we hope you find informative. Janet Gore, Jim Webb, and Jen Rosso have been dedicated in their efforts to help make this the best book it could possibly be.

There have been many important mentors along the way for us both. Dona would particularly like to acknowledge Dan Keating, whose extraordinary intellectual mastery and commitment to the largest best truth will always be a model; Rena Subotnik, whose thoughtfully perceptive wisdom and generous support create bountiful possibilities; Don and Joyce Matthews, whose commitment to learning and engagement in life are the foundation of everything else; and her colleagues at the Ontario Institute for Studies in Education of the University of Toronto (OISE/UT) and at Hunter College, City University of New York, whose friendship and support is invaluable. Joanne would like to acknowledge Debbie Gladstone and Rhona Shulman, who offer ongoing encouragement and latitude in her board-based consultancy practice; her colleagues at more schools than can possibly be mentioned here; the many individuals who have provided guidance and collaborative support at OISE/UT; and Clara and Nathan Stein, and Shirley and the late David Foster, who instilled in her a lifelong love of learning that serves to underlie all personal and professional growth.

We would like to thank our preliminary readers, and in particular, Linda Edwards for understanding, fine-tuning, and helping to breathe life into our manuscript. We would also like to express our appreciation to all of the wonderful educators, parents, and children with whom we have worked over the past 30 years. We are delighted to have this opportunity to share their voices and viewpoints with you. And a special thanks goes to all of our friends and extended family members who were always there to cheer us on and sometimes just to listen.

Our husbands have been an integral part of the process of writing this book. We cannot say enough to thank Stephen Gross and Garry Foster for their boundless support and patience, and for being there with humor, perspective, inspiration, comfort, and love every step along the way.

Finally, we would like to dedicate this book to our children. We have learned more from Robin, Erin, Eric, and Michele than they will ever realize—until perhaps one day when they have children of their own.

Contents

Foreword. xi

Preface xiii

Poem: They Tell Me I'm Gifted xvi

Section I. Being Smart about Giftedness 1

Chapter 1 . Perspectives and Paradigm Shifts 3
    What Is Giftedness? 3
    Two Perspectives: Mystery and Mastery 5
    Shifting Paradigms 13
    Origins: Nature or Nurture? 15
    Domains of Competence 16
    Is Learning Easy? 18
    Other Terms 19
    Historical Perspective 22
    Guidelines and a Definition 24
    Questions 27

Chapter 2. Creativity and Giftedness 31
    What Is Creativity? 31
    Can We Measure Creativity? 35
    Nurturing Creativity 37
    Creative Parenting and Teaching 39

Section II. Being Smart about Testing, Identification,
    and Labeling 41

Chapter 3. Questions about Testing 43
    Who Needs Testing? 43
    What Are the Key Concepts? 46
    What Purpose Does Testing Serve? 49
    When to Test? 50

Where to Test? 56
Why Test? 57

Chapter 4. Assessments and Tests 61
It Starts with the Teacher: Classroom Assessment 61
Standardized Academic Achievement Testing 64
High-Ceiling and Above-Level Testing 66
Intelligence Testing: What It Is and Is Not 68
Aptitude Tests 73
Creativity Testing. 73
Career Interest Inventories 74
Other Information Sources 76
School Reports 77
A Synopsis 79

Chapter 5. Identification and Labeling Issues 81
Identifying Giftedness 81
Processes, Policies, and Problems 83
Recommendations 85
Questionable Approaches 90
Early Identification. 92
The Need for Information. 94
Labeling 98
Accentuating the Positives 100
Parents' Roles 102

Section III. Being Smart about Meeting Gifted Learning Needs . . 105

**Chapter 6. Adaptations: The Gifted Learner in the
Regular Classroom** 107
A Flexible Range of Educational Options. 108
Options in the Regular Classroom 111

Chapter 7. Alternative Educational Options 135
Whole-Grade Acceleration. 135
Gifted Classes 139
Second Language Immersion and Dual Track Programs . . . 142
Specialty Subjects. 145
Specialized and Alternative Schools. 147
Private and Independent Schools 148
Home Schooling 150
Summary 154

Chapter 8. Stretching the Boundaries 157
   Extracurricular Enrichment 158
   Mentorships 159
   Career Exploration 164
   Books 165
   Travel 168
   Do-Nothing Times 170

Chapter 9. Adapting to Change 173
   Flexibility 175
   Support 177
   Choosing a School 179
   A School Choice Experience 182
   Decisions 187

Section IV. Being Smart about Gifted Kids 191

Chapter 10. Motivation and Other Issues 193
   Curiosity 193
   Motivators 197
   Extrinsic and Intrinsic Motivation 202
   Achievement Issues 204
   Practical Ideas 218

Chapter 11. Emotional, Social, and Behavioral Concerns 223
   Gifted Labeling 223
   Self-Concept 226
   Emotional Intelligence 227
   Perspective 228
   Social Concerns 232
   Computer Time 236
   Social Skills 237
   Leadership 240
   Behavioral Concerns 241
   Bullying, Anger, and Conflict Resolution 242
   Well-Being 247

Chapter 12. Gifted Development 253
   Nature or Nurture? Back to Origins 253
   Developmental Pathways 254
   The Importance of Play 256
   Being Smart by Being Funny 258
   "Rot" to "Rotation" 261

Young Gifted Children 263
Adolescence (Sigh) 267
Academic and Career Counseling 274

Chapter 13. Different Ways of Being Gifted. **281**
Differences between Boys and Girls 282
Cultural Differences 286
Extreme Giftedness 291
Learning Problems 294

Section V. Being Smart about Families, Advocates,
and Educators **305**

Chapter 14. Parents. **307**
The Parental Perspective 307
Advocacy: Helping Schools Meet Children's Needs 310
Supportive Parenting 317
Sibling Relationships 321
Gifted Adolescents 328
Seeking Professional Help 330

Chapter 15. Teacher Development **337**
Teacher Development 338
Formats 341
Administrative Support 346
What Can Parents Expect? 348
A Dynamic Scaffolding Model (DSM) of Teacher
Development 351
Engagement in Teaching and Learning 357

Chapter 16. Optimal Learning for All Children. **363**
Trends and Directions in Canada 363
American and International Perspectives. 367
Sharing Resources in a Changing World 374
A University-Based Resource Center 377
Keeping Up-to-Date 381
Conclusion 383

Appendix. **385**
Interpreting Test Scores 385
Assessments and Young Children 393
A Case Study with Excerpts from a Psychoeducational
Report. 395

References 399

Index 413

About the Authors 423

List of Tables

Table 1.1. A Comparison of the Mystery and
Mastery Models of Giftedness 10

Table 4.1. A Synopsis of Assessment Tools 80

Table 12.1. Responding to High-Level Development in
Young Children. 266

Table A.1. Standard Score Classifications 387

Table A.2. Translating Standard Scores into Percentiles 388

Foreword

Psychology has lots to offer gifted child studies and gifted education, and it always has. Most of the patriarchs and matriarchs of the field were trained in the discipline, as were many of their rebellious "sons" and "daughters." This wonderful volume continues that tradition by promoting evidence-based practices that have been carefully culled and vetted through psychological science, education, and evaluation research, as well as by the deep expertise of the authors.

Dona Matthews' and Joanne Foster's conceptualization of "Mastery" versus "Mystery" approaches for gifted education and gifted child studies unveils the source of conflicting outcomes we see in the gifted education literature. They make it clear that unless the preparation provided to teachers and the consultation we provide to parents are grounded in some form of definitional consensus, our field will undermine its ability to play a greater role at the table of school reform and policy development.

The authors explicate the arena of gifted education in a number of constructive ways. They do not accept hearsay or ideology as an excuse for promoting practices in identification, curriculum, evaluation, or counseling services. They provide solid advice to parents, educators, and decision makers in language that is accessible to all interested readers. Every reader, from those with little exposure to the field other than experiences with their own children and their children's teachers, to those who have been immersed for decades in serving the needs of gifted children, will find this book a welcome reference.

Rena F. Subotnik, Ph.D.
Director
Center for Gifted Education Policy
American Psychological Association

Foreword

Preface

This book is about understanding and supporting optimal development in all children. It emerges from our experience with students who have exceptionally advanced learning needs and from our commitment to making sure that all children have a chance to develop their abilities. We consider voices and viewpoints of various stakeholders in the work of educating children, and we look at different ways of supporting optimal development in both those who have been labeled gifted and those who have not.

It is perhaps obvious but nonetheless important to note that there is no one gifted experience. If we are to support gifted-level development for the children in our lives—that is, to provide the best possible guidance, challenge, and encouragement—we must start by reflecting upon individual differences, including emotional, social, academic, developmental, and many others. We can then consider the various factors and possibilities at school, at home, and in the world. There is no single formula for living or working with gifted children. However, there are some perspectives and understandings that can help us make good and informed decisions, and find ways to make a difference so that children experience their world as an engaging place in which to live, laugh, and learn.

We have been involved in teaching as well as in developing gifted education curriculum at several different levels—in the classroom, for initial teacher preparation, for graduate education, and for professional development courses, workshops, and seminars. For many years now we have actively consulted on gifted issues to public and independent schools, and to boards and districts of education. We have done research on and writing about gifted development and have consulting practices specializing in work with gifted children and adolescents. We have addressed parent groups, administrators, and professional colleagues across North America, and we have presented information on a wide range of issues related to educating and nurturing gifted children.

In response to many, many requests for this book over the years, we now want to share what we've learned. The Canadian poet Irving Layton once wrote, "They who are driven dance best." Those six words beautifully convey our passion and enthusiasm for the writing of this book. We have experienced the writing process as a combination of serious committed effort and lyrical pleasure.

Although we direct the book primarily to parents and teachers, we think that the ideas, experiences, and issues we discuss will also be of interest to other professionals, including prospective teachers, teacher educators, school counselors, psychologists, administrators, and policy makers. We discuss a wide range of topics that we have found to be pertinent, including some not often covered in other books about gifted development. For example, we know from our work in the field that the testing, assessment, and identification of giftedness are generally not well understood and are the objects of much interest as well as confusion. We hope you will find our discussions of these topics comprehensive and thought-provoking.

We offer some alternative approaches to gifted programming, ideas about teacher development strategies, advice about advocacy, a consideration of the relationship between creativity and giftedness, and a description of our own dynamic scaffolding approach to gifted consultancy. We also discuss many issues that affect gifted kids' well-being, including social, emotional, extracurricular, and motivational factors. Throughout the book, you will hear real voices that belong to the adults and children with whom we work, and you'll read vignettes of gifted experiences we've lived or come to know.

In our work, and throughout these pages, we focus on evidence-based understandings of high-level development. We challenge much of the conventional thinking about gifted education and include only those policies and practices which are solidly grounded theoretically and/or empirically. As you read this book, you may recognize that some of our perspectives differ from those popularized by others working in the field of gifted education. We hope you find that we make compelling arguments for our positions.

Over the past 25 years, we have been observing a paradigm shift in the field of gifted education. In the first chapter, we introduce what we call the mystery and mastery models of gifted education, and we discuss the movement toward the latter, which we then revisit throughout the book.

We believe that there is a double mission in gifted education. There is an important and primary focus on nurturing exceptionally advanced ability where it is already evident—that is, on understanding and supporting gifted learners' development and education. We also think it is important for those of us interested in this field to use what we know about gifted development and encourage it in children who may not yet appear to be gifted.

By understanding how children and giftedness develop, parents, educators, and others can foster advancement in those whose exceptional abilities might not otherwise be optimally developed. Grounded in our backgrounds in special education, developmental psychology, and educational psychology, we build a foundation in this book for readers to learn more about, and to better understand, many of the complexities of gifted development, and so be better positioned to make informed decisions with and for the children and adolescents in their lives.

This book, *Being Smart about Gifted Children*, comes from our years of work with high-ability children, their parents, and educators, and also from a shared sense of the joys, challenges, diversity, and uniqueness inherent in this field. We believe that the gifted educational enterprise should be encouraging and inclusive, working to support the optimal development of all children, while at the same time paying particular attention to those who are exceptionally capable.

Note from Joanne about the poem:

Some time ago, over the course of many nights, I wrote a poem full of questions about giftedness. I used a flashlight and notepaper that I stashed in my night-table drawer because often the verses would come to me in those early hours when most people are asleep.

As I kept asking myself questions, I realized that I had to crystallize the answers. In order to do this, and to be able to share it with others, I collaborated with Dona Matthews, and we undertook an exhaustive search of what was known about giftedness. Together, we wrote down what we saw as the essentials for those to whom such information matters. The fact that you picked up this book indicates that it matters to you.

So please read the poem, reflect on our text, consider using the reference and resource material, and kindly contact us with your thoughts and responses to this work. We'll continue to look for answers.

They Tell Me I'm Gifted...

They tell me I'm gifted... What does this mean?
Is this something new, or have I always been?

> *They tell me I'm gifted... Congratulations!*
> *But I am uncertain about expectations.*

They tell me I'm gifted... I'm lucky, I'm blessed.
But how do they know that from one written test?

> *They tell me I'm gifted... I'm not quite sure why.*
> *But everyone thinks my "potential" is high.*

They tell me I'm gifted... With increased understanding.
I wonder, will this make my life more demanding?

> *They tell me I'm gifted... Although I'm not sure*
> *If it's something I'm meant to enjoy or endure.*

They tell me I'm gifted... Where do I belong?
They say it's all right, but it sometimes seems wrong.

They tell me I'm gifted... It must be for real.
But it doesn't explain all the things that I feel.

They tell me I'm gifted... New school, new friends...
Is this a beginning, or is it an end?

They tell me I'm gifted... What should I conclude?
Is this why the other kids sometimes seem rude?

They tell me I'm gifted... I wish I were wise
'Cause then I might know what the label implies.

They tell me I'm gifted... And if this is true
Does this signify I have more "gifts" than you?

They tell me I'm gifted... I've so much to learn!
But sometimes I just don't know which way to turn.

They tell me I'm gifted... Who really knows?
Is it something unseen, or something that shows?

They tell me I'm gifted... Can this be outgrown?
What's in my future? It's all so unknown!

They tell me I'm gifted... Yet they don't explain
If it's all of me, or just a part of my brain.

They tell me I'm gifted... The test scores are proof
Yet in lots of ways I still behave like a goof.

They tell me I'm gifted... Is that a fact?
Do I have to change how I think, feel, and act?

They tell me I'm gifted... From whose point of view?
Does this mean that I am no longer like you?

They tell me I'm gifted... Could this be a blessing?
Who knows for sure, and who's only guessing?

They tell me I'm gifted... What should I do now?
Do I shrug? Do I laugh? Do I cry? Do I bow?

They tell me I'm gifted... They say I'm unique.
Do I have to show strengths? Can't I ever be weak?

They tell me I'm gifted... Now I'm in a jam.
Do they think I'm smarter than I really am?

They tell me I'm gifted… Is it destiny?
Controlled by what's inside or outside of me?

They tell me I'm gifted… I don't really see it.
And if that's the case, then how can I <u>be</u> it?

They tell me I'm gifted… What do I need?
Love and support that will help me succeed.

They tell me I'm gifted… I'll take it in stride
'Cause I'm very young, and the world's very wide.

They tell me I'm gifted… I think that means able.
I hope others know they should look past the label.

They tell me I'm gifted… And so it must be,
But I know deep inside that I'm still only me…

Joanne F. Foster

Section I.

Being Smart about Giftedness

Chapter 1

Perspectives and Paradigm Shifts

What Is Giftedness?

Does genius make history or
does history make the genius?
(Tannenbaum, 2000, p. 23)

There is no such thing as a "typical gifted child." We have seen over and over in our work in gifted education that giftedness is an individual differences phenomenon. Developmental histories and pathways, including how a child feels and responds to things and what he needs in order to thrive, are all highly individual and unpredictable. Parents and teachers who understand that there is no single approach that applies to all gifted children are much more likely to make good decisions for the gifted children in their lives than those who think that there might be any one "right" answer to the questions they have.

This book is about helping exceptionally capable children to find a healthy balance in their lives—one that respects and nurtures their exceptional ability and that also fosters their well-rounded development. It is also about applying what we know about giftedness to nurturing optimal development in those who might not be formally identified as gifted, but who can benefit from the principles and practices we discuss here. Parents often have mixed feelings, difficult questions, confusion, and concerns about the term "gifted" that is in use in their children's schools. Here are some questions and comments that we have frequently heard:

> *"How are gifted kids different from other kids, if at all?"*
> *"I need to know what to expect, what I should worry about with my child."*
> *"Now that she's a teenager, she's become impossible. What can I do?"*
> *"My other son isn't 'gifted,' even though he seems to be just as bright as his brother in many ways. Is there anything I should do?"*
> *"Gifted children do not wish to <u>work</u> more, they wish to <u>learn</u> more."*

Teachers have similar kinds of questions and concerns about giftedness. Here are some examples:

> *"How are gifted kids different from other kids?"*
> *"If a so-called 'gifted' student doesn't finish all her work, she really isn't gifted, is she?"*
> *"What am I supposed to do with the gifted kids in my classroom? I have 28 whose work is average or below and just two who are identified as gifted. I can't design a special program for each student!"*
> *"I'd like to know how to help some of these gifted kids improve their social skills."*
> *"I feel that the really bright ones can manage with an extra challenge here or there, so I usually try to pay more attention to the students who are struggling with their work. The slower kids need more help."*

Some of the most poignant questions and comments are the ones that we hear from the children themselves:

> *"How are gifted kids special?"*
> *"If I don't understand the math work, does that mean I'm not really gifted?"*
> *"Why does everyone expect so much of me all the time?"*
> *"Other kids call me 'brainer' or 'nerd.' I'd rather be cool than gifted."*
> *"I'm embarrassed when people ask me questions about being gifted."*
> *"I'd rather not be different."*

If we are to understand gifted children and support them in their development—that is, provide them with the best possible guidance, challenge, and encouragement—we must start by reflecting upon their individual differences. Only then can we consider the various factors and options at school, at home, and in the world. But first we should figure out what it means to be "gifted."

Two Perspectives: Mystery and Mastery

One might think that the question, "What is giftedness?" is one that any expert in this field could answer quickly and easily. Provide a simple definition, and then move on to more interesting things. But unfortunately, it is not so easy. Not only do kids, parents, and teachers all give different explanations of what giftedness is, but experts disagree as well. Here is how some people perceive giftedness:

> *"Smarter than others."*
> *"Born with the ability to learn incredibly fast."*
> *"Has a higher IQ than others, that's all."*

These voices reflect what we call the "mystery model" of giftedness. From the mystery model perspective, gifted children are born with high potential and will usually score in the superior or very superior range of intelligence tests. Their ability stays relatively constant over time.

Teachers and parents who hold the mystery model perspective sometimes describe gifted kids as "scary," or they tell us that they experience such children as inexplicably advanced somehow compared to others, or even that they, the adults, are in awe of what these children know and can do.

The mystery model is implicit in those approaches to gifted education in which children are categorized as "gifted" or "not gifted" without any explicit links to specific educational programming based on their particular strengths or abilities. While we celebrate the mysteries of life itself and respect the fact that there is much more that we don't know about human development than we do know, we think of this approach as mysterious because it is very difficult for us to figure out exactly what giftedness means using this model, and what to do about it when it is identified.

Now we consider some other responses to our question about what being gifted means from kids who have been identified as gifted and their parents:

> *"Smarter in some areas and closer to average in others."*
> *"It's not what you have, but what you do with what you have."*
> *"School is almost always boring, 'specially math."*

These answers are closer to what we call the "mastery model" of giftedness. Under the mastery model, the term "gifted" denotes a mismatch between a child's current developmental level in a given subject area and the educational programming that is usually offered at that student's age and grade level.

The mastery model fits well within a special education perspective. It is about individual exceptionality from the norm, about learning differences at a given point in time that require special educational adaptations. Under this perspective, a child is considered gifted only when her learning needs in any given subject area are so advanced relative to her classmates' that her academic development will be stalled or impeded unless the programming is somehow adapted to meet those learning needs.

There is no mystery about what giftedness means from the mastery model's perspective: it is developmental advancement at a certain point in time in a particular context that requires academic adjustment. We should add that although the mastery model's defining focus is intellectual advancement, it does not preclude attention to other ways of excelling, such as musical or artistic virtuosity or athletic ability.

There are social and emotional consequences and concomitants of giftedness, as there are with other exceptionalities. Just as we pay attention to social and emotional dimensions of learning disabilities and sensory impairments, so we must attend to these issues with exceptionally advanced learners. The best way for us to describe the important elements of the mastery model, and to explain why we are making the distinction here, is to compare it with the mystery model.

1. **Origin.** Genetic predispositions ("nature") and environmental supports ("nurture") are both accepted today as important influences on intelligence by most practitioners working in gifted education. A pure mystery model proponent of the past

would have argued (along with Galton, 1869) that genetic endowment was all that mattered. In current practice, the mystery model tends to incorporate more of the "nature" component than does the mastery model, as well as to assume that some children are born with brains that work better, just as some can become better athletes. In the mastery model, explanations like this are unnecessary and avoided, because this perspective focuses on finding the best educational match. When mastery model practitioners discuss an explanation for superior intellectual ability, they tend to put more emphasis on the child's opportunities to learn—the "nurture" factor.

2. **Duration: Dynamic or Temporal Factors.** The mystery model in its pure historic form implied an intellectual superiority from birth to death and across all contexts: "once gifted, always gifted." From the mastery perspective, a person's exceptional intellectual strengths are seen as current and perhaps only temporary. It is not that mastery model proponents see giftedness as wildly varying across time and individuals, but rather that they make no assumptions about its duration because it is defined as a *current* need for special educational programming—something which could possibly change over time. Under the mastery perspective, giftedness is understood as a relative and comparative term—in some contexts, a person's abilities might be exceptionally advanced, whereas in others, the same strengths would not be seen as exceptional.

3. **Extent: Domain Strength.** The mystery model traditionally focused on global intelligence and assumed that a gifted individual was superior in thinking tasks in most or all domains. One could say, "He is gifted," and it would imply an expectation of excellence across most tasks that require analysis or synthesis, from reading a map to deciphering a Shakespearean sonnet to learning advanced algebra. A main tenet of the mastery model is the practical focus on the fact that for most people, intellectual competence varies considerably across areas. Thus, a person gifted in algebra is not necessarily gifted in reading maps or understanding Shakespeare. Under the mastery model, the term is usually accompanied by a subject area designation;

for example, a child might be described as scientifically or musically gifted.

4. **Identification Timing.** From the mystery model perspective, it is possible to specify which children are gifted and which are not at any given time, as long as the measures used are appropriate and sufficiently sensitive. Under this model, the sooner in a child's life that giftedness is identified, the better, and there is considerable emphasis on early identification to make sure that innate giftedness is not lost or wasted. From the mastery model perspective, which focuses on remedying educational mismatches, the only urgency is to identify exceptional educational needs as they develop. Identification of giftedness is seen as an ongoing process, a natural part of a child's education, and not separate from it. Increasingly, practitioners in the field are moving to this latter perspective.

5. **Identification Measures.** Historically, the best measure of giftedness for advocates of a pure mystery model was the IQ. In a pure version of the mastery model, on the other hand, the best way to identify giftedness would be through a combination of dynamic classroom assessment and high-ceiling tests of academic reasoning to provide targeted teacher-oriented information about appropriate curriculum and educational programming. We should note that most practitioners see the merit in all of the above assessment approaches and would not be dogmatic about one to the exclusion of others. We will talk more about testing in Chapters 3 and 4, as well as in the Appendix.

6. **Identification Implications.** In the mystery model, gifted identification practices and educational programming historically were disconnected from each other both practically and logically. When intelligence tests (or any form of cognitive ability test) were used to identify giftedness, the only educational implication of achieving at or above the cut-off score for gifted identification was the categorical designation of "gifted." This designation was then used to make the child eligible for whatever gifted programming was available in that child's school district. Many jurisdictions still use some form of this approach, although

an increasing number are moving closer to the mastery model, in which identification methods lead directly to educational planning and targeted decision-making. The mastery approach identifies children's areas of exceptional strength (and sometimes areas of weakness) such that targeted curriculum adaptations can then be designed.

7. **Placement and Curriculum Implications.** Historically, the best placement under the mystery model was a segregated gifted class, full- or part-time, or some form of generic gifted enrichment. There were (and still are) several perspectives on how to accomplish this. However, all too often, teachers who were expected to implement the gifted program or devise the adaptations received little training or support. In many jurisdictions now, a segregated gifted class is seen as only one of many possibilities within a broad range of options, with the placement depending on a child's individual special learning needs. This practice is consistent with the mastery model.

8. **Political Implications.** Under the mystery model, even the best-intentioned educators of gifted learners often face considerable pressures relating to charges of elitism; in addition, they may experience the scapegoating of gifted programming, including funding cuts. On the other hand, schools that work from a mastery perspective are far less likely to incur these kinds of social, political, and funding problems. When gifted learning options are (and also are seen to be) flexibly targeted to special learning needs and include all those students for whom they are appropriate, people have fewer problems with gifted education.

In Table 1.1, we summarize our comparison of the mystery and mastery approaches.

Table 1.1. A Comparison of the Mystery and Mastery Models of Giftedness

Factor	Mystery Model	Mastery Model
Origin	Nature focus (i.e., genetic, innate), with nurture/environmental influences	Nurture focus (i.e., appropriate opportunities to learn) in context of genetic predispositions
Duration	Static; "once gifted, always gifted"	Dynamic; changing over time
Competence Domains	Most or all intellectual areas	Domain-specific (e.g., mathematical giftedness)
Identification Timing	Once, as early as possible	Ongoing, as needed
Identification Measures	Intelligence tests; checklists; creativity tests	High-ceiling academic reasoning and ongoing dynamic classroom assessment, supplemented by IQ tests as necessary
Identification Implications	Categorical (gifted or not-gifted)	Special education needs at a specific time in a specific area of functioning
Curriculum/Placement	Enrichment; segregated gifted class if possible	Range of options; regular class if possible
Political Implications	Some charges of elitism, as well as scapegoating, funding concerns	Easily defensible

The following vignettes further illustrate the differences between the mystery and the mastery models. We show how each model might play out in the life of one child.

Raqi's Story, Version #1 (Mystery Model)

Raqi was an early talker and a very early reader. When she entered kindergarten, she was already reading chapter books and more than ready for "real work." She was lucky to have a kindergarten teacher who enjoyed her precocity and who encouraged her to read while the rest of the class participated in learning their letters and other kinds of reading readiness activities. Grade 1 was a good year for her, too, again because of a teacher who knew how to keep her challenged and learning and who was able to be flexible in her demands. Grade 2 wasn't so good; there were no special accommodations for gifted learners, and she just had to wait it out. She had arguments with her teacher, who was irritated by her extraordinary mathematical ability and who tried to trap Raqi by giving her problems she couldn't solve. Raqi made it through the second and third grade until the system-wide gifted identification process was available. She sailed through the gifted assessment process with flying colors, achieving an IQ score of 143. There was no question about her identification as gifted, and she was happy when her mother decided to allow her to attend the full-time gifted program at a school that was outside of the neighborhood.

Raqi loved the idea of going to school with other kids who were as intellectually curious as she was, who were as keen to learn about everything, who insatiably gobbled up books and wanted to talk about them. She waited impatiently all summer and strode off to school on the first day of fourth grade with very high hopes of having a teacher who understood her and friends she could really talk to.

But that first day of school in the gifted class, Raqi came home dejected.

"Mom," she said, "I hate my teacher. She's nice but she's really dumb, and she won't let us do anything."

Over the course of the next few weeks, Raqi's opinion of this teacher did not improve. She was even more dismayed to find that the kids in the class did not share her interests or enthusiasms and that their vocabularies were not much different than those of the kids she knew at her old school. Most of them didn't know what she was talking about unless she talked silly, and of course (being Raqi), she would not stoop to that level. As if all that wasn't bad enough, she had some unhappy experiences in which she discovered that the other kids and teachers in the school openly resented the kids in the gifted program, especially the ones like her who refused to pose as less intelligent than they were.

Raqi's mother went into the parent-teacher conference in October hoping to help Raqi's teacher deal with her daughter, whom she knew to be difficult when she felt that her time was being wasted, but also to be wonderful when she was learning and engaged. *Raqi's mom found that Miss Pinkerton was very young, and this was her first year working with gifted learners. She was an enthusiastic teacher who was following a set of curriculum materials obtained through the District office. The teacher explained very nicely but quite firmly that she wasn't able to create a special curriculum for each of the children in the class, and that even if Raqi already knew the material they were covering, she would be expected to go through it with the class, doing all of the homework and assignments. Raqi would be allowed to do extra work if she wanted to, of course, although Miss Pinkerton would have little time to mark it or to talk with her about it.*

Raqi stayed in a gifted class for the next few years, feeling a bit lost and desperate and even weirder than she had felt in the regular classroom. She had hoped that once she was in a gifted classroom, she would meet kids like her and have teachers who understood her insatiable hunger for learning deeply and broadly. Those hopes were not realized. Sadly, it wasn't until high school that Raqi began to enjoy school again and find opportunities for real learning at school.

Raqi's Story, Version #2 (Mastery Model)

Let's replay Raqi's story and tell it as if her school district were providing gifted education designed to match her exceptional learning needs, consistent with a mastery perspective. We have the same little girl, a precocious talker and reader, hungry to learn everything she can from her earliest days on, gobbling up mathematics and literature, foreign languages and geography.

We don't have to retouch the first two primary school years at all. Her kindergarten and first-grade teachers did all the right things, responding flexibly to what they observed and providing opportunities for Raqi to keep on learning, even though she was advanced in so many ways compared with her age peers.

In this second telling, Raqi's Grade 2 teacher realized that she was out of her depth and called in the special education consultant who worked with her to identify where Raqi's exceptional strengths were. Together with Raqi and her mother, they worked out a plan that compressed some of the aspects of the curriculum that Raqi had already mastered, and they designed a program that allowed her to work with the fourth-grade teacher, who was a math specialist, in a special weekly math challenge group that was working toward participation in a district-wide math contest. Raqi was also given some flexibility around classroom assignments and allowed to choose her own reading material with the help of the school librarian, who worked with her to develop a reading plan for the year.

The special education consultant worked with each of Raqi's teachers for the next several years until she was ready for high school. She had accelerated through one complete grade and was ready to begin doing Advanced Placement courses in mathematics by the time she reached high school. She'd had a very happy and successful elementary and middle school experience. She was looking forward to continuing with the exploration of her interests at a good local high school that had a wide range of subject area possibilities and a flexible administration that was willing to support the development of her many and varied interests.

Shifting Paradigms

By definition, paradigm shifts are disturbances of the status quo. Over the past 25 years or so, we have been observing a paradigm shift in the field of gifted education, an evolutionary movement from a prevailing emphasis on the mystery model to a more generalized acceptance of the mastery model, with some mystery model influences remaining. It is always difficult to identify when a paradigm shift begins to happen; it is more easily seen in retrospect. With its focus on domain-specific abilities rather than general intelligence, the Marland Report (Marland, 1972) laid early groundwork for that aspect of the mastery model. Another early and important influence in this paradigm shift was the work that Julian Stanley and colleagues at Johns Hopkins University did with the Study of Mathematically Precocious Youth (Stanley & Benbow, 1983; Stanley, Keating, & Fox, 1974).

A further significant occurrence was the publication of Nancy and Hal Robinson's paper outlining their optimal match concept (Robinson & Robinson, 1982). These authors argued for providing a range of options for gifted learners and matching programming to individual learning needs. The following year, Howard Gardner proposed his theory of multiple intelligences (1983) which changed the way educators think about intelligence.

Then, in 1989, Jim Borland published *Planning and Implementing Programs for the Gifted*. In this book, he talked about gifted education in very similar terms to those that we use here. He described himself as "a special educator whose population of interest is gifted children" (p. 2). He enumerated the following underlying principles, all of which are consistent with what we call the mastery model:

1. The education of the gifted is a form of special education.

2. Children's current educational needs, not their prospects for future eminence, should guide our practice.

3. The nature of the children served in programs for the gifted will and should vary from school district to school district.

4. No single program model can be appropriate for all school districts.

5. Programs for the gifted should be based on information gleaned from formal needs assessments.

6. The needs of gifted children are best addressed in the company of their age and ability peers.

7. Curricula for gifted students should stress the acquisition of important knowledge.

Borland went on to say, "No other way of conceiving of the education of the gifted, I believe, offers as defensible a rationale or as workable a framework for special programming" (p. 2).

Michael Howe's *The Origins of Exceptional Abilities* (1990) provided further and highly persuasive evidence for a domain-specific developmental perspective on gifted-level ability. About the same time, the inaugural issue of *Exceptionality Education Canada* (1991) contained several frequently-cited and thought-provoking articles, including those by Dan Keating (1991) and David Feldman (1991). Each of these articles made effective and controversial arguments for the need to move to what we are calling here a mastery perspective. They were seminal in our beginning to think about the field in this way. Many other perspectives in gifted education are consistent with important elements of the mastery model. These include the talent development approach (Subotnik, Olszewski-Kubilius, & Arnold, 2003; Tannenbaum, 1983) and the integrated curriculum model (VanTassel-Baska & Little, 2003). Renzulli's enrichment triad model is a widely-used approach to giftedness that we see as providing something of a bridge between the mystery and mastery models (Renzulli & Reis, 1985; 2000).

Over the past few years, many experts in gifted education have written about the need for major changes in perspective (Borland, 2003; Feldhusen, 2003; Rogers, 2003; Subotnik, Olszewski-Kubilius, & Arnold, 2003), with some describing the changes underway as a paradigm shift (Feldman, 2003; Treffinger & Feldhusen, 1996). For example, in discussing his observations of a paradigm shift in progress, David Feldman (2003) wrote, "Recognition that the field of gifted education is holding an increasingly untenable position appears to be growing, perhaps to the critical point at which real change becomes possible, even necessary" (p. 15). He posited (as do we in this book) that it is important for the ongoing viability of the field that educators interested in high-level development pay attention to the developmental aspects of giftedness and the evolutionary movement of gifted education. We suggest that the mastery model provides a good way to do just that, and to simultaneously clarify some confusion that exists for many parents as well as educators.

Origins: Nature or Nurture?

Children's joy in the learning process is the ultimate goal without which, we believe, giftedness will not easily be evidenced.
    (Gottfried, Gottfried, Bathurst, & Guerin, 1994, p. 183)

For many years, there has been an ongoing debate about the relative weight of genetic and environmental influences on intelligence. Current research describes the inextricable and highly complex dynamic interconnection of nature and nurture over time (Keating, in press; Nelson, 1999, in press). The findings on high-level development come together in interesting ways. They suggest that high IQ most frequently results from children with the necessary neurological predispositions being listened to, cared about, respected, and provided with opportunities to learn and explore in age-appropriate ways (Howe, 1999). There is good reason to think that giftedness rarely evolves unless some combination of "cognitive ability, motivation, and enriched environment co-exist and meld together to foster its growth" (Gottfried, Gottfried, Bathurst, & Guerin, 1994, p. 183-184). After a very careful review of extensive longitudinal research findings, these researchers concluded that if parents want to encourage giftedness, they should be careful observers of their children's development, responding to it and enhancing it, but not inappropriately demanding achievement.

Giftedness can develop for other complicated reasons, too. For example, high achievement can be motivated by a drive to overcome some kind of obstacle (perhaps poverty, disability, or social or emotional deprivation). The gifted child may be one who wants to know everything about everything and/or has a passion to excel. In a book exploring the reasons for, influences on, and various aspects of high-level development, Simonton (1994) considers the prevailing "common sense" notions and myths about such development, as well as the research findings for myriad possible effects on it, including (among many others) genetic inheritance, gender, birth order, creativity, age, intelligence, personality, psychopathology, relationships, and opportunities. From Simonton's book, one learns to appreciate that the pathways to gifted-level achievement are as diverse and unpredictable as the achievements themselves.

The research on exceptional ability as it manifests itself in adult achievement outcomes is similarly interesting. Very often, giftedness does not show up until middle or even late adulthood. The majority of those who end up succeeding at very high levels in most real-world domains (with the exception of math, music, and sports) were not recognized by teachers or parents as exceptionally advanced children (Bloom, 1985; Howe, 1999; Simonton, 1994). When children are not identified as gifted, parents should *not* therefore conclude that they are ineffective parents or that their child has less genetic potential than others. Giftedness as seen from the mastery perspective is about exceptional learning needs at a given point in time that require special educational adaptations; it is *not* about predicting future success.

Domains of Competence

Over the last few decades the definition of giftedness has changed from being a one-dimensional conception linking giftedness to

high intelligence to multi-dimensional conceptions acknowledging
the existence of outstanding ability in various domains.

(Schoon, 2000, p. 21)

The concept of intelligence as multifaceted is not new and has been proposed by many people in many forms (Gould, 1981; Guilford, 1967; Spearman, 1927; Thurstone, 1938). Gardner (1983) captured popular imagination with his theory of multiple intelligences. He argued that a solitary measure such as that provided by an Intelligence Quotient (IQ) is inadequate and misleading in describing individual abilities. When trying to understand or assess a person's intelligence, there are many intelligences or ability domains that should be considered somewhat separately.

Gardner acknowledged that the boundaries among the various intelligences are contentious and arguable and that there are many possible candidate intelligences. He developed criteria to designate a domain as an intelligence, including: (a) that there is evidence that the domain is useful and important, at least in certain cultural settings, (b) that it is at least somewhat neurologically discrete, and (c) that it is given psychometric, psychological, and historical attention as a functional domain. He initially proposed seven intelligences that met these criteria: linguistic, logical-mathematical, spatial, bodily-kinesthetic, musical, interpersonal, and intrapersonal. He has since nominated three other intelligences as candidates for this list, including naturalistic, existential, and spiritual intelligences (1998). It is possible that a given individual could be gifted in one, two, or even several of these domains but not in others, and very few people (if any) will be exceptionally capable or gifted in all areas. Gardner's concept of multiple intelligences tends to appeal to educators, many of whom now include instructional activities and teaching methods that incorporate an understanding of various intelligences. Children's profiles of abilities are different, and Gardner provides a model for thinking about that.

Even among those who are identified as gifted because of overall high IQ scores, most are not gifted across all school subject areas. In fact, many children identified as gifted are quite average in some areas. By the time they reach adolescence, gifted young people who are good at everything are more the exception than the rule, and as they get older, there are only a very few who can be considered gifted across most or all subject areas (Matthews, 1997; Matthews & Keating, 1995).

Is Learning Easy?

"I can't get math now. I guess that means I'm not gifted anymore."
"My homework takes me soooo long, and my friend does it in five min-
utes. Could the tests be wrong? Maybe I'm not gifted after all."
"I failed the geography test yesterday. Am I still gifted?"

Contrary to popular belief, being gifted does *not* mean finding all learning easy. Gifted learners may find it simple to achieve or even exceed some or most age-normal expectations, but they experience the same challenges as anyone else in moving from their current level of mastery in a subject area to the next higher one. They may have some advantages in doing so. For example, they often have a larger and more conceptually complex foundation of knowledge than their age-peers, as well as the confidence that comes from previous learning successes. However, it seems that real mastery involves effort. Investigations of the lives of even the most highly gifted individuals inevitably conclude with observations of the tremendous investment of time, energy, and attention to the learning process that has been made. The lives of Beethoven, Einstein, and Picasso, for example, all illustrate the fact that high-level achievement reflects a huge commitment and countless hours spent mastering their respective domains of competence (Howe, 1990).

In their book *Cradles of Eminence* (2004), Goertzel and Hansen discuss various kinds of shaping experiences in the childhoods of hundreds of prominent figures, and they consider what elements might lead to eminence. They find that personal strengths, abilities, and ambition were valued in the homes of many of the individuals described, and their homes were places where ideas and opinions mattered. Love of learning was nurtured, and parents respected and largely encouraged perseverance and achievement.

No matter how easy learning might be for any given child, the moment always comes when a person who has previously found learning to be effortless comes across something that is difficult to master. Some children experience this when they first encounter algebra or a second language; others may become discouraged when they tackle philosophy or creative writing. If they are lucky, they experience some kind of failure sooner rather than later. Sometimes when that first real difficulty is encountered, gifted children might think that they are no longer gifted. We do these children a disservice if we allow them to go through years of schooling without real and appropriate challenges that can help them learn how to work hard, to persevere through challenges, and to surmount obstacles.

The most important component of gifted-level achievement may well be hard work done consistently over many years with an attitude of problem-finding and problem-solving. Opportunities to learn are very important, as are the guidance and supports children find along the way. Exceptionally high-achieving adults are characterized by having more failures than others (as well as more successes) and as having a different reaction to them—specifically, a mastery orientation, wherein they work to master the skills that they are having troubles with, rather than deciding that they aren't capable in that area (Gardner, 1991; Simonton, 1994, 1997).

Another component of whether gifted-level achievement is easy or hard seems to be the age of earliest exposure to a domain such that sensitive periods in brain development are maximized. An important variable is temperament, particularly as it interacts with and is shaped by the environment (Howe, 1990).

Our reading of current research and theoretical literature on the development of intelligence suggests that you can reassure gifted young people who are worried about losing their giftedness by telling them that the best way to stay smart is to work hard at things they're curious about and that no worthwhile learning comes easily. There is no real learning without failure; in fact, it is how we respond to failure that makes the difference between achieving at a high level and being mediocre in our achievements (Bereiter & Scardamalia, 1993). As one of our colleagues who is also the parent of gifted children says, "This is so important! It speaks to our impatient culture of instant success with minimal effort. Kids figure they should comprehend instantly, and they feel stupid if they have to reread something."

Other Terms

"I don't believe in the term 'gifted.'"

This is a comment we hear quite frequently from parents, teachers, and children. It is one that we welcome, because when people say this, it often means that they are doing the serious thinking that is necessary to achieve a better or more complete understanding of what it means to be gifted. The term "gifted" is controversial, and for good reasons. Many of us who work in this field have trouble with the term, because when used as a label to identify certain children, it creates an exclusive category of gifted persons, implying that they share certain characteristics while simultaneously establishing an implicit category—"non-gifted"—for everyone else. There is also a problem with the relationship between "gifted" and "gift," with the implication that the gifted person has simply received a gift and therefore cannot take ownership of it or even feel proud of success. There's a risk of intellectual identity detachment, a feeling that the gift must be used but cannot be owned, and that accomplishments are handed out rather than earned. There's also an unfair burden of responsibility that the person has to use this gift wisely.

There are many other terms used to refer to high-level development:

1. **Precocity** literally means *knowing ahead of time*. Precocious readers, for example, read sooner than expected, and that kind of precocity—or doing something ahead of the age at which it is expected—is commonly thought to be a sign of giftedness. Although reading early does give a child a big advantage in independent mastery of the world of learning, not all precocious readers go on to become gifted learners. Conversely, not all of those who are considered gifted are early readers.

2. **Prodigy** is a word used to describe a child whose *achievement in one area is truly extraordinary for his or her age*, at a level expected of a much older expert. Thus, a musical prodigy might play a violin solo with the kind of technical virtuosity that an older, already-accomplished violinist would use. A math prodigy might have skills usually exhibited by someone who has been studying mathematics for years. For various reasons, prodigies do not always live up to the promise of their youth (Feldman & Goldsmith, 1986; Winner, 1996), and not all of those who achieve prodigiously as adults were prodigies, or even remarkable, as children (Howe, 1990).

3. **Genius** is a term reserved for someone who has *demonstrated enormous achievement in an important field of endeavor*, such as Mozart, Einstein, Gandhi, or Freud. It is usually considered to be inappropriate as a descriptor for a child.

4. **Superiority** relates to a psychometric term meaning *at least one and a half standard deviations above the mean.* "Very superior" is the psychometric category used to refer to scores that are at least two standard deviations above the mean. We discuss these terms more fully in Section II.

5. **Talent** is typically associated with giftedness in the arts or sports, such as musical strength or athletic prowess. Gardner (1983) argued that these aspects of one's development are *integral and not peripheral to human intelligence,* and that in fact, there are many ways to be intelligent. "Talent development" is the term being used increasingly by experts in gifted education as they investigate the dynamic and developmental dimensions of all areas of ability (Borland, 2003; Subotnik, Olszewski-Kublilius, & Arnold, 2003; Tannenbaum, 2000). Most of the work in talent development is consistent with the mastery model approach by virtue of its focus on understanding and supporting domain-specific high-level development and on individual developmental differences.

6. **Advancement** refers to *competence or achievement that is ahead of what is expected* for a child's age and is similar to precocity in that way.

Of the terms listed above, advancement is probably the best description of the mastery model of giftedness. It means, simply, that the child is advanced academically in what he understands and can do, ahead of what is expected for other children his age. However, because "gifted" is the term that is used in most educational jurisdictions, we tend to use it in our work and in our book. We use it somewhat interchangeably with other terms such as "high-ability learner" and "advanced learner."

Very few people would argue with the observation that children demonstrate enormous individual differences in their personalities, abilities, developmental pathways, interests, attitudes, and ambitions. However, not everyone recognizes that this is just as true for those who are gifted as for all others. Addressing the needs of gifted learners means paying careful attention to those individual differences and thinking beyond the widespread misconceptions about exceptional intelligence that are, and have been, embodied in the word "gifted." For these reasons, we do not include any charts or lists of common "characteristics of the gifted," and we tend to stay away from talking about "*the* gifted."

Historical Perspective

"People call you brainer or smart kid."
"I don't like being treated like I'm different."

The concept of "giftedness" was not formally studied by researchers until the early twentieth century. In a longitudinal study called *Genetic Studies of Genius* (1925-1959), psychologist Lewis Terman examined the developmental characteristics of gifted children. He believed that intelligence was genetically determined, a blueprint of a person's mental capacity, and measurable with IQ testing. This view prevails today in much of what is written about gifted education, and many educational jurisdictions continue to rely on IQ as a primary instrument for identifying gifted-level intelligence, which influences the nature of and access to educational programs for high-ability students. Leta Hollingworth, a colleague of Terman's, focused on the guidance and counseling needs of gifted children. Rather than asking, "Who are the gifted?" (which was Terman's focus), she concentrated on finding out, "How can we meet the needs of the gifted?" (Hollingworth, 1926). Her contributions to the fields of psychology and gifted education were numerous and significant. Her work is still highly regarded, and its impact is widespread (Klein, 2002).

In the intervening years since Terman and Hollingworth conducted their studies, interest in giftedness has waxed and waned, and social and educational perspectives on it have varied greatly. One notable influence is the Marland Report (1972). This document focused on problems resulting from discrepancies between children's abilities and educational program offerings, stating that children who are exceptional in one or more designated categories should be provided with special educational services. The Marland Report included these categories: (1) general intellectual ability, (2) specific academic aptitude, (3) creative or productive thinking, (4) leadership ability, and (5) visual and performing arts. These categories have been used by educators for more than 30 years as a broad guideline for determining who might be gifted.

Today, many parents are exhibiting a strong interest in giving their children every intellectual advantage. A huge industry is thriving on marketing educational toys, games, and programs that claim to make children smarter. Large regional talent searches are very popular throughout North America. These programs typically identify academically gifted children at early adolescence and support them into early adulthood.

At the same time that there is great interest in supporting high-level development, however, it is politically incorrect in many places to even mention giftedness, much less to devote educational resources to addressing the needs of gifted learners.

Many people working in the field of gifted education are seriously concerned about the emerging consequences for gifted learners of the American federal *No Child Left Behind* (NCLB) legislation (U.S. Department of Education, 2001), which puts strict rules in place for schools regarding minimum learning outcomes for all students. Unfortunately, this legislation is having unintended consequences. Gifted children and those with learning disabilities (sometimes one and the same) are at the margins of schools' planning, of society's attention, and of policy makers' consciousness in crafting policy. Without appropriately targeted learning opportunities, neither group achieves the depth or breadth of which they are capable. When policy provides disincentives for schools to specifically support youngsters with exceptional needs, valuable contributions to society are lost.

One troubling sign of the times is that many parents are actually embarrassed to discuss their child's intellectual giftedness with friends and family or with their child's teacher at school. Interestingly, they would not be reluctant to discuss a similar level of athletic or artistic exceptionality. Kids are often embarrassed to talk about being smart, too:

> *"I try not to let anyone know I'm in a gifted program."*
> *"It's not fun to be called a geek."*
> *"Some kids 'dis' the congregated gifted, calling us nicknames like 'nerds' and 'smart people.' And sometimes they say we're really stupid."*

Many educators who work with gifted children tell us that their colleagues consider their work with these learners to be peripheral and elitist, and we have certainly seen this attitude ourselves. It is unfortunately true that much that has been done in the name of gifted education is not evidence-based and is in fact peripheral to what goes on in the rest of education. A "gifted enrichment activity" that focuses on building kites might be fun and interesting for some participants, but too often, little or no serious thought or effort goes into connecting the activity with seminal aspects of the curriculum. Students who describe this kind of activity as not only unproductive but also trivial or insulting are not entirely wrong. However, there are many teacher-friendly and evidence-based suggestions for adapting curriculum for gifted learners in ways that are not peripheral and that are well-grounded in theory. We describe these in detail in Section III.

Using the mastery model approach, identification and programming practices work toward matching a child's ability level to curriculum. For instance, some gifted third-graders appreciate the opportunity to read and discuss literature that is typically assigned to much older children. The majority of parents and teachers are not likely to see this as elitist or as a perk that would benefit most children.

If there is a bright future for gifted education (and we hope there is!), the current problems in the field, such as programming that embarrasses children, or invites political sniping, or elicits charges of elitism, must be overcome. One way of doing so is to make it an explicit goal to ensure that the learning needs of all children are known and well-met and that what is understood about gifted development is shared widely.

Guidelines and a Definition

"All children are gifted."

Most people would agree that every child has enormous learning potential and that we ought to encourage the best possible educational outcomes in all children. However, this sentiment—that "all children are gifted"—is problematic. Very few people would consider placing normally developing children in special programs for developmentally delayed learners. Using the mastery approach, those who are gifted are those whose exceptionality from the norm is such that they require specific educational adaptations to ensure a level of instruction that matches their observed performance. By seeing all children as gifted, we rob the word of any useful meaning and greatly reduce the chances that we will address the learning needs of those who are exceptionally advanced.

So what exactly are we talking about when we talk about giftedness? One definition is Ontario's Gifted Definition: "A gifted pupil is one who has been identified as possessing an unusually advanced degree of general intellectual ability that requires differentiated learning experiences of a depth and breadth beyond those normally provided in the regular school program to satisfy the level of educational potential indicated" (Ontario Ministry of Education, 1984).

Another definition is that used by New York State: "The term 'gifted pupils' shall mean those pupils who show evidence of high performance capability and exceptional potential in areas such as general intellectual ability, special academic aptitude and outstanding ability in visual and performing arts. Such definition shall include those pupils who require educational programs or services beyond those normally provided by the regular school program in order to realize their full potential" (New York State, 1982).

While both of these definitions have the advantage of being flexible and tied into programming, there are problems due to ambiguity. For example, what does "unusually advanced degree" mean? Or "general intellectual ability"? Or "potential"? It may seem obvious that the primary mandate of educators is the academic development of all students. Their job is to think about and provide for that which children need for their academic and intellectual development. With that in mind, the business of educators is to offer learning opportunities, rather than to create a hierarchy or ranking of children's potential life achievement. According to the mastery model, educators overstep their boundaries when they think of giftedness as anything other than academic advancement. We recognize there are social/emotional implications of exceptional ability, but here we are working to define the term as simply and clearly as possible. In Chapter 11, we address the important social and emotional issues associated with gifted development and education.

With due regard to how the mystery model has shaped thinking about gifted education over the years, and with a sense that a paradigm shift is well underway, we have formulated a mastery model definition for giftedness. We have developed some basic guidelines, grounded in our work in educational psychology and developmental psychology. The definition must:

- reflect what we know about high-level cognitive development and individual differences

- incorporate the domain-specific nature of intelligence as evident in one or more areas

- respect the dynamic and context-specific nature of intelligence

- make few assumptions about differences in children's potential

- focus on academic proficiency relative to others

- make no generalizations about social/emotional/behavioral or other characteristics of the individual

- lead logically and directly to identification practices

- lead logically and directly to educational programming implications

- minimize the categorical dichotomy between gifted/not gifted

We suggest the following working definition of giftedness—one that incorporates all of the suggested guidelines.

The Mastery Model Definition of Giftedness: Giftedness is exceptionally advanced subject-specific ability at a particular point in time, such that a student's learning needs cannot be well met without significant adaptations to the curriculum.

> *Note: Those familiar with special education for students with learning problems will recognize that this approach is consistent with what is often called "Adaptive Instruction" and the prevailing approach to best practices in special education* (Heward, 2002).

We have observed that schools that use the mastery model (or adaptive instructional) approach to giftedness experience fewer problems (for example, those relating to elitism, political and funding tension, or parental pressure to get children into gifted programs). At the same time, academic curriculum for all students, including those who are gifted, is enhanced. Because the program is focused on matching precious resources to clearly defined and designated learning needs, there is less mystery to the gifted enterprise and consequently less resentment and exclusion from resources from which all children might benefit.

What gifted kids need—like all kids—are learning opportunities that challenge them sufficiently and appropriately, along with the right kinds of guidance and support so that they can meet and enjoy those challenges and feel good about themselves at home and at school.

Before we address creativity and its connection to giftedness, we would like to answer some of the questions that people frequently ask when encountering the mastery perspective for the first time.

Questions

1. *"Are you saying that all children are gifted in some way or another?"*
   No, because giftedness is about exceptionality from the norm. It is an individual differences phenomenon, and each child's developmental pathway is unique. All children have strengths and weaknesses that vary from a lesser to a more profound degree in one or more areas at any given point in time. Whether or not the strengths manifest themselves at the highest levels depends on a great many factors and influences in the child's life, including appropriately targeted opportunities for learning.

2. *"I often see lists of 'the characteristics of gifted children,' but you don't provide any. Why is that?"*
   Since we conceptualize giftedness as being about individual differences, it doesn't make sense to us to compile a list of "gifted" traits or characteristics that may (or may not) apply to any one child. In fact, one of the points that we are trying to make as we discuss the mastery perspective on gifted development in this book is that gifted learners are highly diverse individuals and *not* a homogeneous population. In our experience, they cannot be characterized as like each other any more than we would make a list to describe the characteristics of learners who are *not* particularly advanced. However, if you find lists like this useful, there are many different ones to choose from—which perhaps underscores the point.

3. *"Where do social and emotional considerations come into the picture?"*
   There are many important social and emotional concerns that relate to being smart. The child does not leave her giftedness behind when she exits the classroom, nor does she leave her

social/emotional self behind when she enters it. We discuss the interconnectivity between social/emotional elements and cognition in considerable detail in Chapter 11.

4. *"How do child prodigies fit in?"*

The prodigy is a "more extreme version of a gifted child, able to perform at an adult level while still a child.... There are simply too many interacting factors that shape a child prodigy into an adult creator to be able to predict which ones will make it into the halls of the greats" (Winner, 1996, pp. 279-280). Early expertise in structured or formal domains (such as math, or music, or chess, for example) may have little or nothing to do with high IQ and does not guarantee future success. Ability, passion, temperament, and learning opportunities all fuel the fire for accomplishment. Children grow up and circumstances in life change such that "every prodigy eventually becomes an ex-prodigy" (p. 291) as others catch up.

5. *"I'm really confused about testing and assessments, what they mean, and whether it's important for bright children to be tested. Can you please explain matters to me?"*

Testing, whether formal or informal in nature, can be a very useful way to acquire information about a child's learning needs. Different kinds of tests are designed to yield different kinds of information about such things as a person's cognitive strengths and weaknesses, interests, and learning styles. In any assessment process, whether it consists of one test or more, careful interpretation is of the utmost importance. Results should be communicated to those who are responsible for decision-making and educational programming, and they in turn can use the information to provide the best possible learner-learning match. We discuss assessments, tests, and identification in Chapters 3, 4, and 5, and we provide additional understandings of test-related issues in the Appendix.

6. *"Do children have different learning potential?"*

It is quite possible that some children are born with more intellectual potential than others in one or more dimensions, just as there are some who are born with a greater likelihood that they will be tall or good-natured. The science of cognitive measurement, however, is too imprecise for us to ascertain with any degree of certainty what children's potential actually is and which children have more of it in which areas. In addition, the more we know about brain development (especially neural plasticity), the clearer it is that we have to be very careful when setting any kinds of limits on people's potential for learning. Developmental pathways are highly variable—as individual as fingerprints—and we do well to avoid identifying which children might have more (or less) potential than others. We feel that educators are on firmer ground when discussing giftedness as a need for special education at a certain point in time.

7. *"I think that giftedness really IS mysterious. Are you saying that giftedness is not mysterious and that it is only about school?"*
We agree that human development is mysterious, and we marvel at the achievements of which people are capable in every domain. There is so much that we still don't know about human development, including what fosters creativity, expertise, and exceptional accomplishment. However, we think that giftedness makes the most sense when viewed as a mismatch between what a learner is capable of doing and the learning opportunities provided. The focus then has more to do with *mastery*, which can be addressed directly, and less to do with *mystery*, which by its very nature cannot be addressed directly. Identifying and attending to exceptional learning needs drives the understanding and encouragement of giftedness in children—which is what this book is all about.

Chapter 2
Creativity and Giftedness

What Is Creativity?

*The present belongs to the sober, the cautious, the
routine-prone, but the future belongs to those who
do not rein in their imaginations.*
(Kornei Chukovsky, n.d.)

Is creativity a part of giftedness? Is it essential? Can a person learn to be creative?

Over the course of history, there has always been a fascination with creativity. Toynbee (1967) hailed outstanding creative ability as "mankind's ultimate capital asset." He argued that progress in confronting the problems of our world will be "spearheaded by some of the most advanced thinkers of our times," and that therefore, "to give a fair chance to potential, creativity is a matter of life and death" (Toynbee, 1967). When we consider the riches that humanity has created over the ages in every area—in art, science, philosophy, music, literature, and other domains—we see the achievements of those whose creative work has stood the test of time

People are experiencing more rapid and profound change in their lives than ever before. The nature of the current changes, particularly in communications technology, suggests that this change rate will continue to increase dramatically. One of the educational implications of living in these rapidly changing times is that it is essential for parents and educators to encourage children to develop their ability to adapt to changing circumstances. Creativity and creative habits of mind are vitally important means to that end.

People often see creativity and giftedness as disconnected concepts, thinking of "creativity" as referring to artistic ability and "giftedness" as applying to exceptional academic intelligence. Our work in this area suggests that, in fact, these concepts are symbiotically intertwined. Creativity is an important component of actualizing giftedness in every domain, and domain-specific mastery is a prerequisite for high-level creative work. Rather than thinking of giftedness and creativity separately, our perspective is much closer to that expressed by David Feldman (1991):

> *To be creative means to use your full set of capabilities for some valued and valuable purpose, the consequences of which make a significant difference to an established field of endeavor.... Creativity is quintessentially a matter of devotion, mastery, patience, persistence, and talent...applied in full measure over a sustained period of time (p. 45).*

Over the years, many people have directed our attention to children's creative efforts. Comments include the following:

> *"I want to enter the creative writing contest but I know I won't win."*
> *"Look at my picture! I'm not creative at ALL! You should see the pictures my friend draws. People with three heads, blue monsters, and cars with wings. She's really creative."*
>
> *"Other kids call him weird. I've even had adults tell me they think he's weird. But I think it's because he looks at the world differently, more creatively."*
> *"I don't want to stifle her creative spirit."*

If you talk with creatively productive people, you'll find that creativity is even more challenging to define than giftedness. There is a diverse and fascinating literature attempting to define creativity and exploring the topic, from the deeply philosophical to the frivolously trite. In addition to David Feldman, some authors who have explored the field intelligently are Mihalyi Csikszentmihalyi (1991), Howard Gardner (1993), Dan Keating (1980), David Perkins (1981), Jane Piirto (2003), and Dean Keith Simonton (1997).

A highly contentious position that some of these writers take is that real creativity can only be identified when someone's work has fundamentally changed or affected thinking or practice in a given field. Leonardo da Vinci, Martha Graham, Martin Luther King, and William Shakespeare would all be considered creative by this definition. Such high-level creativity does not occur, however, until someone has acquired a rigorous or high level of mastery of a domain, which rarely (if ever) happens until the person has been working hard in the domain for at least 10 years. Only then is there a large enough foundation of knowledge and skills that the potentially creative individual has mastered the tools and has the complex conceptual understanding required for important and interesting innovation in the field (Gardner, 1993).

On the other end of the rigor spectrum, many people define creativity as divergent thinking, or the production of novel ideas or unusual products. For example, suppose that a teacher or parent interested in encouraging creativity asks a child to devise new ways to depict a character in a story they are reading. If the child generates something that appears to onlookers as unusual and unique, like a poorly-written poem about a person with three heads, then the child and his ideas might be considered creative. Although it would be accurate to describe the poem as representing divergent thinking and to say that this kind of divergent thinking has a place in creativity, it would be a mistake to think it is its essence. Divergent thinking is necessary but not sufficient for productive creativity.

Many years ago, Keating (1980) defined creativity as an interplay of four factors which he called the "four faces" of creativity. His position synthesizes many of the competing definitions that are still in vogue, and it has interesting practical applications. He proposed that creativity involves:

1. content mastery,
2. divergent thinking,
3. critical thinking, and
4. effective communication.

This perspective incorporates the argument that one cannot be creative in any useful or important way until acquiring the knowledge and skills (content mastery) with which to *be* creative. It recognizes divergent thinking as an essential component of creativity, and certainly by most definitions, one must be thinking laterally or "outside the box" and generating innovative ideas in order to be doing creative work. People who are considered creative must be good at divergent thinking, but they must also be good at selecting their most promising ideas from the merely unusual or novel ones. As Keating argues, effectively creative people are also able to analyze, synthesize, and evaluate their divergent ideas. They have to be able to think critically about which ideas are worth further time and energy. And once an important idea has been generated and identified as promising, they must then be able to communicate it effectively enough for others to understand it or recognize its value.

Creativity by this definition applies as well to science, business, and other domains as it does to the arts. If one cannot communicate one's good idea so that others can and want to understand it, then it is not very useful. Poorly written poetry, therefore, is *not* creative. There may be promise, perhaps, that with further work, a writer might be able to do something more, but by Keating's criteria, a poorly executed poem is not in and of itself creative.

Another approach to understanding creativity is to examine the lives of highly creative people and consider how they experience creativity. Creatively successful people in a number of domains often describe an experience of being so fully engaged in their work that consciousness of time disappears and one experiences a profound sense of well-being. This sense of well-being and fulfillment is called "flow" by Mihalyi Csikszentmihalyi, a psychologist who has written extensively about creativity. Flow is the feeling that motivates a person to do the work in which personal creativity is embedded, and it occurs when one experiences a balance between the challenges in a situation and the capacity to take action on them (Csikszentmihalyi & Wolfe, 2000). Csikszentmihalyi identifies the following essential components of a creative flow experience:

- clear goals along the way
- immediate feedback
- a balance between one's challenges and one's skills
- a merging of actions and awareness
- the exclusion of distractions from one's consciousness
- no concern about failure
- no self-consciousness
- a distorted sense of time
- a sense of an activity as its own reward

According to Csikszentmihalyi, these components combine in ways that are complex and absorbing. This occurs to such a degree that a person in a flow state might temporarily lose track of time and place and a sense of the world itself. In a spirit of authentic inquiry, voluntary engagement, and emerging awareness, flow can evolve into surprising realizations. There may be no other purpose to flow than to inspire a person to keep on flowing (Csikszentmihalyi, 1991), thereby fueling intrinsic motivation and furthering creativity.

Can We Measure Creativity?

"How on earth can I grade my students' assignments for their creative worth?"

"I think there is danger in seeing creative activities as somehow distinct from activities that involve careful thought and problem solving."

"I don't think creativity is something that can be packaged, then put on a scale or placed alongside some kind of measuring grid to be given a mark."

Although there are many tests of creativity, none of them comes close to assessing the qualities that we have been talking about here in connection with creativity in any kind of valid or meaningful way. In order to fit into a standardized, paper-and-pencil, group-administered testing mode, standardized tests of creativity focus on decontextualized divergent thinking tasks. That is, these activities are performed in and of themselves with no specific connection to any particular area of study. For example, a child may be asked to do as many things as possible with a circle or a paper clip in a limited time period. There is no sense of authentic challenge involved in such tasks, and those who accomplish truly creative work typically do not find such tasks worthy of much effort. Piirto (2003) and many others who are engaged in creative work and/or the study of creativity observe that truly creative people are not likely to score very well on creativity tests.

A Parent's Thoughts about Creativity Testing

My son, Joel, is in Grade 4. He excels in math, sculpting, and other tactile activities. My younger daughter, Kate, has not really been exposed to many of these things yet, so I'm not sure what her strengths are in those or, for that matter, other areas. For all I know, she may be outstanding, too.

My point is that age and context are big factors here, and in any case, not all creativity is consistent. I'm upset that one of my kids did badly on a creativity identification test. I'm not sure his performance means a darn thing other than the fact that now he's being penalized for it in much the same way that a great author may write a poor book (or a series of books) and be faulted for that. Some people have the potential to think in new and exciting ways but may not be able to show it on cue or in a test situation for a variety of reasons. This is an issue if, in the process of trying to measure or identify my children's creativity, their teachers are using the testing information in figuring out how best to teach them.

Joel's Thoughts about Creativity Testing

I love Lego®! It's my favorite thing. I also like to make stuff out of popsicle sticks, bubble wrap, and duct tape. Sometimes when I'm bored I build forts with the furniture. It drives my mom crazy.

The other day, the teacher gave our class this dumb assignment. She handed me and each of the other kids a piece of paper with a bunch of circles drawn on it. She said, "Make as many things as you can, all different." How stupid! I looked at Sammy. We shook our heads and groaned. So I drew some faces and a couple of bikes and a sun to make my teacher happy.

You're not going to believe this but my mom says I'm not allowed in the gifted program because I'm not creative. She says that circle thing was a test and it proved I'm not creative. Well, I think the test is not creative, so there! Why didn't they ask me to build something?

We agree with Joel and his mom that creativity is hard to measure. Creativity is too idiosyncratic a construct, too rooted in particular tasks and situations to be easily quantified. In response to these difficulties, we know of one educator who has devised her own built-in creativity scale. She judges artwork on the basis of whether or not she gets "tingles" down her spine when she looks at it. Needless to say, there are some who might question the validity and reliability of this approach. Creativity is too complex to be pigeonholed and too interconnected with psychological factors such as motivation, attitude, and the potency of perceived challenges. The best we can do may be to assess the four factors of creativity identified by Keating above—content mastery, divergent thinking, critical analysis, and communication skills—in an authentic problem-solving context that has relevance to the individual test-taker. Although real creativity is too contextual, too individualistic in essence and form to ever be quantified by standardized pencil-and-paper tests, there are recent indications that creative and artistic potential in performing arts talent can be assessed validly and equitably with the *Talent Assessment Process* in dance, music, and theater (Oreck, Owens, & Baum, 2003).

Nurturing Creativity

> *"Creative work can be incredibly difficult for students. I've found that I first have to establish a really supportive and encouraging environment before their creativity emerges."*
>
> *"Students who are simply told 'be creative' often give safe answers first. Only after seeing how far they can go without being 'wrong' do they begin to stretch their ideas."*
>
> *"Creativity is not only important in elementary and secondary schools, but also in many workplace situations. Teachers need to value and respect the idea of adopting and modeling creative approaches to learning."*

In the 1980s, North American educators invested a lot of time, energy, and money in teaching creative thinking skills. The research done at that time demonstrated conclusively that creative thinking strategies do *not* transfer to other tasks. We cannot teach people to be creative, or for that matter analytical, in a vacuum. Creativity must be applied in domain-specific areas, building on rich content knowledge.

As with any expertise, fostering creativity involves nurturing the following habits of mind (Bereiter & Scardamalia, 1993):

- active engagement in learning and experimentation
- the progressive tackling of higher level problems
- a matching of talents and task demands
- *practice, practice, practice* ("the way to Carnegie Hall")

Over the years, many teachers have expressed their concerns to us about how challenging and yet how very important it is to encourage children's imaginations. Namrta Bhardwaj, a teacher, wrote the following:

A Science Teacher's Viewpoint

I fear that there is not enough creativity in science classrooms. Students are rewarded for memorizing or learning facts, not for unique insights or creative ideas. This is very unfortunate, because for someone to develop into a good scientist, unique and creative ideas are truly essential. For example, researchers have to be able to see solutions that are not obvious. If we want students to become effective scientists, we need to develop their creativity right from the start.

Many resources have been designed to help teachers encourage creativity in their students. We provide references for some of these on our website (www.beingsmart.ca). Parents who want to stimulate children's creativity at home may also find the recommended strategies useful.

The optimal environment for fostering creativity is one that paradoxically feels both safe and challenging, which is also what is required for a willingness to take risks. Whether at home or at school, such environments have some common features (Piirto, 1998; Sternberg & Williams, 2002):

- acceptance and celebration of diversity
- errors seen as opportunities for learning
- opportunities for independent learning as well as collaborations
- flexible tasks
- time to listen, reflect, focus, and refocus
- encouragement of children's input
- requirement to defend one's positions with fact and logic
- serious attitude toward children's questions

- opportunities to work with varied materials under different conditions

- rewards for courage as much as correctness and compliance

So how are creativity and giftedness related? When someone is sufficiently competent in a particular domain, that person has developed one of the necessary prerequisites for being creative. The next step is to stretch beyond the domain's frontiers to break new ground and generate fresh ways of looking at the world. It is not necessary to be formally recognized as gifted in order to be creative, but it is helpful to have the rich and complex mastery of a domain that is the essence of giftedness as we define it here with the mastery model perspective. Being gifted is not the same thing as being creative, but it is a very good beginning.

Creative Parenting and Teaching

> *Fostering creativity should not be reduced to a collection of set exercises carried out at fixed times as part of a 'creativity program.'*
> (Cropley & Urban, 2000, p. 496)

> *"I think that children who are given opportunities to play with lots of toys tend to develop more creative problem-solving skills."*
> *"I always enjoyed creative drama when I was younger. I try to involve my daughter in role-playing activities because it's a good way to increase her creativity and her understanding and tolerance of others."*

Being a creative parent or teacher means learning a lot about the content of these domains (i.e., parenting or teaching) and then continuing to learn more. It also means looking at our problems and failures as opportunities to broaden horizons—in fact welcoming problems as possibilities or as ways of identifying what we can do better. By pushing ourselves to extend our competence and by being open to new ideas, we grow, expand, and invent new approaches and ways of doing things. Remember Keating's analysis of creativity as a combination of (1) achieving a high level of mastery in a domain, (2) engaging in critical analyses of our behavior and its outcomes, (3) opening our minds to divergent possibilities, and (4) communicating effectively. They are as valuable in our own work and daily lives as they are when applied to our children's efforts. Being creative in these ways (and, too, modeling all of this for our children) can keep us fresh and learning and enthusiastic about living and working with the children in our lives.

Section II.

Being Smart about Testing, Identification, and Labeling

Chapter 3

Questions about Testing

Parents and teachers have many questions about tests and assessment procedures. We ask and answer several *who, what, when, where,* and *why* questions as they apply to various situations. We address questions concerning *how* to test in Chapter 4.

Who Needs Testing?

"I'm just not sure whether or not to put my son through the testing process."

"Robert tested at 129, so he's not in the gifted class. His friend's score was 130, and so he is identified as gifted. This doesn't seem right. Is there any real difference between them?"

"I dislike the gifted label, but I can see that Adrianna is way ahead of her classmates and bored with her grade-level work."

Parents and teachers often have questions about the whole educational testing enterprise, particularly as it applies to advanced learners and the testing that might be needed for entry into school gifted programs. They have uncertainties about the tests themselves, as well as the cut-off scores that are used to designate giftedness. For example, some jurisdictions use one cut-off score, while adjacent ones may use a higher or a lower score.

The questions and uncertainties raise valid concerns. Adults should think carefully before putting a child through all of the time and trouble involved in the testing process, to say nothing of the time and expense incurred by parents or the school. Nonetheless, for exceptionally capable learners, some kind of evaluation procedure is usually necessary to inform sound educational decision-making. Test results can show where a student's areas of strength and weakness lie, as well as providing guidelines for intelligent curriculum decision-making.

In thinking about the testing process, it is good to begin by asking these questions:

1. "If this child is *not* tested, what is likely to happen?"
2. "If we *do* test, how will the information be used?"

Although these questions can be answered only on a case-by-case basis, there are a few rules of thumb that can help guide decision-making. We present some sample scenarios below.

The Child Who Is Unhappy

> "I used to like school. Now I hate it. Nothing but blah."
> "I like spelling. But the Grade 2 spelling words are too easy, so I write them backwards."
> "I was doing a math experiment I invented in the bathroom. I was counting the number of flushes, but the toilets overflowed and then I got a week of detentions. It's not fair."

If a parent or teacher observes that a child is seriously or chronically frustrated, bored, or unhappy at school, then an assessment should be considered. If there are learning issues and the child's strengths and weaknesses are not identified and addressed, this can lead to more serious long-term problems, such as depression, behavior problems, low academic achievement, low self-esteem, and dropping out of school. An assessment by a psychologist who is trained and experienced in these matters can help to uncover the various interacting factors and reasons for a child's difficulties. When the assessment is followed by a consultation with parents and teachers, it can lead to helpful, specific recommendations for productive learning.

The Child Who Is Doing Well

If a child appears to be learning and thriving at school, and if her developmental needs seem to be well met without making any changes, testing may not be useful at that point in time. Are things moving along happily and well? Do the teachers and school appear to understand the child's learning needs? Are they providing what is needed for her to continue to learn and progress commensurate with her ability level? If so, then why bother going to the time, trouble, and expense of an assessment? If a child does not need the exceptionality label in order to get the education that she needs, it usually makes more sense to wait until assessment information will be more useful—for example, if problems occur with some aspect of her learning or school experience.

In some circumstances, however, a precautionary attitude may help to prevent future problems, and a proactive assessment can be helpful. Sometimes a child appears to be doing just fine but *does* need something more if he is to be appropriately challenged, a possibility to which parents and teachers should be attentive. At these times, a regular school-based administration of a high-ceiling or above-level subject-specific reasoning test (as discussed later in this section) provides a more systematic way of ensuring that children in this category are discovered. Where such tests are not in place, a psychoeducational assessment can be useful.

Individual Differences

> "He feels that he is different from everyone else and worries that others do not accept him for the way he is."
> "Sometimes she seems 'off the wall.' She just sees things differently."

Schools and educators vary tremendously in their readiness, willingness, and ability to consider and address individual differences, even if testing has shown that a child is exceptional in one or more areas. An important factor in making a decision about whether to assess an individual child is whether or not anything productive will be done with the results. This is not always easy to know ahead of time. Some schools pay lip service to diversity and to "educating the whole child" but in reality provide a "one size fits all" kind of education, with little or no adaptations made for individual differences. Schools may have an attitude (and implicit policy) that states, "If you don't like what we provide, you can go elsewhere." Other schools welcome assessment information and work actively with teachers and parents to adapt programming and develop options that facilitate learning for each student.

When wondering about doing an assessment, it is good to ask the question, "Will the testing give us information we can use to develop a better educational plan, and what (if anything) will be done with the findings?" Parents can find answers to this question in discussions with the child's teacher, the principal, special education personnel, and possibly other parents, in combination with their own observations based on discussions with the child. In general, the more open, flexible, and accommodating the school climate, the more likely the assessment recommendations are to be implemented.

Who should be tested, then? To summarize, the strongest candidates for testing are those who are having difficulties that can not readily be investigated or solved by parents and/or educators using their own knowledge of the child, or if a child exhibits problems over a sustained period of time, such as:

- difficulty at school

- boredom or unhappiness at school

- learning needs that are not being matched by the learning experiences at school

Students whose schools are prepared to make the necessary changes once they are provided with information about exceptional ability in one or more areas are more appropriately positioned for testing than those who attend schools with little or no programming flexibility.

What Are the Key Concepts?

"There are so many different kinds of tests. I don't know what any of them are."

"How do we get the test results? Will someone explain them to us?"

"The school wants to test Maya, but I'm not sure if that's a good idea."

Assessment is one of the most complicated and problematic issues in the field of gifted education. There are a number of essential aspects, some of which we discuss more fully in Chapter 4. For those who want a quick overview, we go over some of the basics here. If you want to check on the meaning and usage of terms used in the field of gifted education beyond what we discuss here, go to http://members.aol.com/SvenNord/ed/GiftedGlossary.htm.

Assessment Fundamentals

Tests vs. Assessment

A *test* is a specific instrument, such as the *Stanford-Binet Intelligence Scale*, the *Wechsler Intelligence Scale for Children*, the *Woodcock-Johnson Psycho-Educational Battery*, or any of the academic achievement tests that are routinely given.

An *assessment* of a child's abilities is much more comprehensive than any one test and includes several different measures, many of which may be tests. A full psychoeducational assessment usually includes an intelligence test; one or more academic achievement tests; various measures of learning styles, self-concept, and attitudes toward school; and a consideration of the child's functioning at home, with friends, and at school. It includes visual and verbal interaction and observation of the student, and often an interview/consultation with the parent and/or teacher as well. Parents are usually asked to provide infant and toddler medical and anecdotal history and to comment on the child's interactions with siblings.

Standardized Tests

Standardized tests are designed to allow reliable comparisons of individuals with others of the same age or grade level and to provide standard scores. These tests are standardized in both the administration and the scoring procedures. This means that there are very detailed rules about how to administer and score each item so that the test conditions are as close as possible to identical or "standard" for all those who take the test. The advantage is that it provides a standard against which to measure an individual's ability. The disadvantage is that it allows no flexibility in administration or scoring.

Percentiles

A percentile designates where one person's score falls relative to other people's scores. For example, if a child scores at the 60th percentile, it means that she has scored at or higher than 60% of others who have taken the test. If someone scores at the 98th percentile, she has scored as well as or higher than 98% of others. This does not mean that the child knows 60% or 98% of the information being tested, but rather that she has done better than that percentage of the comparison population.

Standard Scores

Intelligence and academic test results are usually reported as standard scores. A standard score is nothing more than a comparison of that person's functioning on the test with others of the same age. Such a score is based on a test mean that is set at 100. By definition, 100 is the average standard score for people of the test-taker's age. Here, age is specified to the month and year and is not related to school grade.

Standard Deviation

Standard deviation is a statistical term describing the distribution of scores around the test mean of 100. Intelligence test scores typically have a standard deviation of 15 points. Most people (68% of the population) score within one standard deviation (that is, 15 points) above or below the mean of 100 (that is, between 85 and 115). The farther from 100 a standard score is, the more exceptional it is. Mental retardation is usually considered when scores are two or more standard deviations below the mean (70 or below). Giftedness is usually considered when scores are two or more standard deviations above the mean (130 and above, or above the 98th percentile).

Intelligence Quotient (IQ)

Historically, the "quotient" in intelligence quotient refers to the relationship between a person's mental age and chronological age. While that computation is no longer used, the term intelligence quotient (IQ) remains and is widely used to designate a standardized measure of intelligence. The two most widely respected and widely used tests of intelligence for school-aged children are the *Stanford-Binet* (currently in the fifth edition) for ages 2 to 90, and the *Wechsler Intelligence Scale for Children* (WISC) (currently in the fourth edition) for ages 6 to 16.

Group vs. Individual Tests

Group-administered tests can be given to many people at once—in a classroom setting, for example. They are time- and cost-efficient to administer, although they provide little or no opportunity to consider individual differences in response styles or reasons for making errors. The administration of such tests does not require specialized training, though the interpretation may.

Individual tests are administered privately, one-on-one, by a highly trained and experienced test administrator (a psychologist or psychometrist). Individual tests are significantly more expensive than group tests but provide much better opportunities for observation of a child's individual learning style, attitudes, strengths, and problems.

What Purpose Does Testing Serve?

Tests can provide valuable information about exceptional learning needs. Their value lies in the way they are interpreted and in the manner in which they are used to inform educational programming.

A psychoeducational assessment requires a written report (usually within 30 days), which is typically given to a child's parents in a conference where they are free to ask questions. A good assessment report is quite comprehensive—typically several pages long—and it includes test scores, findings concerning the child's areas of strengths and weakness, recommendations for home and school, and conclusions. All of this information is important for parents and teachers to know for purposes of decision-making and program planning.

In cases in which standardized test scores are being reported, it should be remembered that the percentile scores are based on a comparison with the norming population (the hundreds or thousands of people at each age group who were included in that particular test design process). Thus, a child who achieves at the 80th percentile on an intelligence test (or some other standardized test) is considered to have done as well as or better on the test than 80% of all children his age would be expected to do if they all took the test. For gifted identification purposes, scores are generally required to be above the 97th or 98th percentile.

Professionals involved in assessments (including psychologists and educators) sometimes disagree about what cut-off test score supposedly designates gifted exceptionality. However, when a student's score is two standard deviations above the mean (130, or above the 98th percentile), parents and educators must start looking further into the child's educational and other needs. In these circumstances, the school program may not be sufficiently stimulating, challenging, or appropriate. An unusually high intelligence test score is an indicator, a warning flag, for caring adults to investigate the match between the child's ability and the learning opportunities that she is being given.

There is evidence to suggest that children who score above 150 have even more special educational needs, as well perhaps as being at risk for social/emotional difficulties, particularly at early adolescence (Ruf, in press; Winner, 1996). It is also important to realize, however, that when a child's overall intelligence test score is below 130, it does *not* necessarily mean that the child is *not* gifted. Just because a score is below any given cut-off, it does not signify that an educational mismatch does not exist for that child at that time. We emphasize the importance of careful test interpretation. Scores and any other information generated can be useful, provided they are all wisely construed and carefully communicated to those who are making school-related decisions.

When to Test?

To answer the *When?* question, we consider factors such as the child's age, individual level of comfort with testing situations, various retest considerations, the time of year in which testing occurs, and whether advance preparation is required.

Age

> *"We've been told that our four-year-old son is showing signs of giftedness. Should he be tested?"*
> *"Do schools typically test smart kids in the primary grades?"*
> *"My son is 13 and has never had an IQ test. Is it too late?"*

Under most circumstances, a four-year-old child is too young for testing. Tests are not generally considered psychometrically reliable until a child is age six or seven, partly because of the huge individual differences in several dimensions of maturation. Before age six, for example, a lot of independent and curious kids are not much interested in complying with a stranger's requests that they follow the directions to manipulate blocks in a certain way. They would rather invent their own block designs than copy the ones the examiner shows them. In addition, they may have very little desire to do these activities as quickly as possible, which is necessary for high scores on many standardized tests. Although formalized assessments for giftedness can take place in the preschool years, "the reliability of those measures tends to be somewhat questionable" (Toto, 2004). In or around third grade is a more accurate time to test a child. Moreover, a number of schools around the country are appropriately using a more multifaceted approach to rule out the notion that there's just one test that will find any kind of need, let alone giftedness.

Intelligence testing *can* be done when a child is as young as two and a half or three years old or even younger, but generally, it only makes sense to proceed with testing that early when there are specific issues or concerns. If a child's development is generally proceeding well, and if she seems happy and interested in learning, it is not the time to think about testing. We discuss these issues more fully later on in connection with early identification, and we illustrate some of them with this vignette.

When to Test?

Parent

> *Jake is six years old and in Grade 1, and I'm wondering if he should be tested. He is currently reading chapter books around the Grade 3 or 4 level and also enjoys having them read to him. He wants to write his own chapter book and has a title and story idea in mind. His teacher is supportive and is encouraging him to do so. She also goes out of her way to find interesting materials and activities for him.*
>
> *Jake has always been very verbal. He is extremely focused and intense. He gets frustrated, but at the same time, he has a lovely sense of humor. Socially, he is very well adjusted, but we are beginning to notice that a lot of his friends don't have the same desire to remain at various activities for the length of time he does. He appears to be very strategy-oriented (he likes chess) and looks for patterns everywhere. He loves statistics and has taught himself many things, particularly in the sports world—names of all the players, their info, as well as the ins and outs of baseball and hockey. He is very self-challenging (with computer games, he won't rest until he has completed each level of difficulty), and he loves it when he's successful.*
>
> *As Jake is our first child, we really don't know if his attributes are that different from others his own age. So far, he is happy*

and loves school. However, he is quite mature for his age in some areas (he can reason like someone much older, and he's always thinking ahead). He is also the multi-tasking king. He can follow a hockey game (or two) on television while playing on the computer, and he can still carry on a conversation.

If you could shed light on any of this it would really help.

Our Response

Jake sounds wonderful. Although he might well test at the gifted level, we do not recommend testing at this point. As long as his learning needs are being met and he is doing fine in other ways (and he sounds like the kind of child who goes more than halfway to ensure that!), our position is, "If it ain't broke, don't fix it."

As he gets older, if you notice signs of unhappiness, boredom, frustration, aggression, or depression, then it would be a good time to consider testing. In the meantime, it sounds like your instincts are excellent and that he is in home and school environments that are meeting his needs very well. So keep doing what you are doing! You might want to take a look at some of the resources we provide on our website (www.beingsmart.ca) and consider joining your local chapter of the Association for Bright Children (ABC).

When considering whether or not to test a child who is age seven or older, think about the two questions we emphasized earlier: (1) if he is *not* tested, what is likely to happen, and (2) if he *is* tested, how will the information be used? There is no upper limit to the appropriate age for testing, so adolescents are not too old. Even adults who perceive a mismatch between their abilities and learning or career opportunities can sometimes benefit from assessment information.

Level of Comfort

"I had a fever of 101 degrees the day of the test, but I never told anyone I felt sick 'til later."

"When I got tested last time, the lady had an accent and I couldn't really understand her."

> *"I wanted to make sure the stupid test was done in time so I wouldn't miss any of the lunch period."*

A child who is sick or distracted or who decides to rush through the testing in order to do something she really wants to do (lunch, gym, recess, or maybe math) is not going to perform as well as she is able, and her test scores will be lower than they would otherwise have been. A child who feels uncomfortable with the test administrator or is pressured or has trouble understanding the instructions might also not score well. Although important components of professional assessment practice (particularly with individual tests) include that a child is physically and emotionally comfortable and that she understands the instructions, we have nevertheless seen many examples of these rules being violated.

Retesting

> *"Can we have Christopher retested on the WISC?"*
> *"Emily took the Stanford-Binet six months ago. She has matured a lot since then, so we want her to redo it."*
> *"Hunter took an IQ test when he was six. He's going to high school next year. Does it make any sense for him to do it again now, or will the results be the same?"*

Intelligence tests are quite different than content-mastery tests. Intelligence tests are designed to provide information about a child's cognitive processing, including his reasoning ability, when faced with novel puzzles and problems. In order to provide valid scores, the tasks must be new to the child, and because of this, the same test cannot be given too frequently. Not only is this sensible, but the rules governing test practices (with the most valid and reliable tests) actually prohibit re-administration of a given test before a minimum of one year. Some jurisdictions are more conservative than that and will accept the results of a retest only if it has been at least two years since the previous testing using the same instrument. This prevents results being affected by a retest phenomenon that gives an advantage to children who have been recently tested.

If children are assessed when they are young, it is sometimes necessary to repeat the testing later. Generally, assessments that are two or more years out of date are not considered current enough for making programming decisions. Children do grow and develop in ways that cannot always be predicted and that do not follow "normal" pathways, and so of course, children's test scores (including IQ) can change over time, occasionally dramatically, sometimes rising, sometimes falling. At the same time, there is rarely a good reason to do "regular" intelligence testing or to retest a child at all unless there is a decision that requires new information.

Time of Year

> "Should children be tested at the beginning, middle, or end of the school year?"

The best time to test a child is when the need for it is recognized. Experience has shown us that the two peak months for testing are October and May. Because most classes begin in September, problems tend to surface in October, and parents and teachers may identify a need for assessment at that time. In the spring, people begin thinking about and planning for the next school year. There is enough lead time then to incorporate any necessary changes into educational planning for the next year.

If testing is being done by the school rather than by a private practitioner, there is usually little individual scheduling choice. As might be expected, there tend to be waiting lists for individual assessments, particularly if the referring issue is one of giftedness, which is very often seen by schools as less urgent than other kinds of schooling issues.

Advance Preparation

> "What can we do to make sure our child doesn't 'fail' the gifted test?"
> "Are there practice tests our son can work on?"
> "How can we reduce text anxiety?"

Sometimes parents ask how to prepare a child for testing. Our answer: "Make sure she gets a good sleep the night before and eats a nutritious breakfast." There is little that one can study that helps prepare for an intelligence test.

Intelligence tests are designed to assess a child's reasoning ability and knowledge in several areas. Preparation for them is what has occurred all through the child's life up to the time and date of testing. A child who feels loved and listened to, whose curiosity has been encouraged, and whose questions have been addressed is as ready as he can be. If his learning has been supported and he has been exposed to a variety of situations and learning opportunities, then he has done the best homework or preparation possible.

In fact, studying for an intelligence test is more likely to make a child anxious and so reduce the score rather than improve it—that is, unless an unscrupulous person who has access to the test is coaching the child in the actual test items or similar tasks. Even when parents are willing to collude in this unethical practice and find someone willing to prepare their child in this way, they do the child no favor. If they succeed in artificially boosting the child's score into the gifted range, she is likely to find herself struggling to keep up with the others in a gifted program. She runs the risk of going from being one of the most competent members of a regular class to being the least capable learner among those who are more advanced. Even though tests and scores are problematic in many ways, if they are the standard that all children are being held to, it is not usually an advantage to be the least competent in the group at meeting that standard. For obvious reasons, this kind of situation can seriously damage a child's self-esteem, learning, and eventual achievement.

Another concern about test preparation relates to test anxiety. Some children become anxious just because they are being tested or as soon as they see a stopwatch being used to time them. Parents can help prevent or reduce anxiety (and its possible score-lowering effects) by making sure that their child is happy, well-rested, and well-fed on the day of testing. They can also help by modeling a calm, poised, and curious attitude toward the assessment session.

Parents can also help their child do as well as possible in an assessment by explaining the reasons for doing the testing. One way to talk about the testing process is as an exploration of how the child learns. When parents ask us what to tell their child about what he will be doing during an assessment, we suggest saying something like, "We're hiring a learning detective who needs your help to find some clues. You'll be working together to figure out how you learn best. We want to know what you do really well and what might not be so easy for you. Mostly we want some ideas about how you learn and some information that we can share with your teachers. The learning detective will ask you to do some puzzles, thinking games, and quizzes." Most children like the idea of working with the psychologist to help figure themselves out.

The vast majority of gifted children actually love assessment tasks, and many of them ask their parents on their way out of the testing if they can come back another day or do this instead of school. Generally, the only children who really dislike the process are those with serious problems who have had too many bad testing experiences already and who feel that their weaknesses are being investigated and exposed.

To summarize, life itself is the best preparation for such a test, and being fresh and relaxed helps, too.

Where to Test?

> "Are the tests done by the school the same as the ones done by private consultants or psychologists? Will my child do just as well on the school tests?"

> "Jill was tested two years ago, and the school psychologist concluded that she had emotional problems. Since then, none of her teachers has even thought about her giftedness. Instead, all they do is focus on her so-called emotional issues."

> "Does it matter where he takes the test? Will the scores be part of his school record?"

In some school settings, parents who want an assessment for their child have no choice other than to hire a psychologist in private practice. In other settings, there are school psychological services available, and at no charge.

Some parents, however, may have legitimate concerns about testing that is conducted through the school. Once the testing has been done, test results usually become part of the child's permanent school record unless parents request that they be excluded. Requesting their removal is not always an easy process. Whether the results automatically become part of the child's record or not, parents may worry that educators will misinterpret the findings or use them to support programming that they (the parents) don't believe to be appropriate. There is some variation in these practices across jurisdictions, so this is something that parents should check into with their child's school, especially if it is a concern.

For most gifted children, however, there is no reason to be uneasy about the school testing process or to even think about doing the testing privately if it is available through the school. If there are concerns about what the assessment results will be or how they will be used, it is good to discuss matters with the school psychologist, as well as to consider the possibility of hiring a psychologist in private practice to conduct the assessment.

When a private assessment is indicated, it is important that there be a good fit between the child and the person doing the assessment. Choosing a competent, experienced, and caring professional can be a time-consuming and stressful process. It requires some patience and effort, as well as considerable knowledge about what to look for. We discuss how to go about the process of seeking professional help in Chapter 14.

Why Test?

> *"I know my son is smart, but his grades are terrible."*
>
> *"My daughter's really creative, but she's always getting in trouble at school. The teachers just don't seem to like her."*
>
> *"I have this one student who never hands in his homework. He's the class clown. I think he's really bright, but how can I know for sure?"*
>
> *"There's a kid in my class who's driving me nuts with her questioning. She's becoming a real behavior problem. I need to know how to program for her."*

In most schools, there is strong resistance to accelerate or enrich a child's classroom activities—or even consider the possibility of giftedness—unless the child has demonstrated abilities unequivocally in ways that the school considers compelling. In some settings, giftedness means being a "teacher-pleaser," a dutiful student who always hands in top-notch assignments and gets high marks. In other settings, giftedness means being knowledgeable, expressive, and assertive. In yet other situations, it can mean being creative, task-committed, curious, or demonstrating a combination of personality or learning style attributes. Most teachers have little or no training in gifted development, and so they have many and varied personal biases and assumptions that influence their perceptions of what a gifted child is like. Such characterizations can prevent them from recognizing and identifying the advanced or gifted learners in their classrooms.

We know from experience that there are many kids who are exceptionally advanced in their learning ability who do not fit (1) any of the generally accepted "gifted student" types (as so frequently seen in the checklists included in books and articles grounded in the mystery model approach), or (2) the conception of giftedness that happens to be in place in their school. In fact, some of the most capable learners are so bored and frustrated by what they are asked to do at school that the last thing they appear to be is keen, curious, task-committed, or high-achieving—attributes that are often regarded as typical characteristics of "the gifted." Some gifted students' grades are appalling except when they happen to like the teacher, the assignment, or the subject. In such situations, the best way to make the case for gifted learning needs is to provide standardized test scores. These can be used to show:

- exceptional subject mastery relative to age-peers
- areas of strength and weakness
- level and type of educational accommodation needed.

Testing can therefore be useful to indicate a child's areas of mismatch. The important question to ask then is, "What learning opportunities does this child need in the mismatched areas?"

A Sampling of Student Testing Scenarios

Each of the following students was identified as gifted on the basis of assessment criteria established by their individual schools. It is interesting to see that the reasons for testing, procedures used, children's experiences, and consequences were all quite different.

Dana

Dana was a lively and energetic 10-year-old who had always achieved a high academic standard (straight A's). However, her parents had become increasingly disillusioned with the educational philosophy of the private school she had been attending since kindergarten. They believed that a full-time gifted program in the public school system would be comparable to a regular program in the private school, and at considerable financial savings. Accordingly, Dana's parents arranged for a psychologist to administer the

Stanford-Binet during the summer. She met the criteria for her public school's gifted program and was granted automatic entry. Family members treated the test "simply as an entry exercise" required in order for her to move from a private school to a public school. She loved the new environment and found it challenging.

Sheila

Sheila, a fourth-grader, was involved in a weekly "challenge program" in her local elementary school that provided enrichment to a group of children on a pull-out basis. The special program teacher believed that Sheila was a suitable candidate for full-time gifted programming and nominated her for testing. Sheila took part in assessment procedures but divulged that she was confused. "I really didn't understand... I didn't know. I just said, 'Yeah, I'll take the test.'" On the basis of a WISC score above the 98th percentile, Sheila was identified as gifted. Placement then became an issue. Sheila's parents wondered if they should leave her in the part-time challenge program and the regular classroom or move her to a full-time gifted placement. As far as Sheila was concerned, she was ready to "start fresh." After careful deliberation, Sheila and her parents decided to accept the gifted placement for her. From fifth grade onward, Sheila went from being bored to being happily challenged. She compared work demands, reporting that they had previously been "effortless," whereas they became "a lot harder and much better than before."

Corey

Corey was a feisty nine-year-old who described school as "yawwwn, zzzz, ahhh! It's boring, exhausting, and far too much work." His report card indicated a range of achievement levels from A to D and inconsistent work habits. He loved mathematics and all things to do with computers, although his school grades did not reflect that. Corey had almost no friends, and he perceived school as a place that he was obliged to attend but which served little purpose socially or academically. "I like school because it ends." Corey's gifted identification procedure consisted of a group intelligence test at school which he described as "managing bits of information." After a long wait, the school informed Corey and his parents that he had been selected for placement in a gifted classroom. He was hopeful that being in a full-time gifted program would make school more interesting and enjoyable; however, a year later, he said nothing much had changed. He still had not made any friends, and his advanced abilities in math and computers were not being addressed at school. He said, "The only place I learn anything worthwhile is at home in front of my computer."

Although intelligence test scores are not always used intelligently (as in the case of Corey above), when seen in the context of other information, they can help parents and educators understand a child's learning strengths and any problems she might be experiencing. It is important to keep in mind that the only good reason to test children in schools is to understand what is reasonable to expect from them and how we can better meet their learning needs. Testing merely to discover an IQ score does little or nothing to help a child or to help a teacher understand what kind of educational programming is needed.

Now that we've considered the "Who, What, When, Where, and Why" of testing, we look at "How" to understand assessments and tests, and then at gifted identification and labeling.

Chapter 4

Assessments and Tests

In Chapter 3, we established a foundation for understanding assessment and identification issues. We introduced many terms, concepts, and issues surrounding the complex area of assessing gifted learning needs. Here we discuss the way assessments are actually done, the various tests and measures that are used, and how to make sense of the scores and results that are generated.

It Starts with the Teacher: Classroom Assessment

"Madeline absorbs everything I give her. I know she's ready for more, but I don't know where to start."

"I know that all the kids in my class have been identified as 'gifted,' but I don't know what that means when it comes to what math I should teach them."

Learning is a dynamic process that happens in a particular context or environment. Learning in a school setting is deeply influenced by the learner's relationship with the teacher and with other students, and is also impacted by the child's interests, abilities, and personal history. Identifying academic and other needs begins with ongoing dynamic assessment in the classroom.

Dynamic Assessment

In dynamic assessment, the teacher engages with the student as an active partner in an ongoing, cyclical process:

- informally assessing students' learning needs
- teaching to the optimal levels
- assessing learning outcomes
- teaching to the optimal levels
- assessing learning outcomes
- and so on, repeating the cycle

In dynamic assessment, the teacher and student are engaged in a seamless and recurring cycle of assess, teach, assess, teach, assess, and so on. In this way, instruction and assessment inform each other, and both are grounded in a clear understanding of what each individual learner already knows and can do. Once a student reaches mastery level of a section of curriculum or skill area, he is given (or helps the teacher discover or design) new and more challenging material to learn. By keeping close track of student learning in this way, teachers and students can work together to make informed decisions that match curriculum demands to learners' developmental levels. This approach has obvious benefits for all students, but it is particularly important for gifted learners, whose exceptional learning needs might otherwise go unnoticed by the teacher. By enabling students to confront new and appropriate learning challenges, this strategy both encourages gifted students' ongoing learning and helps to prevent boredom, frustration, and tuning out.

Dynamic Assessment in the Classroom

Sean learned everything he could about dinosaurs when he was in kindergarten and first grade, so he had little motivation to study them with the rest of his Grade 3 class. His teacher, Miss Kuna, conducted an assessment of students' knowledge before beginning the unit on dinosaurs and, recognizing Sean's advanced knowledge, talked with him about what else he would like to learn about the topic. She consulted with the school librarian, who was able to find some more challenging books for Sean containing information about the disappearance of the dinosaurs and recent discoveries. Together with Sean, Miss Kuna worked out some meaningful activities that he found stimulating and that kept him happily engaged while the others in the class were learning basic skills that he had long since mastered. She encouraged him to keep everything in a portfolio folder so that he could work on his dinosaur project whenever he wanted to. He began an e-corre-spondence with a dinosaur expert at the American Museum of Natural History and learned about some recent findings that weren't even published yet. He proudly showed his dinosaur folder to his parents and shared it with some of his classmates who were interested.

Dynamic assessment minimizes the need for formal testing, labeling, or withdrawal of students from the regular classroom. There are several advantages to using the ongoing dynamic assessment model with gifted students:

- Curriculum can be much more readily tailored to a child's temperament, personality, interests, and learning styles, including a student's motivational state (Bolig & Day, 1993).

- It significantly reduces the cultural and socioeconomic status biases inherent in standardized testing (as we discuss later on).

- It provides a much more targeted indicator of learning ability in specific areas (such as math reasoning or reading comprehension).

- Most importantly, dynamic classroom-based assessment is directly related to each child's learning needs, providing specific implications for where and what kind of instruction or intervention is appropriate.

The Student Portfolio

One dynamic assessment approach involves the use of portfolios, or compilations of students' efforts that demonstrate their progress in one or more areas. Students are responsible for putting work samples in their own portfolios in collaboration with the teacher; the degree of student responsibility and involvement depends on age and other individual factors (Blumenfeld, Soloway, Marx, Krajcik, Guzdial, & Palincsar, 1991). A personal folder, box, or specially decorated holder can contain whatever the student (in consultation with the teacher) deems relevant and important as artifacts of the learning process. A portfolio might contain, for example, work samples, journals, tapes, pictures, continually-updated accounts of test results, teacher assessments, and descriptions of achievements and learning experiences (including self-ratings or reflections). It is a "purposeful collection of student work that exhibits processes, strategies, progress, achievement, and effort over time" (Schipper & Rossi, 1997, p. 4). In planning for the portfolio, the student is managing her own work and setting personal goals—both important life skills. The student takes ownership and pride in her own accomplishments rather than having to depend on outside evaluation from teachers or parents.

Portfolios generally reflect instruction, responses, and tasks that are authentic; that is, they are personally meaningful and relevant to the individual. For example, a typical student portfolio might contain initial plans for a project; several written drafts; self-evaluations; feedback from peers, teachers, and other experts; finished products; and possibly plans for subsequent activities. These materials can be kept by the teacher or by the student, depending on his maturity, and can always be revisited. By sixth grade or so, a child should be fully responsible for assembling, maintaining, and updating his own portfolio.

Portfolios are particularly useful for gifted young children whose abilities may not be well-assessed using standardized or teacher-made tests. With the portfolio approach, parents and teachers are able to recognize an individual child's abilities and developmental pathways in certain areas over time, as well as the demands of a given school curriculum and the resources the child has used (Wright & Borland, 1993). Portfolios are also useful for artistically gifted learners as they work to develop skills, message, and vision in their work. Increasingly, portfolios are being recognized as useful for both student learning and dynamic classroom assessment purposes, and in parent-teacher conferences to showcase a child's learning. Because classroom-based portfolio assessment is a departure from traditional practice, teachers require administrative support as they learn to use this approach (Kornhaber, Krechevsky & Gardner, 1990).

Standardized Academic Achievement Testing

> *"Tony loves school and does really well, but I'm not sure whether he needs harder work or not."*
> *"I'd like to know the actual benefits of achievement tests."*

Unlike dynamic assessment methods, standardized tests are not flexibly responsive to a single individual or context. By their very design, they cannot reflect the authentic, interactive, and dynamic nature of learning. What they do accomplish, however, is important. Standardized academic achievement tests provide a *standardized* way to measure how well a student is mastering school curriculum compared with the norm for children at her age and grade level. Used wisely, they constitute an important supplement to classroom-based assessment, providing a reference point and source of accountability for parents and educators.

Standardized academic achievements tests are typically pencil-and-paper tess administered by a teacher to an entire class group at one sitting and scored electronically or by teachers. They measure how well a student is learning in specific subject areas, and they indicate grade level of content mastery and reasoning ability in each subject.

Because of the time, effort, and expertise that go into their construction, standardized academic achievements tests are generally much more reliable in their design than teacher-made tests. They can therefore yield direct and useful information about where a teacher ought to be targeting instruction. They are also useful for comparing schools and programs within and among districts and for providing standards of accountability. If, for example, a school discovers that 75% of its fourth-graders are scoring below the fourth-grade mean in mathematics, the school has some important information for thinking about possible reasons for this and for encouraging improvements in fourth-grade mathematics curriculum.

Academic achievement scores can indicate what a child knows about a certain subject area, provided they are interpreted carefully. Because these tests are standardized, they may or may not be directly related to what a given student has been taught in a particular school. A student's low score on a standardized test is not always a good measure of how well he has learned what he has been taught, because he has not necessarily been taught what the test is measuring. As with other kinds of assessment, there are many reasons for a child to score poorly on these tests—reasons that have nothing to do with a child's actual ability. Nevertheless, standardized academic achievement tests provide one important information source for thinking about how best to match individual learning needs and educational programming.

High-Ceiling and Above-Level Testing

"I can see that Juan needs more challenging work in math, but I just don't know how far to advance him."
"I think Zaria is capable of doing sophisticated reading comprehension activities. But she's only in Grade 3!"

When academic achievement tests are used to assess giftedness, they must be able to differentiate between those students who are excellent grade-level students (that is, operating well at grade level) from those whose abilities are far beyond the current grade level. If a child scores the maximum possible score on a test, she is said to be scoring at the test ceiling (sometimes referred to as "topping out" on the test). When that happens, we don't know how much more the child knows, because the test does not have enough items that are sufficiently difficult to measure the upper extent of her ability

Academic achievement tests that are designed to assess students' mastery of one grade-level of curriculum are meant to do just that: assess students' competence at grade-level knowledge and skills. They cannot be used to identify whether students should be placed at higher grades, or at what level. If a child is in third grade but is functioning in his reading comprehension at the tenth-grade level, he will score very well on a third-grade reading achievement test. However, so will the child who is working at an early fourth-grade level. On the basis of the high scores on that third-grade achievement test, we are not able to distinguish between the student who has gifted educational needs (the one who reads at a tenth-grade level) and the one who is doing very well at or slightly above grade level.

However, there are achievement tests which can be used to assess academic achievement more flexibly. These tests assess a wide enough range of grade levels that they are useful for identifying the actual grade level at which a student is functioning in any given subject area. The *Stanford Achievement Tests* are an example of a set of measures (sometimes called a test battery) that satisfy the three essential properties of such tests:

- *very high ceilings*, which means they have enough very difficult reasoning items to allow for differentiation between excellent grade-level students and those whose ability would be better matched by considerably higher grade-level curriculum, and they show the extent to which beyond-grade students are exceeding expectations

- *norming flexibility*, so that students can be compared with their age-peers, and their grade-peers (those who are functioning at the same grade level)

- *assessment of subject area reasoning separately from basic skills or content knowledge*, which provides information about a child's level of conceptual mastery somewhat independently of their opportunities to learn the actual content (that is, the gap between where they are in their learning and the grade level and material they are exposed to in their current studies)

High-ceiling academic achievement tests can therefore provide useful information about which students have gifted educational needs and what curriculum level best matches their learning abilities. Tests that focus more on reasoning than on content knowledge can help identify a younger child who has not yet been exposed to curriculum at higher grade levels but who can easily master it conceptually.

Another approach that is sometimes used to address this assessment issue is to administer above-grade-level tests—that is, tests that are aimed at a higher grade level than the child's age would normally suggest. Consider, for example, two children who score very well on a third-grade test of reading achievement but who are widely different in their actual learning needs. If they were to take a fifth-grade, or seventh-grade, or even a ninth-grade reading achievement test, the difference between their scores would be evident. The resulting information would enable educators to plan ways to differentiate curriculum for them. However, imagine giving a ninth-grade test to a group of third-grade children. The majority of the test items would be completely unfamiliar, and most third-graders would be intimidated by being asked to attempt them. Such tests do not have the same natural flow along the ability spectrum as high-ceiling tests, which are targeted to move seamlessly up from a child's normal age/grade level. Above-level tests do have the advantage, when compared to high-ceiling tests, of being more readily available and easier for teachers to administer and score. However, they do not provide a measure of the child's ability compared with others of the same age and, as noted, can be upsetting to children who are not ready for them.

For curriculum planning purposes, a teacher needs to understand the extent of a child's development in order to provide appropriate learning opportunities. The most important thing is that teachers recognize the necessity of doing this kind of diagnostic testing. Otherwise, there will continue to be too many gifted children languishing in classrooms where they already know the material being taught.

In keeping with the mastery model perspective, children's learning needs can be met if they are assessed using a combination of dynamic classroom-based assessment and standardized high-ceiling subject-specific achievement tests, which would be given routinely to all children. With this approach, students capable of handling and benefiting from sixth-grade work in science or math, for example, would be given the appropriate learning material regardless of whether their age would normally peg them in second grade or tenth grade. They'd be encouraged to study, learn, and progress at an individual pace, going through the curriculum as quickly or as slowly as necessary. Where teachers have the training, perspective, and support required to implement this approach, many of the problems associated with giftedness (and other exceptionalities) are alleviated. In a lot of classrooms, however, there are likely to be children whose learning needs will not be met unless they are identified as exceptional.

Intelligence Testing: What It Is and Is Not

> *"Justin is good at everything he tries. I know he's really really smart, but I have no idea how well he'd do on an IQ test."*
> *"Katelyn used to be smart. She had a high IQ when she was five years old, but I sure don't see signs of that now."*

Intelligence as measured by intelligence tests is a much more limited concept than the name of the test suggests. Many years ago, Stephen Jay Gould wrote compellingly about the limits of intelligence testing and the changeability of IQ scores (Gould, 1981). There have been many scientists since then who have confirmed his findings, including the fact that people's IQ scores can change quite dramatically over time (Ceci, 1996; Howe, 1999; Wahlsten, 1997). How much emphasis should we put on intelligence tests? Many, if not most, important aspects of successful careers and lives are not measured by intelligence tests. These aspects include social/emotional development; creativity; leadership; musical, athletic, and artistic ability; interpersonal skills; decision making ability; and independent thinking. Rather than seeing IQ as a true measure of a person's intelligence and as some kind of "real" indicator of a person's innate and permanent general cognitive ability, it is more accurate to see it as describing a child's functioning at a certain time on a number of specific tasks.

Intelligence tests can be a good interactive tool for assessing how well children and adolescents learn in many important areas. Although they certainly have limitations and miss much of what is important about gifted development (Sattler, 2001), when used in conjunction with academic achievement levels and observations of social and emotional functioning, these tests can provide useful information. By using a combination of assessment approaches that include intelligence testing, it is possible to identify a child's learning styles, strengths, and weaknesses in a way that informs both short- and long-term educational planning.

Group Administered Intelligence Tests

"I'm confused about all the different kinds of intelligence tests."
"Is a group test as good as an individual one?"

Examples of group administered intelligence tests are *Raven's Progressive Matrices* and the *Canadian Cognitive Abilities Test*. Such tests often include the words "intelligence" or "cognitive ability" in their names. They attempt to measure an individual's abstract reasoning ability, differentiated as much as possible from academic opportunities to learn.

Group intelligence tests have the usual benefits of group administered tests—they are cost- and time-effective. However, they are problematic for identifying giftedness. To begin with, there is no direct connection to academic curriculum, so very little information is provided about whether or not there is a curriculum mismatch for any given child. Because they are multiple-choice pencil-and-paper tests, they provide no opportunities for the child to interact with the material or the test administrator. Therefore, these tests miss the divergent or creative gifted thinker who looks at questions differently than others or who thinks in more complex ways than the "right answer" exemplifies. They miss the child whose reasoning ability is exceptionally advanced but whose reading and/or writing skills are not developing as well as might be expected. They almost always miss the child with double or multiple exceptionalities—for example, the child who is both gifted and learning disabled.

Group intelligence tests can perhaps be useful for preliminary screening, with the understanding that there will be some gifted children who fall between the mesh-lines of this screening and who need to be "searched for" at some point below the cut-off score. There are ways to reduce the problems associated with rigid cut-off scores by being flexible in assessment interpretation and identification. We discuss these issues in the remaining pages here and also in Chapter 5.

Individual Intelligence Tests

Individual intelligence tests have several of the same validity problems as group-administered intelligence tests in that they measure primarily the ability to do well on intelligence tests. These tests suffer from some of the same diversity-fairness issues as group intelligence tests, such as cultural differences in opportunities to learn, for which tests simply cannot compensate. No matter how a test is redesigned or the scores adjusted for life experience, children will not do well if they do not know the material being tested or if they have not had a history of embedded learning opportunities that prepare them for effective test-taking. Although test developers have worked hard to meet such criticisms, many observers are concluding that trying to make conventional intelligence tests culture-fair may not be a productive endeavor and that gifted identification itself is fraught with serious problems (Borland, 2003; Ford, 2003a; Robinson, 2003).

At the same time, however, individual intelligence tests *do* have some strengths that justify their being used as part of an assessment of possible giftedness. To begin with, individual intelligence tests are interactive in their design. The test administrator has an opportunity to closely observe a child's learning in a novel cognitive performance situation. Extensive training is required in order to administer individual intelligence tests, and an experienced clinician observes the child's approach to receiving, manipulating, and communicating information. The testing process takes an hour or two (depending on the child and the subtests administered). It consists of oral questions as well as tasks requiring manipulation of various objects and puzzles, with several subtests measuring various kinds of abilities. Throughout the process, the examiner's role is to observe the test-taker's response style carefully, noting interesting and relevant dimensions of cognitive and personality functioning. When considered along with the test scores, these factors can be used to inform placement and programming decisions.

Another important benefit of the major individual intelligence tests is that they are highly reliable measurement instruments. If the scores are interpreted carefully, taking individual and cultural factors into account (such as tiredness, illness, test anxiety, language spoken at home), they can provide an effective indication of a student's exceptionality.

When an intelligence test score (IQ) is extremely high, some kind of exceptionality exists that implies special educational needs. Exactly what cut-off designates exceptionality is contentious and frequently debated. However, when a student's score is more than two standard deviations above the mean (an IQ of 130, at the 98th percentile), there is good reason for parents and educators to examine the nature of the learner-learning match. And an IQ score above 145 (three standard deviations above the mean, as noted in Chapter 3) is even more suggestive of a probable mismatch.

There are two major individual intelligence tests in use, both of which have excellent test design and normative properties: the Wechsler tests, and the *Stanford-Binet Intelligence Scale*. Wechsler tests currently in use include the *Wechsler Preschool and Primary Scale of Intelligence* (WPPSI), designed for children ages 2 to 6; the *Wechsler Intelligence Scale for Children* (4th edition, WISC-IV), designed for children ages 6 to 16; and the *Wechsler Adult Intelligence Scale, Revised* (WAIS-R), for age 16 and over. The *Stanford-Binet Intelligence Scale* (5th edition, SB-V) is designed for ages 2 to 90. Tests in both systems are in a constant state of revision, which is why their names include designations like "4th edition."

Individual Testing: A Case Study

Zachary, a five-year-old, was taking the Stanford-Binet Intelligence Scale. The reason Zachary's parents sought an assessment was to find out if there was something wrong with their son's cognitive processing that might lead to his having problems at school. At home and elsewhere, they observed an insatiable curiosity and appetite for learning in combination with an extraordinary intensity of focus when he was interested in something. However, his kindergarten teacher described him as unexceptional—other than being a behavior problem in her class.

On one of the early items of the intelligence test, Zachary was asked to put together a puzzle that depicted a person's face. He scored close to zero on this item, getting very few of the puzzle pieces in the right place. The test-giver was dismayed. Was the child's visual/spatial perception distorted? Did he have some kind of emotional problem that led him to misperceive human faces?

The little boy, however, seemed quite pleased with himself as he pronounced, "I made a face like Picasso would do it!" He then went on to discuss in some detail Picasso's work, including listing his reasons for preferring the work of Camille Pisarro to that of Pablo Picasso.

Through Zachary's conversation with the test administrator on this and other test items, it was obvious that he was extraordinary in his knowledge and interest in a wide range of areas. If a group-administered test had been given instead of the individual test, he would probably have had the same kind of fun thinking up interesting answers. But items in such a group test would simply have been marked wrong, and Zachary wouldn't have had anyone to explain his answers to. It is likely that his parents would have been informed that his intelligence was average (or perhaps below!) and that his problems were emotional, maturational, and/or behavioral. Although his score on the individual test was considerably lower than he was capable of scoring, it was possible, because the test was administered orally and one-on-one, to provide an intelligent assessment of his exceptional curiosity, knowledge base, and inventiveness. It was also possible to make a strong recommendation for gifted programming for Zachary. He was clearly the kind of child who needed more challenges and who would continue to create his own!

Zachary is now 10 years old. He has had variable learning experiences over the past few years and continues to be a delight and also a challenge to his parents and teachers. It seems that when he has a patient and flexible teacher who enjoys working with a lively, curious, intelligent student, he does very, very well. Otherwise, his school performance drops precipitously. We predict that this pattern of ups and downs will continue for the next several years, until he is finally out of high school and in circumstances in which he gets to choose what he is learning and has more autonomy about how he learns it.

Aptitude Tests

"What is an aptitude test?"
"I'd like to find out Madison's potential. Should she take some kind of aptitude test?"

Aptitude tests are pencil-and-paper tests, often group tests, that include a mix of reasoning and content mastery test items. They are designed to measure children's aptitudes for various subject areas—that is, whether or not they might become good at something. They are similar in their format and appearance to academic achievement tests and group-administered intelligence tests; they are standardized in administration and scoring, and teachers can both give and score them.

Aptitude tests do not provide a measure of a student's actual subject-specific achievement. Nor do they indicate the extent of one's reasoning ability in a given area (which is as close as we can come to predicting an aptitude for learning something one has not yet learned). Aptitude tests have neither the test-reliability strengths of individual intelligence tests nor the opportunity for one-on-one interaction and observation. They also lack the curriculum-based validity of high-ceiling academic achievement tests. We do not recommend aptitude tests; we feel that other testing tools are preferable.

Creativity Testing

Standardized pencil-and-paper tests used to find some kind of generic creativity do not make sense. Pencil-and-paper tests purporting to measure creativity are simply not useful long-term predictors of creative talent, ability, or achievement (Perkins, 1981; Piirto, 2003). The best judges of creativity are those who are experts in a particular domain. If we want to know if a child is artistically talented and creative, for example, the best way to find out is *not* to ask the child to complete a test of creativity, but rather to assemble a panel of experts and ask them to comment on the child's work, just as a teacher might evaluate a child's academic portfolio. The same goes for musical, scientific, and other forms of creativity. And in fact, the extensive literature on this topic shows consistently that domain-specific ratings by experts are the best predictors of subsequent achievement (Amabile, 1996; Czikszentmihalyi, 1996; Feldman & Goldsmith, 1986; Gardner, 1993; Perkins, 1981; Piirto, 2003; Sternberg, 1998). Creativity assessment has very little place in an academic assessment, then, except perhaps as a trait to note if apparent, as in the case of Zachary described above. As we discussed in Chapter 2, although creativity is an important component of high-level real-world achievement, it does not make good theoretical or practical sense to attempt to quantify it as a component of gifted identification for placement in a program for gifted learners.

At the same time, however, there are recently-published findings demonstrating the validity of a systematic approach to assessing creative and artistic potential in performing arts talent. The *Talent Assessment Process* approaches in dance (DTAP), music (MTAP), and theater (TTAP) (Oreck, Owens, & Baum, 2003) have been used in New York City for the past 13 years and are now mandated by the Ohio Department of Education (2000) for gifted and talented identification for students in the visual and performing arts. These are multi-session and multi-observer assessment processes that have proven to be valid and reliable with diverse student populations and limited access to arts instruction. In its focus on "current readiness for advanced instruction" (Oreck et al., 2003, p. 81), D/M/T TAP is consistent with the mastery model of giftedness under discussion here.

Career Interest Inventories

"*Monique isn't sure what she wants to study after high school. There are so many options open to someone with her talents and abilities. How can I help her decide what to do?*"

"*Cole wants to be a lawyer. But he also wants to be a musician. AND he wants to be a scientist. Now he has to make course choices that will eliminate one or more of these possibilities. Help!*"

Gifted children often demonstrate multipotentiality. That is, they often have several areas of exceptional strength and interest (for instance, math, music, and science), each of which is highly promising and would normally be considered an obvious selection for academic and career development. A student with multiple and diverse interests, and with highly developed ability in more than one of them, often has difficulty figuring out which future direction to choose and which areas of interest to sideline. As highly capable children become adolescents and young adults, choosing a college major or a career path can become very confusing and worrisome.

Consider for example the dilemma faced by a student who loves chemistry and is being encouraged by her science teachers to become a pharmacist or scientist, but who also loves writing and has been told repeatedly by her English teachers that she could be an excellent journalist. At the same time, her drama teacher has encouraged her to become a professional actor because of her obvious talent and passion for drama. This young woman is in a quandary, because she must choose high-level courses and focus her attention more narrowly in her areas of serious interest as she approaches the end of high school and considers her post-secondary education.

There are interest inventories and tests designed to help with this process, though they are not generally appropriate for children younger than age 17 or 18. Unfortunately for gifted students, career interest inventories are designed to identify more conventional career paths and so can be problematic for those who are highly gifted or who have high-level abilities in many areas. Career options typically do not include highly specialized occupations such as biochemical engineer, neuropsychologist, or international investment banker—any of which might be appropriate and interesting for a gifted student to consider. Additionally, career inventories cannot help those who have exceptionally well developed abilities in a number of totally different areas to figure out which interest to specialize in. Career decision-making instruments can provide a framework to stimulate a young adult to think more systematically about his options and interests if used in combination with counseling and guidance by someone who understands high-level development.

Although career interest inventories are not typically very useful for highly gifted learners and those experiencing multipotentiality concerns, there are many other ways for exceptional adolescents to do the exploration and get the guidance that they need in order to make good informed decisions. Some of these include mentorships, career days, job-shadowing, or part-time job opportunities in areas of interest.

Other Information Sources

"Jordan has been failing math all semester. I'm afraid his attitude is creating a block for new learning."

Parents, teachers, and students should take into account data from several sources when making decisions about academic programming. One such source might be how a student approaches learning tasks. An analysis during an assessment process can be helpful. The person conducting the test might do an error analysis (noticing where a child is making errors and why) and/or consider the student's reactions to various tasks. These reactions could include her manner of handling the easier and harder items on different subtests, responses to timed tests, reported preferences for certain kinds of activities, etc. This information can help parents and educators better understand a student's learning style and areas of difficulty. For example, several of the very high-ability children we have seen in our practice have performed much better on the harder items on some subtests and made many careless errors on the easier items. This pattern clearly indicates their need to be intellectually challenged. Such children often do poorly when given grade-appropriate work but respond much better to ability-appropriate work, and they experience educational mismatches in classrooms where they are not challenged in their particular areas of strength.

Self-concept and orientation to learning can also be assessed. Harter's *Perceived Competence Scale for Children* (1982) and other measures like it incorporate several design features that make them useful for assessing advancement in specific areas. There are also questionnaires on school attitudes, experiences, and learning styles. They include questions about hobbies and extracurricular activities, preferred school subjects, and various aspects of daily school life. These kinds of inventories are informal and do not provide reliable scores. Nevertheless, they can be useful additions to understanding a child's learning needs in order to make academic recommendations.

School Reports

> *"Corinne's poor marks are becoming a regular thing. How can we break the cycle of negative feedback and change it to more constructive feedback for her?"*
>
> *"I really look forward to getting my daughter's report card. It lets me know how well she's doing in school and how I can help her to improve in some subjects."*
>
> *"It's not fair. I think teachers play around with report card marks and parents don't even know it. I didn't 'earn' an A on my science project because my teacher had a problem with one little part of my presentation, but Dean got an A just for trying!"*

Report cards are another source of useful information and often include recommendations as well as good programming clues. Sometimes report cards are helpful as written, and sometimes they require some decoding. It is not unusual for parents of gifted learners to see comments on their child's report card like, "fails to complete his homework," or "is often disruptive in class," or "spends her time daydreaming." Knowing that the child in question is competent, such comments can signify that he may not be sufficiently challenged by school tasks and needs adaptations to the curriculum.

Teacher-assigned school grades can indicate gifted-level ability, as in the case of students who easily and consistently achieve extremely high marks. However, a problem with using high academic grades is that they do not, in and of themselves, differentiate high achievers working at grade level from those working way beyond it. It is important, too, to remember that children who already know most of the material being presented in class or who are exceptional in other ways as well as giftedness (such as gifted/ADHD) are very often disinterested, bored, and frustrated. As they get older, these students may put little effort into their schoolwork. They may not even pass their courses, much less demonstrate gifted-level achievement. We have known many highly gifted middle and high school students who receive below average or even failing grades. Still others drop out from the futility of seeking a place of new learning, even if it means underemployment in the workforce.

Unfortunately, high academic achievement and high task commitment are criteria for entrance to gifted classes in many schools. Such criteria can be improperly used for gatekeeping, so that students with gifted learning needs are held in standard classrooms. This perpetuates a systemic trapping of students who need to demonstrate motivation in order to have their learning needs met but are who not motivated *because* their needs are not being met. Similarly, they must achieve high grades but are unable to do that because a lack of stimulation has effectively shut them down intellectually.

Consider the comments of classroom teachers who have argued against gifted programming for some exceptionally able children:

> *"She doesn't even DO all her schoolwork, much less do it creatively. And I know that creativity is part of giftedness."*
> *"He never pays attention to what we're doing in class. He's certainly not task-committed."*
> *"She never finishes anything. She'll start a project and then lose interest halfway through."*
> *"He needs to learn good work habits before he goes to a gifted program."*

Rather than showing that a child should not participate in a gifted program, these comments illustrate a desperate need for gifted educational adaptations. In each of the above cases, for a variety of reasons, we had evidence that the child was in fact highly creative, could pay attention for long periods of time, and had all the necessary skills to do work—when given appropriate intellectual challenges. However, student report card marks and comments would not likely reflect this.

Although a grading system does provide a kind of yardstick enabling parents to know how a child is performing at school and in comparison to other children, report card grades can be highly subjective. The underlying message of teachers' comments can be difficult for parents to figure out. And marks are inevitably and directly tied to teacher expectations, which can be quite variable. For example, what exactly is an excellent mark? A? A+? Does a child have to *exceed* grade expectations to earn it? Report card marks are not held to a uniform standard.

Some schools use process folios in place of report cards. Such portfolios represent the learning and efforts of a single individual over time and do not lend themselves to being ranked or compared, because in effect, each student is competing against her own past achievement record. A student will participate in determining the criteria by which work is evaluated and then can use it to reflect upon strong performance, weak performance, and ways to change and improve performance (Schipper & Rossi, 1997). A student learning profile, in the form of teacher-documented descriptions of a child's progress through the stages of the learning process, may supplement the portfolio. A teacher can prepare this using baseline data, annotations from conferencing, and notes on processes, final products, and celebrations of successes.

The nature of the traditional report card is, to some degree, in flux. However, many parents feel that the report card, or a variation thereof, provides concrete and meaningful information about how their child is doing relative to others, and it lets them know whether or not they should be worried.

A Synopsis

We have pulled together into chart form a synopsis of the benefits and drawbacks of the various kinds of tests we discuss.

We conclude this chapter with some cautionary advice: Remember that the real value of test scores is in their interpretation. Only when test interpretation is done with sensitivity to the individual situation and its complexity can test scores be used intelligently to generate recommendations for appropriate curriculum modifications and to inform educational decisions.

For those who would like more information on interpreting test scores, including some components of a typical psychoeducational assessment, how to translate standard scores into percentiles, score conversion, mitigating circumstances with score interpretation, and scoring patterns among high-ability learners, please refer to the Appendix.

Table 4.1. A Synopsis of Assessment Tools

	Benefits	Drawbacks
1. Informal classroom-based assessment		
a. Dynamic classroom assessment	Interactive, reiterative, responsive, elastic method	Lack of necessary teacher training and support
b. Process folios	Cumulative, authentic, evolving, child-created process	Time-intensive, non-systematic, subjective
2. Formal assessment measures		
a. Standardized tests	Comparative approach	No context-specific information; anxiety-inducing
i. Academic achievement	Subject-specific information for curriculum decision-making	Test items may not reflect what has been taught
ii. Group intelligence	Cost- and time-effective; good preliminary screening tool	Lack of responsivity to developmental diversity
iii. Individual intelligence	Valid, reliable test design; individual interpretation possibilities; information on reasoning ability independent of content	High cost; over-weighted in decision-making; lack of school relevance; emphasis on speed
iv. Aptitude	Inclusion of both reasoning and content mastery	Neither curriculum-relevant nor reasoning-based
v. Creativity	Questionable when pencil-and-paper measures are used	Can be misleading
b. Non-standardized measures	Responsivity to individual differences and contexts	Subjectivity; compromised comparison across settings
i. Self-concept	Social and emotional information	Questionable reliability of self-report data
ii. Learning styles	Focus on preferences, motivators, optimal school environment	Superficiality and limited nature of information
iii. Attitudes	Information on experiences, outlook, interests	Artificiality; static measure of dynamic constructs
iv. School reports	Information on actual school performance and work habits	Subjectivity; many reasons for underachievement; variable in format

Chapter 5

Identification and Labeling Issues

In this chapter, we look at various aspects of gifted identification processes, and we present some recommendations for identification that are consistent with the mastery model of giftedness. We start by considering how we think identification ought to be and then discuss the way it really is and what people can do about it. We discuss some of the concerns and issues about gifted labeling and finish this section by addressing parents' roles in supplementing assessment.

Identifying Giftedness

"It would have been interesting to have had someone to go through the test with us so we could've figured out how to cater to her learning by zeroing in on how she learns."

"I'm sure I know more about Morgan than any tester possibly could. Yet it seems to me that schools value those 'official test results' more than what parents have to say about their child's abilities."

"Are intelligence tests the only accepted way of evaluating whether or not my son is gifted?"

We have already addressed the importance of tying the assessment and identification of giftedness as closely as possible to an individual learner's educational needs. And as we discuss elsewhere, identifying giftedness simply on the basis of general intellectual ability, as measured by intelligence or cognitive abilities tests, is inadequate. How, then, *should* gifted educational needs be assessed? Think back to the mastery model of giftedness we presented in Chapter 1—that is, giftedness as exceptional subject-area advancement requiring educational adaptations at particular points in time. Rather than search out some inner, unseen essence of a student's intelligence or creativity, we recommend concretely determining subject-specific capabilities that can be tended by appropriate help and support. This has been called a student's "zone of proximal development" or ZPD for short (Vygotsky, 1930/1978), referring to the zone in which an individual's learning in a particular area is both *challenging enough to be interesting* and *familiar enough to be mastered with some help.*

The major goal of gifted assessment, then, should be to find those students who are working well *past* the learning zone within which the teacher is teaching. These students may be working so far above grade level in certain subjects that they are learning little or nothing from classroom activities and would benefit from studying different material from those who are working very *well* at the teacher's targeted zone. It is only when little is happening of educational value that a student should be considered for instructional adaptations, and that is sometimes hard to see unless you know what to look for and how to look for it.

The optimal assessment approach for *all* learners occurs in a comfortable place and in a way that is sensitive to children's individual differences and developmental levels (Gardner, 1993). For exceptional learners, as well as those who are more average in their abilities, assessment is best when it is an ongoing process, by subject area, and clearly integrated with curriculum (Heward, 2002). With this kind of approach, there is a natural match between a student's developmental level and education, and therefore, there is no need for formal identification or labeling as gifted. Looked at in this way, the identification process— ongoing assessment integrated into the classroom—is seen as formative, practical, and an integral part of the learning process (Hargreaves & Earl, 1990). Current research findings show the educational benefits of assessing each student's zone of proximal development in each subject area and then offering guidance and learning opportunities accordingly (VanTassel-Baska & Little, 2003; Vygotsky, 1978).

How should teachers go about conducting such assessments, and what do they need to know? In order to assess students' mastery and learning readiness that exceeds a current year's programming, teachers need to (a) be very familiar with the domain or subject being assessed, (b) have a good understanding of content and procedures across several years worth of curriculum, and/or (c) have access to support and resources that can provide this kind of knowledge and expertise.

Unfortunately, in most circumstances, teachers have been given neither the training nor the support necessary to carry out this kind of ongoing, flexible, high-level assessment. Professional development is one of the most pressing concerns in gifted education (Council of State Directors of Gifted Programs, 2004). We address teacher training in Chapter 15.

The infrequent but regular (perhaps yearly) use of high-ceiling standardized achievement tests in all subject areas is very useful for determining a student's level of learning. These tests include challenging above-grade-level items, tap into reasoning skills, and minimize penalties due to a lack of familiarity with specific content details. A mismatch of curriculum is then identified for those students who score extremely well. A classroom-based assessment strategy that works very well is student portfolios used in combination with high-ceiling academic achievement tests. This approach enables teachers to identify students' special abilities and provides information for curriculum decision-making in terms of both content and process. It is a sensible and efficient way to figure out who is learning what, and who has special learning needs. However, this is not the approach currently in use in most school districts.

Processes, Policies, and Problems

> *"I never perform well on tests. I get really nervous and tense, and I sometimes have mental blocks, even when I know the stuff being tested."*
> *"What if I throw up?"*
> *"Why doesn't someone tell us more about these tests before they give them to us? It would be nice to know what to expect."*
>
> *"We recently moved, only to find that our daughter is no longer eligible for gifted programming in this district. That makes no sense! What should we do?"*

> *"Demarco was tested in Grade 6 at his new school, and they want to place him in a gifted program. It seems strange to think he suddenly became gifted. Now we wonder what kinds of educational opportunities he's been missing."*

In many jurisdictions, identification procedures take place at one standard age or grade level for all students. Children who at that time achieve the designated cut-off score required for gifted identification become eligible for special programs, and others do not. This one-time-only identification process identifies as "permanently gifted" some children who may be ahead of their peers in certain tested areas at that point in time. Gifted programs that have a single entry point exclude some whose gifted learning needs develop beyond the time of testing, and they may include children whose learning needs would be better met by a regular program later on in their schooling. One-time-only or "snapshot" assessments also miss all those whose need for advanced programming is not evident at the time of identification for any number of possible reasons, not the least of which is the fact that children's maturational timing varies tremendously. Other possible reasons why a child might miss a certain gifted cut-off score (reasons that have nothing to do with a child's actual intellectual ability or with his need for gifted programming) include the following:

- domain-specific (rather than global) ability (such as mathematical or linguistic giftedness)

- maturational differences (there are early and late bloomers)

- poor test-taking skills

- test anxiety

- learning or attention problems

- motivational factors, including a desire not to be identified as gifted

- environmental test-taking factors (such as heat, comfort, or noise)

- personal factors (such as hunger, tiredness, or illness)

- differences between a child's first language and the language at school

- connection with and comprehension of the test administrator

- cultural differences

Another common problem with gifted identification practices occurs when the cut-off scores and/or method of identification differ from one school district or jurisdiction to the next. This causes children to become labeled gifted or to lose the label as families move, something which can be greatly unsettling for those who think that "being gifted" is meaningful. Gifted identification practices even within a single jurisdiction can change frequently over time, leading to situations in which a given child can move in and out of eligibility for a gifted designation. Eligibility standards can be affected by program availability, the school district's financial constraints, changing educational philosophy, educational priorities, and other factors. These kinds of designation inconsistencies provide further rationale for the flexible mastery model perspective on integrating gifted identification and programming applications.

In addition to these and other school policy variables, the child who fails to meet a given school's specific gifted criteria may well have gifted educational needs. There are a variety of possible routes parents can take to ensure that these needs are met. One option is to consider a supplementary assessment, which is particularly relevant where there are test environment or personal factors that appear to have impeded a child's performance. This approach might include an alternative test given by a different administrator or classroom-based assessment techniques. Another approach is for parents and teachers to work together and implement some of the learning options we describe in Section III.

Recommendations

"I bet those tests don't really show how much kids actually know."

In thinking about how identification should happen consistent with the mastery model of giftedness, we have developed three recommendations that are consistent with National Association for Gifted Children (n.d.) standards. Rather than being disconnected from learning and teaching (as many identification practices are), these recommendations lead logically and directly to evidence-based programming:

1. The process should be based on current and grounded theories and conceptions of competence.

2. Gifted education should be an ongoing process, not a one-time only test. As children mature, there should be regular (perhaps yearly) re-evaluations of their emerging abilities.

3. The identification process should be viewed as a means of assessing individual children's learning needs. It should be diagnostic, indicating not only areas of strength, but also areas of weakness, and specifying programming implications. The exceptional learning needs (*not* the child) should be identified as gifted.

Labeling certain children gifted is troubling for a number of reasons, but perhaps most seriously because it implies that other children are not. At the same time, however, from a practical perspective, it can be difficult to make the case that children require special academic accommodation unless we give a name or label to circumstances that require accommodation. When there is no official label, it is frequently the case that programming adaptations are not provided for the exceptional learners who need them.

All labels carry awkward connotations. Labels designating learning problems have their own issues, but the gifted label is particularly provocative for many parents and educators. Perhaps the worst thing about the term is that it implies that the majority of children (all those who are *not* in the gifted category) lack special abilities or gifts. The gifted label can evoke negative reactions from peers, and even from teachers and others (Foster, 2000; Kitchen & Matthews, 2004). It may also lead a child to believe that, because she demonstrates heightened ability, she does not have to work hard at school (Feldhusen & Jarwin, 2000). There is a simple and effective alternative to the practice of labeling students that emerges out of the mastery model approach and is consistent with current best practice in special education (Andrews & Lupart, 2000; Deutsch Smith, 2004; Heward, 2002; Rogers, 2002). This is to label the educational services instead of the students, offering a variety and range of options to those who are interested in and capable of taking advantage of them.

Although these recommendations and conclusions make practical sense, and many educators and researchers have pointed out their importance over the years, they are more frequently ignored than followed. It is true that in some places, students are given repeated chances to qualify for special programming using different tests, or retesting might occur after a two-year interval if parents and/or teachers request it. However, for the most part, the gifted identification process happens once or perhaps twice in a child's schooling and goes something like this:

- A child takes a preliminary screening test, usually a group-administered cognitive or academic abilities test, or a spatial reasoning test, along with his classmates, most commonly in the third or fourth grade.

- If the child achieves above a designated score on the screening test (e.g., above the 90th or 95th percentile), the next step is usually further testing, often on a more complex and better designed intelligence or cognitive abilities test, yielding a norm-referenced summary measure of intellectual ability.

- If the child achieves the requisite score (usually 130 or 135, or above the 98th or 99th percentile), she is designated as "gifted." Other measures may be included in the determination, such as parent inventories, teacher checklists, creativity tests, etc. In practice, however, these additional measures are rarely used for decision-making or programming purposes, but rather to demonstrate that multiple broad measures have been included in the process (consistent with Public Law 94-142 in the United States, and best practice elsewhere).

- Following the school's formal identification process, the child is able to use the gifted designation or label as the required ticket for admission to enriched academic learning opportunities.

Current Theories of Competence

This typical gifted identification process is grounded in a mystery model of giftedness. It assumes a general heightened level of functioning of some children and does not take into account current theories and understandings of competence and talent development in two important ways:

1. Intelligence is not best represented by a composite score whereby a single number is used to reflect many areas of functioning (such as IQ).

2. Individual developmental issues must be considered if educational programming is going to work toward matching a child's real learning needs.

Therefore testing must happen regularly, as specified in our recommendations for evidence-based programming as listed above, and it should be multifaceted. In mastery model thinking, intelligence is domain-specific, and giftedness is dynamic. That is, it occurs in certain areas at certain times and is fluid—set in the context of a child's life and relative to many factors, influences, and circumstances—not a once-and-for-always state.

An Ongoing Process

Identification that is ongoing with repeated evaluations of emerging abilities as children mature is very rarely addressed in any real way in typical gifted identification processes. Instead, once a child is labeled gifted, he is usually then considered to be gifted for the rest of his school career, unless serious problems develop in grades or behavior (which may then threaten programming, not necessarily the label itself). Similarly, if a child does not meet the gifted criteria at the time of testing, the possibility of giftedness-related educational needs is rarely reconsidered unless the parents take some action, such as seeking professional testing outside of the school system. Thus, many gifted learners are lost in the very system that is supposed to discover them, and it can be difficult for them to get the educational adaptations they require.

School districts that offer ongoing testing and assessment opportunities are better positioned to identify high-ability learners who are later in maturing or who do not test well at earlier stages. For information on gifted identification and programming practices in specific jurisdictions in the U.S., see *The State of the States* (Council of State Directors of Gifted Programs, 2004). (No such publication exists in Canada.)

Diagnosing Exceptional Learning Needs

When a school provides accommodations for gifted learners, it is almost always required that a child be categorically labeled as gifted in order to receive special academic or other services. It is unusual to find a school-based gifted identification practice that is *diagnostic*—that is, that uses test data to find areas of weakness, as well as areas of strength, for purposes of specifying necessary adaptations to programming. More often, the assessment for school-based gifted identification purposes is a summary report consisting of scores, along with a simple statement about whether or not the child meets the gifted criteria. This approach fosters a "one size fits all" mystery model approach to gifted curriculum, which is in sharp contrast to the mastery model's focus on matching curriculum to an individual child's areas of strength or weaknesses (if any).

Whether an individual intelligence test or some combination of assessment approaches is used, test cut-off scores are usually the major (and frequently the sole) factor in designating eligibility for gifted programming. Because such overall scores are not diagnostic in nature except in a very broad way, they offer little or nothing to classroom teachers by way of programming implications. On the other hand, individually-administered intelligence tests can be useful when assessing gifted educational needs, particularly in those cases in which such needs are otherwise difficult to assess. When parents and teachers are helped to interpret the test data, they can better understand an exceptional learner's functioning. When an experienced clinician observes a student's test-taking behavior and responses to complex tasks in a carefully regulated setting, this generates important and useful information. This is consistent with best practice in the use of intelligence tests (American Educational Research Association, 1999; Kaufman, 1994).

According to the three recommendations that we have developed, then, most processes of identifying gifted learners leave a great deal to be desired. Too often, exceptional learners' needs are not identified or understood, much less met, whether they achieve the requisite cut-off score or not.

Questionable Approaches

"Our neighborhood school has no gifted identification policy in place."

Far worse than a poor identification process, some schools have no process at all. They may even have an official anti-giftedness policy rooted in a well-meaning but misguided belief that *all* children are gifted and that they do not want to show favor to some children over others. Other schools—often private schools and some of the elite public schools— have the attitude that all children's high-level learning needs can be well met by the excellent education that they provide for all of their students, without adequately considering the enormous individual differences in their students' learning capacity. In these situations, schools take an explicit or implicit (and often uncompromising) position that they do not need to consider gifted-related assessments or provide special gifted education.

A Case Study

Although Logan was gifted in many respects, his parents were concerned that his learning needs were not being met. He had failed to make the 130 IQ gifted programming cut-off score required within his district and so was deemed to be ineligible for any gifted programming. However, the legally-mandated definition of giftedness in his jurisdiction was stated as: "An unusually advanced degree of general intellectual ability that requires differentiated learning experiences of a depth and breadth beyond those normally provided in a regular school program to satisfy the level of educational potential indicated" *(Ontario Ministry of Education, 1984).*

A school administrator indicated that the official criteria for identifying gifted behaviors in children involved the following:

1. *Academic assessment or evidence indicating a student's functioning to be at an advanced academic achievement or level (that is, at least two years or two grades higher than his or her chronological age).*

2. *The possibility of nomination by the child's parent, a peer, or a teacher.*

3. *Evidence of strengths in areas other than those measured by an IQ score (such as social perceptiveness, or advanced social interaction skills, or athleticism).*

4. *Demonstrated creativity.*

5. *Task commitment, as observed in behavior and as related to persistence in activities or pursuits (academic or otherwise).*

However, the determining *criteria for gifted identification pertained to psychoeducational assessment, using a standardized instrument as a means of verifying a student's intellectual ability. A student was required to achieve a performance IQ of 130 or above, corresponding to the 98th percentile, in order to be eligible for gifted programming.*

Logan's parents believed that he was being denied an appropriate education based solely on the result of his composite IQ score and that this was not acceptable. They advocated for their son's right to suitable programming and against the use of IQ scores as an exclusionary criterion, and they won their case at a tribunal hearing. In short, the arguments in support of their position emphasized that one test should never be used as the basis for a decision about a child's educational placement and that doing so breaches ethical standards of the testing profession. Moreover, they argued that identification should be a multifaceted process, reflective of current understandings of giftedness. Logan's entitlement to learning opportunities appropriately matched to his levels of ability could not be denied and, in the end, was not.

The final decision in this student's favor encourages optimism that educational institutions may be in the process of becoming more accountable for the intelligence of their gifted identification policies. This means being less tied to arbitrary, unsound, and outdated practices, less tolerant of bureaucratic arrogance, and more attuned to the needs of individual learners, consistent with the mastery model recommendations.

Too few educators respect gifted education, and too many believe that they have more important activities on which to focus their time and attention. There *are* some schools and educational jurisdictions that approach gifted identification in ways that are consistent with our recommendations. In such situations, a learner's exceptional needs are assessed on an ongoing basis, carefully considered, and intelligently addressed. In the majority of schools and school districts, however, this is not the case. Throughout this book, we offer numerous suggestions for parents and educators who wish to implement and advocate for more enlightened and effective policies of identifying gifted learners and then programming for them.

Early Identification

> *"What is the recommended policy for identifying a very young child as gifted?"*
>
> *"Our 22-month-old daughter is advanced for her age. Her vocabulary is amazing, and she communicates so well that people actually stop me in the street! She prefers to associate with kids age five and up and needs to be mentally stimulated. But the teachers won't place her in a daycare group with the older children. Should I have her tested?"*

One of the most contentious areas in gifted education concerns early identification. In most jurisdictions that have official gifted identification policies and practices, identification for gifted services does not occur until third or fourth grade. We believe that for most children, this timeline makes very good sense. Prior to age eight or nine, much of the learning going on in children's lives concerns their physical, social, and emotional development. Although many gifted learners come to school having mastered basic literacy and numeracy skills quite well and may appear to need gifted identification and programming as early as four or five, there are other skills that are just as important to their future success.

In the early years, the learning foundation upon which subsequent development builds includes a comfort with exploring and understanding the world in the context of family, classroom, and community. This happens best with consistent and dependable adult support for social and emotional strengths that will lead over time to happy self-confidence, enthusiasm for learning, and psychological resilience. The research on high-level development (Bloom, 1985; Gardner, 1991; Howe, 1999; Lieberman, 1993) emphasizes that for most children who will go on to exceptionally high-level achievement and healthy adult lives, the early years of learning (up to the age of eight or nine) in all fields is better characterized as play than as work.

Quite often, then, from this theoretical perspective, parents who are anxious that their young child could or should be learning more are not doing her a favor by advocating for gifted identification and programming. As long as that child is not actively unhappy in the regular classroom, a parent's energies might be better spent ensuring that she has extracurricular activities that engage her enthusiasm for learning, as well as lots of opportunities for spontaneous unstructured play and exploration.

There are some young children, however, who, because of their gifted ability in combination with their temperament, find it difficult to handle a regular classroom and curriculum. Some are impatient with and feel insulted by a teacher's insistence on their doing work they find too easy, for example. In cases like this, it can be very important to assess the nature and degree of giftedness and to look for some kind of solution. If a child is already reading at a level markedly higher than other children in the class, a solution might be to provide single-subject acceleration or enrichment through more materials at the child's level of comfort and challenge, without changing anything else. In other situations, it can be appropriate and beneficial to accelerate the child to a higher grade, which we discuss more fully in Chapter 7. Despite widespread notions to the contrary, the research is strongly supportive of the benefits of early entrance to school or whole-grade skipping for certain children. An instrument has been developed to identify good candidates for such an intervention, *The Iowa Acceleration Scale* (Assouline, Colangelo, Lupkowski-Shoplik, Lipscomb, & Forstadt, 2003).

The research on high-level achievement shows that when parenting or working with young children, what is most important is listening and responding sensitively to the child. There are three points to consider (Courtney, 1989, p. 27):

- "Proficiency and learning come not [only] from reading and listening but from action, doing, and experience.

- "Good work is more often the result of spontaneous effort and free interest than of compulsion and forced application.

- "The natural means of study in youth is play."

The Need for Information

"Now what?"

For anyone, but particularly for a child, gifted identification can convey inconsistent messages. It can be self-affirming and a source of pride. However, it can also be a problem if, for example, the gifted label causes worries about having to do well in everything, or if it evokes unfavorable reactions from other kids. Sometimes it generates an inflated notion of what being smart means, and a child comes to think of himself as superior to others in a whole lot of ways that have nothing to do with what has actually been measured. For some parents and teachers, a child's identification as gifted suggests strengths and abilities that are well beyond the child's actual competence. Being labeled as gifted can be very worrying to a child, as well as an unfair burden, especially if the gifted designation is accompanied by unreasonable expectations or responsibilities. It is important that the child, his parents, and his teachers all understand in what areas the child has exceptional abilities, to what degree, and what it all implies (and does not imply) in practical educational terms.

When a child is identified as gifted, the new label is often mysterious to both the child and her family, raising more questions than it answers. It is important that communication channels among the child, the family, and the school be kept open. Parents and teachers should try to understand the child's feelings about the labeling and program placement experiences. Adults can prevent possible future problems if they remain sensitive to the child's feelings and needs.

Gifted children, for their part, benefit from being informed. This means knowing what might transpire at home and school as a result of the identification. It also means learning to focus on their learning strengths in positive ways so that they can enjoy developing their exceptional abilities as much as possible. The bottom line is that parents and teachers have to explain many things to children, including programming options and what kinds of changes, if any, to expect.

When a Child Is Identified as Gifted

Let's listen in on a conversation between a mother, who has just found out that her daughter has been identified as gifted, and her nine-year-old daughter.

A Conversation about Being Formally Identified as Gifted

"So, Amber, what did you think of that test you took a while back?"

"Do you mean the gifted test?"

"Yes, the intelligence test."

"It was fun. I liked doing the block patterns. Did you get the scores yet?"

"Yes. That's why I was asking you about it."

"SO…HOW DID I DO? DID I PASS?"

"You did very well, Sweetie. In fact, the school is suggesting that you might like to go into the gifted program."

"WOW! Wow. That is actually sorta scary. I don't know if I want to."

"Okay. We'll talk about it later with your dad and see what he thinks about it. We don't have to decide right now. We can think about it for a couple of weeks and talk about the pluses and minuses."

"I don't want to leave Jessica and Lynn's class. Are they gifted too?"

"I don't know. Maybe we should make a chart with all the positives and negatives, and also the questions like that that we need to investigate."

"Does that mean I'm smarter than the other kids?"

"No, not really. It does mean that your mind works very well, that you're really good at solving puzzles and figuring things out, and that you have the brainpower you need to do lots of wonderful learning. All kids have things that they're good at and things they're not so good at, and you happen to be good at the kind of thinking that that test measures."

For several reasons, this is an effective way to tell a child that she has been identified as gifted. The parent is low-key, not enthusiastic or pushing one attitude or another, and this allows the child an opportunity to think about her own questions and concerns. The parent listens actively for the child's questions and then reassures her that they can work together to address them carefully and patiently. This kind of dialogue helps her to know what the test scores and gifted identification do and do not mean. They do mean that the child is particularly competent at certain kinds of intellectual tasks that help her do well at school, but the scores do not mean that she is superior to other kids in all things.

When a Child Is NOT Identified as Gifted

Now let's listen in on a conversation between another mother and her son.

A Conversation about Being Formally Identified as *Not* Gifted

"So, Matt, what did you think of that test you did a while back?"

"Do you mean the gifted test?"

"Yes, the intelligence test."

"It was fun. I liked doing the block patterns. Do you have the scores yet?"

"Yes. That's why I was asking you about it."

"SO…HOW DID I DO? DID I PASS?"

"You did very well, Sweetie. You scored higher than most of the kids your age."

"But did I pass? Am I gifted?"

"It's not a test that you can pass or fail. You are definitely gifted in a lot of areas, but on the overall score, you didn't quite make the score they need for the gifted class. That does NOT mean that you aren't gifted, only that there were some things you didn't do quite as well as you'd have to do to get that label."

"I failed it."

"You did NOT fail it! Matt! You are a VERY smart kid! You did NOT fail that test—not at all! Let's take a look at the scores, and I'll show you where you did well and where you didn't do so well. Actually, there were no bad areas, and there were some

amazingly good areas. Look how well you did on the verbal reason-ing area! 98th percentile! Definitely gifted in verbal reasoning."

"What does that mean?"

"What do you think it means?"

"Maybe I'm good at figuring things out with words?"

"Sounds like it. And 98th percentile means that you did better than 98% of kids your age."

"Verbal reasoning is pretty important if I want to be a lawyer, isn't it?"

"I think so! My guess is that it's pretty important in practi-cally everything."

"So maybe I didn't do so bad after all."

"Exactly. What these scores show is that your mind works very well, and it says what you are especially good at. For example, you are extremely good at solving puzzles and figuring things out, and you have the brainpower you need to do lots of wonderful learning. All kids have things that they're good at and things they're not so good at, and you happen to be good at many of the things that this kind of test measures. You are also great at all kinds of things that are not on that test—you're a dynamite hockey player, a fabulous big brother to your sister, a caring friend to a lot of people, and you're terrific at playing the piano. If there were scores for those things, I think you would be gifted on all of them!"

There are many things to note in the above conversation that make this an effective way to talk with a child about not being identified as gifted. As with the previous example, the mother has parked her own emotional responses off to one side, understanding that the child needs to process this news for himself and that her emotions (one way or the other) will only get in the way of that. She is available and responsive but not expressing her own disappointment, if that is how she feels. As with the previous example, she is helping her son see what the scores do and do not mean. She is emphasizing his strengths, as well as the fact that people vary in how well they do on tests like this.

Unfortunately, many schools don't inform children and parents about the specific test results or the implications of gifted identification, let alone how to go about imparting the news. All too frequently, not enough is said about the kinds of learning or placement decisions that will be required. There are often many unknowns to confront, and children and parents may not know where to turn for information.

Everyone benefits when educators ensure that their policies and procedures for gifted identification and placement are widely and easily available and readily understood. There are many ways to make this happen, perhaps by posting a gifted information page to a website and/or by sending information home with the request for assessment permission. Most parents find it very helpful when schools hold information sessions where they can ask questions and become familiar with gifted education policies and processes. When a teacher and/or the school psychologist is available to discuss the identification process, there is less speculation, misinformation, and misunderstanding.

There are some surprising benefits to schools when they make gifted education information more easily available. These include that their teachers become more familiar with the principles and practices and that in the process of collectively thinking about them, policy can be refined and improved. Many of the schools with which we have worked through the years have found that opening up their gifted education practices for school-wide discussion has led to positive changes in many other areas of the school learning climate, too.

Labeling

"Is the gifted label a good thing?"

"I was so happy when I found out I was gifted!"

"I do NOT want to be one of those nerds! If I pass the gifted test, I don't want anybody to know, and I will NOT go into the gifted class."

Children are often unsure of what to expect once they have been given the gifted label and most other kids have not. They may experience one or more of a number of emotional responses, including pride, confusion, embarrassment, and fear. Many children have social concerns, wondering, "Will I be accepted? Will it be hard to adjust to a new environment? Will I be able to keep pace with other gifted kids?" Other children worry about academic workloads and programming. Many parents have similar concerns and uncertainties about what lies ahead.

We share here some personal perspectives on gifted labeling. First we consider it from students' points of view.

> *"It's a cool thing."*
> *"Because I'm gifted, I can only have one label: Gifted. Not cool."*
> *"I'm not the norm, but I'm not 'gifted.' I feel like I'm the only person like this."*
> *"I don't consider myself smart. I consider myself a quick learner."*
> *"If I had not been identified, I might have considered drugs."*
> *"The gifted label helps university acceptance."*
> *"I feel embarrassed when people ask if I'm gifted."*
> *"People respect me more. It makes me feel good."*

Now let's consider parents' views.

> *"We felt vindicated but worried. He felt vindicated and relieved."*
> *"She was proud and embarrassed."*
> *"He feels that he is different from everyone else and worries that they won't accept him the way he is."*
> *"I was extremely happy and proud."*
> *"She felt special and excited. It's a great opportunity."*
> *"Not a big issue. Not at all surprised. She didn't display much emotion one way or the other."*
> *"The concept of labels should be taken lightly."*
> *"We had a number of questions and no one to put them to."*
> *"I only hope the gifted label opens doors for her in the future."*

It is apparent that there is no single viewpoint on the gifted labeling experience. There are many concerns and questions, many possible answers, and both positive and negative aspects to consider.

Because any kind of change requires flexibility and adaptation and contains many unknowns, parents and children will obviously want to reflect upon what might occur as a result of someone being labeled as gifted. There is wisdom in the old adage: "The way you manage change is as important as the change that you manage." We discuss some of the changes to manage, as well as some sane ways to manage them, in Chapter 9.

Accentuating the Positives

The greatest problem with any school label, official or unofficial, is that the term will begin to take on an existence of its own and over-shadow the actual needs of the child.

(Armstrong, 1991, p. 221)

Although many people think of giftedness as a good thing and of the gifted label as an enviable achievement, it is in fact a mixed blessing and often brings challenges. Like a beautiful rose with surprisingly sharp thorns, the gifted label can be accompanied by unexpected difficulties. It is important that adults deal sensitively and patiently with a gifted child by listening to and communicating honestly with him. Knowing what the concerns might be and how to find appropriate resources can make a big difference in how positive the gifted experience is for a given child or his family.

Most children experience a mix of pluses and minuses to being labeled as gifted, a mix that can change over time with shifting circumstances, opportunities, and maturation. The following benefits came to light in a series of in-depth interviews with gifted children and their families about their reactions to the label and its consequences:

- validation of abilities

- reduced boredom and frustration due to programming modifications

- enhanced learning opportunities

- bolstered self-confidence

- a confirmation and affirmation of feelings of differentness

- opportunities for interaction with intellectual peers

There were also many problems identified by the children and by their parents. Here is a sampling:

- the need to change schools to get gifted programming

- programming uncertainties

- controversy about the label

- unhappiness with the elitism and exclusivity sometimes associated with the label

- dealing with the stereotypic views others have of giftedness

- intensified expectations imposed by oneself, by parents, or by teachers

- inflated self-confidence

- scorn and/or misunderstanding from peers

- envy and rejection from old friends

Each child and situation is unique. In addition to the educational opportunities that result from the label, a child's experience may vary depending on her age, resilience, sensitivity, maturity, social competence, family support, personality, domain(s) and degree of giftedness, siblings who are (or are not) gifted, attitudes of teachers and peers, and the presence of any other exceptionalities.

Although most children experience relatively smooth sailing through the gifted labeling and placement process, many do not. For example, consider a child who experiences serious disruptions in his life because he has to change schools in order to participate in the gifted program. He has to commute to his new school, has less time for extracurricular activities, and has to make new friends. In situations like this, it is important to carefully consider all of the variables before making a decision to attend a gifted program.

Here are some other troubling situations that children experience, along with some examples of their comments:

- misconceptions and misinformation about the label
  (*"Is being gifted like being super smart in everything? I think they made a mistake, because there are LOTS of things I don't know!"*)

- ridicule or a lack of support
  (*"The teacher made fun of me today. She asked the class a question that NOBODY knew, and then she turned to me and said, 'Let's see how gifted you really are. What's the answer to the question?'"*)

- concerns about developmental issues
  (*"I wonder if I'll outgrow my giftedness."*)

- conflicting expectations
  ("My teacher says there'll be a lot more work in my new class. My mom says I won't have to worry about it because I'm gifted and I can handle it. But I'm worried.")

- confusion about roles and responsibilities
  ("I bet I'm going to have to lead all kinds of study groups. I won't be able to do that!")

- fears that the test scores were wrong and that the child is not really gifted, or that he or she won't be able to measure up in the gifted class
  ("I think they messed up when they scored my tests. I won't be able to keep up with all those smart kids!")

In general, if a child can be in a challenging learning environment that matches her learning needs *without* the gifted label, then that is probably best. Labels can cause problems for children and their families. The gifted label's meaning and value reside only in its practical consequence. It should be pursued or accepted only when it is required for entry to the educational programming a child needs in order to maximize her learning.

Parents' Roles

What parents typically know about their children is worth a thousand standardized tests. Parents are constantly observing their children under a variety of changing conditions and over a period of years. Testers, on the other hand, see kids in only one setting: the school.
(Armstrong, 1991, p. 206)

"Parents and teachers who are at odds with one another do a child no favors."
"I really appreciate parents who can provide input and who are also willing to help me put things in perspective."

Children display their learning progress and the richness of their individual growth experiences in many ways. Many abilities and learning accomplishments can be demonstrated through non-testing assessment approaches that will improve the evaluation process and provide valuable information about a child's learning. When parents assist in the assessment process and work collaboratively with their child's teachers, such approaches can help teachers identify learning needs and plan programs and instructional strategies.

We offer the following suggestions for parents:

- Encourage your child's teacher to use a variety of methods of evaluation besides tests—methods that not only provide information about mastery of subject matter, but also give information as to where a child may need help. (Examples include checklists of skills, progress charts, student-maintained journals of learning activities, questionnaires, interview and conferencing records, and student work samples.)

- Keep a record of your child's learning activities outside of school, and share your observations with educational professionals.

- Keep a scrapbook or portfolio of photos, paintings, written material, tape-recordings, etc. that illustrate your child's abilities in different areas and at different ages. Videotape and document special events, presentations, or learning outcomes.

- Encourage your child to become involved in self-assessment— that is, to keep a record of his or her learning experiences and personal accomplishments that can be shared with teachers. This is also a useful strategy to help your child develop self-confidence and powers of self-reflection about what and how he or she learns.

As we noted earlier, test scores are useful only if they are interpreted intelligently. This means *matching the educational provision to an individual's ability on a subject-by-subject basis.* We will be discussing how to do that throughout Section III.

Section III.

Being Smart about Meeting Gifted Learning Needs

Chapter 6

Adaptations: The Gifted Learner in the Regular Classroom

In the first two sections of this book, we provided a context for understanding many of the core issues in the field of gifted education. Now we explore the question, "What educational options can help meet gifted students' learning needs?" Our answers have important implications, and not just for those who have been identified as gifted. We will consider how to use these various educational options to support high-level development in *all* students.

Many advanced learning needs can be met in a regular classroom by a teacher who is well-trained and well-supported in working with exceptionally capable learners, and in this chapter, we discuss nine classroom strategies for meeting gifted learning needs. There are, however, some children and circumstances that require other approaches, so in Chapter 7, we consider a range of alternative options, some of which take the child out of the regular classroom full time or part time. In Chapter 8, we review a range of options that are primarily extracurricular in nature, and in Chapter 9, we address how to choose what is best at a given time in a child's development.

A Flexible Range of Educational Options

Students' education must be appropriate to their strengths, interests, and needs, and must prepare them for the future.
(Ontario Ministry of Education and Training, 1999, p. 52)

"*Our limit should be the world. But then again, it should be the stars!*"
"*I love school because work is fun; work is fun because I like to learn new things!*"

We appreciate the remarkable diversity of ways that gifted learners approach their schooling experiences. From the mastery model perspective, education for gifted students is about matching curriculum to advanced learners' specific academic needs. Our experience is consistent with the findings of educational researchers and theorists who conclude that there are many good ways to meet students' diverse learning needs and that the best programs for gifted learners differentiate for them by providing a flexible range of educational options. In order to challenge gifted students appropriately and encourage their engagement in learning, educators need to consider: (a) possible teaching strategies, (b) expected outcomes, and (c) the proficiencies of the individual child. This can be done on many levels (Tieso, 2003). For example, working with the *curriculum* (think big-scale and broad–based), suitable modification might entail the following strategies:

- Analyze and remove unnecessary or repetitive chunks of content.

- Enhance existing units of study by reorganizing or intensifying content.

- Connect a unit of study to other subject areas or disciplines.

Working with the *program* (think instruction within a classroom), teachers might adopt these applications:

- Use pre-assessment to determine a child's strengths and weaknesses, and then use flexible grouping practices accordingly.

- Increase the breadth of the program (interest, choices, learning style variation).

- Increase the depth of the program (different lessons for different ability levels).

All of these modifications come under the heading *differentiation*, or modifying instruction to match the learning needs of individual students. When differentiating experiences for diverse learners, these practices can and should be combined. In an ideal world, teachers would be differentiating instruction for students all of the time.

Differentiation is not something to do from time to time—it is a way of thinking and should pervade what a teacher does in the classroom.

(Tomlinson, 2003a)

From looking at curricular development frameworks to adapting daily lesson plans, the teacher's goal in differentiation is to engage students fully in their own learning as much as possible at their individual ability levels. The keys to doing this are flexibility and fluidity at all levels, and of course, this requires teacher skill and training.

The inclusive classroom context that we envision here is a welcoming and opportunity-laden environment, one where diversity is respected, where teachers respond to the needs of individuals by offering a range of instructional supports, and where students are systematically encouraged to master their individual learning objectives (Andrews & Lupart, 2000). At the same time that this type of classroom keeps gifted students interested in learning, it also works to meet the learning needs of students with learning disabilities or other specific challenges.

A critical element of the inclusive classroom is the teacher's attitude toward exceptional learners across the learning spectrum. If we want to help teachers implement and practice adaptive instruction while at the same time celebrating diversity, we must provide them with the knowledge, support, and resources they need in order to implement the educational objectives, strategies, materials, and programming applications that can and do work.

We use the term adaptations as an umbrella heading for this chapter, referring to the various programming options available for gifted students in regular classroom placements (Robinson & Robinson, 1983). A bonus for teachers who understand and implement these kinds of options is that they work well not only with children who are identified as gifted learners, but also for those who are not officially designated as gifted. The ideas we present here and in the two chapters that follow interconnect and overlap in many ways. The boundaries between them are not distinct, and implementing one of these approaches almost always means incorporating important aspects of one or more of the others. Parents and educators should keep in mind that the wider the range of learning opportunities available, the more likely they are to find a meaningful and happy educational match for a particular child.

For the past several years, Joyce VanTassel-Baska and her colleagues at the Center for Gifted Education at the College of William and Mary have been investigating ways to integrate differentiated learning experiences into the regular curriculum in such a way that gifted learners receive the accommodations that they require while systematically mastering the regular curriculum in alignment with educational standards. Perhaps the biggest contribution of this group has been the development of the integrated curriculum model for gifted learners. Using this model, they have developed flexible modes of enrichment and acceleration in all subject areas, as well as comprehensive field-tested curriculum resources across subject areas and grade levels (VanTassel-Baska & Little, 2003). Teachers who wish to implement the mastery model for gifted education will find these resources invaluable. (Go to http://cfge.wm.edu.)

The parallel curriculum model (Tomlinson, Kaplan, Renzulli, Purcell, Leppien, & Burns, 2001) is an approach that emphasizes quality curriculum and differentiation working in tandem. This model layers four curriculum areas: one represents a core; another focuses on connections and relationships as applied to subject matter and content; a third addresses practice including authentic problem solving, learning activities, and grouping; and the fourth attends to student identity with an eye to individual interests and differences. Teacher-designed tasks, lessons, and units of study revolve around these parallels, blending and modifying them in accordance with learners' needs and levels of ascending intellectual demand. Throughout her career, Tomlinson has actively encouraged teachers to think about ways of differentiating process, content, product, and learning environments. In a recent publication, she suggests five teacher responses to the needs of students—"invitation, opportunity, investment, persistence, and reflection"—and she describes why these are important and how educators can proceed (Tomlinson, 2003b). Information on the parallel curriculum model can be obtained from the book by that name or through the National Association for Gifted Children (www.nagc.org). Another publication by Tomlinson (with Sally Reis, 2004) offers further insight into differentiation, as well as strategies and practical applications for classroom use.

The National Research Center on the Gifted and Talented offers many resources and publications through their website at www.gifted.uconn.edu. Other sources of information pertaining to curricular models, instructional resources, and the fundamental adaptations discussed here can be found on our *Being Smart* website, www.beingsmart.ca.

Options in the Regular Classroom

> *It is often said that in an ideal world, special education, including gifted education, would not be necessary, because curricula would be sufficiently responsive to individual differences to make separating children into exceptionality categories unnecessary.*
>
> (Wright & Borland, 1993, p. 591)

> *"Have you ever spent time in a classroom? Do you have any idea how hard it is? I have kids coming to school in the morning without breakfast. They can barely function. Now you're expecting me to also think about providing a smorgasbord of possibilities for the extra bright ones?!?"*
>
> *"I can't do everything! It's enough just to keep on top of the mandated curriculum and all of the paperwork. I cannot individualize a program for every child in my class!"*

Inclusive approaches to education involve differentiating programming for individual learners in a regular classroom setting (the child's age-appropriate grade level). On their first encounter with such principles, many teachers express concern, dismay, dismissal, or even anger. Comments like the ones above often focus on the many difficult challenges that teaching presents without adding individual gifted accommodations to their burden. And in fact, we are not suggesting that teachers ought to provide an individualized version of every lesson, targeted especially to each child's developmental level. As teachers ourselves, we fully appreciate the impossibility of that demand. However, we also know the power of providing fundamental adaptations to basic instruction as required and how very effective that can be.

The best advocates for this approach are teachers and parents. Consider, for example, the reflections of Shoshana Cohen-Taitz, a teacher.

A Teacher's Program

I think that one of the most valuable things I learned from the professional development workshop is that meeting the needs of gifted learners is not as difficult as I had previously thought. Actually, many of the strategies that I've been implementing in my classroom are already providing enrichment for the gifted children (and all students), helping them to achieve beyond the simple letter of the curriculum and to experience appropriate challenges. This really makes me feel hopeful and more optimistic about working with gifted children in my classroom. With this in mind, I am now able to look at the strategies that I have begun to work with and think about developing them further. I guess the idea that we do not have to start from scratch, that we do not have to recreate everything, but rather can work with what has already been started, is a very valuable lesson that I've been able to take away from this training and work with in my classroom.

A second thing that I learned deals with the relationship between teacher and student. I have always believed that the teacher is required to offer students a range of options within a structured environment. This is what I have always done in my program. I take a lot of time developing different ideas and extensions for my lessons. However, from this session, I learned that designing the rubric and selecting activities should not be just the teacher's responsibility. Student input is valuable. Balancing what the teacher has to cover with what the child wants to cover can be tricky, but it is essential. I have begun to encourage my students to be active in developing topics and ideas based on what I need to teach. For example, I am currently working with Grade 7 students on designing a book report. I know what expectations I need to cover, but getting their input for the style of the book report and the way it will be presented allows them freedom and a feeling that they are actively involved in the learning process. They are then involved in the decision-making, the presentation of work, and independent and/or collaborative effort. This strategy is effective for all students, and it helps me in my planning.

> *For me, important ideas that were covered in the workshop include student ownership, responsibility, and freedom within the confines of the curriculum guidelines, as well as the fact that children need to be challenged in order to feel successful. I think the strategies we discussed (e.g., guided independent study, project-based learning, and single-subject enrichment) can greatly enhance the learning of gifted students in the regular program. Advanced learners will feel less singled out, less stressed, and they will have more opportunity for open dialogue. These strategies are not threatening and do not place kids in the spotlight or set them apart as different from their peers. I think this will provide a safe emotional setting for the gifted students in my class to work and achieve to the best of their ability.*

Shoshana's story is one that we have encountered and experienced countless times. As teachers come to understand the mastery model perspective on giftedness and acquire the tools they need to provide a flexible range of curriculum options, they are usually pleased and surprised to find (after the initial learning investment) that their workload decreases. Like their students, they usually find themselves enjoying school a whole lot more.

In fact, many gifted needs can be met with adaptations to the basic instructional program, working from a child's placement in an age-appropriate regular classroom. This approach has some obvious advantages, such as being flexibly responsive to changes in a child's development, interests, and circumstances, as well as preventing most of the problems associated with labeling and elitism. It also allows for considerably more teacher creativity.

We will now describe the strategies mentioned by Shoshana, as well as some others we have found to be useful.

Curriculum Compacting

Advanced learners can often acquire the important facts, concepts, and skills of a given curriculum unit or subject area of strength with a minimum of instruction and practice. The practice of carefully assessing a student's subject-area mastery and then condensing curriculum areas so that they can be covered more quickly is called curriculum compacting.

Curriculum Compacting: An Example

Natasha is planning to teach a math unit on four-digit addition. She has ascertained through pre-testing that Xavier, one of her students, has already developed a reasonably high degree of proficiency in adding four-digit numbers. She compacts the assignments in the math unit for him, choosing only a representative few questions, thereby ensuring that he has a solid grasp of all the necessary principles and skills that are covered in the unit, and yet also providing him with extra time that he can invest more happily and productively elsewhere.

Such shortening of the amount of time needed to cover a section of curriculum accomplishes two objectives:

1. It reduces the boredom of unnecessary repetition for students who have already mastered the concepts and related skills.

2. It frees up time and energy that can be much more productively directed toward other student interests and other real and relevant learning outcomes.

Curriculum compacting is a prerequisite for many of the strategies we describe which adapt basic instruction to gifted learners' needs without radically changing programs or schools. It must be done with care, however, so that important foundational skills are not omitted from the child's learning and so that children do not feel rushed in their learning. Several steps are required for successful implementation of curriculum compacting (Rogers, 2002):

1. Identify the essential learning outcomes of a particular unit of study.

2. Develop a pre-test to assess how much of the essential learning the students have already mastered. Pre-tests can be informal or formal, varying from a discussion with the child about what he already knows to a score on a standardized test.

3. Establish the criteria that will be used to designate mastery of the essential outcomes. That is, should the child know 85% of the required material? 75%? Or perhaps 95%?

4. Plan for the time gained by compacting or eliminating the already-mastered material.

And this is where the next several strategies come in.

Project-Based Learning

Many gifted learners enjoy being given opportunities to explore their interests somewhat independently of normal classroom constraints. Project-based learning can be done individually or in a group format and is focused on a target product as an outcome (the project). The value of such learning is enhanced when (Blumenfeld, Soloway, Marx, Krajcik, Guzdial, & Palincsar, 1991):

- the problem is authentic
- the problem is challenging
- tasks are varied
- the students have choices
- the students have opportunities to work with others
- there is an opportunity for closure, and the students have a sense of completing something important

Authenticity is a key concept for those concerned about increasing engagement in learning: one's motivation to learn is greatly enhanced by a feeling that activities have real-world relevance (Bereiter & Scardamalia, 1993; Bransford, Brown, & Cocking, 2000; Keating, 1996; Matthews, 1998). Project-based learning is structured to encourage authentic learning experiences. It begins with identifying a real-world problem or question of interest to the child. This problem or question is then used to motivate her to learn the skills she needs in order to arrive at an understanding of the issues. Some of these skills might include predicting, designing experiments, researching, data management, drawing conclusions, and communicating. The child then creates artifacts or products that address the initial question or problem.

The following example of project-based learning with upper elementary students is taken from an action research project in which we were involved (Matthews & Steinhauer, 1998).

115

Mr. Graham's Project-Based Learning Experience

Mr. Graham was a fifth-grade teacher who observed that his gifted students often "tuned out" during geography class. He had been a teacher for many years and described himself as "cynical about gifted education." He felt that gifted students did not "need anything extra," and he was frustrated with our perspective that he could meet the learning needs of the gifted kids in his class without compromising the time that he needed to spend with the children with learning disabilities. However, he did participate in a professional development session we conducted, and he saw some interesting possibilities in project-based learning. We worked together to design a project that ended up transforming the way he experienced teaching—and the way several of his students experienced learning.

For his project-based learning experiment, Mr. Graham asked his students to work in small groups, together choosing a country of interest and creating a list of questions to explore. He encouraged students to use any resources they could think of for their investigation. What happened next delighted him. Using books and diverse non-text resources (including visual, electronic, and human), Mr. Graham's fifth-graders discovered answers to their questions, as well as several more questions to ask. They interviewed friends, neighbors, and relatives; they found old records and were given treasured mementos to borrow, along with personal histories of what the mementos meant; they scoured libraries and the Internet for answers to their questions. The children then became interested in their classmates' histories and in their own families' histories, and geography class went from being "ho hum, boring" for everyone in the class (including Mr. Graham) to being an active and creatively productive hour.

As the learning continued to evolve, each group of students classified its information into four different categories and created a model of a four-room museum. Each room contained organized artifacts and written information about topics from the research. Groups also took turns presenting a sound-tracked videotape offering a guided tour of the model museum.

All of the students in this mixed-ability class were involved in various interest-motivated educational activities: collecting and managing data, drawing conclusions, and communicating these conclusions in a multimedia final product. Most of the gifted students took advantage of opportunities to learn skills at levels commensurate with their abilities—levels not typically achieved in their regular classrooms. Several students who had previously shown no sign of gifted-level ability achieved exceptionally high learning outcomes. All students experienced the pleasure and sense of competence that can be gained from productive engagement in intellectual mastery, an experience that in itself can lead, over time, to gifted levels of achievement.

Mr. Graham became an enthusiastic advocate of project-based learning and lost some of his cynicism about gifted education.

Project-based learning can be used in any subject area—from history to science to mathematics to literature. It can incorporate scientific methods and concepts (involving, for example, a consideration of the activity's purpose, hypotheses, methods, observations, conclusions, and implications), which makes it an excellent way to teach science in a meaningful and engaging manner to all kinds of learners. The possibility of collaboration makes this kind of approach to learning a particularly attractive option for girls, since many girls respond well when given productive, well-designed opportunities to work together with others (American Association of University Women Educational Foundation, 1998).

Project-based learning experiences like the one we describe here have many benefits for diverse kinds of learners, including but not restricted to those who are gifted. There is one important caveat, however. The project-based learning approach can easily be abused, such as when a teacher argues that he is adapting instruction to meet a gifted child's learning needs when there is actually little or nothing being learned. Sometimes projects are assigned, and the child is expected to do them whether or not she is interested and to pursue them to completion without any further guidance. Sometimes gifted children are simply sent off by themselves to the library or elsewhere to work on a project. When project-based learning is undertaken, the teacher should develop an appropriate framework such that learning is scaffolded and productive, and there is ongoing monitoring and guidance.

A Story of Scaffolding Learning

Jane, a first-year Grade 5 teacher, was working with a group of gifted students on a book study. Each child was reading a different self-selected biography of someone who he or she thought interesting, exciting, or creative. Although Jane had been taught how to scaffold instruction for high-ability learners, she had never actually tried it before. She realized that she would have to try different strategies in order to see what worked best for each child. Some of the approaches she used included the following:

1. *Encouraging the use of certain key words such as* who, what, where, when, why, *and* how *in order to generate questions about the material students were reading. (Jane actually showed them how to do this by using a biographical short story as an example and demonstrating the technique to the class.)*

2. *Encouraging the children to think out loud and to make revisions and choices as they worked.*

3. *Helping children to create and use cue cards for reference and practice as they explored ideas about the person.*

4. *Providing checklists for students so they could self-regulate the quality of their responses to the questions they asked and answered.*

The class enjoyed the experience. By building the learning process upon their individual differences and monitoring and assessing their progress along the way, Jane was able to scaffold the lesson for each of her students. That is, each one was encouraged to work comfortably at the appropriate starting level and then to advance beyond it to the next.

Because portfolio assessment is process-oriented, it can be a good way to assess project-based learning, encouraging children to build ongoing connections across their learning, rather than focus exclusively on the end product. The process of developing a portfolio (as we discussed in Chapter 4) helps students to become organized, reflective, and explicit about what it is that they are learning. It gives them an opportunity to showcase their efforts, to be creative, and to use a variety of expressive and illustrative means to record and chart information (such as conferences with the teacher, interviews, and any resource material they've gathered). Portfolios can be used for a variety of independent learning activities, and they have the advantage of being flexible in design and orientation.

Guided Independent Study

Guided independent study is a term used to describe project-based learning, as well as other kinds of activities in which students identify and explore interests beyond the regular curriculum while working somewhat independently of teacher instruction. It can be used for the study of whatever a student is keen to explore. Some examples are learning a foreign language or a new computer program, studying environmental issues or local history, learning the impact of certain drugs on certain outcomes, or other areas of personal interest with academic merit. Guided independent study has many of the same advantages and problems as project-based learning. To be successful, it is essential that a teacher, parent, or mentor be actively involved with the student in creating and monitoring the study.

The province of Ontario has undergone a major restructuring of its secondary school system, which included moving from a five-year diploma for university-bound students to a four-year diploma. Guidelines accompanying the restructuring process include several provisions that can be used productively for gifted learners in high school, and even earlier in some cases. Wide freedoms are given to teachers to adapt instruction for special needs learners, and there are no restrictions on the number of periods that a teachers may allow for independent study within any one course. This policy is consistent with the research and perspectives reviewed here. Many children would benefit if this policy were widely (and wisely!) implemented.

For younger children, guided independent study can be an exciting way to learn. Ruth Morgenthau, a resource teacher who participated in a professional development program focusing on giftedness, recently sent us the following correspondence describing her plans to strengthen the way this instructional method is approached at her school.

Ruth's Plan

I am a teacher-librarian in an elementary setting (K-8). The children use my library facility at all times of the day. Students from various grade levels are often sent to the library to do independent research on different topics assigned by their teachers. Typically, the assignments are to be researched and written right there in the library, putting undue pressure on students and the librarian.

I think individual assignments should be activities that explore a student's interests beyond the curriculum. These activities should have thought and structure, and they ought to be monitored by the classroom teacher. Now that I've taken the gifted development course and know more about gifted learners, I intend to ask teachers to meet with me so that we can plan children's independent study assignments together.

As librarian, I'm familiar with the material available in my facility and can guide the classroom teacher, suggesting possible topics. With advance notice, I can ensure that information will be available in the library for a student to use in his/her research. Too often in the past, students have come to the library to do research on any topic they wish, only to find that we did not have enough information on that topic or that the question needed a lot more consideration and planning before it could be investigated. Time was wasted and nothing was accomplished. It is important for kids that their projects have closure. Library research assignments need to have a focus and a proper structure with a beginning, middle, and end. When I meet with teachers individually and we plan assignments collaboratively, all related tasks become more meaningful for students, and ultimately, they're better executed. I hope my offer to meet with staff members to help plan independent learning opportunities for children will be welcomed. It would be great to see lots of projects that are not only well designed, but successfully implemented, too!

I know my learning resource center/library can fill many roles for gifted students. For example, independent study can provide enrichment; the resources in the library go well beyond the classroom material. The library is a wonderful setting to work in, and for a gifted child who may have social issues, the library is a familiar and safe haven. Experience has taught me that a librarian can form a special rapport with students who like to study independently, and it's always great when student are able to develop a working relationship with a trusted adult.

Also, sometimes teachers assign book reports using the books in the library, and I have some good reading lists for gifted students. I'm running a reading incentive program second term, and I used the lists to choose books for the brighter students who will be participating.

I would like to meet with you again to learn more about how to incorporate independent research projects into specific subject areas and programs at the different grade levels. I'm always looking for new ideas for all of my students.

With the help of a resource librarian like Ruth or another interested adult, a child can be motivated to pursue a topic and engage in various research and thinking activities. This is not a replacement for what goes on in the classroom; rather, it is a way to enrich a child's learning in a personally relevant and purposeful way, in concert with the rest of the program, when time has been created using the curriculum compacting method we describe above.

Cross-Grade Resources

Schools have within their walls and across boundaries into their sister schools, at both higher and lower grades, many enrichment resource possibilities in addition to what is contained in the regular classroom. Very often, excellent gifted programming approaches are discovered or created merely by considering as resources all locally available teachers, classes, materials, and students at all levels (pre-school through college). For example, a ninth-grade student, gifted in the area of language arts and a keen writer, might find his learning needs met by meeting once a week with an interested English teacher at his school who sets up a workshop for serious writers across several grade levels. Such a student might find that the creative stimulation, support, and discourse provided in the weekly meetings, combined with writing time to substitute for his normal English classes, are enough to sustain his interest in writing and learning about writing. He may actually come to appreciate the fact that much of his other coursework is easy and that he has time and energy to pursue his real passion—writing.

Consider, for example, a sixth-grade student who is outstanding in both math and science. This student might be introduced to high-level algebra by an interested math teacher in the nearby local middle school. If she has a particular interest in, say, lab experiments, she could be given opportunities to work with a middle school or high school science teacher in setting up and conducting research experiments.

There are innumerable similar possibilities, each of which is embedded in the local context. These options cost little more than time and flexibility on the part of the educators and parents. The best way to find what makes the most sense for a given learner is to start by identifying learning interests and needs, and then ask the question, "What provisions might be found or developed that will help meet those needs?"

We view this as a "What are the possibilities?" approach. It provides a contrast with the more usual approaches such as, "This is the program for gifted learners. If you don't want it, we have nothing for you." Or as Mr. Graham said prior to his project-based learning experience, "If a kid is gifted, he shouldn't need anything extra." The best gifted programming often emerges serendipitously from educators working together creatively and being open to opportunities for collaborative solutions.

Single-Subject Enrichment

Very often, educators and parents think that a gifted learner requires adaptations in all subject areas. Sometimes that is the case, but for many students, focusing on just one subject area to enrich at a given point in time is a good way to encourage a (re)connection with a love of learning and meaningful engagement with school. The example used above of providing writing enrichment for a linguistically gifted ninth-grader illustrates this concept. So, too, does the following initiative, described by Nanci Wax Pearl, a teacher who participated in a professional development session.

A Teacher's Plan for an Enriched Math Group

Nanci's Learning Strategy

Nanci selected a small group of students on the basis of their math proficiency to participate in an enriched math program. They have been working together in the classroom on a variety of different math activities designed to extend their regular fifth-grade curriculum.

Nanci's Reflection on the Process

The students were eager to participate in a math group and were excited about being able to explore different ways of applying their knowledge. They were open to any idea and math-related subject investigation presented to them. The parents were supportive and happy that this enrichment idea was being established.

The concept is working, but there is a great deal of refinement that needs to be done to the process. I realize that some students are gifted in one area but not others, even within math, as illustrated by the five different strands in the math curriculum. For example, some children indicate tremendous proficiency in number sense and numeration but not in geometry. Then, within number sense and numeration, they might demonstrate very strong computation skills but struggle conceptually with fractions and percentages.

I've learned several things. I have to keep this small enriched group of more able learners open to constant change in order to accommodate individual strengths and weaknesses. The block of time set aside for the small group has to be flexible. I've discovered that in the future, a more specific set of criteria must be initiated to help indicate which students might benefit from enrichment grouping in various units of study, because I want to be sure I choose the right students without leaving anyone out. Also, I think I need to have better communication with the parent body as a whole about the program.

Single-subject enrichment can be beneficial for students and can be implemented within the classroom or on a pull-out basis. It may be coordinated by the classroom teacher, a resource person, or another individual on staff who is both willing and able to take on the responsibility.

The process is one that requires planning and refinement on the part of the educator(s). Again, the financial cost is minimal to the district or jurisdiction; the only costs involved are planning time and commitment on the part of the teacher.

Single-Subject Acceleration

Acceleration in a single subject area is sometimes the best way to support a child's gifted learning needs. Take, for example, the case of a seventh-grader we know who is exceptionally capable in many areas, but who has a particular interest in math.

Ben's Story

Ben was assessed when he was in the fourth grade. He scored in the gifted range on the WISC-III (above the 99th percentile) and was highly gifted mathematically, operating at that time at the tenth-grade level (six grades above his own) on tests of math reasoning. Although he was eligible for the gifted program at the local public school, his parents thought that his social and emotional needs would be better met at the nearby private school that his two siblings attended. Although there wasn't a gifted program at that school and no accommodations were made for his exceptional ability, things went along pretty happily for him until the end of sixth grade, when he began to be a behavior problem. His parents and teachers were concerned about how he would do in seventh grade and so arranged for an updated assessment during the summer, with a follow-up meeting to be held early in the next school year.

In early October of Ben's Grade 7 year, a team meeting was held that included the school principal, gifted coordinator, Ben's parents, his homeroom teacher, and a gifted consultant, along with Ben himself for the first part of the meeting. It was clear that something had to be done; the behavior concerns were getting worse, and Ben's attitude was becoming disruptive in the classroom.

Team members listened thoughtfully to Ben's concerns, suggestions, and opinions. He was told that the principal and his parents would discuss any plan with him before finalizing it.

Working together, the team then devised an individual challenge program for Ben. In subject areas other than math, his teachers agreed to enrich and extend the curriculum and assignments for him, as well as for a small group of other highly capable seventh-graders. However, Ben's mathematical ability and interests were so advanced that they knew they would need something else for him in math. His temperament was an additional complication (as temperament so often is!). His impatient personality meant that he was at serious risk of dropping math altogether if he didn't feel like he was progressing as fast as he wanted to without wasting his time.

On the recommendation of the gifted consultant, Ben was allowed to take the seventh-grade end-of-year exam to demonstrate his competence. Because he did well (the criterion was set at 85%), he was excused from attending all seventh-grade math classes. Instead, Ben was provided with a combination of independent study and tutoring help to work his way through the eighth-grade math curriculum, and he was encouraged to participate in regional and national math competitions as well. The advantage of this independent study approach from Ben's standpoint was that he was excused from work that provided no real learning for him and that he found deadly boring. He was allowed to finish the eighth-grade math curriculum at his own pace, and he was then free to move to higher-level or enriched mathematical work as he wished.

The math teacher who was tutoring Ben (an extra that the parents paid for) spent two or three hours weekly with him and mentored his progress in the eighth-grade math curriculum to ensure that everything was moving along smoothly and that Ben was understanding the work. There were a few glitches along the way. For example, for a time, Ben thought he'd been given a "spare" for math class, and he let his classmates know what a good time he was having while they were slaving away. However, over the months that followed, there was a dramatic change in his attitude. Ben moved from being noticeably bored and unhappy at school and causing trouble both there and at home to being the happy, keen, and engaged boy he had been as a younger child.

> *Most importantly, Ben felt respected and became committed to making his program successful.*

Postscript on Ben

> *Ben has now moved on to a competitive high school where he has been allowed to accelerate mathematically. He participates in math classes with students who are a few years older than he is and who are also excellent math students. For the first time, he is experiencing real competition, and he is thriving on the challenge. He is doing well across the curriculum.*

Optimally, as in Ben's case, an elementary or middle school will have enough flexibility and a strong enough relationship with a local high school that an arrangement can be made to grant high school credit for any courses that a highly competent student completes ahead of time. The student may need an advocate to negotiate on her behalf if the higher learning institution is reluctant to follow this kind of individual plan. For example, if a student is willing to take the Grade 9 end-of-year exam or an informal assessment given by the math coordinator in order to prove her competence, and high school administrators are agreeable, then arrangements for an individualized math program can be made, as occurred with Ben. As such a student gets older, she might be helped to find advanced placement courses and other university-connected high-level options that will allow her to continue to pursue her learning interests at her own pace.

Ontario legislation allows elementary school students to take high school courses when they demonstrate the necessary capability (Ontario Ministry of Education and Training, 1999). This approach requires a high school principal to assume responsibility for the evaluation and recording of credits. A note of caution: although student are sometimes allowed to reach ahead, in most jurisdictions (as in Ontario), they are not given high school credit for the skipped-over classes and will have to make up the necessary credits for matriculation in another way. What students gain through this process is the freedom not to be bored by doing courses well below their competence and the opportunity to take more courses at higher levels. What they usually do not gain is credit for courses they have not actually taken.

With mathematically gifted children, subject-specific acceleration is particularly important for a number of reasons. First, the subject area itself tends to build more sequentially than many other curricular areas. It is therefore harder than with other subjects to create enrichments that do not also move beyond the child's age/grade level. Second, there is solid research evidence supporting this approach, grounded in the widely renowned Study of Mathematically Precocious Youth (SMPY) conducted for the past 30 years at Johns Hopkins University in Baltimore (Stanley & Benbow, 1983; Stanley, Keating, & Fox, 1974). Third, most important breakthroughs in the field of mathematics are made by individuals in their twenties. For students who are truly gifted in mathematics, appropriate early acceleration is necessary for them to build the foundation of skills and knowledge they will need to make their contribution to the field while still young.

Career Exploration Built into the Curriculum

> *"Whenever we travel as a family, I always take my "gifteds" to explore the local university campus. They've seen Harvard, University of Toronto, McGill, Queen's, etc. This summer, one goes to Oxford. It helps them keep their eye on a better intellectual place than high school, reminds them that school is a long process that they have to learn to function in, and through university catalogues, exposes them to non-typical fields of study."*

Students with exceptional ability should be encouraged to explore a wide range of appropriate and unconventional career possibilities. This should begin earlier in their education rather than later to increase the likelihood of their choosing the appropriate high school courses and, in some cases, prevent dropping out of school. Gifted young people who have talents in many areas will need adult help in prioritizing their interests and activities and in exploring possibilities for combining two or more strong interests—for example, learning about bioengineering as a way of combining strong interests in both math and science, or medical engineering for combining medical research, math, and science.

Gender roles in careers is a topic for discussion with gifted students as well. Research on gifted girls shows that they very often opt out of the higher level mathematics and science courses necessary for the pursuit of careers in which they may ultimately have an interest. If girls don't sign up for high school math and science classes, they may unknowingly be closing the door to careers in the health sciences, psychology, business, architecture, computer technology, and engineering, to name just a few. Similarly, gifted boys should keep a variety of career pathways open for ongoing consideration.

We include an excerpt from a report by Laressa Rudyk, a teacher candidate who chose to study gifted girls at the senior high school level, investigating their perceptions of their abilities in computing science. Her observations were made over the period of her student teaching from September through November. You will see that, initially, she found the girls' self-perceptions to be more negative than the self-perceptions held by boys. We found it interesting to see what she did and what she thought about it later.

A Research Investigation on Girls and Computing Science

Initial Observations

1. *Girls in the computing science class were initially very quiet compared to the boys.*

2. *Girls hesitated to ask for help when they were having trouble with an assignment.*

Findings

I administered a questionnaire to students at the beginning of the school year in September. The data indicated that girls lacked confidence in their abilities in this subject area, as compared with the boys in the class.

I administered a second questionnaire at the end of November, asking the same kinds of questions. Results showed increased confidence among the girls, bringing them closer to the boys' confidence level. I also noticed a change in the girls' behavior; there was more vocal participation and greater comfort with experimentation. Perhaps most importantly, girls' achievement levels were higher at the end of November than they'd been earlier in the term, and they expressed more enjoyment and interest in the course than they had earlier.

Strategies I Employed in Class from September through November

I made it a point to give the girls lots of praise and encouragement and kept the idea of confidence-building in mind. I asked leading questions that directed students to draw conclusions on their own. I tried to help the girls unobtrusively so they would experience the confidence-building joy of figuring out things for themselves.

Personal Reflections on the Investigative Process

This study was relevant to me because I was the only girl from third year on in my own college math and computing courses, and my experience was extremely positive. I was quite confident and enjoyed battling wits with the boys and my professors (all male). The idea that girls are underestimated, or otherwise discouraged, in math or computing was foreign to me before beginning to teach and then investigating the girls for my study. I was quite sad to see that the girls thought so little of themselves back in September when I first administered my questionnaire. I was glad to see some positive change and hope that my conscious confidence-building efforts contributed to this.

I think the issue of whether these gifted girls perceive themselves as "good at computing science" has broader social implications. Most careers with higher compensation levels require a formidable knowledge of computing, and girls are unlikely to pursue careers in areas where they lack confidence. The skills developed by learning programming are valuable in their own right. Programming teaches students how to articulate (and follow) a set of unambiguous instructions to perform a task. As such, students learn extremely important communication skills that can be applied in other areas.

I may take up the cause of promoting computing science to teenage girls!

The next step in the process that Laressa began in her practicum would be to set up a class forum to discuss the experience, including engaging the students in discussing the value of achievement in computing science and the kinds of careers that would be open to individuals with these skills, as well as areas that might be closed to those without computer skills.

Another important reason to encourage career exploration in exceptionally capable adolescent learners is to support their understanding of the relevance of schooling. Interest in a possible career path can sustain academic engagement in those who need their learning to feel meaningful and worthwhile. Sometimes gifted kids can endure high school better when they see that it can take them to a better place.

Peer Coaching

One of the reasons that peer coaching works so effectively is that it combines pressure and support in a kind of seamless way.
(Fullan, 1991, p. 91)

"I believe that the best way to learn is to teach."
"Peer coaching gives my gifted learners a chance to see how 'normal' children think. It should make them grateful that learning comes so easily to them, rather than resentful that they have to do it."

While peer coaching can be used in a number of ways to support gifted learners' educational needs, it has many pitfalls and a justifiably bad reputation in many circles. For some students in some settings, being a peer coach can consolidate knowledge, encourage high-level discourse, and support the development of both intellectual and social skills. Working together with others in a group of mixed strengths can also encourage respect for diverse kinds of ability. It can facilitate the development of alternative skills as well.

All too often, however, when teachers who lack training in gifted development are faced with a gifted learner in a regular classroom, they ask the gifted learner to work with a student who is having problems with some aspect of the curriculum. These teachers think they are not only giving better learning opportunities to the child who is behind in his work, but they are also providing the gifted student with an opportunity to develop social and communication skills. As might be predicted, however, if the gifted learner is neither a natural teacher nor unusually altruistic (in other words, a typical child), and if peer coaching is used too frequently, the gifted student becomes a resentful teacher's helper. She may come to think of the peer coaching experience as an irritating and unfulfilling annoyance, especially if she feels neither intellectually stimulated nor enhanced in her social skills or reputation.

Alternatively, the gifted student who is used too frequently as a peer tutor may come to identify too closely with the teaching role and take that as an unexamined career path, coming to see himself in the helper/mentor role and never comfortably stepping to the fore. He may learn to downplay and hide his abilities out of sensitivity to those he must help. Worse still, working with struggling students may normalize their abilities for him and reinforce concerns he might have about himself being abnormal.

For peer coaching to work well, each participant must be gaining something from the activity and must perceive that that is the case. The process of negotiation between the teacher and the potential peer coach is important for building success into the experience. The teacher needs to have private preliminary discussions with each of the prospective participants in the peer teaching experience. These discussions should include whether or not each one is interested in participating in the activity and what the teacher's role will be. It is helpful, too, to discuss procedural basics such as how to respond in various situations, how to recognize when the peer teaching is not working out, and what to do if that should occur. In some jurisdictions, students can receive course credit for doing peer tutoring under a teacher's guidance. They can function very much like a teaching assistant, helping with some administrative duties, planning and preparing materials, and working one-to-one monitoring seat work.

As with all of the strategies discussed here, and perhaps even more so, peer coaching must be undertaken carefully, with the teacher available to step in at a moment's notice if requested. Peer coaching must be tailored to individual learning needs and to the personality profiles of the students involved, as well as the learning objectives of the task. It must be used sparingly. When the conditions and supports are in place to ensure that it works for everyone concerned, peer coaching can indeed satisfy many educational needs all at once.

Cyber-Learning

> *Every learner can, at his or her own choice of time and place, access a world of multimedia material.... Immediately the learner is unlocked from the shackles of fixed and rigid schedules, from physical limitations...and is released into an information world which reacts to his or her own pace of learning.*
>
> (Salmon, 2000, p. 11)

The frontiers of learning extend into cyberspace. Technological possibilities have advanced to the point at which different learning styles, curriculum requirements, and individual educational objectives can be met online by even a very young aspiring techno wizard, as long as she has a computer available for use. (In fact, as most adults realize, students often surpass their parents and teachers when it comes to e-learning.) By going online, kids can navigate discussion threads, access a never-ending and far-ranging supply of resources, and supplement material that's being covered in class, thus deepening and broadening their knowledge. Students can become part of a community of learners, a community that knows no boundaries.

E-possibilities and electronic learning resources are growing almost too quickly to comprehend. There are countless homepages that offer links to learning activities. Software programs and online course dynamics continue to be developed and refined. Textbook companies have interactive materials on the web. There are opportunities to be part of a collaborative group, or to be a facilitator, or to work independently, all at an individual pace. In just a few keystrokes, one can find web-forums and pathways to learning that were not available just yesterday. People everywhere are surfing the Net to explore interests, answer questions, develop new understandings, and motivate one another across culture, age, time, and space.

Here is one prospective teacher's experience with e-learning.

E-Learning in Action

Many educators are already using cyberspace for gifted learners. For example, in my English class for secondary education, the professor took our whole class and put us online with a high school English class. We helped the tenth-graders write by providing immediate online feedback during their writing process. It was totally interactive and gave us a solid sample of the power of the medium. Another example is that last summer, my ninth-grade daughter fast-tracked through a required tenth-grade civics course online. Such courses can be pretty tedious for the high-ability kids, especially when they are already clearly on a path because of their talents. She did the courses in one month instead of five and was able to take a Grade 11 psychology course in her Grade 10 program, giving her much more interesting content to study. Her gifted friends were quite envious once they realized they had missed the opportunity to fast-track through a required course. E-learning isn't just coming; it's here!

For a gifted child, online possibilities hold many obvious benefits, as well as some risks. Parents' and teachers' monitoring concerns and limits should be made explicit from the start of any kind of online application. Many high schools are developing "edlines" and encouraging students, parents, and teachers to log on regularly. For example, on one site, you might find educational resources, technical support, library catalogues, study skills and tips, a virtual reference desk, web-adventure-learning experiences, instructions for building web pages, and more. There are also e-moderating guides for those who want to hone their e-skills (Salmon, 2000). We are witnessing an unprecedented range of learning and teaching possibilities, including innovative processes and far-flung connections. What is already "a potentially powerful teaching and learning arena in which new practices and new relationships can make significant contributions to learning" (Palloff & Pratt, 2001, p. 25) promises to become even more powerful and expansive.

Now that we have reviewed some fundamental adaptations that can be implemented in a regular class setting at a child's age-normal grade level, we discuss options that require high-ability students to move into other learning environments. Some of these are part-time placements, and some are full-time.

Chapter 7

Alternative Educational Options

Although many gifted educational needs can be met in a regular classroom by a teacher who is well-trained in working with gifted learners, as we described in Chapter 6, some children require other approaches. In this chapter, we discuss a range of alternative options, some of which take the child out of the regular classroom full time or part time. The approaches include various kinds of acceleration, full-time and part-time gifted programs, second language immersion and dual track programs, specialty subject focus, specialized and alternative schools, private schools, and finally, home schooling.

Whole-Grade Acceleration

Whole-grade acceleration is the practice commonly known as grade-skipping.... The decision to whole-grade accelerate a student is one of the more difficult and controversial issues that educators and parents encounter.... However, a great many gifted and talented children clearly need additional educational challenge that can only be obtained by allowing them to advance at least one grade, sometimes two.

(Assouline, Colangelo, Luplowski, Shoplik, Lipscomb, & Forstadt, 2003, p. 9)

> *"I really don't like to hear the word "skipping" used when referring to moving children ahead a grade in school. It makes it sound frivolous, when in fact it's a serious decision for parents and children."*
>
> *"I didn't know that Elizabeth had skipped a grade until mid-October, when her mother told me. I just thought she was rusty on her fourth grade math."*
>
> *"What on earth were they thinking when they decided to skip Jon? He may be smart, but his behavior is completely inappropriate, and the other kids don't like him. His social maturity is WAY behind his intellect."*

Whole-grade acceleration or grade-skipping moves a child ahead of his age-peers by a year or more with the idea of allowing for instruction to better match his individual mastery levels. The process itself can be done quickly with little or no special preparation or planning—for example, skipping right over the fourth grade straight from the end of third to the beginning of fifth.

On the other hand, full-grade skipping can also be done thoughtfully and well through a strongly supported process in which, prior to the grade skip, the pace of learning is faster than usual for a time, and the child is helped systematically to master grade-level content and skills more quickly than usual. This helps to eliminate gaps in knowledge once the child is placed in the higher grade. There are many different scheduling possibilities, including doing two years of work in one, which is the most common; doing three years' work in two; covering one year's work in one semester and then moving into the next grade level for the second semester; or doing a more radical acceleration of three or more years in one. We discussed single-subject acceleration in Chapter 6 and focus here on full-grade skipping across all subject areas.

Although whole-grade acceleration continues to be controversial and is currently not much used, it is the gifted education option with the strongest and most robust research validation. Over and over again it has been shown to be an important programming option for educators to consider (Assouline, Colangelo, Luplowski, Shoplik, Lipscomb, & Forstadt, 2003; Feldhusen, 1995; Rogers, 2002; Shore, 1991; VanTassel-Baska, 2003). When done thoughtfully and with attention to many factors, including children's physical, social, and emotional development, in addition to their academic levels, it can be both highly effective academically and cost-efficient.

At the time of this writing, the upcoming publication of The Templeton National Report on Acceleration is being announced. *A Nation Deceived: How Schools Hold Back America's Brightest Students* (Colangelo, Assouline, & Gross, 2004) reports on an investigation of acceleration practices in America. The authors document that schools, teachers, and parents have not accepted the idea of acceleration, in spite of 50 years of solid evidence that supports this practice. They discuss the reasons why schools hold back America's brightest students:

- schools' unfamiliarity with the research on acceleration
- the philosophy that children must be kept with their age peers
- the belief that acceleration "hurries" children out of childhood
- the concern that acceleration could hurt students socially
- political concerns about "equality" for all
- the concern that other students will be offended if one student is accelerated

The report shows that none of these concerns is supported by research. This document is being made available to schools, the media, and parents requesting copies. It can be viewed online at www.nationdeceived.org.

As a general rule, in order to choose full-grade skipping for a given child, the costs of *not* accelerating the child at a given time (boredom, frustration, alienation from school, behavior problems, depression, to name a few) should be higher than the potential costs of doing it. The benefits include a faster and more appropriate pace of learning, less time wasted in classes where content has already been mastered, and a level of challenge that is better matched to a child's capacity to learn. Potential costs include creating a situation in which a child's social, emotional, and/or physical maturity puts her at risk of social isolation or rejection, or alternatively of feeling a need to conform to older social norms, such as moving into dating behavior before feeling ready. Another potential cost when the whole-grade acceleration has not been well-planned or well-chosen is that a child won't succeed at the new advanced grade level, such that a previously successful student experiences a sense of failure.

Generally speaking, a student who is self-directed, is achieving well beyond grade-level, is comfortable working ahead of age-peers, and is socially, emotionally, and physically mature for his age is an excellent candidate for full-grade skipping. A teacher should be available to monitor and guide the process, crafting a good ongoing match between the child's ability, the curriculum content, and the pace and depth of learning. Although some exceptionally capable learners appear to have very few gaps and some educators believe that any gaps that they might have can be addressed at higher grades, it is important that both the pre-acceleration and post-acceleration teacher monitor possible problems that may later compromise the child's knowledge or skill-building. As we emphasize throughout this book, children's learning trajectories are highly individual, and even the most exceptionally gifted learners can have gaps in foundational knowledge or skills that can cause problems for them later.

It is important that the child who is learning faster nevertheless learns all that he needs to know. Schools can facilitate a successful whole-grade acceleration experience by providing teachers with the professional development and support options that they need and by creating a school climate that respects diversity and individual differences. Some schools choose to develop non-graded and/or multi-grade classes which allow for a seamless kind of acceleration where appropriate, with children moving along through the curriculum at their own pace.

Full-grade skipping is a more radical approach to addressing gifted learning needs than the strategies we described in Chapter 6 which are rooted in a regular classroom placement. It requires careful decision-making and planning in order for it to work well. There are certain times in a child's life when this option is simpler and less disruptive. Examples of natural transition times include entering kindergarten or first grade a year early; advancing a grade when a child is changing schools anyway, whether because she is moving or entering middle or high school; and early entrance to college. Whole-grade acceleration works best and the problems associated with it are minimized when a small group of students goes through the process together. An obvious advantage of the group approach is that, as students move quickly through the curriculum, they do so with a peer network. This is beneficial in every way, from academic support and discourse to friendship-building.

Full-grade skipping options must be considered on a case-by-case basis, with attention being paid to the age of the child, assessment information, learning profile, attitudes about school, motivation to learn, other stressors in the child's life, and social and physical maturity. School factors to consider include the nature and degree of support provided, as well as the school's culture and respect for individual differences.

The *Iowa Acceleration Scale, 2nd Edition* (Assouline, Colangelo, Luplowski, Shoplik, Lipscomb, & Forstadt, 2003) is a tool for generating recommendations and guidelines for decision-making about high-ability students who require special learning accommodations well beyond what is available in their current educational environments. This resource, consisting of the IAS Manual and IAS Form, is designed for use by an interdisciplinary team of educators, parents, and the student when considering acceleration. The guide is targeted for students in grades K-8 and includes case study examples and pertinent information. It describes key elements for decision-making, emphasizes the importance of discussion and planning, and specifies certain critical standards that must be met. For good discussions of the research concerning acceleration, including practical issues, best practices, and process monitoring both during and after a grade-skip occurs, see Rogers (2002) or VanTassel-Baska (2003).

Gifted Classes

"*Finally! I found other kids just like me!!*"

"*By the time I get home and finish all my work, there's hardly any time left to relax or do other things like skating or swimming or playing the piano.*"

"*Betsy used to be what her teachers called a 'lazy learner.' But once she joined the gifted class, she began working harder and enjoying it more.*"

"*It seems as if the gifted class has revved Rob's learning a few notches, but he doesn't seem any happier. He's just more—I don't know— 'driven.'*"

Full-Time Gifted Classes

For some children, particularly those with exceptionally well-developed linguistic skills, a full-time self-contained gifted class can be a good way to offer additional stimulation along with the chance to interact with intellectual peers. In some cities, there are entire schools for gifted learners, sometimes affiliated with university campuses and teacher education programs. We are very familiar with two such facilities, University of Toronto Schools in Toronto, and Hunter College Campus Schools in New York City, each of which has an excellent track record in providing accelerated and enriched learning opportunities for students who are able to take advantage of them.

Many parents and teachers involved in the field believe that self-contained classrooms are the best way to provide appropriate intellectual stimulation, as well as opportunities to meet and interact with others of like mind and interest. There is also considerable support for this option in the gifted education literature. Nancy Robinson describes self-contained classes as "singularly inexpensive and...probably constitut[ing] the easiest and most effective way to meet the needs of many (certainly not all) gifted children" (2003, p. 256).

At the same time, it should be noted that problems have been identified with full-time segregated gifted classrooms. Concerns include the labeling issue. In a self-contained class, the gifted label is made explicit on a daily basis, exposing the child to possible experiences of social ostracism from students who don't have the gifted label, former friends, other kids' parents, and even from other teachers in the school (in cases in which the entire school is not devoted to gifted education). Another potential problem is transportation. Participation in gifted classes may require commuting to a new school outside of the home neighborhood, which cuts into the time and energy a child has available for other activities. Commuting time can jeopardize opportunities to participate in after school or co-curricular programs, and it also reduces the time available for sleep and leisure activities that are very important to optimal developmental outcomes.

When considering the option of a self-contained gifted class, parents and educators should remember that within each such class, half the students will be below the class average. A child who moves from being routinely at the top of his class to being below the class average can suffer serious blows to self-esteem. Another social/emotional problem identified with participation in full-time self-contained gifted classes is the "hothouse effect." A segregated gifted class is an artificial environment in many ways, and it may not provide sufficient opportunities for the child to learn to cope effectively with the broad variety of people and situations that he will have to learn about later.

An academic concern with full-time gifted classes is that individual domain-specific learning needs are not always taken into account. For example, a child who is exceptionally gifted in math may not be provided with a math curriculum appropriate to her ability, which is highly advanced relative to the mathematical ability of her peers in the gifted class. Another often-overlooked fact of self-contained classes is that sometimes exceptionally gifted children are deeply disappointed to discover that they are still "weird" even within the gifted class, that their interests and methods of discourse are still not understood, and that their learning needs are still not being met. This can increase the burden of feeling different and somehow wrong.

In spite of these concerns, there are many children for whom full-time placement is both socially comfortable and academically stimulating. Some important benefits of this option include the greater probability that the teacher has had more training in gifted education, and the increased likelihood of students finding intellectual peers. A child's learning needs may be better met on a consistent basis in a self-contained gifted class, facilitating a higher level of motivation to learn and subsequent personal achievement. Many parents have told us that the full-time class is a very good way for children to receive the kinds of challenges they need and the depth of learning experiences that they enjoy. As with all placement decisions, the emotional, social, academic, and motivational implications of joining a full-time gifted class—where one is available—have to be weighed carefully during the decision-making process.

Part-Time Gifted Classes

"I'm not gifted just on Tuesdays from 2-3 P.M."

In our experience, and according to the literature in the field (Cox, Daniel, & Boston, 1985; Robinson, 2003), part-time gifted placements are rarely a good option for a number of reasons. As some children have said to us, they're not gifted just on whatever day it is that their pull-out gifted class is scheduled. Others complain that their regular classroom teachers penalize them for their absences by sometimes planning for treats and fun activities during the time when the gifted kids are gone or by giving tests or assigning work that they are expected to make up later.

Additional problems with part-time programs are that regular teachers often resent the pull-out class or teacher, thinking, "I can teach that child as well as another teacher. Why does my top student have to leave to have his needs met?" And sometimes, the work in the gifted class does not truly represent differentiated study, but rather is something that might benefit all students. Part-time programs are rarely well-integrated into a child's regular learning experiences; instead, they tend to be add-ons that take children out of the regular program for enrichment activities that may or may not be targeted to individual areas of giftedness or interest. Too often, such programs do little to meet gifted-level learning needs other than to reduce boredom for a few hours a week and to bring together for short periods of time those who are more likely to be intellectual peers.

Second Language Immersion and Dual Track Programs

"Miguel is able to talk fluently with his grandparents now!"

"Victoria gets a big kick out of school these days. When she hears an Italian expression, she immediately figures out how it translates into literal English. The other day she came home from school and said, 'Do you know how you say "Nobody's around" in Italian, Mom? It's "Non c'e un cane," which literally means "There's not a dog."' She liked that."

"I had hoped that the Immersion program would challenge Zoe. Instead, what I found was that she became even more bored than before."

Extended opportunities to travel abroad can provide a child with opportunities to become immersed in another culture and to experience, perhaps even learn, a second language. This not only provides powerful learning experiences, but it also broadens and enriches a child's life and thinking forever. However, given that extended travel experiences are not realistic possibilities for most families, second language immersion programs provide an interesting alternative, and they are often recommended for bright students who need extra challenge. Dual track programs are another approach, in which students learn to speak two or more languages over the course of many years of studying, usually in a schedule that divides the day into two separate parts in two different languages. In immersion and dual track programs, math, science, social studies, and/or other subjects may all be taught in a language other than English, beginning at the preschool level and continuing on through high school.

Canada is officially bilingual, and all children are provided with both French and English language instruction, although the age at which second-language instruction begins and its extent varies somewhat across provinces. In some jurisdictions, parents can choose to have their child enrolled in a language immersion class starting at kindergarten in French (or in predominantly French-speaking areas, in English), and many parents of high-ability children choose a language immersion class as a way of enriching their child's learning. Sometimes learning parts or all of the core curriculum in a second (or third, or fourth) language provides sufficient additional challenge to keep a gifted child interested in school, while at the same time developing another area of skill (the language itself, such as French, Hebrew, Chinese, or Spanish).

Such programs, however, are not always good choices for gifted students. Consider, for example, a child whose strengths are her reasoning skills and conceptual mastery and who thrives on high-level discourse. In a French immersion program, her French vocabulary will not keep pace with her ideas and concept formation, and she will not be able to express herself effectively at the advanced level at which she thinks. She won't be able to have meaningful discussions with her teacher or classmates until she achieves fluency in the new language. This can make her school experience frustrating and boring for the first few years, rather than stimulating and challenging.

The general conceptual level of classroom instruction in non-language subjects (science, geography, history, etc.) is typically significantly lower in foreign language classes than what can be provided in first-language classes. We have discovered that for children whose reasoning skills are exceptionally advanced, it is often best to provide second-language instruction as a subject area on its own rather than as a medium for learning in other areas, at least until a high level of second-language proficiency has been acquired. This is particularly true for those children who are not much interested in second- and third-language acquisition.

Another concern with using language-immersion schooling as a way to address gifted educational needs is that the child will be at a disadvantage for a few years in standardized testing situations. It is unlikely that he will have had the same opportunities as others his age to learn some of the facts being tested. He will not have had the same opportunities to discuss matters in his first language, certainly within his schooling environment. Therefore, his test scores are unlikely to be as high as they would otherwise have been. While there is evidence that this disadvantage evens out over time and is eventually converted into an intellectual advantage, this can be an important consideration if a language immersion program is being considered as a temporary enrichment measure until the child is old enough to participate in another program of interest that requires him to meet standardized test score criteria.

In some communities, dual track programs have been developed that provide a compacted version of the regular age-appropriate curriculum in one part of the day, with a separate course of studies for the rest of the school day. For example, the students might spend half of each day on the normal general studies curriculum of math, language arts, science, history, etc. The other half of the school day is spent working on various aspects of religious studies or humanities and on alternative language learning.

Educators in dual track and immersion programs often argue against additional provisions for gifted learners, observing that the programs themselves are challenging enough to meet gifted learning needs. Moreover, because of the time pressures involved with such an intensive curriculum structure, they usually question the practicalities of adapting instruction for gifted learners, even if it were deemed desirable or necessary.

A dual track program can work very well for those gifted children who are keenly interested in the particular focus of the second track and who don't mind spending less time on other subject areas. However, for gifted students who are less interested in the second-track focus or who experience some difficulty with it, such programs can be seriously problematic. The sheer breadth of the curriculum leaves little room for in-depth study of areas of interest (math, science, English literature, etc.). Similarly, creative and intrinsically motivated learners often experience frustration due to the narrowness of focus necessitated by the amount of material being covered. Such students can benefit when teachers in the two streams of study (the dual tracks) participate in professional development initiatives designed to help them modify curriculum and adapt instruction for gifted learners in dual track programs.

Overall, we have found that an immersion program or parallel curricular track is not in and of itself sufficient to address most gifted learning needs. However, when teachers are given the professional development opportunities and support they need to learn how to implement adaptive instruction, they are well able to meet gifted learning needs in these programs. We discuss teacher development approaches in Chapter 15.

Specialty Subjects

> *"Joey amazed everyone, even himself, when he joined the Drama Club. Up until then, he hadn't been doing particularly well and was having some trouble with reading. But once he discovered drama, he became engrossed and completely engaged. He had a reason to become an excellent reader. Now I can't keep him away from books and theatrical activities, and English has become his best subject."*

> *"Collin was one of those typical science/math nerds until he joined the school band. Previously, he had no friends and really no interests outside of academics. He has discovered a talent for music, and now he's got a much broader set of interests, as well as a group of kids to do things with."*

Throughout this book, we concern ourselves primarily with those whose learning needs are not well met without some kind of adaptation to the regular curriculum, those whose time will be wasted in school if no accommodations are made for their exceptionality. In Chapter 1, we defined giftedness relative to schooling as currently practiced, emphasizing a mismatch of ability and curriculum in the traditional academic subject areas. There are many other learners who are highly gifted in one or more "specialty areas" such as art, music, drama, leadership, or alternative language study. We know that there is tremendous diversity in patterns of gifted development. Many people are surprised to learn of the extensive range and diversity within the gifted population. Thus, a child who is mathematically gifted may or may not be linguistically gifted. Similarly, those who are academically gifted may be quite average in one or more of the specialty areas. And those who are highly gifted in one or more of the specialties can be average academically.

Gifted programming for specialty areas such as drama or dance can be designed and selected to suit individuals in much the same way that differentiated programming can be developed for the more traditional academic subjects. It can be used both to support gifted development in those who show evidence of talent in certain specialties and also to provide high-ceiling learning opportunities for those whose academic giftedness is not otherwise being addressed.

Consider a child who is musically gifted, or one who is academically gifted and interested in challenging herself musically. Such a student can be given opportunities to hear, play, and perform advanced pieces, to compose her own work, and to incorporate music into school projects and activities. She can be encouraged to participate in extracurricular bands, orchestras, and other musical venues. There are infinite possibilities for parents and educators interested in finding challenging learning opportunities in the arts. We know of one student who played a violin solo with the local orchestra when still a teenager. Another had a lead in a production of *The Nutcracker Suite* ballet. Others sometimes find vehicles to develop their talents, interests, and love of learning through various community-based theatre productions or festivals, rather than in traditional classrooms.

Specialty areas can be tapped to successfully explore a gifted child's abilities and interests. This approach can provide opportunities for challenge and engagement to students who might otherwise focus too narrowly on their areas of expertise. For example, someone who is advanced in and passionately engaged by science but unremarkable in the arts might be asked to dramatize a scientific discovery in drama class, draw a scientific invention in art class, or research physical responses to athletic activities in physical education classes. Developing a cross-curricular attitude helps to broaden children's scope, discoveries, and understandings.

Other strategies that work well in specialty subject areas and that strike us as useful for all teachers of gifted learners include:

- flexibility in program design, allowing for individual differences
- open-ended assignments that encourage gifted-level exploration

- student participation in planning and choosing learning options that they find relevant and engaging

- individuals working at their own level, no matter where this falls on the ability spectrum

- children not being pushed to operate at the gifted level in every subject area

- availability of a variety of resources, with openness to finding more

- authentic collaborations that are carefully guided and facilitated

Specialized and Alternative Schools

Some school boards and districts establish schools, or programs within schools, that specialize in the performing arts, pure and applied sciences, technology, languages, or the International Baccalaureate. Sometimes, alternative schools are established in which the approach to learning is more flexible and individualistic, or more structured and traditional, than is usually the case. These kinds of schools vary greatly across jurisdictions and are worth investigating when one is considering the needs of a gifted learner. Most are aimed at the high school level, although some jurisdictions have specialized and alternative programs for younger students, too.

These facilities frequently operate on a magnet school basis, attracting those who are interested and can demonstrate their ability to participate in the programming offered, independently of any prior official designation as gifted. There is almost always some kind of audition or application process involved and/or other prerequisites for admission. We have seen many cases in which a good match has been made and a particular alternative school has provided exactly the right kind of education for a particular student. New York City is rightly famous for many such schools, such as the Bronx High School of Science and the LaGuardia High School for Performing Arts (featured in the movie *Fame*). Many communities have similar kinds of schools. For example, in the Greater Toronto Area, there are several high schools for performing arts; there is a high-level science program at Marc Garneau Secondary School (the TOPS program); the National Ballet School provides exceptional training in dance along with regular schooling from an early age; and Gordon Graydon Secondary School in Mississauga features an international business, computer, and technology program.

Something to think about when considering a specialized school is the possibility of a premature narrowing of a child's interests and focus. For a child with diverse intellectual enthusiasms, it can be a mistake to narrow the focus too soon. For such a child, a good, challenging traditional school may be the best learning environment in which to hold open as many options as possible for as long as possible. Another factor to keep in mind when considering specialized and alternative schools is that while they provide excellent challenge and stimulation in the targeted areas, they are not always as strong in other areas. Schools for the performing arts, for example, are sometimes less demanding in the traditional academic subjects than they should be for an intellectually gifted learner. And while some students thrive on the competition that is part of many specialized schools, others find that they do better in a more collaborative atmosphere. Finally, there is almost always extra travel time and other commitment required in these choices, which could be either resented or appreciated, depending on the individual.

Private and Independent Schools

"What is a Montessori school?"
"Private schools charge a lot of money. I would think they'd have to be better. Otherwise how could they justify that?"

Some independent schools work toward facilitating high-level development in an atmosphere that values achievement and excellence in a wide variety of areas without using the gifted label. A small private school with a low student to teacher ratio that provides a context of academic support and appropriate challenge is a good choice for some children. For example, Montessori schools are often very suitable for independent, intrinsically-motivated young learners who need to have their individual learning needs and interests respected.

The theoretical framework of the Montessori method is an excellent foundation for nurturing children's individual and developmental diversity, including supporting gifted-level abilities, but it should be remembered that the actual schools vary considerably in how well they translate Montessori theory into practice. The Montessori approach focuses on encouraging children's unique learning needs within a context of independence and structure. Children are given many opportunities for sensorimotor experiences, manipulative play, social skills development, and independent and leisurely pursuit of various learning activities. Some Montessori programs work exceptionally well at addressing gifted educational needs and encouraging high-level development in different kinds of young learners, and others do not. Many are independently operated facilities with little or no ongoing commitment to maintaining authentic Montessori standards. Because Maria Montessori and later her family did not patent the name, some schools with the Montessori designation practice only a few of the methods. Parents interested in supporting high-level development in their children should definitely consider Montessori schools, but should do so carefully and thoughtfully, including inquiring about teacher training and certification. The true Montessori school will have teachers with International Montessori certification.

The same cautionary advice applies to any school that bills itself as a learning academy or institute. Sometimes these schools publish attractive brochures and advertise exciting or unusual learning opportunities such as theater outings, rock-climbing excursions, ski trips, archeological digs, museum visits, and so on. Experiences like this appear enticing to parents who are looking for challenges for their exceptionally capable child. However, as with any major purchase, parents will want to investigate marketing pitches carefully and not take glossy brochures too seriously. For example, what does a "global curriculum" or "child-centered approach" really mean in a particular context? What exactly is a school promising when it claims to provide a curriculum that encompasses "a wide body of knowledge all children need in order to develop into successful and self-confident individuals?" Many independent schools *do* provide supportive learning environments, but parents must do some research to find out if a particular school will actually be a good fit for their child. This can be a very challenging task—one we consider in more detail in Chapter 9. We suggest that parents take the time to visit any school being considered, ask lots of questions, be attuned to what is happening in classrooms and hallways, and find out what kinds of programming adaptations are available for children with the kinds of needs, interests, or abilities that are of particular concern to them.

The specific qualifications of teachers in independent or charter schools may not fall under the same regulatory body as those in the public sector. Therefore, parents should inquire about teachers' certification and experience, including specialized training in gifted education, whether there is a gifted consultant and an appropriately targeted support network in place, and what sorts of gifted professional development services are readily available and used.

Home Schooling

Home schooling seems to require the same formula for success as parenting, which is to say, it can work when the parents are loving and open-minded and dedicated.

(Cloud & Morse, 2001, p. 45)

Many parents commit to educating their children at home. Their underlying motivation is the conviction that this is best for the moral and spiritual development of their family, and it is the best way to provide a solid education for their children. They are concerned for the spiritual and character development as well as the social and academic welfare of their children.

(Home Schooling Legal Defense Association, www.hslda.org)

"How do I teach things I really don't know myself?"
"We'd like to home school our son because we don't think the educational system can provide him with the kinds of opportunities we can offer by teaching him at home. But how do we design a curriculum?"

Sometimes students just don't fit into a traditional school situation. Thomas Edison, Florence Nightingale, and Agatha Christie were all taught at home, as were countless others who have achieved at very high levels in one or more areas. Some children may be too advanced or otherwise unsuited to the learning environments of the classrooms available locally. If the parents of a gifted child are willing and able to invest the necessary time and effort, and if they have the inclination to provide home schooling, then this can be a viable alternative. However, there are a number of factors to consider.

Although home schooling is legal in Canada and the United States, regulatory practices vary from place to place. Parents who wish to teach their children or who plan to hire an education professional to do so will want to investigate government policies on home education in their district or jurisdiction. In order to meet local requirements, parents may simply have to inform local educational authorities of their intent to home school, or they may have to fulfill more detailed regulations. Home schooling policies are under a constant state of review and revision.

Home schooling support groups have sprung up across North America and act as networks to provide parents and children with information about all aspects of home schooling—from establishing goals, expectations, and limits to legislative issues, curriculum, extracurricular options, and most importantly, the chance to interact and share resources with other parents who have chosen this alternative. In Canada, for example, approximately 80,000 students are educated at home; the Canadian Centre for Home Education (a division of the Home School Legal Defense Association of Canada) can be investigated at www.hsldacanada.org and offers many valuable supports and links to other networks.

There is a continuum of learning in home schooling practice. It ranges from mirroring what might go on in a typical classroom (such as doing some kind of library or Internet research and then going to the zoo to find out about llamas) across the spectrum to extremes of various kinds (such as buying and caring for one or more llamas). What goes on in a home schooling program is as individual as the children and educators or parents who design it, which is the biggest advantage of this educational approach, as well as the biggest potential problem with it.

Many parents who home school choose to do so because of their objections to practices in public schools which they view as too permissive or too constraining. Many choose to home school because of religious convictions. One large study found that "the most common motivation for home schooling (up to 85%) is to achieve superior results in three diverse areas: (1) family relationships, (2) children's moral environment, and (3) academic achievement" (Van Pelt, 2003, p. 2). Additional parent concerns revolve around safety in school, frustration with the educational system, wasted time, and children's special learning needs. Depending on the parents' focus, values, and personalities, a home schooling program can be nurturing, challenging, motivating, and directly targeted to a child's domain specific strengths and weaknesses; or it might be rigid, constraining, and authoritarian.

A child who is home schooled has the ability to progress at his own rate and immerse himself in areas of interest. Typically, there is less peer pressure and competition, with plenty of opportunity to develop independent thinking and feelings of self-confidence. And certainly one might expect fewer disciplinary issues. Some of the common difficulties include parents not having sufficient time, energy, or know-how to provide optimal learning experiences, lack of commitment on the part of parents and/or children, social pressures, and financial costs involved.

Home schooling advocates are increasing in number, and heightened technological possibilities are making it more attractive today than previously. Curricular flexibility, parental involvement, and academic effectiveness are also draws. There are many strong examples of home schooled students who have achieved very well in college and in various life pursuits. It is interesting to note that the standardized test scores of home schooled children may be *higher* than those of the general student population (Van Pelt, 2003). Life-satisfaction and well-being research are other rapidly emerging areas of study.

Parents of children being home schooled often work collaboratively to develop meaningful programs and to advocate on behalf of their children. There are many aspects of home schooling that have to be carefully considered, preferably ahead of time, so it is helpful to have other parents with whom to confer. We touch on a few aspects here.

Parents should be mindful of various approaches to curriculum. They should be attentive to record-keeping, such as maintaining portfolios of children's work and ongoing progress assessments, including children's academic credentials, especially as they get older, if they hope to attend postsecondary education. Social development is also important. Children may benefit from opportunities to take part in a local school, attending one or more classes and/or participating in extracurricular activities so that they can interact regularly with age-mates. Home schooling support groups often provide planned and informal social interaction opportunities, and students often become involved in community and volunteering pursuits.

Designing a curricular framework in different subject areas and at different levels of advancement is a complicated endeavor, and one that requires considerable planning. Parents who choose to teach their children at home have to be proactive and able to access the kinds of information and materials that enable them to perform the instruction-related activities that are required, including preparing daily lessons; individualizing instructional and assessment practices; researching curricular content; setting objectives, expectations, and timelines; and more.

Lisa Rivero, in *Creative Home Schooling: A Resource Guide for Smart Families* (2002) discusses many aspects of the process, including how to begin, with starting points, program planning tips, curriculum resources, sample learning units, and ways in which individual learning styles can be met. She suggests ways that parents can acquire the necessary materials and resources for successfully tackling what at first seems daunting but gets easier and more comfortable as one goes along. Many good references are included.

Parents who home school also need to pay attention to their own needs and to monitor whether they are becoming too stressed by the responsibilities of managing and implementing an educational program in addition to the other responsibilities in their lives. Teaching gifted learners is, after all, not an easy undertaking. (Otherwise, more schools would have perfected it by now!) On the other hand, with some children, it is actually easier than one might expect because they become self-directed learners. Consider the following letter, sent to us by a parent.

Home Schooling: A Mother's Perspective

Home schooling is going very well for us. There are days when I feel like pulling my hair out, but then I had days like that when Derek was still in school! The real difference now (and what a positive difference!) is that if something isn't working, we can just sit down, talk it through, and try something else.

I have found the TAGMAX listserv discussion group under the www.tagfam.org umbrella. It is very interesting to read and exchange e-mails with other home schooling parents of gifted kids. There is something quite refreshing about the been-there-done-that advice/comments, even when you know each kid is a unique being. The group is also extremely useful for advice and evaluations of book and curriculum alternatives since there is almost always someone who has had some relevant experience.

We are still having some of the behavioral issues with Derek that we experienced while he was in school. I believe that they are largely the result of the poor socialization and emotional "hurt" he suffered while at the private school. We certainly aren't completely blameless in that we were more lenient with Derek than would have been optimal with 20/20 hindsight. I am reasonably hopeful (most of the time!) that we will get through this phase.

On the educational front, Derek is soaring ahead. He really loves the ability to focus on topics in as much detail and for as long as he wants (at least until he has exhausted his mother for any single sitting). We quickly evolved an approach that is quite eclectic. I think the "classical education approach" is often too rigid for gifted kids, so we are relying on the basic framework for guidance but not on the structure for day-to-day planning. One of my biggest challenges is how to find the appropriate balance of a predictable schedule and routine for a kid who loves many things while at the same time letting him pursue a specific topic for as long as he wants to, rather than shutting it down simply because it's time to do something else. My feeling is that getting a well-rounded education is something like eating a well-balanced diet: you don't have to have something from each food group every day to remain healthy so long as you don't go for too long without spending some time with each group.

Derek wants to keep on home schooling until he is ready to go to college. I'm keeping a more open mind, although I must confess that I'm not sure if a school exists that can accommodate his wide range of skill levels.

Summary

The variety of approaches that can be used to nurture giftedness is enormous. Some are intended for use in regular classrooms, and others are designed to be implemented in many different kinds of special learning environments. As we emphasize throughout this book, it is important to remember that what works well for one child does not necessarily work at all well for another. When selecting or constructing a program from such a large variety of possibilities, the main task is not to find the right or the best option, but to find the one that is most appropriate for a given child at a particular time in her development, given the constraints of a particular situation and context.

We have looked at many specialized educational alternatives for high-ability learners. We have also emphasized the importance of ongoing interactions among the student, parents, and teacher in designing and implementing approaches to meet the dynamic learning needs of the individual. In addition to the many options reviewed in these last two chapters, there are out-of-school experiences for parents and educators to consider when thinking about ways to meet gifted students' special learning needs. We describe some of these in the next chapter.

Chapter 8

Stretching the Boundaries

With a little bit of creativity and a resourceful attitude, there are many opportunities for high-level learning outside of the more conventional approaches to schooling that we discussed in Chapters 6 and 7. In fact, sometimes all that is required to meet the gifted learning needs of a child at a given point in time is that the parent, the teacher, or the child himself, takes a curious look around at the world and sees what possibilities are out there waiting to be explored. Sometimes the right course of action is to combine educational alternatives and/or to complement them with supplementary learning experiences.

Thanks to current technology, educators and parents can readily learn what's happening in classrooms close to home and far afield. School walls are much less constraining than they have ever been; the innovative supplementary options of today may be part of schools' basic repertoires by tomorrow. For example, students in North America can take part in online math and science programs offered at facilities elsewhere in the world, such as the Weizmann Institute in Israel. We know adolescents who have networked, enrolled, and participated in summer learning programs in Greece (archaeology), at Oxford University (English literature), in Italy (art), in Costa Rica (biology), and elsewhere. The list is extensive and growing every year as the technological possibilities increase, and students find that these can be wonderful ways to learn and acquire school credits. When educators and parents work together to take advantage of what's new, interesting, and potentially useful, and combine and take advantage of varied possibilities, they greatly increase the likelihood of keeping gifted learners engaged in learning. In this chapter, we propose some supplementary learning activities for parents, teachers, and children to consider. These are just a sampling; there are really no limits to the learning possibilities!

Extracurricular Enrichment

"How can I supplement what's going on in my daughter's school?"
"What else should I do to make sure Bryan's getting the right kinds of learning opportunities?"

Extracurricular enrichment activities can help keep learners intellectually challenged and developing. At the same time, however, it is important to remember that children and adolescents also need time to do nothing, to find out more about who they are and what it is they want to do with their time and their lives. The research on high-level development suggests that over-programming kids can be counterproductive in the long run. The key is to find a healthy balance that affords opportunities for relaxation. That being said, there are many extracurricular options to consider:

- **Music:** playing an instrument and/or participating in a choir, band, or orchestra

- **Physical Activity:** dance, gymnastics, martial arts, sports

- **Theatre:** costumes, makeup, acting, clowning, script development, sets, lighting, and puppet plays

- **Art:** painting, drawing, sculpture, photography

- **Crafts:** woodworking, sewing, pottery, model-building, knitting, jewelry design

- **Recreational Reading:** anything of interest

- **Writing:** stories, poems, articles, for pleasure or submission for publication

- **Classes or Tutoring in a Second or Third Language:** also summer language-learning experiences

- **Performance:** high-level professional concerts and showcases in different artistic media

- **Math and Science:** special science, math, and engineering programs

- **Computers:** advanced web-related activities

- **Community Service:** health-related associations, youth organizations, global causes, political affiliations

- **Leadership Opportunities:** tutoring, interest groups, religious and community organizations

- **Clubs:** chess, astronomy, cooking, photography, etc.

- **Camps:** summer and/or weekend recreational or specialized by area of interest, such as sailing, dance, language immersion

- **Competitions:** local, regional, national, and international levels, in different subject areas

More information on these and other possibilities can be found on the *Being Smart* website (www.beingsmart.ca), through the Internet, in local newspapers, and from active parent associations.

Mentorships

Mentoring is a supportive relationship between a youth or young adult and someone more senior in age and experience who offers support, guidance, and concrete assistance....

(Reilly, 1992, p. 7)

"Our 14-year-old daughter had an incredible mentorship experience last year. She worked with a doctor who helped her design an experiment having to do with pediatric testing for chicken pox. She learned how to structure a research study, and her results were compatible with findings from other studies. Her work is being sent to a medical journal for possible publication."

Understanding Mentorships

The term "mentor" comes from Greek mythology: Odysseus' son Telemachus was entrusted to the care of Mentor, who was a wise advisor. History and literature abound with examples of mentorships in every field, including politics, business, science, the arts, and education. Philosophers

Plato and Aristotle had a very effective mentoring relationship, and those who are less serious about their cultural references might think of Mickey Mouse in *The Sorcerer's Apprentice*. A mentoring relationship can be established in any context where there is a learner and someone with more experience who has the patience and willingness to support, challenge, and guide the individual along the way to greater knowledge and understanding. Reilly (1992) emphasizes that a mentoring relationship should be built upon a foundation of shared interests, and it should be mutually respectful, responsive, and gratifying.

Mentorships offer potential benefits for both parties. Benefits to students include:

- enriched perspective on a topic or area of interest
- increased competence
- encouragement and guidance for self-directed learning
- new connections between one's learning and the real world
- discovery of resources beyond the classroom
- personal growth (confidence, persistence, empowerment, self-efficacy, autonomy)
- career path awareness
- respect for expertise
- relationship-building experiences
- model for enjoyment and accomplishment in the chosen area
- introduction to other individuals who might provide insight and support
- increased exposure to and visibility within a field of interest
- preparation for taking on roles within society

Benefits to mentors include:

- continued learning
- rejuvenation of spirit
- sense of self-satisfaction

- sense of respect and being valued

- fresh perspective

- involvement and enjoyment

- vicarious satisfaction through accomplishment of the protégé

- contribution to skills and expertise of those entering the field

- establishment of a connection to the educational system

Though the format of mentorship programs vary, all involve a student in some kind of relationship with an adult whose work he respects and who can inspire and guide the student in his own development. In any mentorship arrangement, expectations should be clarified and agreed upon by both the mentor and the student. In formal academic situations, it's a good idea to prepare a written agreement that specifies the intent and responsibilities of each party, including the right to withdraw from the arrangement. Periodic review of this written "contract" helps to ensure that expectations are being met by both parties.

Mentorships are an excellent way of providing students with gifted level challenges while enabling them to stay in regular classrooms. There are many models for and levels of mentorships. For example, they can take the form of job-shadowing programs, in which students prepare for the mentorship phase in school classes and then spend a certain number of hours in the career setting of their mentor. Alternatively, mentorship programs can consist of visits to the school from community experts who increase the depth of programming that classroom teachers are able to provide. A graduate student in mathematics, for example, might be a paid mentor for an hour or two per week, working with one or more middle school or high school students who are advanced mathematically. Under the guidance of the teacher, mentors can individualize academic programming, offering an opportunity to design a program together with the student that targets specific needs and interests more precisely than a classroom teacher can hope to do given the normal constraints of a classroom of 20 or more students. Students can be assisted in finding individuals in the educational or broader community who are (or have been) actively engaged in working productively in areas of interest. Although they need careful monitoring, mentorships can also work well in elementary schools and are quite popular in many schools across North America.

To encourage the formation of such learning partnerships, teachers or parents can get in touch with other teachers and parents, asking for nominations for possible mentors—that is, people who are willing to work with students who want opportunities to explore their interests in some depth with knowledgeable people. We have seen such drives recruit retired and active musicians, actors, doctors, chefs, professors, business people, artists, artisans, architects, and others, each of whom was willing to help a keen and able student to explore and develop his or her particular interests and abilities. Some communities that have active mentorship programs circulate registration pamphlets and maintain links on their district websites for prospective volunteers to access.

A good mentoring relationship is built on mutual respect. A shared sense of humor is an important bonus. Ideally, a mentor's teaching style and personality provides a match for the student's learning style and personality. The mentor should possess good communication skills and be comfortable working with young people. She should be willing to help the student learn to recognize problems and find solutions, and provide some opportunities for career exploration. It is best if the mentor has a flexible attitude and is willing to offer constructive evaluation and feedback. She should be prepared to invest the time and patience required to make the mentoring relationship work.

Structuring Mentorships

When developing a framework for a mentorship arrangement, there are a number of questions to consider (Reilly, 1992):

- Will there be a safe atmosphere for learning?

- What is the student interested in?

- Is the student receptive to the learning opportunity and, in particular, to the suggestions and proposed mentorship approach?

- Is the student willing and able to commit time and energy?

- What is the student's current level of expertise? What can the student do independently, and where does he or she need help?

- What community resources relating to the student's interests have already been accessed and used wisely?

- How does the student learn best?

- Are there any special issues to be aware of (for example, pertaining to personality, resiliency, emotional or social issues, maturation, multipotentiality, etc.)?

- Does the student demonstrate a high level of motivation? Self-management skills? Task commitment? A desire to learn about the field? Responsibility?

For those who are thinking about implementing a mentorship program in a school, there are important time and energy factors to consider. Organizing, maintaining, and monitoring mentorships is time-consuming and must be carefully and responsibly done. Teachers who want to support mentorship activities must think about the form that they want these experiences to take and what their own roles will be in the context of their other responsibilities. Our experience, which is consistent with research findings, suggests that school mentorship programs work best when the major responsibility for coordinating them is assumed by a member of the special education or administrative support staff working in collaboration with teachers, parents, students, and mentors. The coordinator monitors the student and the mentor to ensure that the mentorship is going along smoothly. If there are problems, he helps to resolve them. Mentoring does not stand alone. The arrangement will be successful and mutually rewarding if it is embraced and valued as an integral component of the individual student's overall educational plan. It can be even more effective when academic credit is granted.

Female and minority mentors do triple duty; they challenge gender and cultural stereotypes and serve as alternative role models, in addition to providing the mentorship experience itself. For girls and minority students, bringing nontraditional minority professionals such as female black and Hispanic mathematicians, scientists, and other experts into the classroom as mentors is an excellent approach to enriching and accelerating education while providing authentic connections to important domains of competence. If such people are not available as mentors, girls and minority student can certainly benefit from interactions with other mentors, and this can be supplemented by discussions of gender and minority issues.

In the end, after finding one another, the student and mentor select an appropriate learning environment and then shape that environment to the individual situation. They develop a shared focus for the mentorship activities and, in the most successful mentorships, experience many rich and mutually productive hours.

Career Exploration

> "*Last fall, a lady from the Humane Society came to the school and described how they look after all the animals. I've been volunteering there twice a month ever since. I want to become a veterinarian when I get older.*"
>
> "*A forensic diver told us all about his underwater diving job. It was awesome!*"

Students with diverse exceptional abilities need to consider wide-ranging and exceptional career possibilities. This can take many forms, both in the classroom and outside of it. Some ideas that we have observed to work well:

1. Career days are held, in which people in various occupations are asked to address interested students and provide a forum for discussion. Students choose to hear speakers from a list of offerings.

2. A variety of speakers visits a class over the course of a semester to discuss different kinds of careers.

3. A career resource center is set up in one area of the school library with books and other materials about careers, providing a place for students to access information and discuss ideas with others.

4. Students spend time visiting someone in a career of interest (also known as job shadowing).

5. Students consider possible career alternatives in a systematic and guided way during courses or parts of courses.

6. Students follow a structured interview form to investigate a career of interest and then share their findings with their classmates.

7. Students have informal opportunities to meet and talk with people engaged in diverse kinds of pursuits.

8. In consultation with guidance counselors, parents, mentors, or teachers, students are encouraged to construct skills-based personal growth plans.

Some gifted students have problems with abilities and interests that take them in too many directions, a situation which is sometimes called multipotentiality. They can experience internal conflicts about which skills to develop to a high level and which to let slide. We address multipotentiality and career decision-making further in Chapter 12.

Books

With a book, you are never alone.

(Anon.)

"Books are NOT like broccoli."
"Other kids just don't realize that books are way better than TV."
"It only took me two days to read the last Harry Potter book. I can't wait till the next one comes out!"

From childhood on, it is through reading that we develop and expand many of our interests, whether they are related to work, hobbies, our families, or the world around us. Reading is the best way to learn about almost anything, and people who don't read well or don't enjoy reading are at a disadvantage in a lot of ways. Books can nurture, inform, stimulate, and soothe. They can be used as a basis for sharing, thinking, learning, sensitizing, dreaming, inspiring, and exploring. Why is recreational reading important for children? There are many reasons and several interconnected principles based on current understandings of teaching, learning, and brain development. Reading has many benefits:

- optimizes the match of learning opportunities to an individual's level of knowledge and understanding

- stimulates reflection and high-level thinking

- increases engagement in relevant, self-directed learning

- broadens and extends children's knowledge and understandings

- contributes to a feeling of connection to different communities

- strengthens home and school connections
- alleviates loneliness, especially for children who feel different or who suffer social isolation, abuse of any kind, or rejection
- provides an escape from stressful or troubling circumstances
- inspires and motivates
- illustrates alternative possibilities in various circumstances and contexts
- provides models for life
- stimulates thinking about values and life choices
- provides peaceful relaxation

Recreational reading is an integral part of the learning process and a compelling, personally relevant, and exciting way to enrich children's lives. Often children prefer fiction, but many gifted children also enjoy nonfiction, and there are books of both types on every topic to capture children's attention and imaginations in ways that challenge young readers' minds and vocabularies, but that are also age-appropriate. Halsted (2002) has written a resource guide aptly titled *Some of My Best Friends Are Books: Guiding Gifted Readers from Pre-School to High School*. She describes how books help children develop an identity, and she offers advice and suggestions for children reading at various levels, as well as annotated bibliographies and foundational references.

Some books are particularly useful for helping children come to terms with their problems (such as friendship issues, feelings of differentness, etc.). Given the right book, a young reader can identify with a character in a story and experience some kind of kinship following that person through a difficult situation and toward a successful resolution. A child can gain insight by applying what happens to a character to her own life, learning how to handle similar kinds of circumstances. Reading can lead not only to greater knowledge, but also to better understandings, changed attitudes, increased motivation, deeper insight, and altered behavior. Books can help children think about what matters to them and how they want to live their lives.

Bibliotherapy, a psychological term, refers to a specific therapeutic process whereby selected reading material is used for dealing with one's personal problems. As a reader interacts with a literary character, he learns about himself and can achieve some insight about his own difficulties, if only to feel that he is not alone. Parents and educators should keep in mind that bibliotherapy, like any therapeutic technique, should be approached with caution: some children experience problems that are deeply rooted and require the help of a mental health professional.

That being said, educators and parents can use books to address many of children's concerns related to their giftedness and other aspects of their lives (such as adjustment to changes and challenges, personal growth, values, identity, social and cultural concerns, family issues, etc.). For this approach (sometimes referred to as developmental bibliotherapy) to be most effective, the adult should be very familiar with the book that the child is reading and be prepared to generate and respond to questions and to promote meaningful discussion. The adult should choose the book carefully, avoiding poorly written material and stories that might make the child feel too exposed or uncomfortable. Reading can also be useful as a preventive measure to anticipate and solve problems before they manifest. Additional information about bibliotherapy, its origins, benefits, and processes, as well as recommended book titles for use with gifted children can be found in Halsted's guide.

As children get older, more and more of their learning is presented in written format, until they reach graduate school, where most programs are heavily reading-intensive. The child who grows up loving to read is at an obvious advantage. Reading can provide an endless source of intellectual and creative stimulation for people of all ages and should be encouraged (and modeled) whenever possible. There are some excellent booklist websites that have been developed with gifted learners in mind (see our website at www.beingsmart.ca).

A final word about books for avid readers and gifted children: librarians are often the richest and least used of our available resources. They know a lot about books and where to find good ones. Librarians and the personnel in reputable book stores are usually pleased to offer suggestions and discuss both new books and the classics on their shelves.

Travel

> *...it was a beautiful map, in many colors, showing principal roads, rivers and seas, towns and cities, mountains and valleys, intersections and detours, and sites of outstanding interest both beautiful and historic. The only trouble was that Milo had never heard of any of the places it indicated, and even the names sounded most peculiar.... He closed his eyes and poked a finger at the map. "Dictionopolis," read Milo slowly when he saw what his finger had chosen.... Suddenly he found himself speeding along an unfamiliar country highway.... "Welcome to Expectations," said a carefully lettered sign on a small house at the side of the road.*
>
> (Juster, from *The Phantom Tollbooth*, 1961, pp. 14-17)

> *"MOM! I just looked up the route from Rome to Paris on Mapquest.com. I found out that it's 875 miles or 1450 km and that the total driving time is only 13 and a half hours! I'm going to plan a trip, in case we ever want to go!"*

Travel is another horizon-stretching approach to consider as a possible springboard for extending learning and to supplement the more conventional learning methods. Whether it is actual, factual, virtual, or whimsical, travel is one of the best ways to learn. Although long trips to foreign lands are not viable possibilities for many families, travel is worth mentioning as a way to stimulate children's intellectual development. Family excursions can cover short or long distances and can last a few days or a full year or more, depending on individual circumstances and constraints. A family might take a one-day hike in the mountains, plan a day in a nearby city, or visit a museum or a historical site. The learning benefits accrue much more from the attitudes and perspectives of family members than from the financial cost, duration, or destination of the trip. Although traveling can be expensive, it can also be experienced by creative families with a limited budget. Ideas mentioned here can be implemented by a family touring Europe, taking a daytrip to a town a few miles away, exploring their own hometown, or even taking a "virtual vacation" on the web.

Before You Go:

- Encourage all family members to spend some time looking at an atlas or maps, tracing possible routes (Mapquest.com is a great website for this purpose).

- Buy a travel guide or download an online version, and spend some time with it. Discuss information, observations, and ideas with other family members.

- Spend time on the Internet, and browse travel magazines or newspaper sections, investigating what might be interesting and what each family member might like to explore.

- Include everyone in family decision-making regarding places to visit.

- Pay particular attention to areas of interest to family members at home. For example, if one child is enthused about a particular sport or art, make sure there are opportunities for some kind of exploration of that interest while away. And if new related interests are found, these can be followed back at home.

While You Are Away:

- Encourage the children to notice and discuss differences they see in food, houses, scenery, and other sights and influences.

- Think about what captures your own interest in the new environment. Act as an authentic model of engagement in learning and exploration.

- Ask questions that stimulate higher-order thinking about the experience and environment. For example, if a family spends a weekend at a cabin on a lake, discover what everyone likes best about this new place. What do they like better at home? What aspects of life in the new environment would they like to take home?

- Encourage children to keep a diary or sketchbook or both to record their impressions.

- Look for ways to make the experience productive. For example, write articles for a website, a local newspaper, or for a school assignment.

- Create a collaborative travel document or scrapbook. For example, consider compiling a photo journal, where one or more members of the family takes pictures of personal interest (not necessarily the usual tourist sites), someone else takes responsibility for writing, and another person puts together the final product. This can be assembled upon returning home, to be shared with friends and other family members.

No matter where you've come from or where you're headed, your thirst for adventure never ceases. It's an insatiable desire to experience the unknown, to test your own limits, to explore further than your imagination has ever ventured.

(Silvertown, n.d., from *Virtuoso, The Travel Network*, 2004)

Travel offers a world of opportunities to learn and acquire fresh perspectives on other places, cultures, and languages. As with the project-based learning we described earlier, many gifted kids love the detailed organization of actually planning a trip (doing the research, planning the itinerary, thinking about the budget, etc.) And for those who think creatively, planning a virtual foray into another era or into space or beneath the seas is yet another way to "go." Just planning a get-away can be a wonderfully motivating learning experience—and if you actually take the trip, well, so much the better!

Do-Nothing Times

"Mom, I've got way too much to do!"
"I never have time just to think anymore."

These comments are typical of children who may need some down-time. In encouraging optimal long-term development in children, it is just as important that they experience periods entirely devoid of scheduled stimulation as that they have appropriate and adequate intellectual stimulation. We all need some unprogrammed time and space in our lives to figure out what we enjoy doing, to explore the scope and shape of our interests and pleasures, to consider and reflect upon our experiences, our successes, our failures, and our preferences. If we don't invest time in this kind of reflection, we will eventually find ourselves quite out of touch with our goals, our hopes, and our dreams. One of the most important tasks of childhood and adolescence is discovering who we really are, and this requires an investment of time that is not otherwise required for homework or participating in scheduled activities.

"Mom, I'm BORED!"

From another perspective, parents should try not to rescue their child from boredom. Figuring out what one wants to do with one's discretionary time can be a valuable learning experience. Children need unscheduled time in order to develop time management skills and to learn to set priorities. Many conscientious parents, in an attempt to provide appropriate stimulation, take full responsibility for keeping their children engaged and happy and organized. However, too much programming can deprive children of something vital. It can prevent them from learning what it is they enjoy doing and who they really are. As with adults, children whose lives are micromanaged lose their zest and enthusiasm. Even more than adults, children who are over-programmed can get stale and stressed.

And so, having considered many of the learning options available for high-ability students in Chapters 6, 7, and 8, it is now time to think about choosing the most fitting ones for a given child and set of circumstances—which is what we do in Chapter 9.

Chapter 9

Adapting to Change

We should no longer even be thinking about "a program" in gifted education for which testing is required to "get in." Rather, we should be thinking about how to collect a variety of information on individual children in order to best match their demonstrated needs with any of a variety of options our particular setting can offer.
(Rogers, 2003, p. 318)

The important issue in gifted education is finding a good match between the learning needs of an individual child and the range of learning opportunities available in the child's particular circumstance. We gave considerable thought in Section II to information about children's learning needs and, in the first three chapters of Section III, to the kinds of educational choices available. In this chapter, we consider the factors involved in choosing the best option or combination of options for a child at a particular point in time. To begin with, we briefly review the many interrelated gifted learning options we have already discussed.

In Chapter 6, we described:

- fundamental adaptations to basic instruction, such as:
  - curriculum compacting
  - project-based learning
  - guided independent study

- ○ cross-grade and cross-panel expertise and resource access
- ○ single-subject enrichment
- ○ single-subject acceleration
- ○ career exploration built into the curriculum
- ○ peer coaching
- ○ online and cyber-learning

In Chapter 7, we considered:

- whole-grade acceleration
- gifted classes in the public or separate school system (full-time or part-time)
- second language immersion and dual track programs
- curriculum adaptations for gifted needs in special subject areas
- specialized and alternative schools
- private and independent schools
- home schooling

In Chapter 8, we suggested supplementary learning options, such as:

- extracurricular enrichment
- mentorships
- career exploration
- books for gifted children and adolescents
- the community and beyond
- discretionary (do-nothing) times

So many possibilities! How does one make an intelligent decision? To begin with, in most cases, appropriate learning options for exceptional children cannot be decided upon with any degree of finality or permanence. Instead, the more exceptional the child, the more likely parents and educators will find themselves in an ongoing process of educational decision-making. It will involve monitoring regularly, at least annually, how a child is doing and what aspects of her education need tinkering with or changing entirely in order for her to keep developing optimally. This concept of carefully focused, ongoing attention to special learning needs is written into special education practice and law in both the United States and Canada, whereby exceptional learners' individual education plans (IEPs) must be reviewed and revised at least yearly.

An IEP is a written plan that outlines the special education program or services that a child requires. It identifies learning expectations that differ from those described in policy documents for the child's normal grade expectations. It is *not* a daily lesson plan that details every aspect of a students' education. It *does* list important information on individual accommodations and programming modifications that are needed in order to assist a student to achieve optimally. An IEP provides a framework for monitoring student progress and for communicating updated information and learning expectations across various subject areas. An IEP typically consists of (Ontario Ministry of Education and Training, 2000):

- reasons for developing the document

- student profile information (such as age, grade, any medical conditions, and relevant previous assessment data)

- a description of the child's strengths and needs, based on appropriate current educational, psychological, observational, or health assessments

- a program description, including the student's current level of achievement in different domains, recommended annual program goals, and specific skills or learning expectations

- special strategies, accommodations, resources, and equipment required

- recommendations for methods of ongoing evaluation of student progress

Additional components of the IEP may include transition plans, consultation specifics, timelines, and alternative informational sources. Most districts have established standards and documentation for Individual Education Plans, and schools are expected to comply with them.

Parents can find out more by contacting their local school or district education office.

Flexibility

"My son's school just doesn't know what to do with him. What do you suggest?"

"We're thinking about changing schools. But I know Jenna will have a really hard time making that adjustment. What should we do?"

It is an unfortunate but predictable reality that education systems designed to meet the needs of the majority are often less effective in meeting the learning needs of exceptional students. Even the most highly competent educators do not always have the knowledge or support they need to work effectively with gifted learners, including checking their progress on an ongoing basis, as mandated for special education IEPs. Being flexibly open to change can be very difficult, and most people prefer to make a current decision that will work for a several-year period. In certain circumstances, with planning and good luck, that can be possible, but it is wise for parents and educators to approach decision-making for exceptional learners as an ongoing work-in-progress.

In making program-related decisions, children, educators, and parents should consider the anticipated benefits of change. Before altering or challenging the status quo, it is good to address the following questions:

- Is change really needed? (Why?)

- What are the advantages and disadvantages of each of the options under consideration (including those of maintaining the status quo)?

- If changes are made, will the process be supported by the parents and the school administration? (How?)

Some of the factors to consider when analyzing the options available are short-term and long-term goals, perceived learning provisions, assessment issues, attitudes, social/emotional concerns, and the anticipated fit between the individual and any proposed changes. There are many other factors, too, that relate to particular circumstances, including health, travel schedules, parents' work schedules, etc.

School-change decisions are rarely clear or easy. For example, a change may involve moving a child from a school where there are no gifted programming provisions to another school where a better learning opportunity exists but where travel demands mean that the child will not be able to play the sports that he loves. It may mean moving a child from an environment where she has lots of good friends but that offers no targeted programming to one where she worries about not knowing anyone. It may involve transferring a child from a good-enough learning situation to one that appears to be better but has unknown elements or perhaps financial ramifications. Maybe parents are considering home schooling and are concerned about the time demands for them and the social dimension for their child. Or if a mentorship program is being newly established, decisions about mentors and questions about the level of support being provided have to be resolved.

Change takes many forms. It can be comfortable and smooth, or it can be rocky.

Contemplating change, however, is a necessary fact of life for most exceptional learners and their parents as they encounter educational situations where there is a not a good match between a child's domain-specific abilities and the learning opportunities that are available. Being smart about education change from a mastery model perspective means staying attuned to the individual child's learning needs and well-being, as we discuss below.

Support

> *"We need to accommodate Lee working above her grade level while remaining with her age group, which we think is important for her. Her mind never seems to take a break, and she is starting to tell us that she feels different from other kids. How do we strike a balance?"*

Parents and educators are instrumental in children's lives in a great many ways. Two of these have to do with charting educational courses and helping children adapt well to the changes in their lives. Of utmost importance is that parents and teachers remain available to offer children ongoing support by responding to questions, allaying concerns, and providing information so that making school-related choices and implementing change are experiences that are as positive and affirming as possible. Children's adjustments to change, whether at school or at home, with peers or with siblings, will vary from one person or situation to the next. Support might be needed on a short- or long-term basis. Sources of potential support for children include parents, other family members, teachers, neighbors, community members, faith-based contacts, classmates, and friends. Supportive measures at times of stress include engaging children in activities that they enjoy and encouraging them to develop competence in skills they value.

Adults can help to demystify giftedness by understanding and talking about it from a mastery perspective, emphasizing the naturalness of exceptional ability within the context of education and human development, and focusing on the very practical idea of facilitating a better learner-learning match. This can help a child understand the nature of his exceptionality and accept the changes it may bring with it.

During times of change, how can parents and teachers support a child in feeling as self-confident, motivated, engaged, and content as possible? The best supports depend very much on the way the individual child experiences the particular situation. For example, a child about to begin attending a full-time gifted program might express concerns about being viewed differently and making new friends, or about the amount of work that may be required, or about finding her way around a new school. Her parents can try to learn about the specific circumstances involved in the change process, get a sense of the social milieu, familiarize themselves with the teacher's expectations for learning, and in general become as knowledgeable as possible to support their child's concerns during the adjustment. They can reassure her that experiencing change is an ever-present part of everyone's life and natural development, and they can remind their child of changes that she has successfully navigated in the past (such as when she first entered school, or began a new activity, or conquered a challenge that she had worried about). They can also discuss with her the fact that she has demonstrated sufficient competence to be recommended for the new program. Most importantly, perhaps, they can remain patiently attentive throughout the change process and be ready to respond supportively as she makes the change, remembering (and reminding their child as necessary) that there is more in her life that is *not* changing than *is* changing.

When only one child in a family is identified as gifted, parents should anticipate the possibility of some reactive behaviors and responses within the family circle. Jealousy, annoyance, sibling rivalry, and provocation can all be minimized if parents use their anticipatory antennae; ensure that all their children feel valued, competent, and supported; and act quickly at the earliest sign of trouble. For example, if one child is working with a mentor, brothers and sisters will likely want to know why they, too, are not involved in such an arrangement. Perhaps alternative learning opportunities (such as outings, books, extracurricular activities, etc.) can be arranged for them. We discuss the important dimension of gifted identification and education as it relates to siblings in Chapter 14.

Parents of children experiencing adjustment difficulties of one sort or another may benefit from learning how other families deal with similar situations, remembering that the viability of a certain approach depends on the particular context. Local parent associations can provide helpful support groups, information, and opportunities for parents of gifted children to network with one another. Parents can also find useful information in books, on websites, or from professionals experienced in working with giftedness-related issues. Again, this topic is dealt with in considerably more detail in Chapter 14, in which we address family issues associated with gifted development.

Choosing a School

> *"In a large city like Toronto where there are lots of options, the question is: Which are the best ones?"*
> *"We live in a rural setting, and the only school nearby is not working out at all well for our child."*

Mapping out a child's education means a lot more than selecting a program. It's also necessary to think about the school itself—the advantages and disadvantages, the larger picture. Some families live in communities where there are many possible choices; others live in areas where there are limited options. Either way, there are schooling decisions to make.

A good choice to consider for most young children is the regular classroom in a local publicly funded school—for a number of reasons. Such a placement facilitates finding local friends who children can play with informally and casually on their own initiative. For those who live in urban communities, going to the local school encourages a sense of belonging to a neighborhood; it assists in a feeling of autonomy and mastery to be getting to school on one's own. These factors continue to be important as the child matures, and at the secondary level, extracurricular sports, drama, music, student government, and other school-based activities make proximity important as well.

Regular public school classrooms tend to be diverse and provide a wide spectrum of experiences of people and life. These settings encourage a child to consider and develop his own way of being in the context of lots of possibilities, with fewer predetermined boundaries than are experienced by children in more select or exclusive circumstances. Educators working with students in regular classrooms in publicly-funded schools are frequently more willing than others to be flexible in accommodating children with special learning needs. Although we believe that the experience of social, cultural, and economic diversity and the development of authentic individuality are important goals, this perspective reflects our philosophical bias and is not one that all parents share. We also recognize that in order for this approach to lead to healthy developmental outcomes, it must be balanced by strong family values and support.

On the other hand, gifted learners sometimes need stimulating learning opportunities beyond those that are available in a particular regular classroom. The educational match we envision for high-ability children in their neighborhood school may be ideal, but it just does not happen in some situations. For example, there may be little support for addressing gifted learning needs, or there may even be a school climate that makes gifted children feel unwelcome or weird.

As with all exceptional children, choosing a school for a gifted learner is a highly complex and often challenging decision. When a family is lucky enough to have a choice between two or more possible schools, they have to consider many factors, including proximity, affordability, after-school options, stability, and the needs of others in the family, to say nothing of the highly variable and often unpredictable needs of the learner herself. When this is complicated by the fact that it is very difficult to know exactly what kind of education a given school really provides and how that might change over time, decision-making can feel like a nightmare. Some parents we know have become immobilized in their deliberations over selecting schools for their gifted children.

When we are asked for help in school (and program) decision-making, we suggest that parents consider the following questions.

#1 Assessing Teacher Characteristics:

- Is there support for teachers' ongoing professional development, including opportunities to acquire and update an understanding of the special needs of gifted learners?

- Are teachers encouraged to learn about differentiating instruction for gifted children?

- Are there indications that teachers' content mastery is valued in the school? For example (in high school choices), do any hold graduate degrees in their subject areas?

- Do teachers display intellectual curiosity themselves? Do they welcome and implement innovative approaches?

- Do they provide appropriate and scaffolded intellectual challenge?

- Do teachers focus on children's abilities and strengths, as well as on any learning problems that need to be addressed?

- Do teachers display a sense of humor?

- Do they listen? To parents? To children? To each other?

- Do they respond promptly to children's questions and behavioral issues, and with patience and understanding?

#2 Assessing Programming and Classroom Characteristics:

- Are academic standards high?

- Are expectations clear?

- Is programming both flexible and challenging? That is, does it accommodate and support children's diverse abilities, interests, and learning styles?

- Are gifted students given ample opportunity to interact with intellectual peers, as well as with age peers?

- Is there an emphasis on classroom activities which encourage creative expression?

- Do problem-solving activities allow for many possible answers and lots of exploration?

- Do children have sufficient time and opportunity to muddle through problems and work them out by themselves and/or with others?

- Do teachers and students appear to be engaged and stimulated by what they are doing?

- Do teachers and students display mutual respect?

- Are there open channels of communication across grade levels and subject areas?

#3 Assessing Administrative Characteristics:

- Are the priorities of the program's administrators consistent with your needs and concerns?

- Do the administrators have accepting, positive, sensitive, and appropriately nurturing attitudes toward high-ability children?

- How does the administration support teachers in becoming more knowledgeable about theories of child development, instructional methods, and course content?

- Does the administration encourage parental involvement in the school?

There are always unknown elements when choosing a school, and no school or teacher can realistically be expected to meet *all* of the criteria we list here. However, if parents do what they can to become well-informed about the various aspects of the possible learning environments and the teaching professionals in them, the decision-making and change processes can be smoother for everyone. In Chapter 14, we discuss ways that parents can find the kinds of information they need to answer these questions and be good advocates and decision-makers for their child, including seeking out other parents and students in the programs under consideration and contacting schools.

A School Choice Experience

> *"I hear lots of talk in the neighborhood park, and the assumption is that no enrichment is necessary at private schools, but it is necessary at public schools. Is that true?"*
>
> *"We've narrowed it down to three possibilities. How do we know which school is the best one for us?"*

We know that it can be very difficult to make the necessary school or program choice. Consider the following e-mail that we received from Jeane. Her older son, Thomas, had shown many signs of giftedness and, at the time, was in kindergarten at the neighborhood public school.

Jeane's School Decision-Making

Here are our latest thoughts on schools. I'd love your comments.

Idea #1: We keep Thomas at Boxwood, the nearby public school, and I make a special effort to supplement his studies through my own form of teaching, such as trips to the library with his little brother Edward (which we should do anyway) on a regular, scheduled basis to study different things and then have him do projects. Also augment the math, etc. I'd do this in conjunction with what he's learning at Boxwood, and I'd talk to his teacher about appropriate topics. I'd also have scheduled study times for Thomas every day at home, and Edward could color or do something else. And then he'd have some time during the week for play dates and other extracurricular activities. Also, family trips to the Science Center, etc.

My husband wonders if this is too much for me to take on, but I'd be doing most of it right after school, when I'd be carpooling anyway if he was at a school farther from home. I think this might challenge Thomas enough, while giving him a nurturing home and neighborhood environment. I've heard that the Grade 1 teachers at Boxwood are excellent. They have different styles, but both run good, organized classes.

Idea #2: The other option is Lancaster (the private school), along with programs which augment the curriculum, maybe a form of enrichment once a week after school. What do you think? I continue to hear terrific things about Lancaster. It apparently has a lot of individual attention for the kids, they work hard, etc. But will he get tired of the same small school in the later grades?

Right now we're talking to a few people, both with kids at Boxwood and at Lancaster. But all in all, I think we're spending far too much time on this! When Thomas is in college, we'll laugh about how much time we spent worrying about his Grade 1 education! I mean, he's only five!

It almost makes one's head spin to think of all the variables and issues here, and as Jeane wrote, we are talking about a five-year-old child who has not had any problems with school. Jeane's analysis of how to supplement the education at the public school is excellent, including her description of spending time with her children doing interesting things instead of carpooling. One of the themes running below the surface is the differences that parents often have with each other. Both parents love their children and are seriously committed to their well being; any conflict reflects the complexities of the decision-making process and the fact that no school is likely to be perfect. In this case, the conflict is a minor problem that the parents resolve (as you will see). In some families we've worked with, it can take on larger proportions and become a problem much bigger than the school choice itself.

The most important thing in children's lives, especially at this early stage, is not which schools are chosen, but that they feel loved, encouraged, and respected, particularly by their parents. Generally speaking, the more traditional the school environment, the less likely it is to accommodate a highly gifted child's independent spirit and love of learning. However, as long as the child is not being harmed by his school environment (which does happen sometimes, but is rare), extracurricular activities can often supplement what might be missing from the formal curriculum. Knowing this can help make the decision process less anxiety-provoking for parents. It is also helpful to remember that much of a child's important learning does not happen in classrooms. Most of the people who go on to interesting gifted-level achievement did not have exemplary or unusual early schooling experiences.

In the end, Jeane and her husband decided on Lancaster (a private school with an excellent academic reputation), which they thought would be better suited to Thomas' creative, intense, and intrinsically-motivated learning style. An interesting postscript to the story is that Thomas spent two and a half years at Lancaster (with his little brother Edward joining him for the second year and a half, and a third boy having been born into the family in the meantime). However, sometime in first grade, the teachers began to express concerns about Thomas' poor handwriting and his troublingly enthusiastic behavior, which was described as a problem with impulse control and following school rules. He had a hard time restraining his curiosity when he had a question, for example, and found it very difficult not to blurt it out in class, something that we frequently see in gifted primary school children, particularly boys.

These concerns did not disappear in second grade, and Thomas' parents were informed that Thomas might not pass into third grade. Told by the school that he might have learning problems and worried about their son's academic ability, they had him tested by a private psychologist. They discovered that he had no learning problems whatsoever, and was, in fact, highly gifted. After sharing the assessment results with Lancaster and working with the Grade 3 teacher to implement the educational recommendations regarding their son's giftedness, they still felt that Thomas' learning needs were not being well met. The school's position continued to be that he needed to work on his penmanship and social maturity and that he might fail the grade if his printing did not improve. Jeane and her husband decided to move both boys to Boxwood Public School. We have since received this message from her.

Jeane's Decision-Making Experience Revisited

Boxwood Public School is great; in lots of ways, better than I'd anticipated, in some ways, the same as I'd thought. As for Edward, he is in his element. The kids love him, find him funny, and the teacher can see that he's very clever.

Now for the really interesting part. I could go on and on about this, but in a nutshell, here it is. The Lancaster School must have an amazing public relations person to have developed such a great reputation for itself as being so academically advanced and challenging. Parents believe that only the brightest kids are accepted and do well. As you know, this just isn't the case. Both Thomas and Edward are being challenged more at Boxwood. They are asked to do more stimulating and harder things, while using the same textbooks as Lancaster in a lot of cases. Plus, they have the huge advantages of being able to get up an hour later in the morning, come home for lunch when they want, and they don't have the drives at both ends of the day. All in all, they're learning as much as I'd hoped while having a lot more free time. It's ideal! The funniest part is that Thomas is asking us to let him go back to Lancaster, even with the longer days, because the work is too hard at Boxwood! Ha! With his scores on the assessment, I think he can handle it!

Anyway, I find this most interesting in light of the fact that a lot of parents around here assume that private schools have better academics, the kids learn more, etc. Yes, they often have better art programs, some have better sports programs, but $16,000 a year is a high price to pay, not to mention the lack of neighborhood feeling!

Jeane's story is a true one, and we have heard different versions of it over the years. The parents of exceptional learners often discover that the experiences of other parents cannot be directly applied to their circumstances and that many factors go into finding a good fit between an individual child and a learning environment. Yet there is much to be learned from the decision-making experiences of others. In Thomas' case, he was clearly not well-understood or appreciated at the traditional private school, where the focus was on his learning problems (his penmanship and exuberant curiosity) rather than his exceptional intelligence and his love of learning. By switching to the local public school, Jeane and her family gained many advantages, including a more relaxed lifestyle, in addition to a better educational match and considerable financial savings. This story illustrates the flexibility required and the need to see educational decision-making as an ongoing work-in-progress when dealing with gifted learners.

It might also be helpful for parents to think about the following set of criteria for school excellence that we extracted from a recent reader survey conducted by *Maclean's Magazine* and *Today's Parent*, two widely-read Canadian publications. Parents across Canada were asked to nominate schools that they thought were exceptional. The magazines' editors consulted 60 experts about what parents should consider and then settled on the following criteria (*Maclean's Magazine*, 2004).

Ten Things that Make an Exceptional School:
1. High-quality classroom teachers
2. Principal's leadership skills
3. Teamwork
4. Parent communication and involvement
5. A caring, respectful, orderly, and secure school environment
6. Community involvement
7. High student expectations
8. Student engagement and leadership
9. Academic excellence
10. Excellence and innovation in non-core programs

We include this school selection process because it is a useful set of reference points for parents to think about when seeking an exemplary learning environment for their children.

Decisions

"Below a certain age, isn't school choice really the parents' decision? When does it become more the child's decision? I know some families who seem to give far too much weight to their kids' opinions at a very young age."

"I'm not sure if the decisions we make are binding or if there's a grace period. What if Emma hates the new school?"

"Is there something special I need to know for this school meeting we've been summoned to?"

The best educational program for a gifted child is one that provides learning opportunities that are appropriate to his mastery level and pace in a context that supports his optimal development. *The objective should be to find the best-fit program on an ongoing, year-by-year basis, taking into account both the available options at that level and the child's educational, social, and emotional needs at the time.*

Each approach has its own goals, content, problems, and advantages, and choosing the most appropriate one at a given time for a child is a complex process involving research, advocacy, and collaboration between home and school. Parents or educators wanting further help in thinking about this might consult Karen Rogers' (2002) *Re-Forming Gifted Education: How Parents and Teachers Can Match the Program to the Child* for some additional and thoughtful guidelines for decision-making. Rogers identifies important criteria for considering various educational options and also profiles gifted students of various ages and abilities, showing how certain kinds of programming might be suitable for them. Finding the best-fit program requires ongoing flexibility from parents and teachers, most likely involving a combination of some of the options we list in this section and/or changing programs from time to time as circumstances change. In the process, remember that children who possess high-level skills in one or more domains are very often asynchronous in their development—that is, although they might be intellectually gifted, they function closer to or within the normal range in some areas, and they may have cognitive, physiological, and psychological developmental constraints. Academic advancement is not always the most important factor in choosing the right program for a gifted learner.

There are several basic principles that should be considered in the decision-making process, as suggested by VanTassel-Baska (2000), an eminent scholar in the field of gifted education whose work is seminal to the mastery model perspective:

- Curriculum opportunities should allow all students to attain optimal levels of learning.

- Gifted learners have different learning needs compared with typical learners. Therefore, curriculum must be adapted or designed to accommodate these needs.

- The needs of gifted learners cut across cognitive, affective, social, and aesthetic areas of educational experiences.

- Gifted learners are best served by an approach that allows for accelerated and advanced learning *and* enriched and extended experiences.

- Educational experiences for gifted learners need to be carefully planned, written down, implemented, monitored, and evaluated in order to maximize potential effect.

- Curriculum development for gifted learners is an ongoing process that uses evaluation as a central tool for future planning and for the revision of curriculum documents.

Beyond the complexities of identifying the appropriate curriculum for a child is the process of learning *within* a chosen curricular framework. This is a multifaceted process in its own right. It is a matter of the student listening, consolidating, applying, and extending herself, with the teacher guiding the process. It is a complicated endeavor, even for advanced learners, and especially for those who have difficulty with certain subjects or modes of instruction. Program planning undertaken by a student, teachers, and parents involves careful consideration of the child's individual needs and learning profile. It also requires considerable administrative support. When all facets come together well and the child experiences a happily successful learner-learning match, it becomes very worthwhile for all concerned.

An exceptional student's education requires ongoing monitoring and usually has to be modified from time to time. School-based team meetings, both formal and informal in nature, can be extremely useful for doing just that and for working through and arriving at programming decisions. In many jurisdictions, there are official processes in place for such purposes. In the U.S., monitoring exceptional learning needs is the responsibility of child study teams, although these are not generally put into place for the gifted exceptionality. Across Canada, there is also some variability in how official meetings are established in order to assess student functioning and review special program viability. In Ontario, for example, it is the responsibility of identification, placement, and review committees (IPRCs) to monitor such processes.

In these school-based team meetings, typically the parents, teachers, principal, psychologist, and consultants gather to consider the child's needs; in some cases, the child is also included. Everyone gives input during what is usually a structured discussion. Samples of the child's work are reviewed, the psychologist presents any test results, educators describe their views of the child, and parents (and possibly the child) express their concerns and suggestions.

Rogers (2002) offers a selection of inventories pertaining to student interests, learning style preferences, and attitudes about specific subjects, as well as teacher and parent inventories designed to reveal information that can be useful during these kinds of meetings. Everyone has a chance to speak, and then there is an opportunity to consider recommendations and (in a well-run meeting) to engage in further discussion. Such a meeting can help to identify and clarify the issues involved and to provide a multidimensional consideration of a child's educational programming needs.

For parents or educators who feel bewildered by all of the learning options and placement possibilities that we present, remember to take your time when making or advising choices. There may be lots of distractions because of different perspectives on giftedness, on the child, and even on education itself. One of the best techniques for keeping sane and focused in times of consternation and stress is to keep bringing the discussion back to the most important question, "How do we create the best possible learning fit for this particular child?"

Listen carefully to the child's opinions, and think about his personality and his views. He should feel a part of the decision-making process. However, be sensible. A child may prefer a school simply because the playground looks better! Not a trivial reason, for sure, but not necessarily the highest priority in the decision. The older the child, the more input he should have and the more his preferences should be considered. Think in terms of what you already know about the child, including his areas of strength and weakness, favored learning styles, interests, and personal preferences. Find out the advantages one school might have over another by considering those factors we've mentioned, including the range of academic facilities, extracurricular programs, the student-to-teacher ratio, the "personality" of the school (your gut feeling about the social atmosphere and the learning environment, combined with others' perceptions and observations), and the way the system does or does not accommodate children with special learning needs.

Remember also that educational placement decisions are rarely irrevocable. Make your best effort at a decision, try it out for long enough that you can distinguish between adjustment problems and problems with the actual setting, and if it isn't working, you can change your mind. There is no magic formula for figuring out how long should be given to the trial. Although this can vary tremendously from one situation to the next, a family usually knows within the first six weeks whether a change is going to work or not. Remember Jeane's experience that we describe in the vignettes. Although she and her husband did all their homework (and then some!), they made a decision that they later realized was probably a mistake. By being flexible and paying attention to their children's learning experiences, they rectified it. Yes, it cost them quite a lot of time and money, but there was no permanent damage. In the end, they learned a lot, and their children are all doing very well.

The school choice experience should work to include *everyone's* best interests and aspirations. It is vital that parents and children talk about the possibilities and listen to one another. They are wise to openly share their feelings, perspectives, and concerns and to consider the implications of any choice, including the motivational, emotional, social, behavioral, and developmental factors. We address these factors more fully, along with a number of other concerns, in Section IV.

Section IV.

Being Smart about Gifted Kids

Chapter 10

Motivation and Other Issues

*Students who are highly motivated to learn value
the learning process, which leads them to find joy
in understanding and mastery.*
(Good & Brophy, 1994, pp. 288-289)

In Section IV, we discuss some of the learning, emotional, and social implications of giftedness in children, including developmental and diversity issues. We begin by focusing on motivation, its role in the learning process, and some achievement-related concerns.

Curiosity

"I try to encourage students to learn by capturing their interest in the subject being taught, showing why it's important and how it'll be useful to them."

Although motivating learning is often considered to be a basic element of a teacher's job, we know that it can be a real challenge figuring out how to do that most effectively. Motivation involves initiating, maintaining, and governing goal-directed behavior (Bowd, McDougall, & Yewchuk, 1998). How can teachers stimulate and sustain students' motivation to learn? When given opportunities to think about it constructively, teachers can generate creative ideas about ways to sustain motivation. As expressed by teacher candidate Chris Healey:

> *Students need to know where they stand relative to expectations, as well as their strengths and weaknesses.... Teachers must effectively set goals for their students based on their individual needs and motivation levels.... This may require more creativity/ resourcefulness on the part of the teacher but consistent, constructive feedback is especially important (for maintaining interest, keeping their situation in perspective, etc.).*

Motivation is tied to an individual's expectation of success in combination with a valuing of the task at hand. A student who believes that math is important, but also believes that she cannot do it, may behave in a variety of self-defeating ways. She may skip class, avoid doing homework, or give up very easily when asked to solve a difficult math problem. All of these behaviors will contribute to poor performance, which in turn will reinforce her low expectation of future mathematical success. Similarly, a student who does not value the achievement of the assigned learning task can be expected to invest very little effort, if any, in doing it, even if she feels fully competent to handle it.

The theory and research in the literature on motivation for learning point to two simple but important criteria:

1. First, teachers and parents should try to *match tasks to a child's ability*. Tasks should be both challenging and manageable.

2. Second, and just as importantly, *learning opportunities should be authentically relevant* to the individuals engaged in the learning process. Learners should see the tasks as valuable and as enhancing their self-esteem.

The implications of these criteria for parents and teachers are that academic expectations are much more readily met, and even exceeded, when students experience the kind of motivation that results from personal engagement in learning.

In one study on motivation for learning, 100 high school students were asked the question, "How can teachers motivate students?" The students offered many interesting answers, but three distinct themes emerged from their responses. Teachers can motivate students by: (1) encouraging students' expectations of success, (2) facilitating their understanding of the value of learning and relevance of the tasks, and (3) maintaining and enhancing their self-esteem.

Encouraging Students' Expectations of Success

1. **Facilitation of Accomplishment (Content Mastery)**
   Content mastery, which leads to a feeling of accomplishment, is a powerful motivator for learning.

   "A sense of accomplishment makes us feel like we're really good at something, so we try to keep up great marks."

2. **Teacher's Confidence and Expectations**
   Teachers' confidence in students translates to students' increased confidence in themselves. Students who sense that their teachers have faith in their ability are more motivated to work toward academic success.

   "A motivating teacher makes us feel that we can do anything. A teacher needs to believe that we are competent and never underestimate us."

Facilitating Students' Understanding of the Value of Learning

3. **Use of Relevant and Authentic Examples**
   Relevant illustrations of curriculum content make learning more interesting and encourage a deeper level of thinking and discussion about a topic. Personal connection to a topic area is a potent motivator for learning.

   "It helps when the teacher applies real-life examples to illustrate a point."

4. **Teacher's Enthusiasm for the Subject**
   If students perceive that a teacher finds the lesson content highly valuable, they are more likely to take the course seriously and be motivated to learn.

   "It won't work if a teacher who hates chemistry has to explain about carbon dioxide. When a teacher loves what he or she is teaching, students are likely to be motivated, too."

5. **Variety in Teaching Methods**
   By incorporating group work, activities, games, and field trips, teachers can bring the content to life.

   "A teacher can keep students motivated by doing different things and not always using a textbook, or the board, or talking on and on."

6. **Explicit Discussions of Why the Learning Is Important**
   Teachers can initiate discussions of applications and implications of material or skills taught in class.

   "Talk about the importance of what we're learning. How will it affect our future?"

Enhancing Respect and Self-Esteem

7. **Respect and Rapport**
   When students perceive a teacher as being caring, respectful of them, available, and willing to help, their motivation increases.

   "Try to remember that some of us have things on our minds. Take the time to get to know us. And please remember our names!"

8. **Teacher's Sense of Humor**
   A teacher's sense of humor is an important component of a classroom climate. It is one way of showing respect for students' individuality.

   "I find that I always pay more attention when the teacher talks in a good-natured way, like we're real people."

9. **Positive Reinforcement**
   Praise, when it is earned, increases confidence, involvement in learning, and risk-taking. Conversely, criticism can be demoralizing, works toward alienating students, and reduces their motivation to learn.

   "If a students gives a wrong answer, a teacher can still say, 'Nice try.'"

10. **An Atmosphere that Allows Autonomy**
    Students feel respected when rules are relaxed a little. At the same time, it should be remembered that students only feel safe

when the teacher maintains sufficient authority and control over the class:

"Be nice. We won't take advantage of you. It's one thing to be in charge, but if you're too strict, I'll skip class."

Most of these traits are highly consistent with the literature on the distinguishing characteristics of teachers who make a difference (adapted from Torrance, cited in Webb, Meckstroth, & Tolan, 1994):

- promote interaction with others
- encourage inquiry
- support enthusiasm and self-confidence
- foster competence
- communicate understanding
- accept the whole child
- facilitate effort, cooperative learning, and the pursuit of special interests
- respect the unique qualities of the individual

Most importantly, "Encouragement, acceptance as a person, sharing of interest and excitement—these are critical to the healthy development of a person's sense of self-worth and to his obtaining a life-long desire for learning and creating" (Webb, Meckstroth, & Tolan, 1994, p. 35). Although conceived with teachers in mind, this information applies to all adults who work with kids, including parents, coaches, mentors, and others.

Motivators

"What incentives will encourage gifted children to complete enrichment activities?"
"I try to make sure that the work's fair, interesting, and fun."

We suggest a number of evidence-based strategies that parents and teachers can use to motivate children.

Suspense, Intrigue, and Wonder

Give children opportunities to connect intellectual effort with the joy of discovering solutions. For example, you might ask a child, "It's a hot summer day, and all of a sudden, the weather turns nasty. Big hailstones and ice pellets start to fall. Ice! On a hot summer's day. How can this happen?" Children may not know the answer, but they are likely to be curious and uncertain, and they may have some hypotheses to share.

Guessing and Feedback

These two processes work well together. For example, suppose you start a science investigation with the question, "What do people require in order to live?" Consider how guesses can motivate learning and how appropriate feedback can guide and stimulate further inquiry.

Working with Children's Previous Knowledge

Draw links between new material and what children already know. By connecting new learning to already consolidated knowledge (for ourselves as with children), we greatly increase the likelihood that it will be accessible later when it is useful. For example, if you want children to learn about a historical event, you might start by talking about links with current similar circumstances. This will help them to understand the dynamics and put the situation into a meaningful perspective.

Controversy and Contradiction

There are usually several points of view on any given topic, and awareness of controversy can motivate learning. A teacher or parent might ask a child to consider the relative importance of one thing as compared to another. For example, "Which is a better form of transportation, a car or a bicycle?" Or one might ask whether a regulation should be rewritten (such as allowing dogs in restaurants). Adults can help children gather information and engage in reasoning, critical listening, and refutation. By encouraging students to give serious consideration to alternative perspectives, controversy and contradiction can be motivating and stimulating (Bowd, McDougall, & Yewchuk, 1998).

Conducive Learning Climate

Other important considerations for motivating children to learn pertain to whether or not a climate is accepting and conducive to learning. High-ability children are more likely to be motivated when provided with these factors:

- an atmosphere of challenge and support that helps students master knowledge and skills

- an environment that values persistence and goal-directed activity

- an environment where student interests are respected and curiosity is fostered

- opportunities to participate responsibly in program planning and evaluation processes

- expectations appropriate to students' abilities and developmental readiness

- reasonable timelines for task completion

- an appreciation that external factors (distractions, social or emotional concerns, physical health) influence students' ability to participate in class

- a challenging, relevant curriculum that involves higher-order thinking and problem solving

- an environment where students feel safe enough to risk making mistakes

Self-Regulation and Autonomy

Self-regulation and autonomy are primary goals in a child's maturation process, as well as important tools for fostering motivation to learn. When students are allowed and helped to make their own meaningful choices, as well as to feel that they have some control over their activities, they tend to perform the given tasks better and to experience more joy in getting them done. They are also more likely to be engaged by the topics and to feel more committed to their decisions and more responsible for any consequences. Giving students as much autonomy and control as is developmentally appropriate increases the value that they place on the results of a task at hand. Other ways of encouraging autonomy include giving children and adolescents opportunities to evaluate portions of their own work, to choose personal goals with the guidance of parents or teachers, and to help decide household and classroom rules and goals.

Authentic Learning

Another key to motivating learners is to ensure that what they are learning matters in some real-world way that it is authentically connected to their own lives and concerns. Students are far more likely to want to master and apply complex concepts when: (a) at least part of the time, success or failure is determined by their actual performance in a real-world situation, and (b) mastering a skill provides its own rewards and a sense of accomplishment. Teachers can motivate students by structuring learning experiences that involve direct interaction with experiences and objects in their natural context.

Positive Reinforcement and Constructive Feedback

Positive reinforcement and constructive feedback enable children to recognize their accomplishments and to feel proud of them. When adults praise children's worthy performances and do not over-react to mistakes, they inform and enhance the children's perceptions about their developing capabilities. A child who is helped to be competent at tasks that she values and to recognize her growing competence will be motivated to continue the learning process at a higher level. Teachers and parents who are supportive and who value persistence and achievement help motivate continued learning. It is important, though, to make sure that praise is targeted and genuine and that there is solid evidence to back it up. Consider the words of teacher candidate Siow-Wang Lee:

> *Students prefer to be praised only when they actually succeed in doing something challenging, and when they know they measure up to their peers. Put another way, a teacher's praise can be like a mother telling her daughter she is beautiful—a comment that means nothing unless it comes from the boyfriend!*

In other words, keep it honest and make it matter.

Innovative and Expansive Approaches

A discussion on different ways to motivate learners would not be complete without mention of innovative approaches. In schools all across North America, there are countless creative educators nurturing children's confidence, generating excitement about what's happening in their classrooms, and trying out new ways to engage students in learning. For example, programs involving art partners in education have been found to increase children's motivation (Ferguson, 2003). In a project launched in more than 50 schools across Canada, arts-driven programs have captured children's enthusiasm through meaningful collaborations between classroom teachers and artists (including songwriters, fabric artisans, and others). The different programming designs use art to complement such subjects as math, language, science, and social studies; in fact, the underlying premise is "to bring creativity and interactive thinking into the core of the curriculum—to demonstrate that the arts are powerful" (Elster, 2003, p. 18). Children and teachers say that they enjoy an integrative approach in which the arts are not peripheral but are literally woven into a curriculum's foundational subjects.

Another program in use in approximately 150 schools in Canada and globally is the computer-based software called *Knowledge Forum*, which supports students in constructing knowledge, building on concepts and questions, and connecting with others around the world. It motivates students to develop and become part of a global community of learners and to experience the joy of sharing ideas (Scardamalia, 2003). There are also many other excellent computer-based programs being used by parents and teachers to augment children's learning.

Instructional integration is another approach, one that is not necessarily new but is now being seen through a fresh set of lenses. Today's "integrationists" view teaching as opportunities to combine "instructional skills, tactics, and strategies in progressively complex ways...to construct, weave, integrate, and create...intersecting multiple possibilities in the design of powerful learning environments" (Bennett & Rolheiser, 2001). What this means is that teachers (and parents, too) consciously and thoughtfully play with a mix of approaches, integrating and stacking or building them appropriately in order to address children's interests, needs, and learning styles. For details about this kind of approach, see Bennett & Rolheiser's (2001) *Beyond Monet: The Artful Science of Instructional Integration* (www.beyondmonet.com).

Yet another movement is that of "slow schooling." There are those who think that education is not a race and that the approach of offering more information and rapid-paced or intense learning is not necessarily the best way to teach children. Many people are afraid that too much pressure on children to perform or to acquire facts and figures can be counterproductive and take the joy and motivation out of learning. Educators in countries around the world are thinking about how to infuse excellence *and* enjoyment into the learning process, and many are advocating taking a slow route. Slow refers to a different way of learning, "exploring something deeply and thoroughly, learning how to learn, how to ask questions, how to understand, how to apply that understanding to other areas of study" (Mitchell, 2003, p. F1). Students use nonstandard textbooks, seize moments and opportunities to learn without curricular constraints, take time to think about matters, experience learning rather than studying facts, and are given ongoing support so as to sustain their enthusiasm and engagement.

Parents and educators are asking, "If more rigorous curricula and tests take the excitement out of learning, are schools these days preventing kids from realizing their potential?" (Ferguson, 2003, p. 19). Researchers continue to study what makes kids proactive and ready to learn. The answer so far is that authenticity, reinforcement, realizable goals, fun, innovative and integrated subject matter, and pacing are some of the most important ingredients.

Extrinsic and Intrinsic Motivation

New teachers often make insightful observations about motivation. Teacher candidate Karen Lew stated:

> *My colleague gave his students a lecture about self-discipline in the senior grades. I don't know if it was getting a surprisingly low mark or getting a lecture that did it, but the students took their homework very seriously from then on, even though the homework was never collected.*

Another perspective on motivation is to distinguish between extrinsic and intrinsic goals and rewards. Extrinsic motivators include all of those factors that are external to the task itself, and to the person who is completing it, and that other people put in place to encourage an individual to complete a given task. They include grades, scholarships, praise, money, gifts, trips, and many other kinds of treats, awards, and prizes. In order for such motivators to be effective, the student must value the reward, and she must believe that she can be successful in attaining it.

Intrinsic motivators for learning are internal to the person experiencing them and a natural part of the learning process itself. They include such things as a feeling of competence, pride, autonomy, self-actualization, and internalized values (such as working hard).

We have to be careful when providing extrinsic rewards, because there can be unintended and counterproductive consequences. For example, grades are often used to motivate students' learning and are usually highly valued by parents and teachers. A student might want to earn high grades and the praise that goes with them, but if she doesn't believe that she has the necessary ability, she might choose to take easy classes rather than more challenging ones, or she might decide to achieve the high grades she wants (or feels she needs) by cheating. Paradoxically, then, rewards can sometimes work to undermine rather than motivate effort, achievement, and real learning.

In spite of these problems with extrinsic rewards, when parents or teachers use them wisely, they can facilitate intrinsic motivation to learn. Although extrinsic motivation is generally short-term (that is, once the reward is no longer offered or loses its cachet, the desired behavior ceases), an extrinsic reward can sometimes be used to motivate a student to begin or persevere with his learning. For example, a child who is told that he will earn some kind of outing if he does all of his piano practicing for the week may, in addition to collecting the prize at the end, find himself very happy with his musical achievement. Extrinsic rewards can provide opportunities to experience the intrinsic rewards of learning or the pleasures inherent in a sense of growing competence and mastery. Parents support a very powerful form of intrinsic motivation to learn when they encourage and help children and adolescents to think about who they uniquely are, and then guide them in finding good pathways to develop their skills and enthusiasms.

Once a value like honesty, diligence, kindness, or integrity has been internalized, it becomes an intrinsic motivator, and extrinsic rewards or punishments are no longer needed in order to sustain a desired behavior. For example, if a child internalizes the value of diligence, she may find pleasure in working hard academically and become intrinsically motivated to read and study. It should be noted, however, that valuing hard work is unlikely to sustain itself through self-reinforcement alone. For that kind of value to be consistent, it usually needs to be supplemented by other motivators, such as competence (feeling a sense of mastery of material learned). This usually happens naturally, but parents and educators should be careful to pay attention to it.

People enjoy becoming competent, because it allows them to deal more effectively with their environment and enhances their self-esteem. By providing children with opportunities to experience the pleasures inherent in developing and exercising competencies, from proficiency with mathematical calculations to mastery of a second language to computer keyboarding skills, we can encourage their intrinsic motivation to learn. If a task is perceived as being *too easy* (that is, the individual already knows the material or skill very well), then it will have little value, and there will be little or no intrinsic motivation to complete it. On the other hand, if a task is perceived as *too difficult*, then the individual will not expect to succeed and so once again will not feel intrinsically motivated to attempt it. As one might expect, the research on motivation to learn shows that students who are free from external constraints prefer activities that are *moderately* difficult. If a student is not responsive to a task, a teacher should reconsider the design and intent and check to see that it is not simply more work or inappropriately targeted work.

Learning issues that have a direct impact on student motivation and achievement include academic mismatch, learned helplessness, frustration and boredom, underdeveloped study skills and work habits, and academic overload. We consider each of these in turn.

Achievement Issues

Achievement motivation is the need or desire to do something well...gauged against a standard, either according to how well their group is performing...or against their previous personal performances. This evaluation presents both a challenge to succeed and a threat of failure.

(Bowd, McDougall, & Yewchuk, 1998, p. 290)

It's about joy. Joy is what gives us achievement.... We need a curriculum that makes kids happy to go to school.

(Upitis, R., cited in "The ABCs of Classroom Fun," *Maclean's Magazine*, Sept. 22, 2003, p. 17)

> *"I don't understand why our son, who has been identified as gifted, isn't getting high marks in school."*
>
> *"You'd never imagine or know Trevor was gifted if you saw his English homework assignments!"*
>
> *"Rae used to LOVE school. Now she refuses to do her homework and is getting C's and D's when all her friends are getting A's."*

Although it is often assumed that being gifted means being a faster and better learner in all subject areas and classroom situations, that is certainly not always the case. Indeed, many parents who consult with us have serious concerns about their children's grades. Their concerns might center on a recent drop in interest or achievement in a particular subject area; sometimes they are much broader and more pervasive. These are not necessarily new problems, nor are they always simple to resolve. In fact, if smart kids were consistently happy and successful at school, there would be little reason to write (or read) this book. There are many reasons why highly capable learners may not do well at school.

Parents and teachers of gifted children should realize that highly capable learners do not automatically get high marks on their report cards, and that low achievement and low grades do *not* necessarily mean laziness, willfulness, or lack of ability. Neither do low grades always indicate a problem; sometimes they simply reflect the temporary but intentional disengagement of a self-directed learner who finds himself in a boring classroom environment. There are times, however, when gifted learners, just like other exceptional learners, require educational or psychological interventions. We discuss some of the issues and considerations for those trying to figure out a gifted learner's achievement problems.

Underachievers

> *Historically, underachieving gifted students in the classroom have been viewed as defective merchandise in need of repair…. Future research needs to move away from the "fix the broken" mentality of working on students, to one of working with students to develop understanding and learning—acknowledging and accepting cultural, social, economic, and spiritual differences that confound attempts to interpret reality from only one perspective…. Something more than measurable academic or cognitive outcomes must be addressed.*
>
> (Shultz, 2002, p. 193)

"There are two ways to think about gifted underachievers. The first is to focus on the tragedy of the wasted intellect, and the second is to re-examine the labeling process."

"To what extent are some of these students set up to fail by their placement in gifted programs where there's increased competition and task-orientation?"

"Underachievement" is a term generally used to describe an individual's academic achievement when it is significantly below that which is predicted or expected. There are problems with the term "underachiever" and the political implications and personal repercussions that sometimes go with it. The term is typically applied to a child who is doing poorly at school and who is perceived as very capable (the "smarter" student), but not to another who is achieving similar grades and perceived as not so capable (the child of whom less was expected to begin with). The child who is the designated underachiever often feels confused and criticized by this designation. Very often, such a child actually wants to do well and, when told that she is not working to her potential, feels even more pressure than she did before. Conversely, for the student in the same school environment who is *not* given the underachiever label but who has similarly poor grades, there is an implicit decision being made that low grades are the best she can do, and a cycle of low expectations is thereby reinforced for her.

This selective designation of some children as requiring attention as "underachievers" while others are just fine because they are "low achievers" is problematic for two reasons. First is the assumption that school grades matter in an important way and that school learning activities are relevant to all learners (and that there is, therefore, a problem when an apparently capable learner does not achieve well at school). Secondly, it assumes that methods of assessing intellectual potential and learning are sufficiently valid and reliable to distinguish the "underachiever" from the "low achiever." In addition to the fact that these assumptions are questionable, neither the underachieving nor the low achieving student benefits from these assumptions. The underachiever often feels confused about what is expected of him and why, as well as being unsure about how to meet the higher expectations, and the low achiever feels that he is not expected to achieve academic success, so why bother to work harder?

At the same time, however, although we are uncomfortable with the selective use of the term "underachiever," we acknowledge that there are many very smart kids who do not do well at school and that it is important that parents and educators try to understand the reasons for this.

Linda Edwards was once an underachieving gifted student. In her present role as a successful secondary teacher, she designed a "learning strategies" program and field-tested it with a group of gifted high school students who, "regularly arrived in a disheveled manner, flopped into their seats, and read novels regardless of what was requested of them." The program Linda created may be helpful to other teachers.

Linda's Program for Gifted Underachievers

Program Design

In order to entice the students to participate and break through their output blockades, I developed three separate activities for the classroom teacher. Each program featured content that met the following criteria:

1. *interesting, current, and significant in the students' non-school life*

2. *not traditionally presented in schools*

3. *technology-based*

4. *understandable with common knowledge but offering challenging breadth*

5. *targeted toward development of effort rather than achievement or evaluation*

Briefly, the three projects involved:

1. *listening to and interpreting the song lyrics from various eras of twentieth-century music (auditory note-taking skills)*

2. *decoding text-messaging poetry (literacy skills)*

3. *looking at cell-phone copyrights to make detailed descriptions and diagrams of objects (observation, language, math, drawing skills)*

The Results

These were all very successful projects. The students were engaged and cooperative. The "cool" factor was way up, and the output blockades were gone. Students have since returned to more traditional activities such as web quests on study skills, personal surveys on time management and learning styles, readings on study habits, and traditional homework help.

Reflection

As teachers, we should offer non-motivated, underachieving students acceptance and patient friendship, gently leading their education by exposing them to the widest possible array of relevant, concrete subject matter. In a relaxed, non-judgmental environment, intellectual sparks may fly, and students may willingly engage directly with the material. We need to provide smaller student-teacher ratios, content that focuses on unlearning negative attitudes and behaviors, and as much student choice and freedom as is reasonable. I also think that teachers have to be creative because standard rewards and motivational tools will not be potent enough for students who reject achievement-based responses like praise and grades. They need more encouragement and personal approval.

Adults often lecture these students to work harder and to rise to their intellectual potential, when clearly they intend to direct their energies toward their own objectives and live according to their own requirements. Some of these kids endure school bitterly, but may opt for invisibility by skipping classes or dropping out. (I know; I did that.) In the classroom, they drain motivation from their peers and teachers, and they spark frustration and anger as others try to motivate them to overcome the apparent inertia. These students may emit a wave of rejection toward things that others deem valuable (e.g., education, direction, goals, rules, evaluation). The challenge to educators is not to personalize this rejection and then instinctively counter by rejecting or ignoring these students. Rather, we must monitor them and make ourselves available for patient personal connection and support and be flexible about the non-essential elements of education. Their condition is not terminal.

By recognizing and confronting underachievement in creative ways, teachers may be able to engage learners who have temporarily lost the drive to learn.

Academic Mismatch

> *"Is it wrong of me to expect my gifted child to do better than others in his class?"*
>
> *"If she's so smart, why isn't she getting higher grades in math and science?"*
>
> *"I think Sonia should take full responsibility for her poor grades. She blames the teacher, the school, the system—everyone but herself."*

The simplest, most straightforward, and most obvious reason that a gifted learner experiences low academic achievement is that there is a mismatch between the curriculum being offered and the child's learning needs. In some instances, the child is being asked to do work that is so easy that very little is being learned and he feels there is no point in doing it. In other situations, the gifted programming being offered entails either more work or harder work with no attendant benefits. We discuss ways of identifying and addressing curriculum mismatches in Sections II and III.

When the problem of curriculum match is addressed as carefully as possible and a child is still not doing well at school, we must look for other possible reasons for academic problems. An important area to investigate in circumstances like this is that of possible cognitive processing problems, including learning disabilities and attention deficits (which we address in Chapter 13). Other frequently seen reasons for low achievement in gifted learners include learned helplessness, frustration, boredom, poor study skills, or academic overload, all of which we describe below. In still other situations, children may underachieve due to one or more outside factors such as a variety of environmental, physical, and psychological stressors, including isolation, poverty, physical or mental illness, minority issues, linguistic barriers, or even power struggles with parents or a teacher. In cases in which a child is both gifted and experiencing an additional serious outside stressor, it becomes even more important that parents and teachers consider the giftedness perspectives we address in this book with flexibility, sensitivity, and concern for the individual situation.

Learned Helplessness

> *"The work is too hard."*
> *"There's pressure to perform."*
> *"Lavonne will not accept anything less than perfection within herself. She hates failure."*
> *"Our daughter has trouble dealing with pressure, disappointment, or big challenges."*

Sometimes a child decides to avoid work that is causing her trouble and chooses to tackle only work that is "safe." Children who are uncomfortable with open-ended tasks, or who demonstrate a lack of initiative in problem-solving, or who will only put effort into safe learning activities may have acquired a perspective on learning called "learned helplessness." These children believe that they might as well not try something that appears at first glance to be difficult because failure is quite probable.

Learned helplessness, when adopted as an operative mode, is a self-fulfilling prophecy and works very effectively to actually increase the likelihood of mediocre performance or failure. When confronted by an unfamiliar or challenging task, the child who has developed the learned helplessness pattern shuts down and says to himself, "I can't do this," and then finds a reason why he cannot learn or will not try the new skill. He might complain of a stomach ailment, explain that he is already working too hard, or state that he "can't do math," or isn't athletic, or is somehow incapable. Learned helplessness is characterized by an avoidance of anything new or challenging.

Individuals with a mastery orientation to learning, on the other hand, tend to welcome and even thrive on challenge. Like the brave little engine in the children's story *The Little Engine that Could* (Piper, 1930), they can take on big challenges and are far more likely to risk failure. They look for opportunities to expand their range of skills and knowledge, and they enjoy being challenged. They expect to encounter difficulties and tend to see problems as opportunities for growth rather than as blocks to further progress. In general, they feel much better about themselves and are more successful, regardless of their actual ability. Research in this area shows two major differences between people in these two groups (Dweck, 1998):

1. Those with the *learned helplessness* pattern tend to believe that people are either smart or not smart, that each of us is born with a fixed amount of ability or intelligence (the "entity" theory of intelligence).

2. Those with a *mastery orientation* tend to believe that learning is incremental (that is, intelligence develops systematically over time through effort).

Many intellectually competent children (particularly girls) develop the learned helplessness pattern, and some interesting research work has been done investigating ways to combat it. One very effective approach is to help the child challenge her beliefs. Students can combat learned helplessness by:

- learning to define success in terms of improvement and progress instead of grades and prizes

- viewing errors as a normal and essential part of the learning process rather than as unacceptable embarrassments to be avoided

- orienting themselves toward the process of learning, rather than the products that are a result of it

- finding the pleasure in learning itself rather than in doing better than others

Three aphorisms illustrate the incremental theory in action:

1. "When life gives you lemons, make lemonade."

2. "Some people see stepping stones where others see stumbling blocks."

3. "You can see the glass as half full or half empty."

We often see gifted children who are extremely hard on themselves, with expectations so high as to be unrealistic. All children should be encouraged to welcome errors, false starts, and failures as constructive learning opportunities, remembering that learning happens incrementally, one step at a time, and that no one is gifted in everything. Mistakes become gifts when we use them to help us understand something about what we need to learn.

Frustration and Boredom

Consider the following three perspectives:

"My daughter does okay in school, but she says she dislikes it. I want learning to be exciting for her, not some kind of heavy task that weighs her down."

"He seems to resist learning, and he acts willfully. If he's gifted, why isn't he a better student?"

"I just can't be bothered. It's all so tedious! It tires me out! It's boring."

Academic instruction that is far above or below a student's ability/challenge level induces frustration, boredom, and alienation. However, when students are allowed to demonstrate their competence and are given appropriate and interesting learning opportunities, they are far more likely to stay engaged by school and learning. When previously keen and gifted learners show signs of being bored or frustrated, the first thing for parents and teachers to determine is whether or not there is an appropriate educational match for ability.

The question of relevancy should also be examined. Authentic learning experiences are particularly important for many gifted learners, especially for those who are bored or disaffected. All too often, the kinds of activities that most characterize real life learning are not well represented in academic programs, and it is up to teaching professionals to bridge the gap between the sterility of the official school world and the vitality of real life.

Another consideration when dealing with a gifted learner's frustration and school boredom issues is the degree of his exceptionality and whether it might actually be outside the realm of a given school's capacity to address his learning needs. Considered to be a genius as an adult, Albert Einstein found much of his schooling to be deadly boring. He failed courses, was considered a mediocre student by most of his teachers, and was not accepted into the university program of his choice. It is probable that the nature and degree of his giftedness was a major contributor to his lack of engagement at school. One might speculate that the only thing that might have made school more interesting for Einstein would have been opportunities to explore his creative potential and interests with experts and mentors. A school would need to be truly extraordinary to recognize and address the degree of giftedness of such a person. One response to situations like this is to create individualized schooling experiences, such as those described by Derek's mom, in the home schooling vignette in Chapter 7.

In addition to working to create a better educational match for a gifted learner, sometimes the best way to address boredom, frustration, and even alienation is to help the child find engaging extracurricular activities. It can be very motivating to participate in extended learning opportunities with other kids who are as keen about her areas of interest as she is, no matter what those are. Examples include high-level music or dance classes, chess clubs, and other kinds of interests or pursuits. A mentorship arrangement can also be a wonderful learning experience. Finding one area of happy shared enthusiasm to investigate and develop often infuses other areas of life, improving a student's feelings about learning, herself, and life itself, as well as leading to improved school engagement and achievement.

Study Skills and Work Habits

> "Nobody ever taught me how to properly organize notes or how to write a composition. Now I'm in high school, and even when I know the subject matter, I can't put together a decent essay!"

Gifted learners very often have trouble with study skills and work habits. Because so much learning comes easily for them, they manage to get by very well with little effort. At some point in their education, however, they may find that they have to invest some effort in acquiring the habits and skills (such as organizational, time management, note-taking, etc.) that less capable learners had to learn much earlier.

There are many ways to do this. What works for a particular student depends on age, temperament, and context, as well as other individual factors. For some, it may be best to work with a private tutor who can help in a one-on-one relationship and in an environment that is conducive to learning. The tutor can teach a student how to address his particular issues and concerns, adapting instruction to meet any changing needs over the school year. The tutor might be an older student with expertise in the necessary skills, or possibly a retired teacher or a professional tutor.

For other students, a peer study group works well. The group can be organized according to what members feel will be most beneficial to them individually. Participants might do the following:

- agree on a preliminary read-through of assigned text material
- work collaboratively to organize material into themes
- devise conceptual frameworks
- take turns analyzing and synthesizing what has been read

A structured approach like this can help students develop study skills. Students can meet more or less formally, weekly or as desired, depending on circumstances. Study sessions may include teachers, parents, relevant experts, or other students from time to time.

Some students prefer to devise and develop their own approach to studying and then to work independently, perhaps with some guidance from parents or teachers. They might work with study skills workbooks or other resources, many of which can be found on the Internet (by conducting a search in the area of concern). "How to" books on developing organizational skills and study techniques can also be found in libraries and at reputable bookstores.

Teachers can show students how to pair difficult work with more manageable exercises. They can explain ways of designing simple frameworks that enable students to follow tasks through to completion, and they can encourage students to set achievable standards for themselves when first learning new material. Teachers should guide effort, encourage collaborative learning, and help to scaffold work appropriately, as we discussed in Chapter 6.

Academic Overload

We had considerable difficulty paring down the number of voices raised about this prickly topic, but we settled on these:

"Watch out for the homework!"
"It's a lot of pressure. Everyone expects so much of me. I HATE IT!
    And if I make one mistake, I never hear the end of it."
"I've got way too much work! The pile is as big as a chair!"

"He was expecting different work in the gifted program, not more
    work."

> *"Complete tension. I feel like tearing at the books and throwing them out.*
>
> *"I see her struggling with the amount of work in the full-time gifted program. I wonder if it's fair."*

Schoolwork should be engaging and appropriately challenging, but it has to be balanced with other activities. Just as with an adult's life, there can be negative consequences if a student's work becomes too burdensome or all-consuming. Increasingly, even normal academic expectations are so arduous in some school settings that kids and parents are stressed, and the quality of family life is adversely affected. A differentiated curriculum for gifted learners sometimes requires them to produce more work, and at a more sophisticated level, than that required of their age-mates. When academic overload results, it is imperative that teachers and parents pay attention to a child's balanced development and adapt the demands accordingly. Teachers can stagger due dates and encourage interim goal setting so that students can pace themselves more comfortably.

Sometimes it is not the academic program itself that is burdensome but a child's extracurricular commitments that are causing overload. Some gifted and talented learners juggle school with commitments for lessons, practicing, games, and social, family, and religious expectations, as well as other activities. One way to address the problem is to pare down the extracurricular commitments somewhat so that the child experiences some breathing room and some "do nothing" times, and so can enjoy the learning that is his education.

A sense of academic overload may accurately reflect demands of school and other assignments or obligations. The same feelings can also be triggered by the expectations of others. For example, parents of identified gifted learners who derive a sense of pride and accomplishment from their children's achievements may have very high performance expectations for them. These expectations may enhance a child's academic self-concept and achievement, especially if parents become appropriately proactive in the school and provide good opportunities for ongoing development. On the negative side, however, the child may experience an overwhelming burden of having to achieve in order to continue to please her parents, enhance her parents' self-esteem, and thus earn their approval. Parents must seriously consider a child's giftedness in the context of what can reasonably be achieved and how much the child wants to achieve. It is essential for children's long-term development that parents not add to their children's pressures unduly, but rather help them balance the pressure to develop their abilities with the other aspects of their lives.

Undue stress can also result from demands that gifted learners impose upon themselves. Some children's personalities include tendencies to be too self-critical or to search too relentlessly for complexity, perfection, and/or order. Others have learning problems, so that they experience academic overload in situations where classmates might not. Many children and adolescents are not able to recognize their own limitations and need help from the adults they trust in order to put the demands in their lives into a healthy perspective.

No matter the sources of stress and academic overload, at some point in time, students with oppressive workloads may begin to procrastinate, lose initiative, or become alienated from school altogether. In addition to their academic problems, such children may also find themselves experiencing social problems as their anxieties and concerns interfere with their ability to relax and interact with classmates and friends. Parents and educators who live or work with children who feel overwhelmed by work or who push themselves too hard must be sensitive to the signs of overload. Some things to watch for include (Hannell, 1991):

- a drop in grades or markedly lower levels of academic achievement

- procrastination, reduced initiative

- tension, stress, short temper

- anxiety, worry, nervousness, fear of failure, sleep problems, lack of communication, change in appetite

- academic burnout, which may include giving up and extreme exhaustion

Parents and teachers can help overburdened children and adolescents relax and feel more comfortable about learning demands by helping them to pace themselves, to set learning priorities, to break tasks down into smaller parts, and to establish reasonable goals.

Although it can be rewarding to pursue excellence, it is unhealthy to pursue it to extremes of overload or exactitude or to the point where one becomes disappointed or disillusioned with oneself or one's capabilities. Children who struggle with heavy academic burdens or perfectionism can be helped to feel more satisfied with their learning agendas and accomplishments. Like children who are low achievers, those who exhibit learned helplessness, and those who are disenchanted with learning because of boredom or frustration, children who become distraught due to heavy workloads can be shown how to see learning in a different light. When they are helped to experience their learning as meaningful and as appropriately challenging, and when they are given targeted opportunities that they can comfortably take ownership of in partnership with their teachers and parents, they are a lot more likely to be motivated and happily engaged than to be overburdened and overstressed.

Teachers and parents can help kids cope with academic overload and avoid academic burnout by encouraging them to do the following:

- pause and step back from work in order to get a healthy perspective on what really has to be done and when
- work with teachers and/or guidance counselors to manage, reduce, or rearrange academic loads
- think carefully about what can and cannot be accomplished within a given timeframe
- maintain a sense of humor, especially when things get tough
- develop better organizational and study skills (the Internet is a good source for tips)
- increase emotional intelligence in order to learn about ways to handle stress
- choose one or two areas of perfection; try not to be perfect at everything
- talk to someone about plans and concerns (parents, teachers, a guidance counselor, or a psychologist)

Good communication links between teachers and parents of gifted students are very important; informed home and school support systems that work cooperatively with one another are most effective in helping children overcome academic difficulties. Parents and teachers should be ready to intervene as necessary, and sometimes professional counseling is warranted.

Practical Ideas

> *"The curiosity level for each student varies, and it can be a race for a teacher to keep up with the demands of individual students."*
> *"It is far better to focus on process and improvement, because that's where achievement can be seen, measured, and felt."*

Some approaches for motivating high-ability learners seem to work especially well. We close this chapter with an interesting teacher's vignette sent to us by Linda Edwards, and then with a collection of practical ideas (adapted from Stipek, 2002), many of which we have already touched upon. These ideas, directed at teachers, can be adapted for use at home by parents.

Motivation and Context

I had a bright student who was always tired in class because he worked the night shift in order to help his family pay the rent. I think in cases like this, we obviously have to modify the requirements of the classroom as much as possible in terms of deadlines and such. But beyond that, we can acknowledge (reward) the value of a student's work experiences in class. I praised this young man's work ethic and was impressed by his attitude amid tough circumstances. He put his head down quite a bit in this first period class, and after I had given an assignment, I always went over to him to make sure he had heard and understood it, and I made a point to show him ways to work smart rather than hard. I would show him shortcuts and ways to be precise with his effort. Efficient and effective time and work management will help him get through the load he has to carry.

Ideas for Maximizing Motivation

Nature of Tasks

- Explain the demands and purposes and the real-world significance of any skills.

- Assign work that is appropriately challenging and achievable.
- Assign tasks that are multidimensional and open-ended.
- Provide learning opportunities that are enticing and invite active participation, exploration, and experimentation ("hands-on" activities that also involve substantive learning).
- Design tasks that are novel and incorporate an element of surprise or wonder.
- Link learning to children's interests, curiosities, and experiences.
- Value children's perspectives regarding particular instructional practices.

Student Involvement

- Encourage children to make choices in their day-to-day work.
- Invite individuals to express their opinions or respond personally to content.
- Provide enriching activities for those who have completed their work.
- Make it safe to ask for help.
- Give help in a way that facilitates children's own accomplishments.
- Connect new or abstract concepts to familiar or concrete ones.
- Give children opportunities to collaborate.
- Include problems and questions that challenge those with the highest level of mastery.
- Involve *all* children productively.
- Give children as much discretion and autonomy as they can handle.
- Maintain a realistic pace.

Evaluation

- When grades or other forms of evaluation are given, base them predominantly on effort, improvement, and achieving a standard, rather than on performance relative to others.

- Make grading criteria and timelines clear and fair.

- Provide informative feedback and genuine reinforcement.

- Allow children to participate in the design of their tasks, in choosing the level of difficulty of assignments they work on, and in self-evaluation throughout the learning process.

- Allow children to correct some of their own assignments.

- Involve students in personal goal-setting.

- Monitor learning and understanding more than behavior.

- Hold children accountable.

- Treat errors as a natural part of learning. Emphasize the information value of errors, and incorporate wrong answers into discussions as productive contributions.

The Teacher as a Model for Learning

- Create a community of learners, which includes teachers as well as students (e.g., teachers can model using resources, taking courses, reading books).

- Convey to children that not knowing something is not a reason for embarrassment (for example, many teachers seek help from students with expertise in technology).

- Model enthusiasm.

- Attribute successes to effort as well as competence.

- Give tasks that can be completed at different levels (convey the value of different kinds of skills, that there is variation in skill levels, that skill development builds over time, and that it is domain-specific).

- Evaluate, fine-tune, and re-evaluate your practices.

Parents and teachers can motivate children by modeling and providing them with many, varied, and relevant learning opportunities. They can help children to develop a mastery orientation by teaching them to think, choose sensibly, act responsibly, self-reflect, and be respectful of learning, Most importantly, they can convey that they believe in a child's ability to learn and achieve—and really mean it.

Chapter 11

Emotional, Social, and Behavioral Concerns

Emotional, social, behavioral, and academic factors are not separate from one another in people's life experience, but rather are intimately intertwined and interconnected in myriad complex ways. Our emotional reality influences our social perceptions, experiences, and behavior. How we think about and define ourselves affects not only what we do, but also how we perceive others thinking about us. We begin this chapter by addressing separately the emotional, social, and behavioral considerations that pertain to being very smart, and then we bring them together to provide some recommendations for promoting gifted children's development.

Gifted Labeling

"Why do I have to be gifted? I was happier when I was normal."
"Being gifted is like getting in a serious car accident. I mean, you get two points off your driver's license, your insurance rate goes up, and you have a broken car. Being gifted is NOT good for my social life."

Emotional well-being promotes healthy learning and development; conversely, emotional upset, turbulence, and anxiety can short-circuit it. As with all children, a gifted child's sense of self and emotional balance is affected by many different factors. First, we look at some of the issues pertaining to the emotional functioning of gifted children.

Gifted identification, labeling, and placement processes (which we discussed in Section II) can have an impact on the emotional development of bright children. This is an emotionally charged time for some children and their families, one they may experience as exciting, stressful, or confusing. Thus, it is important for parents, teachers, and kids to be as well informed as possible about potential emotional implications and experiences that might ensue.

The gifted label can cause children to question not only what lies ahead, but also their identity and abilities, asking, for example, "Am I really different than other kids?" "Do I want to be different?" It can trigger introspection, self-questioning, and even worries that they have been mistakenly identified as gifted (sometimes referred to as the "imposter syndrome"). Some children react to the label by working very hard to continually prove their intelligence; some worry about their ability to manage unknown academic expectations ahead, or unfamiliar or uncomfortable social situations (such as being teased or left out). When a child is identified as gifted, it is important that the adults in his life talk with him about his fears, discuss specific circumstances and implications, answer his questions as well as they are able to, and offer truthful reassurances.

Children are not the only ones with concerns. Many parents have unresolved feelings and questions about their child's giftedness. Sometimes the questions and comments we hear are said half in jest, but they usually reflect some kind of concern:

> *"Does this mean that my daughter is smarter than I am?"*
> *"I was never a good student. The giftedness gene must come from my husband's side of the family."*
> *"Now that we have a gifted child, I guess that means we have to sacrifice everything for him, right?"*

Teachers voice similar kinds of questions and concerns when working with gifted students. Some of the comments we hear from teachers include:

> *"I'm not nearly as intelligent as those gifted kids."*
> *"She's so smart, it makes me nervous."*

"If he's really gifted, why do I have to give him special help? I have kids to work with who need a lot more help than he does."

Parents and educators should pay attention to their own self-doubts, questions, concerns, and even jealousies. Otherwise, underlying unresolved issues can seriously hinder the important task of supporting the children in their lives. Adults should keep in mind that a gifted child, like any other, needs lots of help growing into a healthy adolescent and ultimately into a happily self-sufficient adult. No matter how apparently smart or confident, each gifted child is still a child, with all the anxieties that go with being young, vulnerable, and inexperienced in life.

As parents and educators begin to address their own issues, perhaps the most important thing to remember is that each child is unique. Caring adults can increase their chances of making good decisions with and for a child by learning about giftedness, networking with others to enhance their understandings of key issues relating to being gifted, and considering a variety of strategies for addressing them. Parents and educators should also remember that giftedness does not define a child, but is merely one aspect of what the child is all about on any given day.

One way to avoid labeling giftedness and to get around problems that have to do with labeling is to encourage exceptionally capable children to participate in learning opportunities with others who are as keenly interested as they are in whatever it is that they are interested in. If this can happen without giftedness entering the picture explicitly, as with high-level music classes, chess clubs, or other extracurricular activities, that is great. Challenging activities that do not carry a gifted label as a prerequisite are an excellent way to provide the learning opportunities that a child needs without the problems associated with the label. However, when such activities cannot be arranged without the gifted label, or when a child has trouble with a learning opportunity because she feels problematically different, it becomes important to discuss with her the nature of her exceptionality from others. An open, honest, yet careful response to the child's questions and sensitivity to her level of understanding can be helpful—even essential—to self-acceptance, self-awareness, and healthy self-concept.

Attention to both giftedness and a well-rounded ability to fit in with what is typically perceived as "normal" may seem to be irreconcilable opposites, yet both are important. Every circumstance has its own best way to resolve this apparent conflict so that a child can feel good about himself.

Self-Concept

"When they told me I was gifted, I felt sort of funny. I don't know why."
"Other children say, 'Gifted? Ha! Ha!'"
"Some kids 'dis' the gifted kids, calling us nicknames like 'brainers.'
And sometimes they say we're really stupid."

A person's sense of self is constructed in an ongoing and complex process. It emerges from a dynamic interaction of (Harter, 1999):

- the perceived opinions of others
- available support mechanisms
- personal history
- developmental maturity

How we feel about ourselves greatly influences how we approach the situations and people in our lives. People who feel confident about their competence are far likelier to experience successes than those with troubling self-doubts.

As with intelligence, there is considerable research evidence demonstrating that self-concept is domain-specific—that people tend to see themselves as competent in some areas and not so competent in others. In general, it seems that children have different self-concepts for the academic, social, behavioral, appearance, athletic, and global dimensions of their lives (Harter, 1999). A person's global self-concept is the most important predictor of her emotional well-being, and it is closely connected to self-concept subdomains that are most valued by the individual. These are, of course, affected by a person's age and developmental history. Early adolescent girls tend to care most about the social and appearance dimensions of their lives. This means that, in general, if a girl between the ages of 11 and 14 feels good about her friendships and her appearance, she is likely to feel pretty good about herself. If, on the other hand, she doesn't feel competent in those areas, it tends to be harder for her to achieve a healthy and strong global self-concept.

Although there is considerable research on giftedness and self-concept, it is highly inconsistent. Some studies demonstrate that gifted children are at serious risk for low self-esteem, to the point of being vulnerable to depression and suicide; others show that gifted children feel better about themselves than others and are at higher risk for an inflated sense of their own worth than for low self-esteem. A synthesis of the research on social/emotional development and giftedness suggests that, generally, gifted learners are no more or less likely than others to experience problems with self-concept and other social/emotional dimensions.

It appears that giftedness can be both a *risk* factor and a *resiliency* factor when it comes to self-concept. Gifted children are at risk of self-esteem problems because of their exceptionality from the norm, their differentness from others. Being exceptional increases the likelihood of feeling isolated, as well as being rejected by peers because of that difference. This can have a negative impact on a person's social self-concept. In addition, academic self-esteem may be reduced when a child goes into a full-time gifted program. When comparing himself with others who do just as well as or better than he does academically, a child who was previously the best student in his class can feel a lot less capable and become unsure about his intellectual ability. At the same time, however, giftedness is often seen as positive, conferring advantages and respect from others, as well as heightened self-respect. It is also associated with higher academic self-concept, particularly for children who are not in full-time gifted programs.

How these various possibilities play out depends on individual circumstances and situations and on the social supports that are in place to help a child figure herself out.

Emotional Intelligence

> "I'd like to be in the 'cool kid zone,' but I just haven't found the way to be cool."

> "Most of my students are happy and productive, but I have a few who are very intense and won't mix, and a couple who are loud and bossy and don't get along with anyone."

Daniel Goleman wrote a bestseller called *Emotional Intelligence* (1995) that provides a good foundation for understanding many problems faced by all of us in our emotional lives. In this book, he discussed how our cognitive and emotional intelligences affect each other, and he described how emotional competence in different areas (for example, self-motivation, mood regulation, and hope) can be learned. These understandings may be particularly relevant for parents and educators of gifted learners.

Goleman described windows of opportunity when certain emotional skills and habits can more readily be taught or encouraged. He also reviewed some emotional literacy programs in which school curriculum and extracurricular activities are designed around children's and adolescents' experiential issues, helping them to acquire and consolidate emotional competence in a number of different areas. Programming that enhances emotional functioning can help students understand and manage their feelings about issues, such as adjusting to a new label, classroom setting, or peer group.

Applying Goleman's ideas to the topic at hand, an emotional literacy program could be used to support identified-gifted children in thinking about the gifted identification experience, how they feel about social difficulties in the schoolyard, or any uncertainties they have about their ability to meet academic expectations. Within a mixed-ability classroom, teachers can design emotional literacy experiences that foster increased understanding and social interaction among diverse kinds of learners, including those who are labeled as gifted. A discussion or role play about a hypothetical collaborative learning activity whereby everyone contributes something personally relevant to a group project might be helpful.

Parents can also learn to systematically support and reinforce their children's emotional intelligence. Like educators, parents increasingly appreciate the value of fostering children's emotional literacy. We are living in a time when social support networks are fragmenting, our sense of security is threatened, and rapid change seems to be the only constant in our lives. Families and educators who pay attention to children's emotional development help children to relate to others more effectively, to cope with their uncertainties and insecurities, and to make wiser decisions in their personal and educational lives.

Perspective

It is a psychological truism that it is not the experiences that we have in our lives that matter so much as the *way* we experience our lives. Perspective and attitude can make a big difference for gifted children, as well as for others. We discuss some perspectives that can cause problems for gifted learners.

Fear of Failure

> *"There's no way I'm going to enter that Math Olympiad. What for? Just because I'm good in math doesn't mean I have to compete and work myself to death. I wouldn't win anyhow."*

Somewhat paradoxically, gifted children who experience consistent successes can develop a fear of failure. It is human nature to fear the unknown, and people who never learn how to recover from failure often come to fear it. Conversely, those who've fallen flat on their faces many times and who've had the support and resources to pick themselves right up again learn to trust that they can not only recover from failure, they usually learn something, too.

You know that a child is becoming afraid of failure if he doesn't want to try new activities or if he stops looking for challenges and selects only safe tasks that will lead to easy victories and successes. Children who opt out of challenging opportunities and competitions, such as the child in the quote above, are showing signs of developing a fear of failure. If not remedied, the fear of failure can be debilitating. Although this kind of attitude can result in a child being able to achieve good academic grades for many years, it nevertheless minimizes real learning and reduces the likelihood of subsequent successes at higher academic and professional levels.

A key to high competence in any area is purposeful and meaningful engagement over time in that area, with an understanding that risks, explorations, and failures are essential to the learning process.

Children who purposefully tackle challenges and who welcome setbacks as learning opportunities can achieve successes that those who are afraid to fail cannot. In Chapter 10, we discussed ways to address the fear of failure in connection with learned helplessness, and at the end of this chapter, we provide some additional strategies for enhancing emotional health and social/behavioral competence. These strategies can be used to help children work through this kind of fear, as well as some of the other potential difficulties we discuss here.

Fear of Success

> *"I don't need to study. Only nerds study."*

Gifted children and adults may be prone to a fear of success. Doing well leads to ever-increasing expectations from others and (often worse) from themselves, perhaps even to ridiculously high or unachievable expectations. Sometimes it feels easier just not to try. Not infrequently, highly able learners pre-empt their own possibilities of success by not studying for a test, not investing much effort in a project, or not applying for an award that they might win.

Although fear of success might appear to be the other end of the spectrum from fear of failure, it is actually quite interconnected and oddly similar. For some individuals, success experiences can lead to doubts about whether they've actually merited the achievements with which they've been credited, or whether they will be able to achieve at that level in the future (the imposter syndrome again!). In cases like these, success can be more anxiety-provoking than more average achievement so that, over time, some people develop a fear of doing very well that is just as debilitating as the fear of failure.

The goal with such individuals (as with others) is to encourage their healthy self-awareness and self-acceptance so that unconscious barriers and defense mechanisms do not impede their optimal functioning. The recommendations for supporting emotional health that we offer at the end of this chapter provide strategies for meeting that goal—for situations that are not too serious. Sometimes fear of success (as with fear of failure) becomes so debilitating as to require professional help, a topic we address in Chapter 14.

Perfectionism

> *"How can educators foster growth and high expectations for high-ability students without this leading to the extreme anxiety and perfectionism that these students sometimes evidence?"*
> *"Sylvie always has to get a 100 on every assignment. Last week, she got 98% on a test and asked if she could retake it!"*

The desire to get things right and to do them well is conducive to high achievement and should generally be encouraged. It would be good if more children learned to take pleasure in meeting high standards in what they do. Some children, however, establish unrealistically high standards for themselves, becoming anxious, dissatisfied, and discouraged when they don't meet them. As with all dimensions of physical, cognitive, and emotional well-being, the objective for children who have perfectionistic tendencies should be to find a healthy balance in which there is enough challenge that there is growth, but without undue and debilitating stress. (We discussed balance in relation to academic overload in Chapter 10.)

Sometimes highly able students with signs of perfectionism simply need extra reassurance and encouragement, including a friendly and clear delineation of realistic expectations, in addition to some consistent and supportive modeling about when to say, "It's good enough for now; it's time to stop and let it go." Other times, however, perfectionism is a sign of deeper problems, requiring professional attention.

Arrogance

> *"Everyone knows that Mesopotamia was the cradle of civilization."*
> *"That question was too hard. Nobody could get it right. Or maybe you didn't ask it right."*
> *"Mrs. Bell, 'success' has two c's. You wrote it on the blackboard with one."*

Sometimes what looks like arrogance from a gifted child really isn't. One of the stereotypes about gifted children is that they are intellectually arrogant, that they think they are smarter (and, by implication, better) than others. Neither research on gifted development nor our clinical experience with gifted children supports this position. In fact, it is quite the reverse; many gifted children who are annoyingly superior in their manner have serious self-doubts underlying their apparently inflated self-regard.

Rather than thinking that they are better than others, some exceptionally capable learners are actually afraid that they are not as smart as others might think, or they feel that they are valued only when and if they are clever, and therefore, they need to constantly prove how smart they are. Such children usually have trouble admitting that they are wrong, and they suffer real embarrassment when they cannot understand something quickly. The embarrassment is sometimes masked by blaming someone or something else, or by anger, impatience, or annoyance, all of which look and feel like arrogance to the recipient. In situations like this, it is particularly important that the child feel respected. She should be helped to learn how to welcome failures and mistakes as opportunities for learning and to see them as something that everyone experiences.

There is another very different reason for apparent arrogance that leads to the stereotype that many people hold of giftedness. It is that some children who are passionate about learning and want to know everything assume that other people (including classmates, siblings, parents, and teachers) also want to be made aware of personal errors. Such children are particularly likely to get into trouble with peers who are not always receptive to having their mistakes pointed out to them, and with teachers who have control or self-esteem issues of their own. Arrogance here lies in the other person's perception, of course, rather than in the child's attitudes or perceptions; the child is not seeing himself as superior, but rather making the assumption that the other person is as hungry for knowledge as he is. At the same time, this kind of child does need to learn some tact. He needs to understand that people do not always appreciate having their errors identified and that it is usually better to wait until you are asked before correcting someone. This is not always an easy lesson for a child to learn, but eventually, most do learn it and mange to get along better as a result.

Social Concerns

Humans are social animals, and as such, acceptance and belonging are important to us. For children, peer pressure, neglect, and rejection can be particularly brutal. Although giftedness signifies cognitive strengths, it is not a predictor of social competence, and it sometimes actually interferes with peer acceptance.

> *"Why won't they be friends with me? I'm like yanking my hair out!"*
> *"The schoolyard is like when Germany was East Germany and West Germany. It's like an Iron Curtain between the gifted kids and the others."*

*"He wants friends more than anything, but he doesn't know how to
go about it."*

*"The children in Megan's class are VERY hard to handle. They tend
to form cliques, and lately she's been the odd one out."*

Take a moment to think about a child's social milieu: the classroom, the playground, the places she goes outside of school, and the
people she encounters each day. Is the child a valued member of her
social group? Is there a sense of belonging, or does she feel at odds with
others in her life? Over the years, many gifted children have talked to us
about their social experiences. We've listened to them discuss ways of
maintaining friendships, as well as confide their concerns about relationships, adjustment problems, and how giftedness sometimes separates
them from others.

Social competence varies as much as mathematical or linguistic
competence. As with adults, some children attract friends like magnets,
easily and effortlessly, while others seem to repel them. Some children
have trouble socializing in certain situations and yet manage fine in
others. And some children try very hard to get along with their peers but
just can't seem to make it work and decide that it's not worth the effort.

Short-Term

*"We really had no idea. He left his local school, classmates, teachers,
and a set of rules that he knew to go to a distant neighborhood
into an already established pecking order with no support from
anything known."*

*"After viewing the gifted class, we walked away having a crisis. We
came out frazzled. Are we doing the right thing?"*

*"I had to decide about going to the gifted class, but I didn't know any-
body or anything they did there. It was like a big surprise."*

*"I felt like I could start fresh at a new school because I had no friends
at my old school."*

"I didn't tell them I was confused."

Adapting to school-related change involves social challenges in
addition to changes in curriculum. For example, many children feel
uncertain, confused, or anxious when they are invited to join a full-time
gifted class in a different school. Parents may feel that way as well.

Any child who is given a new learning opportunity that requires changing his educational setting has to figure out how to be *a part* of things in the new place, rather than *apart* from them. He has to assess the new social landscape and adjust to it—that is, learn how to behave in the new milieu. School culture and the attributes that are valued (such as attractiveness, interpersonal skills, intellectual abilities, or athletic proficiency) vary from one school setting to the next. Fitting in can require a child to work on adjusting his "likability." For example, he might need to adjust his vocabulary, or take more (or less) care with his dress or personal grooming, or become less (or more) eager to volunteer with an answer in class. Some children find these adjustments very difficult. Some don't perceive the need and do not understand why they are suddenly more (or less) popular than they were before. Others perceive the change in culture and expectations but refuse to conform, seeing it as annoying or insulting. Still others see adjustments like this as simple and temporary inconveniences, or even a fun challenge. It is wonderful for all concerned when a child quickly finds the new environment more in keeping with his happiness and what he feels to be his natural self.

It is important that adults recognize that changes in educational programs almost certainly bring with them hidden and unexpected social adjustments. By being aware of this ahead of time, and by being responsive to children's concerns and observations as they make the change, adults can help children anticipate and manage change in ways that increase their resiliency and sense of competence, rather than undermining them.

Long-Term

> *"She prefers the new classmates, and she is much happier."*
> *"She's part of a whole group of kids who think like she does. They seem to feed on each other's talents."*
> *"The gifted program provides a structured relationship toward learning, and especially the chance to socialize with peers."*
>
> *"I so much wanted to go to the smart class, so I took a chance. It was good."*
> *"They think the way I do and go through the same stuff as I do."*

Taking a longer view, in the whole scheme of things, change is often a positive learning experience. Children generally manage to adapt to new surroundings or circumstances and, in many cases, flourish. Sometimes a change works out so well that everyone is delighted, and they wonder why they worried about it in the first place.

For many children, well-chosen new classes, programs, or peer groups represent a kind of beginning *and* an end—a timely conclusion perhaps to what was, and a fresh start toward what might yet be. Children, like adults, have a need to feel accepted, to be affiliated with others with whom they share some kind of commonality, and to be recognized for their accomplishments without being socially disadvantaged as a result. This may take time, effort, acquired social skills, support, compromise, and self-confidence, all of which can be encouraged and reinforced by parents and teachers who care.

Transition Experiences

The following comments, first from children and then from parents and teachers, illustrate children's variable social experiences after moving to a full-time gifted class.

> *"It was really bad for me in my old class. They pretended to be my friends. They're no longer my friends."*
> *"I'm definitely more open now, and I have way better friends."*
> *"My friends are my friends, and I don't care if they're gifted or not."*
> *"Mean kids from your school who aren't gifted tease you and bug you more."*

Parents' views are also highly variable and sometimes disturbing.

> *"It wasn't cool to be smart, so they started to ridicule my daughter in the regular class. She was always miserable when she came home from school. Always."*
> *"Even now in the gifted class, he still doesn't have a close friend at school."*
> *"She has gained personal confidence in social situations."*

Teachers' comments confirm the need to pay attention to children's social concerns.

> *"I have a whole class of gifted kids, and it's a real jumble, emotionally and socially."*

> *"I have three really smart students who don't want to participate in group activities. They're kind of isolated. It's sad, and it's frustrating for me, but it's their choice."*
>
> *"The kids in my gifted class don't socialize much with kids in other classes. There's not a whole lot of opportunity for that, I guess."*

It is important for teachers to establish a supportive classroom culture in which individual differences are accepted, diversity is seen as a strength, and students are helped to understand themselves and others. All children should feel welcome, respected, and appreciated and have opportunities for positive interactions with others in the school.

It is not possible to predict how a child will respond to a new social milieu. However, it *is* possible to enable children to collaborate and engage in satisfying social interactions and to find out about relationship building. Even children who experience isolation or who purposely distance themselves from others (for example, by immersing themselves in music, books, or computer activity) can be helped to feel good about themselves and what they can do.

Computer Time

> *"I've been called a 'geek' and a 'brainer.' So I enjoy working on the computer! I like doing other stuff, too, you know."*

One gifted stereotype is of the nerd who does not interact much with people and spends a lot of time peering at a computer screen. Whether or not excessive computer usage is a problem depends on the context and the balance. A key question is, "What else is going on in the child's life?"

For some children, the Internet and e-friendships provide opportunities for positive social interactions that they would not otherwise have. These relationships can be a good way for socially awkward young people to learn enough about relating to others that they become interested in applying their knowledge to real human contact. In such cases, virtual experiences are actually productive, and the amount of time spent with a computer keyboard is a good investment in healthy, long-term development. Sometimes parents and educators need to ease off on their concerns and nagging about computer time. (They should, of course, pay attention to which websites and chat rooms are being visited, and their content.)

In other situations, children, like adults, can retreat farther and farther into a virtual world. By choosing electronically mediated interactions over other kinds of social activities that they find difficult, some children may become more isolated over time and less comfortable in social situations. For such children, it is obviously important to think about ways to intervene so that the downward spiral of way too much time spent on the computer does not continue. A good general principle is to find a social activity that uses the child's interests and strengths and therefore: (a) is intrinsically motivating, (b) provides opportunities for success, and (c) requires at least an element of human interaction. For example, a child could join a computer club, or work collaboratively on a team that is building some kind of software, or act as a computer consultant or mentor to other kids. Although each of these suggestions requires an individual to spend more time in front of a computer screen rather than less, such activities can also act as the thin edge of a wedge that provides positive experiences with social interaction, and they open the way over time to increased engagement with people.

It is important that adults do not overreact to the heavy use of computers, that they consider computer-related activities in the context of what else is occurring in a child's life, and that they ask themselves if these activities are serving a useful function or meeting the child's needs in some way. If the problems obviously outweigh the advantages for a particular child's development, the adult can look for ways to use the attraction to computers as a motivator to nudge the child into healthier activities. Those who are online with others are at least putting themselves into a quasi-social situation and are demonstrating a need for interaction, which, with some patience and appropriate support, can be channeled productively.

Social Skills

> *"I don't know why, but I don't seem to have friends over at my house anymore."*

Many gifted children have trouble with social activities because the nature and degree of their exceptionality is such that their age peers do not understand their particular interests, enthusiasms, or language use. No amount of social skills training will fix that. Children like this often find it relatively easy to interact with adults or others who are engaged by and knowledgeable about their areas of interest. When a person's interests are profoundly different and her communication skills are several years ahead of her grade-mates, it can be very difficult to forge a meaningful friendship with an age-peer. In these situations, it is best if her individuality is respected and she is allowed to find interactions when and where she can.

Many well-meaning educators and sometimes parents exert pressure on socially awkward gifted students to take socials skills training so that they can learn how to behave more "normally" or so that they can "fit in better" with their age-peers. In our experience, this is almost always a dismal failure (at best) or a traumatic experience (at worst)—an experience in which the child's perception of himself as some kind of bad kid, eccentric, or misfit is only reinforced and his social skills therefore further eroded rather than enhanced. It is usually better to ensure that the child's learning needs are well met and that he has opportunities for high-level engagement in areas of interest. We provide other recommendations at the end of this chapter for supporting emotional health and social/behavioral competence.

Consider the following e-mail exchange with an acquaintance.

Developing Social Skills

Parent:

> *Our son Ahmed is eight years old. Are you aware of any resource groups or programs to help gifted children deal with social skills issues? Any ideas would be appreciated. Thanks.*

Our Response:

> *To be honest, one should be leery of social skills training programs which may focus upon "niceness" by trying to fit wonderfully individualistic square little pegs into conventionally round and very uncomfortable holes—where children may come to think that there is something wrong with them. Our recommendation is to ask these questions:* Does Ahmed experience social skills as a problem area? Whose problem is this?

When children have trouble getting along in social circumstances, sometimes it is because they need extra help figuring out the rules of social interactions, just like some kids need extra help learning to read. For these children, a well-run social skills group can be beneficial.

If, however, the problem is about teachers' notions of Ahmed's need to have (more) friends, it might be because his age-peers do not understand or share interests with him, and this is not something that will be rectified by social skills training. It may be resolved over time. If it is about Ahmed's own desire to make and have friends, well, there might be something gained by participation in such a group, as long as there is a good personality fit with the group leader, and as long as the group leader respects and values his individuality (which may not always be the case).

If Ahmed seems happy enough with his social situation, then social skills groups can cause even more discomfort and be seriously counterproductive.

There are many strategies for building social skills that you can use, however. Here are a few ideas to help make Ahmed's social experiences more positive and reaffirming:

1. Consider his own social preferences and tendencies (some children do not need or want more than one friend).

2. If he has no friends, help him find one person with whom to share a common interest.

3. Assure him that any feelings of differentness he might be experiencing are often a function of age and school program, and will probably improve over time.

4. Reinforce positive social behavior whenever you see it; do this privately, however, as it is very important not to embarrass him publicly.

5. Look for ways to increase his self-confidence in social situations in and out of school.

6. Encourage him to participate in extracurricular activities, cooperative play and learning, and shared activities within the community.

These suggestions are good for children who are very smart and have trouble fitting in. In situations in which children have more serious social skills deficits, such as with regard to Asperger's Syndrome and Nonverbal Learning Disabilities, other approaches may be required. (See www.beingsmart.ca to acquire reference information about these disorders.)

Leadership

There are many opportunities for leadership activities and community service in which students can become involved. Such involvement can be personally rewarding, as well as socially beneficial in lots of ways. For instance, these activities can:

- provide ways to put an individual's strengths to practical use
- allow children to test and further develop their skills
- offer a chance to acquire leadership experience
- enable a child to feel a sense of responsibility, fulfillment, and competence
- foster productive and meaningful interactions with others
- provide preparation for future work endeavors
- help with the career selection process
- lead to references and networks that may prove important later on

Somewhat counter-intuitively, leadership activities can be particularly important for children with emotional, social, or behavioral concerns. When well-chosen to match an individual's abilities, such activities can provide authentic outlets for children and adolescents to acquire better social skills, learn about their strengths, prove their competence, develop a sense of responsibility, and learn to behave in socially acceptable ways, all of which enhance self-esteem.

Behavioral Concerns

"I'm fed up with all of the disciplinary problems in my daughter's class. Some of the kids are off the wall!"

"I think gifted kids are too impatient. Sometimes everyone wants to lead or contribute to a class discussion at once."
"Rafe has been the class clown since he started school. He gets bored very quickly and loves to make things happen."

When thinking about behavior issues and giftedness, it is important to distinguish real behavior problems or conduct disorders from high-spirited attempts to make school more interesting and relevant. Many creative, well-adjusted, and intelligent students are frequently charged with the former when engaged in the latter, such as often seen in the "class clown." Teachers who are rigid or who tend to be less flexible in their attitudes are much more likely to be troubled by this kind of activity from creatively gifted students. In these cases, it is often the teacher who should be identified as in need of assistance to better understand the student, in which case a student-teacher conference may be warranted. The child may also be wise to learn to appreciate the teacher's point of view.

When they encounter badly behaving children, many adults begin by wondering what is wrong with the child, even going so far as to look for some kind of pathology within her. However, there are many possible environmental situations that can lead children to have the kind of trouble that results in bad behavior. When a child's learning demands do not match her developmental level, for example, we can expect her to be bored, frustrated, and unhappy, and perhaps to misbehave. In some ways, acting out is better than internalizing frustrations, a situation which can lead to depression and other emotional problems. The learning issues we discussed in Chapter 10 (achievement problems, learned helplessness, frustration, boredom, weak study skills, and academic overload) can all contribute to negative behavioral patterns and should be investigated by adults who are trying to understand the causes of a child's misbehavior.

Although many gifted children experience no social difficulties, making and keeping friends is a problem for some. Kids with behavioral problems are not tolerated by their peers for very long, especially if they repeatedly disrupt classroom activities or compromise their classmates' learning. Behavioral issues can contribute to or result from social or academic problems. A child having difficulty adjusting to special programs, peer groups, or increased academic demands may exhibit inappropriate behavior in class. This might involve, for example, incessant calling out or disobeying classroom rules. When badly behaved children are ostracized, which is often the case, it tends to increase both their emotional and their behavioral problems.

Sometimes, however, behavior problems become more aggressive and serious, such as when a child hurts or intimidates peers or causes property loss or damage. Conduct that is persistently disruptive and aggressive may indicate serious underlying problems. When a child is violating the basic rights of others, breaking fundamental rules, or ignoring major age-appropriate societal norms, it is time to seek professional help, as we discuss in Chapter 14.

Parents and teachers who are sensitive and responsive to social and behavioral problems can help to minimize the likelihood that such problems will escalate. As we outline at the end of this chapter, there are many strategies that can be implemented, ranging from listening attentively to a child's concerns to acquiring professional assessment and support. When an intervention is required, its success depends on cooperative efforts by parents and teachers, the child's willingness to comply, and of course, time, patience, and commitment.

Bullying, Anger, and Conflict Resolution

"Being bullied really traumatized her. It was difficult for us to resolve."

"Ryan was suspended yesterday for kicking a classmate. He's always been very sensitive to perceived injustice. The way he tells it, the other kid had been ridiculing him all year, and the teacher refused to do anything about it, and so he had to do something to put an end to it."

"I'm not sure why exactly, but Lateesha seems to get picked on an awful lot."

People disagree all the time. People see and value things differently, and they have different expectations and ideas. Conflicts occur as a result of our differences and are, in fact, a natural part of life. Children need to learn how to handle conflict, as well as how to prevent unnecessary conflicts. This includes finding good ways to manage their feelings of anger and annoyance, learning to respect and understand others' feelings and views, and thinking about how to attack problems, not people.

Aggression

The term aggression refers not only to physical attacks on others, but also to verbal attacks, including gossip, ridicule, slander, and slights. Boys and girls tend to handle their negative feelings differently. Whereas boys are more prone to be physical in their attempts to deal with anger, impatience, frustration, disappointment, embarrassment, and sadness, girls are more likely to internalize their feelings or be verbally or indirectly aggressive.

We have worked with children who have been labeled by parents, teachers, or peers as aggressive, as chronic victims, or (not infrequently) as both bullies and victims. Many adults take a morally superior tone of righteous indignation when they confront what they interpret as aggressive behavior, and a tone of caring, protective empathy for those they perceive as victims. Neither of these attitudes is likely to yield the best possible outcomes for the children in question. It is useful to realize that those who are perceived as aggressive by others are often highly sensitive, feel a strong need to be respected, and are seriously committed to justice. When their sensitivities, need for respect, and commitment to justice are acknowledged and channeled productively, they can become highly effective leaders. Those who are chronic victims are sometimes unjustly victimized because of their differences from others, but sometimes they are good manipulators. These children have learned that they will get attention if they appear to be vulnerable and poorly treated. It is important to know the difference and not to become complicit in reinforcing this pattern.

Bullies and Victims

Whenever bullying or victimization shows up, it is a warning signal that children do not feel safe, and this must first be addressed at both school and family levels. Safe environments are inclusive and respectful of diversity. People in healthy nurturing environments feel that their strengths are recognized and that they are valued for who they are. When children are being bullied because they are perceived to be different than others, they need our protection. The best protection we can give is to work to change the culture of the environment in which the bullying is taking place. It is important that everyone knows that there is no tolerance for mocking, insulting, or mistreating people because of perceived weaknesses or differences.

On the individual level, there is a complex connection between bullying and victimhood. What appears to be bullying behavior is very often the so-called bully's response to real or perceived victimization, reflecting a choice to be the winner instead of the whiner. There are many variations of this. One that we have encountered frequently in our work with gifted children is that an independent, sensitive, and intelligent child feels that he is being bullied by another child, when in reality, he has taken another person's actions or words too personally or misinterpreted their intent. For example, a classmate has said something in jest, and the gifted child has perceived this as aggressive or hurtful. This seems to him to justify a defensive but aggressive reaction on his part (which others see as bullying), because the only other alternatives that he can identify are sadness and victimization, and he does not want to give that kind of winning power to others. Remember that threats, blame, bossiness, or antagonistic or aggressive behavior can be used defensively, as well as being perceived as bullying.

Getting past the destructive and downward-spiraling aspects of circumstances like this—on both the giving and receiving end of aggressive behavior—means that the child who is considered a bully or a victim must learn to feel safe. She must be protected by a secure environment (as discussed above) and then learn to recognize that she has the necessary resources to make herself safe without resorting to aggressive or pathetic victim behavior. The next step is for the child to learn to reinterpret the actions and words of others. This involves looking for what is helpful, positive, or useful in what they say and do and not taking offense quite so quickly. Many of the recommendations made throughout this book are designed to help children develop a sense that their world is fine, that they are safe, and that they have some control, all of which help with the transition away from bullying and from being the victim of bullying.

Strategies

A child who has been involved as a bully or a victim or both needs to learn how his actions and reactions contribute to his social problems.

This learning is best when it happens in a nonjudgmental, unemotional way and when it is provided as exploration and education rather than as punishment. In order to encourage bullies and victims to take a positive look at others' words and actions (a crucial first step in moving past this behavior), it is imperative that they feel they are being listened to and that their words and actions are being seen in the most positive light possible. When a child has a bad social experience or behaves poorly, it should be viewed by the adults in his life as an opportunity to learn something together about how he is processing his experiences. Very often, this means reviewing the circumstances and asking what else the other person might have meant by his actions or words, as well as asking if there is a possible innocent or even good motivation behind them. If not, then it becomes a matter of learning how to recognize those actions and words that really matter in the whole scheme of things and how to be tolerant.

A child can be encouraged to think constructively for herself by focusing on the problem, learning to separate the key issue(s) from the personalities involved, keeping an open mind, being respectful of others and tolerant of diversity, and taking responsibility for her own actions. It is obviously essential to the learning process that one or more of the adults in her life model these attitudes.

Children can be supported in developing a new set of habits that gets them out of the bully/victim/aggression loop. Whether a child's problems have been as a victim or a bully or both, parents and teachers can help the child maintain dignity and build positive relationships. We suggest a four-point strategic approach.

1. Help the child learn to observe when he is making a negative attribution of another's actions or words.

2. Encourage him to refrain from responding immediately.

3. Suggest that he ask himself if there is an innocent or reasonable motivation underlying the other's behavior.

4. Help him think of ways to respond to the possibly good intention of the other person rather than the possibly bad intention.

Children begin to feel very good about themselves as they implement this reflective and positive pattern. They enjoy surprising their peers, parents, and teachers by their more mature actions and their reactions. The learning process is even more effective if the conflict resolution skills are developed and practiced on a wider scale, as the following vignette illustrates.

A Justice League for Children

Jack was a gifted child in a regular program in a kindergarten-to-Grade 6 school. From his youngest days, his parents had noticed an intense concern for issues of justice and fair play. He felt it very deeply when he perceived an injustice, either against himself or against others who might have trouble defending themselves. Partway through fourth grade, Jack was given a three-day suspension from school because he used physical means to defend himself against a teacher he thought had intervened unfairly and aggressively. Jack felt that his point of view had not been listened to and that the teacher had used undue force against him. He decided to take advantage of his suspension by inventing what he called a Justice League for Children. He designed this as a school Grievance Court to ensure that children got a fair hearing from a panel of their peers and a teacher, should there be similar cases in the future in which a teacher and student disagreed about something, or in which two students had a serious disagreement and wanted to be heard. His mother helped him write a manifesto for the Justice League for Children, and when he got back to school, he set up a meeting with his teacher to discuss it.

After the meeting, Jack's teacher announced in class that there would be a lunchtime meeting to discuss forming a Justice League for Children. She said that Jack had had a very good idea and that it was an opportunity for the fourth-grade class to take some leadership in the school. Over the next few days, Jack's teacher made time in class for Jack and a few of his classmates to work together to figure out the details and write a serious proposal to the principal.

The group of five fourth-graders who worked on the proposal met with the principal, who loved the idea, and before long, Jack and his team were going into each of the classrooms in the school to discuss their concept.

Simultaneously, Jack's parents were working with him (with the help of a counselor) to help him learn some better anger management and conflict resolution skills. By the end of the next school year, Jack was feeling much happier about himself. The teacher reported that the school had benefited in all kinds of unexpected ways by Jack's proposal and that many parents had observed some subtle and not-so-subtle changes in school culture, as people (including the primary children!) were talking more openly about how to solve problems together. By the end of fifth grade, Jack was perceived as a leader and was looked up to by many of the other students in the school. Children across all of the grades often went to him when they had problems that needed solving. Based on his earlier problems with sensitivity to injustice and with conflict resolution, he shared ideas to help students learn how to resolve matters themselves.

With some help from his parents, teacher, classmates, and principal, Jack had converted what started out as a terrible situation for him into an opportunity for learning and growth.

We have seen other circumstances in which a school climate became friendlier and fairer because one family responded creatively to ensure a healthy, school-wide approach to conflict resolution. Interestingly, when these kinds of situation are addressed constructively, students like Jack who have had problems with aggression often become much better than others at resolving situations collaboratively and productively.

Those who wish to read more about bullying, conflict resolution, and tolerance may enjoy Barbara Coloroso's books on these topics (Coloroso, 2000, 2002).

Well-Being

"I think she has learned to be happy."
"He carries a weight on his shoulders."
"She enjoys her peers, her teachers, her work."

"What strategies can be used to encourage gifted children to interact with other children in the class?"

There is usually more social support and understanding for the "disadvantaged different" child than for the "over-advantaged" gifted child, but the inner reality and feelings of differentness and rejection are similar. Parents and teachers should watch for these feelings and respond to them with understanding and acceptance. Counseling about the normalness of those feelings under the circumstances and the likelihood that they will change as a child moves forward in her education and life can also be beneficial. At the same time, gifted children should be helped to understand that they have areas of relative weakness, that everyone has variable strengths and weaknesses, and that in fact, others are more like them than different.

Parents and educators who work together are in a much stronger position to help children become more emotionally knowledgeable and secure, as well as more socially responsible, competent, and caring.

An attitude of nurturing the whole person as a unique, valued, and valuable individual is essential. Pair this with sound instructional methods that help children to acquire an understanding of themselves and others, relationship-building, and ways to manage their feelings and behaviors.

With this in mind, we offer parents and teachers the following 10 suggestions for supporting children's emotional health and social/behavioral competence:

1. Consider the whole person beneath the gifted label. A label is an arbitrary and artificial category, but the child or adolescent is a unique individual whose sense of self is affected by many different interacting factors.

2. Learn how to be a good listener. Work toward positive, open, and engaged adult-child communication, so that the child feels respected, safe, and secure and has someone to trust and confide in. This means listening carefully to what the child says without interruption or judgment.

3. Be tolerant, patient, and flexible, remembering that your child or student (like the rest of us) is doing the best he can do to be the best he can be.

4. Encourage positive interaction between home and school.

5. Encourage and model personal resilience.

6. Try to reduce sources of anxiety in the family, in the classroom, and in the child's life. Consider the causes, nature, intensity, and duration of the stressors that are encountered. Work together to minimize or eliminate those that impede healthy functioning.

7. Understand that it is healthy and normal to experience failures and setbacks in one area or another of development. Generally, such experiences are damaging to a child's sense of self and emotional well-being only if not understood and mediated by a trusted adult.

8. Make a relationship with the child a priority. Listening, encouragement, attentiveness, responsivity, and guidance are fundamental to optimal development and should not be compromised by the stressors and demands of daily life. Regularly send positive messages that affirm the child's ability to learn and succeed at school and beyond. Tell the child what you appreciate about him.

9. Learn more about emotional and social issues as they pertain to gifted children.

10. Remember that some situations require professional help and that there are people with the necessary training and expertise to assist with more serious problems.

Parents and teachers may also want to visit this website: www.SENGifted.org. SENG (Supporting the Emotional Needs of the Gifted) is an organization dedicated to helping gifted individuals, their families, and the professionals who work with them.

And finally, we would like to close this chapter with the following piece which arrived in the mail from the Kids Help Foundation without author attribution (unfortunately, because we would very much like to acknowledge the writer). Although all of the ideas listed in the piece are good and important to all children, we've put in italics some of the most noteworthy for encouraging gifted level development.

Ways to Love a Child

Give your presence
Laugh, dance, and sing together
Listen from a heart space
Encourage
Understand
Allow them to love themselves
Ask their opinions
Learn from them
Say yes as often as possible
Say no when necessary
Honor their no's
Apologize
Touch gently
Build lots of blanket forts
Open up
Fly kites together
Lighten up
Believe in possibilities
Read books out loud
Create a circle of quiet
Teach feelings
Share your dreams
Walk in the rain
Celebrate mistakes
Admit yours
Frame their artwork
Stay up late together
Eliminate comparison
Delight in silliness
Handle with care
Protect them
Cherish their innocence
Giggle
Speak kindly
Go swimming
Splash

Let them help
Let them cry
Don't hide your tears
Brag about them
Answer their questions
Let them go when it's time
Let them come back
Show compassion
Bend down to talk to little children
Smile even when you're tired
Surprise with a special lunch
Don't judge their friends
Give them enough room to make decisions
Love all that they do
Honor their differences
Respect them
Remember they have not been on earth very long

We would also like to add a few more which are slight variations on some of the ones above:

Respect their individuality
Respect their independence
Nurture their enthusiasms
Learn alongside them
Connect

We invite you to consider some additions of your own.

Chapter 12

Gifted Development

Nature or Nurture? Back to Origins

Inherited influences on people's achievements are
not direct, not reversible or immutable,
not inevitable, and not inescapable.
(Howe, 1990, p. 57)

People are not simply passive beings waiting
for their biological destiny to be played out,
but active yet oblivious seekers....
Nature-nurture interaction is dynamic.
(Coleman & Cross, 2000, p. 206)

"Where does intelligence come from?" This is a question that researchers, the popular media, and the rest of us have been debating for at least a century. As we noted in Chapter 1, current findings in the neurosciences, as well as in developmental and cognitive psychology, are strong in their conclusions that we cannot effectively separate inherited from environmental influences and that it is the dynamic interaction between nature and nurture that leads to intelligence. It makes little sense to assign percentages to the relative influences of innate inheritance (nature) and environment (nurture) on an individual's intelligence. It seems that who we are and what we eventually become, including our intelligence, is a result of all that we experience, mediated and shaped by *how* we experience it, and influenced by myriad genetic predispositions.

Individual intelligence is a result of a person's early nurturing experiences, the various environments that she inhabits, the surrounding cultural milieu(s), her educational circumstances, her life events, and other factors, as interwoven with her inherited genetic patterns and as organized by the individual herself as an active agent in creating her own intelligence.

Because one's intelligence is a result of dynamic interactions over time, it is considerably more mutable than it was once thought to be (and than some people still see it as being). Several noted researchers (Bloom, 1985; Feldman & Goldsmith, 1986; Gottfried, Gottfried, Bathurst, & Guerin, 1994; Howe, 1990) have conducted and analyzed comprehensive studies of high-level linguistic development, for example. Based on their work, it appears that linguistic giftedness develops where it is systematically encouraged, nourished, and nurtured. This shows that environmental differences in children's opportunities to learn from their earliest days can be critical. Where language use is valued in the child's home, community, and/or scholastic experience, *and* where time, attention, and opportunities are provided for its ongoing development, then, barring major biological or psychological constraints, a high level of linguistic competence (or even, perhaps, linguistic giftedness) can be seen as a logical, predictable, developmental outcome. This is not to say that genetic predispositions for certain kinds of intelligence are trivial or nonexistent, but rather that the human brain's capacity for learning is much greater, much more amenable to learning and growing, than most of us realize.

Developmental Pathways

Listen, there's height that people never see. Some guys are 10 ft. tall, only their bodies don't know it yet.
(Hawkeye Pierce to Radar O'Reilly, MASH)

If we could understand the developmental foundations for both the "nipped bud" and the "late bloomer," we would have a much more firm idea about how best to intervene in the growth of talent— especially within our educational systems, where society's involvement is most direct and potent. Thus, we might learn how to

> *prevent the promising youth from going astray, and we might grasp*
> *how to accelerate the flowering of a latent talent.*
>
> (Simonton, 2000, p. 118)

Each child's route to maturity is highly individual and is influenced by many factors (such as culture, supports, and opportunities to learn and explore). Moreover, a person's development is not an even path. The more exceptional a person is in one domain, the more likely it is that there are wide discrepancies across other domains and over time.

A child's abilities do not develop in lock-step fashion. Someone who is labeled as gifted is not likely to be gifted in all subject areas or even in all components of a single subject area.

For example, picture an 11-year-old boy, with heavy physics and biology texts peeking out of his knapsack, holding a comic book and a toy wrestling figure in his hands. Imagine the nine-year-old girl who can sing intricate musical passages but whose fine-motor skills are impaired. Or think about a primary student who can solve complicated math equations but has trouble mastering multiplication tables. These kinds of differences across areas of ability are far more frequent than most people realize.

Now consider children's development over time. What are we to make of a 12-year-old girl who reads and appreciates the complexities of Shakespeare, yet fails to do well in high school, or the boy who barely passes middle school, but later becomes an extraordinary graduate student? How do we account for such disparate patterns of development? Scientists and researchers are still far from fully understanding the way environmental, genetic, and individual factors and forces interact. The developmental pathways that lead to the individual differences that characterize giftedness remain complex and fascinating scientific puzzles.

In spite of political forces working toward educational standardization both in Canada and the United States (as well as other countries), educators are increasingly realizing that they must target instruction to individual patterns of interest and ability in order to be effective. This requires vision and courage at a time of increasing standardization, but many schools and school systems around the world are making important inroads and implementing flexible and responsive approaches to individual learning needs.

Over the next few pages, we consider some of the key issues concerning individual developmental differences, including the importance of play and humor to gifted children's development, the "early ripen, early rot" syndrome, young gifted children, issues in adolescence, and academic and career counseling for gifted students.

The Importance of Play

As today's children move into the twenty-first century and continue to experience pressure in their lives, play becomes even more crucial.

(Santrock, 1994, p. 481)

Play is perhaps the most basic outcome of a child's natural genius....
As children lose touch with their instinctive tendency to be creative in using free time, their social, emotional, and intellectual lives, as well as the destiny of the human species as a whole, may suffer the consequences.

(Armstrong, 1991, p. 123)

Think about those times in your life when there has been too much work and too little play. As unhappy and unhealthy a situation as that is for an adult, it is an especially troubling reality for many gifted children. Many well-meaning parents who over-program their gifted children don't realize that play is the most important work of childhood. In many of the families we work with, children's schedules are so full that they have very little time for real play. In addition to school, which sometimes involves long commutes, children may participate in various organized activities that require practicing, performances, and homework. This leaves little or no discretionary time for play—very few hours when kids have the time and energy to think about what it is they actually want to do. Then, in those moments when play might be possible, they all too often find that it is far easier to turn on a television, computer, or electronic game than to invent their own play activities or engage in play with others.

We have been emphasizing the ways that good teaching and parenting skills can foster feelings of successful mastery and stimulate a young child's engagement with learning. However, parents and educators should also be sensitive to the fact that such engagement need not be constant or intense. In fact, it really should be turned off from time to time. Ample unstructured time, in a context that's nurturing, is a basic requirement for the kind of play that leads to self-discovery and skill development. Although parents and educators of gifted children often feel a sense of responsibility for keeping their children entertained, occupied, and stimulated, it is sometimes better to let children be bored so that they are motivated to create their own fun. The child who is bored is in the right place to discover who she is and what she wants to learn next.

Play is not only a pleasurable activity that is engaged in for its own sake, it is an essential part of children's development for a number of reasons. It is a species-characteristic pattern (also known as instinct) of all mammals (Oatley & Jenkins, 1996) and therefore must have an adaptive function in our evolution. Play serves many purposes in people's lives, including friendship-building, tension release, cognitive stimulation, sensorimotor development, and the exploration of possibilities. Children learn the mechanics and specifics of social interaction through play. They learn about possible ways of being and the consequences of different ways of behaving. Through play, they practice the various roles that they will assume later in life, and they have opportunities to imagine and try out possible roles. In play, children practice and exercise their social, cognitive, and physical competencies and skills, and they test their limits with less anxiety than is associated with many other pursuits. Imaginary play encourages the development of creative habits of mind.

One writer makes the point succinctly: "There is plenty of evidence…much of it from the arena of science, which increasingly shows that children who are stuffed full of factoids and expected to perform don't do as well as children who are allowed to play. By a dreadful irony, trying to make your child smarter can backfire" (Mitchell, 2003, p. F.10). Too much emphasis on academic drilling and intensive attempts to hasten children's education are detrimental when they erode play opportunities or compromise the important aspects of social, emotional, and cognitive development that play affords.

Gifted children's play activities are sometimes more independent of adults, more complicated and broader in scope than that of their age-peers. We've known seven-year-olds who have devised neighborhood theatre companies, working together with a couple of friends to develop the scripts, invent costumes, find props, and then stage, rehearse, and perform their productions. A parent writes the following about her gifted daughters' playtimes.

Beware! Gifted Child at Play

I used to notice the complexity of my daughters' self-designed games. Many times, the activity would be continuous over several days, and the complexity might demand considerable space. One of my kids used to create parallel worlds/lives requiring several rooms to delineate the sections of her play world. She might create a town with rooms as various shops, or a school with classrooms. Or she'd have a family and have to run errands, like take them swimming on the blue bedsheet in the living room that substituted for a pool, then get groceries in the basement. The bathroom might be the bank, and so forth. Another one of my kids used to take ropes and wool and strings and tie up everything in a room to create a maze for us to physically navigate. Now when I go to a movie and see scenes created using laser beams, I smile to think of my good furniture all strung together with ropes.

Although we are emphasizing here the importance of play, we don't want to overdo it. We are advocating plenty of do-nothing times when children are free to invent their own play, without encouraging a tyranny of playtime in which children are forced to play games or participate in activities that adults think are fun and playful. Every child and every developmental pathway is unique, and one child's play can be another child's misery. Some children so love to acquire academic skills that school-learning really is play to them. We know children who spend countless hours inventing play-school games in their free time; it would be counterproductive to take away their books and blackboards and insist that they play with dolls or trucks instead. What is important is to strike a happy and respectful balance with the type and amount of play in children's lives.

Being Smart by Being Funny

While students with musical aptitude may be shown to the music room, students with humor ability are often sent to the principal's office....

(Higgins-Biss, 1995, p. 58)

As with play, humor can be critically important to gifted children's healthy development. It can provide an essential outlet for difficult feelings, a way to cope with stress, or a means to connect with others. It can also be the natural product of an unbelievably fast linguistic mind.

Karen Higgins-Biss, who has taught gifted learners for 20 years, investigated the role of humor (1995). In the context of a larger study, she administered a combination of questionnaires and interviews to 135 children in Grades 6, 7, and 8 in self-contained gifted classes. She learned that humor was highly valued by these pre- and early adolescents and that the identified-gifted children in this study viewed humor as a good way to advance and manage a variety of social goals. Those who were perceived as funniest by their classmates used their humor consciously to achieve and maintain social status, and indeed, Higgins-Biss found that perceived funniness and social competence were strongly linked. Students who received high funniness rankings from their classmates tended also to rank well on other indicators of social competence (peer-evaluations, social skills measures, and teacher-rankings). Young gifted humorists were cognizant of their advanced ability to make people smile and used this proficiency to serve various purposes in myriad social contexts.

When interviewed, the students who were considered extremely funny by their classmates expressed their pleasure. They described themselves as "proud," "honored," and "glad" to receive this confirmation that "people aren't laughing out of politeness." Almost all of the interviewees openly admitted that they deliberately tried to be funny because it felt good and was fun. They reported that engaging in humor is stimulating. They said that their need for excitement is met by entertaining others and themselves. If funny people are around, they said, it's not dull, because humor creates variety and interest.

Being humorous helps initiate social interactions and establish friendships. A sixth-grade boy explained, "When you're funny, people like being around you." Some interviewees discussed how their talent for humor had facilitated the move from their neighborhood school to the special gifted class at a new school. Humor helped ease them into a new social group, as well as deal with the sense of loss experienced by leaving old friends. According to one girl, "Being funny breaks the ice since people can't hate you if they're laughing with you." W. C. Fields would concur: "The pleasure which I cause them tells me that at least for a short moment they love me." A funny child is less likely to be classified as boring, which is a dreaded designation. Once a friendship is formed, that same humor serves to solidify and enhance intimacy, particularly when private jokes are shared.

The gifted children in the study were keenly aware of humor's contribution to their mental health. One eighth-grade boy explained how he used humor to laugh off stressful or hurtful circumstances, especially when he felt self-conscious. Others agreed that humor helped them to consider various perspectives on a situation, and it stimulated creativity. One girl expanded on this theme: "It's so much easier to deal with problems and stuff. If you have a problem, just look at it from a different perspective and you can laugh at it." A boy in her class concurred: "It's easier to deal with something if you're on the bright side with humor." These children reported that it was easier to cope with life challenges when they considered different vantage points and laughed at their own foibles.

Many of the children in the study focused on the inappropriateness of "negative" humor (for example, using it to belittle or malign others). Rather, they frequently communicated a desire to use their talent for humor to make the world a better place. One boy explained, "A group of people are standing around all depressed and bawling their eyes out. If I say something funny, they're going to get happy!"

Some of the gifted humorists admitted to deliberately using humor for manipulative purposes to achieve social control or power. Making a joke can help extricate a young comedian from a difficult situation, especially with peers, but also with parents. Several interviewees complained that these techniques weren't usually as effective with teachers. "Teachers don't want you to be funny. They think you're making fun of them and trying to disturb the class, and you're just trying to relax everyone. Be mellow." Many children saw humor as a potent force that can be used to change both circumstances and people. They knew that they could change the atmosphere in a classroom by employing humor.

These gifted children were quite aware of their talent. They recognized humor as an easy way to irritate, cajole, empower, change, help, or control others. A means to elicit happiness. A social lubricant. For many reasons, it is important that students who are gifted humorists have opportunities to exercise and develop their special talent. Teachers can recognize the contributions class comics are able to make by encouraging their leadership and creativity. When educators and parents appreciate children's humor and comprehend its possible meanings and functions instead of punishing the child for his distracting behaviors, they simultaneously take advantage of a wonderful, enlivening resource at home and at school, and they support the optimal development of those who bring smiles to so many.

"Rot" to "Rotation"

"I'm trying to figure out how much I have to prove, who I have to prove it to, and for how long."

"Our daughter was an amazing athlete when she was little. Now she'd rather just sit around and listen to music. She won't even exercise. What happened?"

Some people believe that children who learn to read or think or do mathematical calculations too well too soon will later experience a decline in their abilities that leads to their never achieving the promise that they showed when young. This view was a common belief in the early 1900s and is called the "early ripen, early rot" syndrome. While it is true that there are people who achieve exceptional proficiency in their early years in one or more areas and end up later achieving in the normal range, most who start out ahead of their age-peers actually increase their initial advantage over time. The early ability to read, for example, leads to early access to a broad range of more complex ideas, which leads to the ability to formulate more complex concepts. This, in turn, enables the child to master increasingly higher-level understandings ahead of her age-peers.

There can sometimes be a certain truth to the nasty fruit metaphor, however. There are many kinds of potential problems along the way that can damage the development of children who show early promise. One way of making sense of the metaphor is through its connection to our discussion of play. An exceptionally capable young child (the early ripener) who is over-programmed or controlled by his parents may later experience some problems and never live up to his early brilliance (the early rot part of the quotation). There are many unhappy life stories of highly talented childhood movie stars who had overly ambitious and controlling stage mothers or fathers managing their careers. Musical prodigies and others can experience problems when early giftedness is accompanied by too much parental pressure and involvement, rather than by a responsive provision of opportunities to explore and develop the child's own interests (Howe, 1990).

Sometimes children's early ripening leads to rot by way of a rut. Highly talented children who are channeled too narrowly and deeply into one area of concentration (whether math, music, sports, or anything else) may decide that it is too much too soon and that they cannot handle it—or that they do not want to handle it. After decreasing the amount of effort and involvement in their area of proficiency for a period of time, they may find themselves unable to easily regain the same heightened level of competence later on. A champion runner who opts out of practicing for an extended period will lose her momentum and edge and may never be competitive again. Moreover, she might not care, and she may have moved on to something else by then that she finds more interesting or motivating. As the mastery model indicates (and as we described it in Chapter 1), there is a temporal nature to intelligence and ability. If the drive to excel in something dwindles, so too, over time, will the level of mastery. Parents or educators who want to support long-term, high-level development should be attentive to the "rut" possibility as a potential source of the "early rot" phenomenon.

There are of course other stories of eminent people whose parents were very pushy (Goertzel, Goertzel, Goertzel & Hansen, 2004). As we emphasize throughout this book, the important facts to keep in mind are that high-level development is diverse, every pathway is individual, and context is everything. Early intellectual ripening is not likely to lead to debilitating problems unless it is forced past bearing, unless the early-ripening fruit is severely over- (or under-) watered and over- (or under-) cultivated. Knowing the difference is an imprecise science. One of the things we do know is that a child who shows early promise is more likely to do interesting things later and experience personal and professional successes if his individuality is respected and if he is given the necessary familial and educational supports along the way.

Many children find their interests changing over time, affected by internal or external factors, and then veering off in unforeseen directions. This may not be a bad thing, just unexpected, possibly disappointing to parents or educators, but also perhaps the best thing for the child's long-term development if it is perceived that way. It makes good sense for adults to look beyond the ostensible rot and think about it as a possible "rotation," a turn-around or evolution toward something different. The proficiencies that a young gifted child develops will forever be a valuable part of her experiential history, whether she builds on them in a straightforward sequential way or spins them around and takes off in a different direction entirely.

Young Gifted Children

> *"I'm having a lot of trouble with my daughter. She's in second grade and refuses to do her homework. She dawdles, procrastinates, and won't get down to work, no matter what I do."*
>
> *"Our school's position is that children need to learn good study habits, and the sooner the better. Steve is only in Grade 1 and has a lot of trouble sitting still and doing his work."*
>
> *"Mae-Lin came home from her first day in kindergarten in tears. She said that all they did at school was play. She is ready to work hard, and I think she feels insulted when the teacher treats her and the others as if they were little children."*

It is an old saying but nonetheless true that gifted children are *children first* and *gifted second*. The developmental principles (not necessarily the timetables) that apply to all children apply to them, too. By responding to children's individual interests, respecting them, listening to them, playing with them, and providing opportunities for them to learn what they can do and want to do next, all in a context of predictable stability and support, the adults in their lives can provide the optimal environment for their development.

In many situations, whether or not a young child is formally identified as gifted is irrelevant. Up to and through the primary years (from birth to about age seven or eight), most of a child's real learning is about the pleasures to be found in exploring and understanding the world in his family, playgroups, classrooms, and community. This very much includes social and emotional skills. The most important achievements of these early years are the construction of a foundation of secure self-confidence, enthusiasm for learning, and resilience, all of which can usually be accomplished without a formal gifted identification or assessment process.

Parents naturally look to the future, and many wonder if their children will grow up to be proficient, high-achieving, or even eminent in one way or another. If a young child is advanced for her age or seems to be exceptionally creative, does that signify great things to come? Most experts in the field of creativity say, "No, not necessarily." As with intellectual prowess, one's destiny depends on many factors, not the least of which are environmental influences, learning opportunities, temperament, and good old-fashioned hard work, along with some good luck, all of which must converge in an effective way over time.

Needs

Much more than formal academic learning, a young child needs activities that engage his enthusiasm for learning in a number of different areas, as well as lots of opportunities for safe and spontaneous unstructured play and exploration. As a strong foundation of competence and confidence is built, the child becomes ready, willing, and able to establish and follow schedules and acquire the discipline necessary for high-level achievement.

Some young children are independent, creative, experiential learners. They may have problems with structured learning in school, and they may not acquire good work habits and study skills until they're engaged in work that they find personally meaningful. Other children are intrinsically drawn to structure and organization and really like the idea of working hard at school and doing homework, sometimes as young as age three or four. These children are impatient with or feel insulted by academic tasks that are significantly below their zones of competence or levels of comprehension.

Some young children think about deep philosophical issues at an early age. They become preoccupied with death or war long before they have the cognitive abilities to put these ideas into perspective (Yalom, 1983). These worries can become exacerbated when they try to share their thoughts with others and discover that their peers are quite happily focused on their daily lives and toys, or that adults don't want to discuss ideas like this with them. Not finding anyone who understands or who wants to talk with them can leave such children feeling more isolated and troubled than before.

No matter what the child's temperament, ability, or concerns, the best thing parents and teachers can do is listen actively and sensitively, ensuring that the child experiences her environment as secure, predictable, and dependable, and that she feels listened to. The younger and more exceptional the child, the more important it is that parents and teachers respond to her individual development with flexibility.

Sensitive Periods

All that transpires during the months and years before a child enters the educational system is not just a prelude to real learning; in fact, there are good reasons to think that the most important learning in a person's life occurs before he goes to school at all. Language acquisition, motor development, social interaction, and play are just a few of the early learning activities that shape a child's future. However, whereas all infants have the potential to learn, not all young children receive the kind of nurturing and learning opportunities that are likely to optimize their healthy overall development across the years.

Although there is currently considerable debate about developmental timing constraints (variously referred to as critical or sensitive periods or optimal windows of opportunity for certain kinds of learning), the scientific community generally agrees that the early years are tremendously important in an individual's development. At least for some competencies, there are periods when a child may be more sensitive to certain influences—times when neurological development best supports specific kinds of learning.

One of the ways that exceptional learners are exceptional is in their maturational timing—they experience the sensitive learning periods earlier, later, or differently than other children. In the case of gifted learners, they tend to be advanced relative to average, with some (but not all) aspects of their development occurring relatively earlier. Because learning happens according to highly individual schedules, parents should recognize that from infancy on, and regardless of age-normal sensitive periods, it is important to respond to children's curiosity and encourage their engagement in learning.

Children thrive when they have access to a variety of learning possibilities and when they are encouraged and empowered to gain competence in various domains. Self-confidence, a positive attitude toward learning, and the drive to achieve are all strengthened when parents encourage their children's curiosity, creativity, and emerging needs to know and experience more about themselves and the world.

Important Concepts

> *"I'm curious about a lot of things. I must have a million questions."*
> *"Parenting a child like mine is somewhat like attempting a jigsaw puzzle when someone keeps throwing in extra pieces and you've never seen the finished product!"*

Many parents of young children ask us for advice. Our suggestions include those we made in Chapter 11 about supporting children's emotional health and social/behavioral competence, as well as the list of ways to love a child. What follows here is a summary chart of some important principles that apply to young children during times of trouble *and* at times when things are running smoothly (Zeller, 1993).

Table 12.1. Responding to High-Level Development in Young Children

What a Child May Exhibit	Provisions
Insatiable curiosity	Limitless opportunities to explore
Intellectual-social/emotional gap	Flexible learning environment
Polymathy (learn a lot easily)	Help organizing/establishing criteria for decision making
Advanced perception and emotional responses to justice and fair play	Help rationalizing seemingly unjust events and outcomes

And a final list of suggestions that we have gathered:

- Listen to your child.
- Be flexibly responsive to your child's individual interests.
- Encourage an attitude of playful exploration.
- Create an environment of predictable stability and support.
- Respect your child's personhood and right to have opinions.
- Play with your child.
- Provide opportunities for her to learn what she can do.
- Provide opportunities for her to learn what she wants to do next.

- Be proactively available to offer guidance, support, and encouragement.

- Help your child set reachable goals.

- Provide a variety of age-appropriate play materials, thinking about as many domains of development as possible (including physical, musical, social, mathematical, linguistic, and visual/spatial).

Adolescence (Sigh)

You can't direct the wind, but you can adjust the sails.

(Anon.)

In this segment, we discuss early adolescence, giftedness as an adolescent risk factor, and issues for parents of adolescents. There are endless topics pertaining to adolescence that we could address (for example, limits and responsibilities, teen culture, communication, trust, etc.), but this book is primarily about giftedness, and so we will stay focused on that.

Early Adolescence

An important fact about coolness: It cannot be achieved through trying. Coolness is a form of cultural grace that descends upon those chosen few.... You can't aspire to coolness; you can't contrive to attain it. In fact, once you try to be cool you are caring what people think and that makes you, ipso facto, uncool.

(Borowitz, 2003, p. 25)

"I got through my own adolescence, but I'm not sure I can make it through my daughter's."

Eleven- to 14-year-olds are engaged in the complex and sometimes overwhelming experience of handling puberty. Everything in their lives is changing all at once: their body shapes, hormones, sexuality, emotions, and cognition, to say nothing of their changing relationships with parents, siblings, friends, and others. Some children experience this vulnerable period in their lives more easily than others. This is mostly because they are "on time" relative to their peers, because they have strong social support networks and resources, and/or because they have few other stressors operating simultaneously in their day-to-day existence.

It is important that adults who are dealing with adolescents realize that, in addition to the obvious physical, hormonal, and sexual changes that occur at this time, there are many invisible cognitive changes in progress. To begin with, an adolescent is still quite egocentric and seeing the world through her own eyes, but she is also becoming better at realizing that others are also looking at her and have their own perspectives on who she is and what she is saying and doing. This can result in a temporary imbalance between the child's social and personal understandings. For example, a young teen may see herself as the heroine of her own unique, fascinating, and poignant life story (her own personal fable), and at the same time be worried about an "imaginary audience" (everyone else), who she imagines as having a primary focus on her actions, physical flaws, and perhaps even her thoughts. You may remember that adolescent feeling of thinking that everyone in the room is looking at you, and more specifically, at that blemish on your forehead.

An early adolescent is also moving from predominantly concrete to more fluid, abstract thinking. This shift usually starts in childhood with gifted children, but it becomes much more solid at this time. With the development of stronger abstract reasoning abilities, early adolescents become more cognitively flexible, more capable of simultaneously considering several dimensions of a problem. That sounds like a good thing, and in the end, it usually is, but in the process of giving up the naïve but comforting certainty of childhood, with its clearly defined notions of right and wrong, good and bad, early adolescents tend to undergo a period of doubting almost everything. They frequently come to believe that reliable conclusions cannot be drawn about anything. This has been described as "rampant relativism" (Keating, 1990), in which nothing seems trustworthy or dependable, including, and perhaps especially, one's parents' statements and ideas.

Complex changes in identity are also occurring during this period, including sex-role orientation and gender identity. Identity formation is a lengthy process which involves moving toward an eventual separation from one's parents. To facilitate the separation, children initiate stronger peer affiliations, experiencing a need to be like their peers and to be liked by them to fit in with what is considered typical for their age at that time and place. This is when being cool, or conversely, being a *dork*, can mean everything. Peer relationships are very important to the developing self-concept of an early adolescent.

Given the complex and interacting changes occurring at early adolescence, one might expect a variety of problems to become more prevalent at this time, and this is indeed the case. Researchers have observed the following problems:

- heightened self-consciousness

- greater instability of self-image

- lower global self-esteem

- lower opinions of themselves with regard to the qualities they value

- reduced conviction that parents, teachers, and same-sex peers hold favorable opinions of them

- greater likelihood of depression

It has been documented that life stress steadily increases through childhood and into early adolescence, which is a time of heightened risk for a number of problems, including depression and suicide. For example, children experiencing the divorce of their parents at this time of their lives are more vulnerable, less adaptable, and suffer more side effects than those who experience it at other times. Parents who have survived their children's early adolescence are usually not surprised to hear that this is a time when parents are at increased risk of stress, insecurity, feelings of inadequacy, and diminished marital satisfaction. And as if all that wasn't hard enough, all too often, children's early adolescence happens to coincide with their parents' midlife reappraisals.

Early adolescence, then, tends to be a difficult phase in a young person's life. Everything is changing; it is a period of social and emotional vulnerability, and it constitutes in itself a developmental risk factor. Somewhat surprisingly, however, most children do not experience serious problems at this juncture, and many young people really enjoy this time in their lives. Nevertheless, there are factors associated with giftedness that can combine with early adolescence to heighten the risk of problems for gifted children going through this period.

Giftedness: A Risk Factor

> *How do we manage to survive the anxieties, the heartache, the worry, the exasperation? Well, I've repeatedly asked my husband to knock me out with a blunt, heavy object and then wake me when it's all over, but he refuses.*
>
> (Borowitz, 2003, p. 3)

Identity formation is a major challenge at adolescence. At early adolescence, there is a strong need to be just like one's age-peers. Yet there is an equally powerful need to be unique, a desire to be completely and unmistakably oneself. These conflicting pressures are demonstrated in the conformist nonconformity of young people who see themselves as expressing their individuality through their clothes and music, but who dress just like their chosen peer group and who listen to the same songs. Students who have been identified as being academically exceptional (such as gifted) can experience more anguish than others in their attempts to identify with their age-peers. Some of them experience more pressure to be just like everybody else because there's an official designation that indicates otherwise.

Educational exceptionality labels used to describe individuals' learning needs can pose difficulties, but there are other concerns as well. Being different in such an important peer-interactional area as the way information is processed can give added weight to the usual cognitive distortions mentioned above (the "personal fable" and the "imaginary audience"). A young person who really *is* different from his peers in such a basic way as how he learns and understands might be expected to see himself as truly different than others and therefore as the subject of uncomfortably intense scrutiny. An added burden of loneliness and ostracism can ensue from the self-consciousness that results from that kind of real differentness from one's peers.

Those gifted adolescents who retain their passion for learning can have an easier time at this often-difficult stage because ongoing high-level achievement can help to compensate for that emerging sense of differentness. The suggestions for supporting emotional health and social/behavioral competence that we presented in Chapter 11 are also beneficial for this age group.

Risk does accumulate, then, when one has physical, learning, or attentional difficulties and is intellectually highly able at the same time that one is attempting to negotiate the critical period of early adolescence. It is certainly not the case that every exceptional learner has serious issues during this developmental period. When the risk factors of early adolescence and educational exceptionality interact with other risk factors, such as gender identity issues, cultural conflicts, or family disruptions, they create a situation of greater potential for problems. In such cases, it is more important than ever that the principles we discuss here of active listening and support are in place.

Parenting

> *"That's it. I quit!"*
> *"We used to discuss things, and I was able to reason with her. Now we barely communicate."*

> *"They won't quit!"*
> *"We used to discuss things, and I was able to reason with them. Now we barely communicate."*

The same parenting skills that foster gifted level development in early childhood can become problematic in certain situations and at other times in kids' lives. Parents who are very involved in their young child's life—parents who are aware, caring, stimulating, and responsive, and who provide lots of opportunities for learning—may experience developmental challenges of their own as their child becomes an adolescent. Parents of pre-teens and teens have to learn to back off, to become reactive instead of proactive. They have to find ways to understand that decision-making is a skill that must be acquired, like all others, through practice, including some trials that result in errors. They have to trust that their child has the resources necessary, including parental support and guidance, to deal with the consequences of the wrong decisions that she makes. This kind of developmental challenge is not an easy one, particularly if a parent has concerns about a child's development or well-being. Although mothers tend to have more trouble letting go of their children than do fathers, we have certainly seen fathers challenged by this, too.

In our clinical work with high-ability learners, we encounter a lot of families experiencing difficulty with these issues. We have observed that when a child perceives one or both parents not respecting his individuality or autonomy, troubles ensue one way or another. Sometimes the problems don't show up until later, often in an adult who is dependent and/or who has trouble making good decisions for himself. But more often, problems show up earlier in the form of a surly or rebellious teenager and a frustrated and confused parent.

One way to put this in perspective is to think about adolescence as an opportunity for a young person to acquire and practice the skills and habits conducive to a successful and independent adult life. By the time a teenager is ready to leave home at age 18 or so, it is best if she does not need someone else to take care of her room, clothing, and food; to make sure she gets up on time; to tell her how many hours of homework she has to do; or to make other kinds of decisions about what to do and with whom. Having achieved puberty, then, it is time to practice being an adult. If she is lucky, she will be able to have this practice period in the context of a safe, supportive, and caring environment, in a home with adults who love her and are able to provide respectful and helpful guidance as she demonstrates that she needs it.

With all of this in mind, we offer a number of pointers for the parents of gifted adolescents.

Power/Conflict Issues	These cannot always be avoided, and that's all right. In fact, the best long-term developmental outcomes occur in families characterized by lots of warmth, as well as lots of intergenerational discussion, much of it heated and conflictual in nature.
Decision-Making	Gifted adolescents' ability to handle sexual intimacy, decisions about drugs, and other potentially dangerous peer pressures is not improved because of their intellectual or reasoning ability, no matter what they tell you.
Rules	Make rules only about those things that really matter. Pick your battles!
Parent Development Issues	Parents of gifted children often have real problems letting go of the desire to direct their child. Not letting go can prevent a child from achieving the independence that is an important developmental task at this stage.

Identity Issues	Work on relating to the *person* and respecting the adolescent's need to experiment with different identities. Do not ridicule or demand what *you* think is a more "appropriate" outfit, haircut, or behavior.
Gender Identity	Continue to support your children in their intellectual endeavors while accepting and understanding their gender identity desires, some of which may strike you as superficial or even troubling (for example, your daughter's yearnings to be attractive and to develop her own sense of style, or your son's aspirations to be athletic and popular).
Sex Differences	Adolescents, particularly daughters, tend to reject their mothers at this period and are often more interested in identifying with their fathers. And while girls don't typically cause as many problems as boys when they are young, this can change at early adolescence.
Cultural Issues	When the family background is different than the surrounding culture, recognize that the child is growing up in the society that the family is in or has moved to and that healthy identity development depends on peer identification. Try to minimize the child's problems with conflicting cultural values.
Academic Underachievement	Encourage the adolescent to find something that he really wants to learn about and to keep as many educational and career options open as possible. Many underachievers metamorphose into high achievers as adults.
Unpredictability	What a gifted adolescent needs is predictably unpredictable and changing all the time. This means that a parent's job is very often a challenging balancing act, requiring constant vigilance and flexibility.

Academic and Career Counseling

At a fundamental level, the gifted develop as individuals in a recip-
rocal relationship with their society; thus their creative work carries
meaning beyond themselves whether it is fully intended to or not.
By the same token, society is enriched by having individuals actively
engaging in self-chosen creative endeavors.

(VanTassel-Baska, 2000, p. 360)

We began the discussion of career exploration back in Chapter 6 when we addressed possible curriculum adaptations for gifted learners. We revisited it in Chapter 8 in thinking about ways to further stretch the learning boundaries for highly able learners. We come back to this topic once again here as a frequently-experienced issue in gifted development. There are a lot of different reasons that so many gifted adolescents and adults have ongoing problems with finding or creating satisfying careers for themselves. .

Guidance Approaches

The very fact of a gifted person's exceptional learning and thinking ability means that the kinds of careers that will be stimulating and engaging are likely to be different for her than for others. Generally, the only adaptation for giftedness that is seen in academic and career guidance approaches is the suggestion of jobs that require a longer time in school, such as engineering, medicine, or law. While this is excellent advice for some gifted students, it is not appropriate for others. As is true in so many other areas, academic and career guidance for exceptional students must be tailored to the unique interests, strengths, possibilities, and constraints of their highly individual situations.

Unfortunately, few guidance counselors have the training or experience required to do this tailoring, and published materials (such as career interest inventories and career decision-making guidelines) do not have a wide enough range to encompass the needs of those who are exceptional in their abilities—on both ends of the ability spectrum. Exposing students to possibilities through mentorships and by making connections with colleges and universities in an area of interest can be helpful.

Multipotentiality

Multipotentiality is the name given to the situation of having many areas of high-level ability and interest that, with development, promise to provide interesting and successful careers. Although it sounds like a wonderful bonus to be able to select from several possible areas of high-level achievement, multipotentiality can cause real confusion and unhappiness as a multitalented adolescent or young adult contemplates which of his favorite pursuits he will continue to focus his energies on and which he will have to let go or develop only to a mediocre level. Sometimes multipotentiality results in "burnout" from trying to do everything well, and other times it results in "rustout" from doing nothing very well.

Sometimes, with a little creative thinking, two or more disparate areas can be combined very happily and productively. The student who is a gifted athlete and loves science might become involved in sports medicine, or the student who is gifted in both mathematics and social awareness might become a psychologist, sociologist, or demographer. In other situations, one interest can be developed into a vocation, while another continues to be developed as an avocation, as can be seen in the lives of the many doctors who play instruments in community orchestras, or the many professors who write fiction or poetry in their spare time.

Amy's Story

Amy loved music, and for many years, she seriously considered becoming a classical musician. However, she also thought she'd enjoy being a physicist or a university physics professor. She was particularly fascinated by the possibilities of metaphysics as it intersected with astrophysics. Amy had some surprising publishing successes while she was still a high school student, and her English teachers told her that she should be a writer. She also thought seriously about studying law and medicine.

Amy won scholarships out of high school and took a mélange of courses in her first year of college. She dropped out of college her second year because she felt that she really needed to do some serious learning, and she was frustrated by her feeling of not having accomplished anything useful. She has spent the last year traveling a little and working part time. It is yet to be seen what she will end up doing with her talents, but it is probably safe to say that her

multipotentiality has made her career path much more complicated and difficult than it might otherwise have been.

Uncertainty

"I'm going to be an astronaut. For sure."
"I wish I had a better idea of what to study. Everyone else in my class
seems to know what they want to be when they get older, but I
really have no clue yet."

Some children decide on a future career when they are very young
and never deviate from that. But for many others, this kind of early commitment forecloses other possible options and leads to an unhappy
sense of being trapped in a career without ever having fully explored
other possibilities. Early commitment reduces uncertainty and anxiety,
both for the child and her family, and enables her to move smoothly
through her schooling, but it can also carry a very heavy price later.

Many gifted people go through prolonged uncertainty and exploration that lasts into early adulthood. In fact, there is some evidence that
most of those who go on to do noteworthy things with their lives and
make major contributions to society in one area or another experience
this kind of career moratorium. Rather than going directly from kindergarten to graduate school, it is sometimes healthier to take one or two or
more years off school somewhere in the period between 17 and 25 years
of age (Kaufmann, 1981). The "time out" can be spent working and/or
traveling and simultaneously engaging in active self-exploration, thinking about society, observing oneself in interaction with others, and
figuring out how to be independent, interdependent, and happily productive. As much as possible, this career and self-exploration period
should be a time of learning about various kinds of responsibility,
including financial, emotional, and social. Once a young adult has worked
out some of these issues of self and society, choosing a career becomes at
least somewhat easier.

Idealism and Self-Actualization

An equal valuing of cognitive, affective, aesthetic, and social development of the gifted, and a concern for both individual and social
contributions must be satisfied.

(VanTassel-Baska, 2000, p. 360)

Many gifted learners are frustrated in their career decision-making by their (often unconscious) drive to find something meaningful to do with their lives or something that will satisfy their sense of purpose. Many of the careers they think about do not appear to have enough room for idealism, enough opportunity for making the world a better place. Many careers appear to have little room for creativity or self-actualization, or for becoming one's strongest and best self. Although some parents and teachers see these problems as youthful folly that will be outgrown with maturation, it is probably healthier to help the young adult figure out a way to combine his interests and his idealism, his need to consider practical goals such as financial self-sufficiency, as well as his need for self-actualization. This can mean moving the emphasis away from *choosing* a career to *creating* one.

Tom's Story

Tom, a highly gifted and affable young man, thought about many different career possibilities throughout high school and college. He studied languages and economics in his undergraduate university years, not knowing where this might take him, thinking perhaps of going into business or becoming a professor of languages. He had always been very creative and was interested both in language use and art. He had frequently thought about advertising as a career, but had dismissed this idea because he saw it as being antithetical to his social idealism.

After completing his undergraduate degree, Tom worked for a non-profit agency for a year. During that period, he realized, somewhat paradoxically, that advertising is one of the best possible ways to make a difference in people's lives and that, although much advertising works by encouraging people's baser feelings— lust, greed, and insecurity, to name a few—responsible advertisers can work very effectively to shape public opinion in positive ways. Tom is now enthusiastically involved in the early stages of a career in advertising and finds himself engaged in the work and excited by its creative, financial, idealistic, and self-actualization possibilities.

Many observers have noted that career education is particularly important for gifted learners. Opportunities to consider systematically and with guidance the problems and conflicts involved in combining challenging careers with family, other interests, and responsibilities can help these adolescents make informed academic and career decisions. We offer some suggestions and ideas to facilitate this process.

Recommendations

The future will require individuals who are able to formulate new problems, come up with new solutions, and adapt readily to the new ideas of others.

(Csikszentmihalyi & Wolfe, 2000, p. 91)

As we discussed in Chapters 6 and 8, we recommend that gifted students learn about the education requirements and likely salaries of a number of traditional and non-traditional careers, and that they be helped to consider the social, motivational, cognitive, emotional, and aesthetic issues that influence career satisfaction and achievement. Adults involved in supporting exceptionally capable students through academic and career decision-making processes should not only recognize their exceptional thinking ability, but also take into account other potentially complicating factors such as learning styles, interests, values, habits of mind, and temperament.

One method of encouraging thoughtful reflection on these important topics is to create a career exploration series of talks, inviting people who work in different fields to come to school to speak to students about their work. Parents, as well as friends, neighbors, acquaintances, and relatives, can be asked to discuss some of the issues that they have experienced in making career and life decisions. Considerations in planning such events include making sure that a range of representative possibilities is explored, including both conventional and unconventional occupations; that the speakers (both men and women, as racially and culturally diverse as possible) are asked to discuss how they became interested in what they ended up doing in their lives and what kinds of paths they followed to make it happen; and that the students are helped to see ways that career interests can be both supported and damaged by choices and factors along the way.

Other methods for facilitating career exploration include job shadowing and asking students to investigate occupations that interest them. They can conduct interviews with practitioners and share information with classmates. Activities like these make good topics for social studies and other subject area assignments and can be used to stimulate meaningful classroom discourse that benefits all students, while supporting gifted learners in thinking about a wider range of possible futures than they might otherwise have done.

Further activities that can help diversely gifted learners consider alternate career paths include mentorships, extracurricular camps and clubs, and contests or fairs at local, regional, national, and international levels that enable students to engage intensely for a short period of time in areas of strength and of possible future interest. Scholarship opportunities abound at career fairs.

Scholarship Possibilities

> *"Beth is still rocking the math world, and she's thinking about applying for an academic scholarship. I have no idea where to even start. Do you have any clue where she should begin looking?"*

When a parent asked us this question recently, we explained that these kinds of things are in flux all the time. However, our suggestions, which follow, may be helpful to other students and parents who want to tap into the various scholarship possibilities available.

- Talk to the counselors in the guidance department at your local high school.

- Think about which programs and schools are of interest, perhaps starting by getting a copy of the most recent edition of the annual review of universities published in *Maclean's Magazine* in Canada, and *U.S. World and News Report* in the U.S.

- People tend to know some of the best schools, at least by reputation (in math, this might include the Massachusetts Institute of Technology, Stanford, the University of Waterloo, Carnegie-Mellon), but which school is best for a particular student will depend on her specific interests, as well as many other factors.

- When considering the various schools and programs of interest, spend time on their websites and begin the process of finding out about available scholarships.

- Very often, it is the most prestigious places that have the best scholarships in place, so apply to the programs that are most interesting, regardless of prestige, and let the schools make the selection rather than doing that for them.

- Check with regional or national gifted associations (such as ABC or NAGC), as well as the various talent search and/or development websites. (Davidson Institute for Talent Development at www.ditd.org provides information on services and scholarship opportunities.)

Here are some ideas for those who may be struggling with academic and career decision-making:

- Think about what you're good at and what you enjoy doing.

- Think about what you're good at and what you enjoy doing that might be useful to others and that might in some way be productive in society.

- Think about ways you can make money. (After all, someone is making money from almost everything under the sun.)

- Do not restrict yourself to standard conventional professions or careers. Many of the most interesting jobs are created by the person doing them, frequently custom-made patchworks of activities rather than easily defined occupations.

Most importantly, if someone—anyone—wants to be happy and successful in a career, he should love his work or find work to do that he can learn to love.

Chapter 13

Different Ways of Being Gifted

I was different. I was always different.
Why didn't anybody notice me?
(John Lennon, from a poster)

Giftedness is not a problem to be solved
but a unique challenge to be nourished.
(Colangelo & Assouline, 2000, p. 605)

For all their complexity, people can rarely be better understood by neatly pigeonholing them. Developmental pathways are highly individual and diverse. Broad categories such as *gifted* and *female* can sometimes assist parents and educators in thinking about how to proceed with a child's education and development, but it is critically important not to lose sight of the unique person behind any label or grouping.

In this chapter, we discuss diversity within giftedness and ways in which uniqueness can influence individuals' lives. In other words, we consider how to optimize "circumstances gone right—the powerful combination of mixing ability, with preparation, opportunity, and timing" (Renzulli, 2003).

Differences between Boys and Girls

The ideal culture is one in which there is a place for every human gift.
(Margaret Mead, cited in Pipher, *Reviving Ophelia*, 1994, p. 22)

When each gifted boy is free to create his unique masculinity, and each gifted girl is free to create her unique femininity, they will also be liberated to fulfill their dreams.
(Kerr & Nicpon, 2003, p. 502)

In recent years, it has become a little more politically correct than it used to be to discuss differences in ability, and there are many interesting findings to consider in this regard (Kerr, 2000; Kerr & Nicpon, 2003). The research continues to show males ahead of females in some aspects of mathematical reasoning ability, particularly spatial reasoning. On certain mathematics and science tests, boys do tend to score higher than girls, and the more competitive the test in its construction and administration, the truer this is. In addition, the higher the ability level, the greater the difference (Lubinski, Benbow, & Morelock, 2000). At the same time, girls tend to do better at school, particularly in verbally oriented tasks and tests, right through to the end of high school. Girls begin to read at an earlier age and tend to be smarter in areas of social and emotional intelligence. There is also some interesting new evidence suggesting that exceptionally capable children (both boys and girls) tend to be more androgynous in their interests, incorporating elements both of the feminine and the masculine stereotype into their preferences and activities (Kerr & Nicpon, 2003). Gifted children are more likely than others to choose interests without regard for traditional gender stereotypes.

Gifted Girls

Wholeness is shattered by the chaos of adolescence. Girls become fragmented, their selves split into mysterious contradictions.
(Pipher, 1994, p. 20)

"She used to be much more enthusiastic about her school work. She still gets A's, but now it seems as if she couldn't care less."
"She has to fake a little bit just to sort of blend in."

282

> *"She just doesn't want to be herself anymore. It's as if some other being has taken over her disposition and attitude toward everything. She's just...changed."*

Typically, smart girls start off their school careers doing better than their male peers. They mature at a younger age and are better able to sit still and do what teachers want them to do. When they are young, they tend to be more interested than boys in typical school tasks like reading and writing. Girls' academic advantage over boys disappears, however, as they enter adolescence and gender identity becomes important.

Although some gifted girls go through adolescence apparently oblivious to the feminine stereotype that excludes high intelligence and ambition, others "dumb down" their academic performance or behavior for the sake of social acceptance or popularity. This has serious consequences because choices made early on can influence the availability of subsequent choices. If a girl decides not to take trigonometry, calculus, or physics, she cuts off many future careers, such as medicine, engineering, architecture, and the sciences. A gifted girl may not want to be smart or gifted anymore if she thinks it reduces her popularity or social attractiveness.

Alternatively, for some girls, participation in gifted learning opportunities and commitment to authentic self-discovery gets them through an otherwise painful adolescence. One sixth-grade girl said this:

> *If I had not been identified [as gifted], I might have considered drugs. It has made me a happier person, a person I never knew was there. I am more creative, I try harder, and I enjoy life.*

Here are some suggestions for supporting ongoing giftedness in girls:

- Encourage gifted girls' development, and raise their aspirations in subjects that they perceive as weaker by means of group work, projects, and authentic learning activities.

- Discuss and illustrate with real-life examples the importance of math and science to subsequent career choices.

- Find or create academic and career development workshops and speaker forums, ensuring that nontraditional and non-stereotypical choices are explored and encouraged.

- Provide job shadowing and mentoring opportunities with accomplished females who enjoy their work.

- Encourage gifted girls to be themselves, to explore who they really are, not who others think they should be. Support girls in their achievement-oriented behaviors and activities while understanding their desire to be attractive and popular. Help them see that it is possible to be feminine, attractive, popular, *and* intellectually curious and competent.

- Consider interventions that are specifically aimed at overcoming girls' high-risk behavior, internal conflicts, and/or social pressures that affect achievement and motivation.

- Provide access to counseling when needed.

Encouraging bright girls to build, maintain, and be proud of their intellectual ability is an important and sometimes daunting challenge for parents and teachers. One gifted girl conveys her feelings about this metaphorically when she says, "I'm a perfectly good carrot that everyone is trying to turn into a rose. As a carrot, I have good color and a nice leafy top. When I'm carved into a rose, I turn brown and wither" (Pipher, 1994, p. 22). What a wonderful way to express the importance of respecting children's individuality! And in fact, respecting individuality was one of the fundamental principles emphasized by researchers investigating talent development in girls and described in an article entitled, "To Thine Own Self Be True" (Noble, Subotnik, & Arnold, 1999).

Gifted Boys

Gifted boys are often held to rigid stereotypes of masculinity.
(Kerr & Cohn, 2001, p. 106)

"Jared is busy with chemistry, photography, and computer graphics. He doesn't want to socialize or participate in sports, and he has no close friends. I worry because he seems to be more interested in products than people."

"I'm not sure what to do about Zack. I know I should let him play with dolls if that is what he wants to do, but really…. That's his favorite activity, and it worries me…."

Active, curious boys who are enthusiastic hands-on learners often have a lot of trouble in the first few years of their schooling. They do not like to sit still and do what the teacher asks them to do, and some decide that they hate school when they are very young. Many of the suggestions and recommendations we discussed in relation to young gifted children (in Chapter 12) apply to these boys.

Generally, as gifted boys get older, they are more likely to participate and stay in gifted programs than girls. It is consistent with the masculine stereotype to be a high achiever, and parents are more inclined to invest time and money on support for high-level educational and career aspirations for sons than for daughters. While gifted boys tend to stay connected to their academic and career ambitions through adolescence, some have trouble with their social development.

Gifted Boys

Marcus is 12 years old, in a regular Grade 7 program, and highly gifted. He isn't interested in sports, finds himself isolated on the playground, and can't relate to the other boys since they have little or no interests in common with him. Outside, nobody wants him on their team because he is inept or disinterested. His isolation continues in classroom situations as well. Inside, no one wants to work with him because he is a loner and not good at working with others. When the teacher assigns him a place or task in a group, it usually ends badly, with him bossing the others or doing his own section of the project with little or no interaction with his classmates. Instead of improving his social skills, group interactions often tend to reinforce his social anxieties and rejection.

Throughout history, and in most cultures, boys have been given more encouragement than girls to develop their independence, self-reliance, and responsibility, all of which help to facilitate high-level academic and career achievement. For some gifted boys, like Marcus in the vignette above, this can be too much of a good thing; the challenge of learning can be far more rewarding and far less demanding than the rigors of socializing. For boys like this, and for others who are not inclined to work at peer acceptance or who lack the social skills to become part of a group of kids, parents and teachers may want to consider the social and behavioral suggestions we discussed in Chapter 11 and check our website (www.beingsmart.ca) for other resources.

Gifted boys are more likely than their female peers to have problems with low academic achievement and dropping out of school (Kerr & Cohn, 2001; Kerr & Nicpon, 2003). Stereotypes may be to blame. Although stereotypes for women have relaxed considerably over the past 30 or 40 years, stereotypes of masculinity regarding acceptable interests and behaviors for boys and men remain troublingly rigid. There is still a belief that boys should not consider professions that are associated with stereotypically feminine attributes of artistic sensitivity and caring about others, including, for example, dance, fashion design, social work, and teaching. Gender stereotypical views like these can undermine boys' motivation to explore and develop their gifted abilities. It may actually be tougher for boys than for girls these days to be true to themselves.

Gender Stereotypes

A home or classroom climate that is conducive to optimal development for children of both sexes is one in which parents and educators are aware of the nature of differences between boys and girls, but are also unbiased in their expectations and values. Parents and teachers who realize that it is normal for boys to be delayed relative to girls—in their ability to sit still, for example—will be patient with primary school children (both boys and girls) who are restless, and they will offer plenty of opportunities for them to exercise and explore. They will provide stereotypically girl-friendly activities and resources (such as books and dolls), as well as stereotypically boy-friendly ones (such as trucks and building toys). And they will be equally supportive of choices that children make, whether it is to play in ways consistent with their own gender's usual interests or not. All of this becomes more interesting and difficult at early adolescence, when gender stereotypes are at their strongest.

Cultural Differences

Gifted and talented students come from all cultural, linguistic, and economic backgrounds.

(Castellano, 2003, p. 76)

*Abundant data suggest that gifted programs are the most segre-
gated educational programs in the United States.*

(Dickson, 2003, p. 53)

*Racial inequalities in the identification of gifted students have
been a constant throughout our history, and they persist today.*

(Borland, 2003, p. 116)

In Canada, as in the United States, students from many cultural
minorities are seriously underrepresented in gifted programs, as are students from lower socioeconomic backgrounds. People have been calling
attention to this situation and attempting to address it for decades. In
1950, the U.S. Education Policies Commission described the "tragic
waste of talent" in minority children (Ford, 2003b). Many who have
investigated this issue have identified two underlying problems: (a) too
narrow conceptions of intelligence, and (b) an absence of respect for
multicultural perspectives on intelligence in our schools.

Donna Ford, an expert in the area of diversity and giftedness,
describes American schools as "places of inequity and barriers to talent
development" (2003a, p. 147). She has suggested that there is a "pervasive deficit orientation" (2003b, p. 507), in which group differences are
interpreted as shortcomings of minority group members, rather than as
opportunities to enrich society through embracing diverse ways of being.
Margie Kitano (2003), another expert in the field, describes racism as a
potent force that we should not overlook in our attempts to understand
the underrepresentation in gifted programs of children who are growing
up economically disadvantaged and/or as members of certain minorities.

According to J. J. Gallagher (2000), the very nature of gifted education has been "wavering back and forth" between equity and excellence.
Gallagher writes:

> *The last two decades has seen the pendulum swing strongly
> in the direction of equity as we have become aware of the many
> problems facing young children growing up in poverty and
> social disorganization, and most of our initiatives have been
> designed to use the educational system to counterbalance some
> of the negative social forces. The new millennium is likely to see
> a swing of that pendulum back to more emphasis on excellence
> as we become more and more embedded in the information
> age. It becomes more and more important for bright students*

287

> *to be using their abilities to stimulate this new era with economic and political productivity. But this will not happen if the current 'laissez-faire' approach to gifted students continues into the next decade (p. 691).*

We will now examine ways of supporting gifted-level development in economically disadvantaged and minority children, emphasizing the need to prevent the laissez-faire attitudes described by Gallagher above from eroding our educational systems or compromising provisions of what is fair, possible, enabling, and constructive.

Supporting Gifted Level Development in Poor and Minority Children

> *We must rephrase the persistent question of minority student under-representation in gifted education from "How can we identify more minority students?" to "How can we provide opportunities and rewards for students of all degrees of ability from all backgrounds so that all will realize their full potentials?"*
>
> (Ford, 2003a, p. 156)

> *If we forgo the process of sorting children into "gifted" and "not gifted" groups...large-scale equity problems in education will not disappear. However, the problem of under-representation...would become a moot point, for program placement...would no longer be a concern. Discrepancies in educational achievement would and should, of course, continue to be a concern. However, addressing these as issues of educational achievement instead of gifted or nongifted status strikes us as a slightly, but significantly, more tractable matter for educators.*
>
> (Borland & Wright, 2000, p. 592)

The underrepresentation in gifted programs of certain groups is a thorny problem that has proven highly resistant to change. Many solutions have been proposed, tested, and discarded through the decades since this underrepresentation was targeted as problematic. The Jacob J. Javits Gifted and Talented Students Act, passed by the United States federal legislature in 1988, provided funds to promote research and demonstration grants to increase the inclusion in gifted programming of students in underrepresented populations. The Javits Act includes those from racial minorities, those who are economically disadvantaged, those who have limited English proficiency, and those with other learning exceptionalities. Since the passage of this Act, tens of millions of dollars have been spent addressing issues of access to gifted programs, support for minority learners, and optimal ways to provide appropriate opportunities to learn. There are several interesting perspectives being proposed at the present time.

To begin with, many of the experts who have been working with gifted learners in minority populations recommend comprehensive, multifactored assessment approaches that attempt to discover minority students' strengths, especially when these diverge from mainstream notions of intelligence (Castellano, 2003; Ford, 2003b; Richert, 2003). Another suggestion is to provide those who show promise of being exceptional (in the absence of meeting gifted cut-off criteria) with "pregifted" programs (Aguirre, 2003) that foster their talents and enable successful transitions to gifted programs.

An innovative way to address cultural, racial, and linguistic equity concerns is to turn the question around, as suggested in the above quotes from Borland and Wright (2000) and Ford (2003a, 2003b). Rather than putting our efforts into finding ways to label more minority students as gifted, perhaps we ought to be working to ensure that all children have the kinds of opportunities to learn that research shows lead to gifted developmental outcomes. This approach certainly makes sense within the mastery perspective, since responding to diversity in individual development is the essence of the mastery model. Other recommendations made by those who are experts in diversity issues in gifted education, and that are also consistent with the mastery model of giftedness, focus on the need to provide flexible grouping and choice within a wide range of programming options (Castellano, 2003; Ford, 2003a; Richert, 2003).

A final but important recommendation is to ensure that all teachers receive the professional development opportunities and ongoing support that they need. "If programs for the gifted are to survive, it is essential that we...fund intensive staff development to improve the effectiveness of all teachers in evoking maximum cognitive, emotional, and ethical potential" (Richert, 2003, p. 156).

Our perspective is that the more inclusive and flexible the giftedness policies and practices of a school or school system, the more likely they are to support gifted level development in those students who are disadvantaged in different ways and who are less likely than others to be included in gifted programming. Minority numbers may increase if such an approach is started early in children's lives. Rather than worrying so much about underrepresentation of minority students in gifted programs, then, many of the experts who are working in this field advocate that we put more effort into ensuring high-level outcomes in all learners.

The key is that by opening up a wide a range of options to as many students as possible and working to provide them with opportunities and support for gifted-level development, educators can work to rectify some of the historic inequities in gifted education.

Value Conflicts

"*Patti was one of the brightest students I'd ever had. But her parents wouldn't let her go into the advanced math and science courses because they said that they would take too much of her time. She was needed at home to take care of her younger siblings and do the housework.*"

"*Rafael was exceptionally talented in language arts. He refused to participate in the Advanced Placement courses or in any of the extracurricular arts or drama programs. He said they were for losers and sissies and that only white boys would go there.*"

Even when we succeed at being more inclusive in gifted identification and programming, being gifted or having certain high academic and career ambitions conflicts with some cultural and gender stereotypes. Minority group members may experience internal conflicts between loyalty to their families and cultures on the one hand, and high achievement goals on the other (VanTassel-Baska, 2000). This is a very difficult and unhappy circumstance, and it can lead to a situation in which nobody wins, undermining both individual achievement and family cohesion.

Parents can minimize the impact of problems with conflicting cultural values by being available for open-minded discussions. Informal talks can provide ways for the family to consider together the strengths and weaknesses of the dominant culture in which they live, as well as the family's perspectives, behaviors, and values, especially as these might conflict with their children's possible social, educational, and career goals. If parents are flexible and accommodating in some respects and do not insist on too rigid an attachment to their own culture-related expectations, it can free their children to develop their abilities while simultaneously feeling happily connected to their family and culture of origin.

Teachers sometimes observe their students experiencing conflicts between the family's or culture's values and the school's or mainstream society's values to which they themselves adhere. For example, a family in which no one has ever gone past high school may want the student to follow in the parents' footsteps and work in a family business, while the student may have college and graduate school ambitions. In cases like these, it is very important that the teacher respect the family and cultural value system, even though it might conflict with the teacher's view of the student's best interests. By proactively supporting a student in developing her giftedness in contradiction of her family's values, for example, a teacher is only fueling conflict for the child and putting her in a more difficult position. If such a teacher is successful in encouraging the student to stay connected with her ambitions, it may be at the price of her connection to her family—too high a price, and one that may well not be in the child's best interest. What a teacher can do is to encourage safe and accepting classroom discussions about the various ways people can choose to lead their lives.

Extreme Giftedness

...the problems of social isolation, peer rejection, loneliness and alienation which afflict many extremely gifted children arise not out of their exceptional intellectual abilities but as a result of society's response to them.

(Gross, 1993, p. 188)

"I feel even weirder now. When I entered the gifted program, I thought the other gifted kids would be like me."

"She's too smart. She's only three. She's actually scary!"

"I'm a researcher by nature and profession. Please don't hate me 'cause I'm gifted. That's code for a fiercely intrinsically motivated curious and wandering mind."

As we discuss elsewhere in this book, low intelligence test scores are far more challenging to interpret wisely than are high scores. There are many possible reasons for capable children to perform poorly on standardized tests, but high scores *always* mean that the person being tested is extremely capable at the tasks that have been assessed. We consider now those children who score between 145 and 160 on individual intelligence tests—that is, those who score more than three standard deviations above the population mean. The major intelligence tests have a test ceiling of 160, which is four standard deviations above the mean, and above the 99.99th percentile. Although some tests provide scores higher than this, at the extremes, the individual scores become less and less reliably meaningful. (Please see our discussion of tests and assessments in Chapter 4 and in the Appendix for more on this.)

Although school districts and jurisdictions vary, when giftedness is defined by intelligence tests, it generally refers to those who score two or more standard deviations from the mean—that is, above 130 IQ, or above the 98th or 99th percentile. The major reasons for concern about those who score above 130, or in the top 1% to 2%, relate to: (1) education (educational programming designed for average learners won't meet their learning needs), and (2) social experience (children who are different from others often experience social anxiety and isolation).

For those who are even more exceptional, who score above the 99.9th percentile on intelligence tests, these educational and social concerns may become pressing. Scores above 99.9% suggest that these children are more competent at intellectual tasks than 999 people out of 1000. They are exceptional even within the gifted exceptionality. In terms of their intellectual ability (at least as measured by IQ), they are as much out of step with other gifted learners as gifted learners are from the norm. In a gifted class, such children can feel even more alone and different than they did before, finding that they *still* have to restrain their minds and communication, that the so-called gifted learning opportunities are still nowhere close to meeting their needs, and that neither the other kids nor the teacher understand their thinking unless they "dumb down" their communication. Since adults and other children have no prior experience to draw on, they very often respond with alarm or rejection to children who show truly prodigious intellectual insight or knowledge.

Researchers who have examined the particular difficulties experienced by extremely gifted children have found that the differences in their abilities in different domains is even more pronounced than is true for other gifted learners. According to Winner (1996), more than 95% of highly gifted learners show a strong disparity between mathematical and verbal competencies, and extraordinarily strong mathematical and spatial capability often accompany average or even deficient verbal abilities. Because they are so asynchronous in their development, if they receive "globally gifted" instruction, such children can experience frustration both in their weaker and their stronger subject areas. It is especially important that extremely gifted children be provided with domain-specific learning opportunities adapted to their particular strengths as well as any possible weaknesses.

Extremely gifted children can become socially isolated and dismissive of conventional schooling. They may have difficulties because their social and emotional maturity do not match their intellectual sophistication. They can experience anxiety due to heightened self-expectations, their extremely asynchronous development, and a sense of alienation and differentness which they too frequently interpret as something being wrong with them.

Just as those who work with profoundly retarded learners must tailor their expectations and attitudes, parents and educators of extremely gifted learners must work hard to be sensitive to these children's extreme exceptionality and high-level learning needs. It is important that adults recognize that the minds of these children work differently than their own, and so try to find the right mix of motivators, instructional methods, and learning options. This means allowing them opportunities for content mastery and higher-order thinking, as well as supporting them in finding ways both to relax and to use their high abilities productively. Some strategies to consider include the following:

- Look for mentorships in areas of special interest and ability, and/or opportunities to be a mentor to others.

- Create with the child project-based learning that involves independent guided study on topics of interest. Such projects should be given school credit and should be assigned instead of (not in addition to) other school assignments.

- Support self-directed learning. Encourage children to create their own activities and discover and build upon their interests.

- Provide diverse and flexible learning possibilities, including acceleration; in-school, cross-subject, or cross-grade learning; and extracurricular enrichment activities, such as university-affiliated, community-based, or business-sponsored programs.

- Focus on bolstering areas of relative weakness.

- Facilitate opportunities to develop other skills, such as athletic or leadership abilities.

- Encourage involvement in community, regional, national, and international contests and activities.

- Allow these children the luxury of time and space to explore naturally their area of extreme giftedness.

Because of the degree of their exceptionality, exceptionally gifted learners have highly individualistic schooling needs. In some circumstances, home schooling is the best possible option for a certain time in their lives (see the vignette about Derek in Chapter 7). In other cases, a highly gifted child may go through reasonably normal school pathways until he reaches college and then diverge widely from the norm. In yet other situations, there may be a variety of options tried through the years, from radical acceleration through special projects through contests and extracurricular activities, with some options working better than others and some years going better than others.

Supporting exceptionally gifted children means working to understand and meet their individual developmental needs. As with all the other aspects of giftedness that we address throughout this book, it means seeing these individuals as unique, providing as wide a range of learning options as possible, finding a way to balance their needs for both autonomy and support, and staying responsive to their changing needs over time. There are many books and websites devoted to exceptionally gifted learners. (See our recommended references.)

Learning Problems

Giftedness can exist in many guises.
(Baldwin, Vialle, & Clarke, 2000, p. 570)

In this segment, we discuss a number of issues, including uneven profiles of abilities, learning disabilities, and giftedness as it applies to learning disabilities.

Uneven Profile of Abilities

> *"If Jonathan didn't read until he was six, he's probably not gifted, right?"*
>
> *"Latonia is not at the top of the class, so how could she be gifted?"*

As we note throughout this book, gifted children can vary tremendously in the maturational timing of their development, their degrees and domains of advancement, their learning styles and interests, their test-taking skills, and their social/emotional development. Therefore, it is not at all unusual to find gifted children who have trouble with one or more aspects of schooling, especially among those who show a markedly uneven profile of abilities. And children who function in the normal range or higher in all cognitive or academic areas may show a substantial discrepancy across different academic areas, even though they have no learning problems when compared with age-peers. Their varied academic performance can cause some gifted children to feel frustrated. Rather than exhibiting task commitment, which is a criterion often used in gifted definitions and identification, such children may become so dejected or self-critical that they do little or no work in class or at home.

Children who find learning much easier in some academic areas than others or who do not want to risk failure can develop patterns of avoiding tasks that involve their weaknesses or appear difficult. For example, some children we know have very highly developed reading and verbal reasoning skills but closer-to-average fine motor skills (as in Jeane's vignette about her son Thomas, in Chapter 9). These children find that their thoughts come faster than they are able to write them down, and they are never happy with the way their ideas look on paper. When this ability pattern is combined with an impatient, perfectionistic, or difficult temperament, it can lead to real frustration with writing. Not surprisingly, children with this profile of being very strong in their reading and reasoning strengths but with average or lower fine motor skills tend to hate writing and find ways to avoid tasks that require it. Over time, this can become a serious problem that can undermine their learning and achievement.

It is best if this sort of concern is addressed sooner rather than later. Everyone has areas of strength and weakness, and those who have domains of exceptional advancement are statistically more likely to have large discrepancies across areas. That is, the more exceptional a person is in one area, the more likely she is to experience a wide gap across areas of competency. Learning to deal well with this situation—to enjoy developing the strengths while mastering the challenges—is an important achievement, and one that is essential to high-level accomplishment over time.

There are many ways parents and educators can help children accept their disparities across ability areas. One of the obvious recommendations in the specific discrepancy example we describe above, with the child who is advanced in reading but closer to age-normal in penmanship, is to make sure that he has access to a computer from a very early stage and that he has a chance to acquire effective word processing skills. Another recommendation is to investigate writing programs such as *Callirobics* that help children develop the fine motor and other skills necessary for fluent writing. In cases like this, in which there is no real disability, it is not the discrepancy itself that is the problem, but rather the child's (or parents') reaction to it. If parents and educators address this reaction early and compassionately, they can prevent a discrepancy from becoming a serious academic problem.

Learning Disabilities

> *"She's so bright, but she can't read!"*
> *"The restaurant in our neighborhood bookstore has great treats. We start there, and we end up there, but we read together in between. That's the best part of all!"*

Defining the term "learning disability" (LD) is as contentious as defining the term "gifted," and there is a considerably larger body of work devoted to learning disabilities. Most LD experts are as tentative about the use of the term learning disability as we are about the term gifted. The position we take on the subject of learning disabilities, which is consistent with our approach to giftedness, is that there are naturally occurring variations in all aspects of all children's development, and that to be successful learners, different children need different teaching strategies at different times in their schooling. Just as with the gifted exceptionality, for a variety of reasons, some children have serious learning difficulties if instruction is not adapted to meet their needs.

The majority of learning disabilities concern problems with reading, and current research findings suggest that when children do not have a precise awareness of the sounds in a language (and, as a consequence, are not hearing exactly how spoken language is broken into distinct sounds), they have trouble with reading, writing, and diction. Parents and teachers can devise games and other more structured activities to encourage such children to learn to be more careful in attending to the sounds in the language, to language processing, and to their enunciation. They can use age-appropriate songs, poems, rhymes, and tongue twisters; the reading activities we describe below can also help. Adults can draw the child's attention to the way others speak and sing, pointing out various accents and different characteristics of speech of radio and television announcers or favorite actors in movies. Diction is important for its own sake as an essential communication tool (causing frustration when not easy and clear), and perhaps surprisingly, diction is also closely intertwined with reading and writing skills.

Giftedness and LD (Dual Exceptionalities)

> "Gordie is great at math computations but struggles every time he encounters a word problem."
> "Jin-Lee is six and very advanced in reading, classification and fact retention. However, his motor skills are delayed. What can we do?"

Identifying giftedness becomes very complicated when a child is gifted and has learning disabilities as well, because one exceptionality can mask the other. The child might exhibit her strengths in conversation and extracurricular ways but does not appear to be gifted in her schoolwork. Her teachers might describe her as lazy, tuned-out, or as a disturbance in class, rather than as keenly and effectively engaged in learning. All too often, parents or teachers will suspect or assume that the child is not working hard enough, and they insist that she just try harder, when in fact, she is already trying very hard. The child feels that something is not right but doesn't understand why. She usually blames herself or gets angry with the adults in her life. Quite predictably, she may begin to have emotional or behavioral problems. Not infrequently, the reason for gifted/learning disabled children coming to the attention of school psychological services is because of emotional or behavioral problems, with neither giftedness nor learning disabilities suspected (Silverman, 2003).

Depending on the nature, severity, and extent of the problems that the gifted/learning disabled child is experiencing, as well as how entrenched his sense of frustration or even despair, such a child will not achieve the necessary test cut-off scores to qualify for gifted identification even if he does come to someone's attention for possible giftedness. This is sometimes a problem of psychometrics and test interpretation practices when scores are averaged across several ability areas. As we discuss in the Appendix, when someone scores very high in one area and very low in another, they will appear to be "average" if those scores are combined to yield one composite score such as the IQ. Although all too widely employed, this tactic is clearly ludicrous. Would we say that Magic Johnson was an average athlete because although he was a great basketball player, he couldn't swim or play hockey well? Yet this is exactly what is done when IQ (or some other score that represents a combination of several abilities) is used to identify giftedness. Thankfully, there are indications that increasingly, professionals are paying attention to a breakdown of separate scores, particularly when they are widely discrepant.

There are three common patterns of giftedness as it combines with learning disabilities:

1. *Learning disabilities are masked by the giftedness*; the child is seen as gifted and is able to use her giftedness to compensate for her problems.

2. *Giftedness and learning disabilities mask each other*; the child is seen to be average.

3. *Giftedness is masked by the learning disabilities*; the child appears to have learning problems, while the giftedness is not seen.

Which of these patterns applies to any given child will depend on his personality and coping skills, as well as on the nature and degree both of the giftedness and the learning problems. Sometimes children move across these categories, with the problems getting more apparent as they get older and interfering increasingly with gifted-level functioning. The gifted/LD pattern is almost always characterized by a high level of frustration and unhappiness. It can lead to serious problems with self-esteem, depression, and behavior, often spilling over into other aspects of the child's life and later into adult life. In cases like this, it is critical that an assessment be done sensitively by someone who is experienced in working with children with multiple exceptionalities. It is sad when a learning disability is not discovered until adolescence or adulthood, because early diagnosis means early intervention and help.

A Visual Arts Dilemma

Question:

> *My nephew (age 11) has had reading problems ever since he started school, but at the same time, he's designed his own comic strips of excellent "adult" quality and has created beautiful drawings since he was four or five. Is that normal?*

Our Answer:

> *Pablo Picasso is a famous example of this combination of artistic ability and reading problems. Some people are strong in both reading and drawing, but most of us are at least somewhat discrepant in our reading and drawing abilities, with one area stronger than the other, sometimes dramatically so. In schools, we often designate as learning disabled those individuals like your nephew (and Picasso). But we're less likely to do that with those on the other end of the spectrum, those who are good readers and poor drawers.*

As with all children, but particularly those with extreme patterns of strengths and weaknesses, it is essential that parents and educators emphasize creative and imaginative possibilities and that they encourage the development of individual strengths in as many ways as possible, creating a strong foundation of learning, confidence, and self-esteem:

> *Use...materials rich in ideas and imagination coupled with a focus on higher level skills.... Both self-concept and motivation are in jeopardy if prolonged use of compensatory strategies and basic level materials are used in the educational process of these learners. Challenging content with a focus on ideas and creative opportunities are essential to combat further discrepant performance (VanTassel-Baska, 2000, p. 358).*

When parents and teachers address children's weaknesses in the context of their strengths, learning is far more pleasurable, motivating, and successful. For example, if a child enjoys art, that interest can be used for developing her reading skills. The child can create books, illustrating others' words or her own, if necessary enlisting the aid of someone else (a parent, friend, older child, or teacher) in writing the words or the captions for her pictures, which are collected and assembled in story format. She can dictate the story to a parent or older child and read it back. She can be exposed to beautifully illustrated books for children on topics that she finds interesting. She can be asked to draw, trace, copy, and/or design letters, words, names, and signs. These kinds of activities can be encouraged in the classroom and at home. Dramatic enactments of plays and stories are another way to encourage a child's development of more fluent reading skills.

Becoming a Reader: A Dramatic Change

Nadia was in fifth grade. She had experienced serious reading problems from early in first grade, but with considerable help and effort over several years, she had managed to get over the hump of learning the decoding basics of reading. However, she was not yet fluent in her reading, and she avoided it as much as possible. As might be expected, this was beginning to have a serious impact on her academic marks in all subjects. Because of the emphasis on word problems, she was even declining in her mathematics grades. But she loved drama, which gave her mother an idea.

Nadia's mother helped her daughter create a theater group with a few friends. The children held script workshops once a week, and over a few months, they wrote a play together. They rehearsed, made costumes, found props, and rehearsed some more. After a few more months, in addition to continuing with their script workshops, they started to give occasional performances for family and community members, and later as part of charity events. This drama group was a great success in many ways. Nadia was highly motivated to do well at the script workshops, and over the course of the year, her reading and writing improved tremendously, as did her academic self-confidence. By becoming involved in a reading-intensive activity that she loved doing at a time in her reading development when she could participate actively, she became highly motivated to become a more fluent reader. With the combination of basic skills, scaffolded support along the way, and the right motivational activity, she developed skills and self-confidence that changed her experience of school and herself. She was still a slow reader, but her learning disability was no longer holding her back in the way that it had before.

Trips to bookstores and libraries can be planned as enjoyable and exciting excursions.

Becoming a Reader: A Library Expedition

Stacey's favorite time of the week was Thursdays after school. Her Aunt Lena would come over and they'd go to the library. Stacey used to feel that the library was a stuffy kind of place. "There are too many fat books, and I'll never be able to read them in a million years!" she told us. However, she soon learned that reading could be a wonderful adventure. Each week, on the way to the library, Lena would ask Stacey what topic she wanted to explore, and Stacey always tried to pick something interesting. One time it was sea turtles, another day it was clowns, and on one particularly cold afternoon it was hot chocolate. Lena and Stacey enjoyed the time they spent together researching the chosen topic, reading about it, and making a shared journal entry. Stacey would select a book to take home. It was always her choice, even though Lena would make suggestions.

Stacey's teacher, who was helping her with reading problems, encouraged Stacey to bring her library books to class. Stacey would read a book (or parts of it) over the weekend. Then, on Mondays, she would share bits and pieces with her teacher. In this way, there was a link between reading activities happening inside and outside of school. Stacey was enthusiastic about the learning experiences, felt pleased with herself and her reading progress, and said, "I might get through lots of those fat books after all."

There are many other ways to create pleasurable reading activities, all of which involve the child spending some time with another reader, usually an adult, who is willing to encourage his selections and share reading-related pleasures. Seeing others enjoying books and hearing them talk about their reading with one another encourages a child to further develop a love of reading, which is so important to many kinds of learning. Another idea is to have a child help someone who is younger and whose reading skills are not as well-developed. By helping a younger child with reading, he will consolidate his own skills and learn where some of his own reading problems might lie.

The following strategies can benefit all students but are particularly useful for those with gifted/dual exceptionality learning needs.

Mostly for Parents:

- Cultivate sources of ongoing expert support.

- Create a home "office" or workspace for independent work time.

- Be patient with one-on-one instruction. Embed it into learning opportunities that daily life presents and that the child welcomes.

Mostly for Educators:

- Repeat directions.

- Ask the child to think about what might help her learn.

- Pay attention to the *emotional* and *motivational* aspects of learning.

- Promote and model collaborative activities and idea sharing.

- Teach social cues.

- Demand quality rather than quantity of work.

- Break large tasks into smaller, more manageable ones.

- Monitor progress and give frequent feedback.

- Seek out and underscore success.

- Teach outlining and underlining.

- Model prioritizing.

- Simplify

- Color code.

- Make a game out of things.

- Structure learning activities so that they include previews, reviews, limits, and reminders.

- Take advantage of technological advances.

- Teach memory aid strategies (such as mnemonics).
- Teach test-taking skills.
- Reduce or eliminate timed tests.
- Consider small group or individual mentorships.

For Parents and Educators:

- Make rules and expectations as explicit as possible. Post them in clear view.
- Encourage structure.
- Help the child create strategies of self-reminders. This will help him to develop organizational and time management skills, and to create homework schedules.
- Set boundaries, maintain a predictable schedule, and minimize variance.
- Take charge *kindly.*
- Make frequent eye contact and personal connection.
- Introduce novel concepts and approaches, but don't over-stimulate.
- Incorporate the arts as an outlet for furthering creativity and expression, and as a way of integrating experiences.
- Encourage the child to take pride in his accomplishments.
- Help the child to design "escape valves" by fostering self-awareness and self-modulation.
- Show him how to handle stress, to vent in healthy ways, and to make time to unwind.

You'll see that these strategies take into account the individual's affective and social development, as well as any cognitive issues. It is important to think of the child as functioning within a particular context, and to remember that the best interventions capitalize on all of the available strengths and resources, including those in the home, school, community, and the child herself.

There is not enough room in this book to discuss in detail other exceptionalities that may combine with giftedness. For information about Attention-Deficit/Hyperactivity Disorder, Non-Verbal Learning Disorder, and Asperger's Syndrome, we suggest you check our website (www.beingsmart.ca), where we have listed many resources on these and other learning issues that can complicate giftedness. *Misdiagnosis and Dual Diagnoses of Gifted Children and Adults: ADHD, Bipolar, OCD, Asperger's, Depression, and Other Disorders*, a publication by Webb, Amend, Webb, Goerss, Beljan, and Olenchak (2005), is of particular interest.

As with other kinds of learning problems that we do address within this book, an effective approach for parents and teachers is to develop and use children's strengths and interests as catalysts for strengthening their weaknesses, remembering that there are many, many different ways of being gifted.

Children who are gifted and otherwise exceptional provide wonderful examples of the tremendous diversity in individual developmental pathways. Seen through the lens of the mastery model, we realize that if we attend carefully to their learning needs, they can guide us to flexibly creative ways to understand the nature of and possibilities inherent in learning and teaching.

Children with diverse learning needs, including those with dual exceptionalities, can thrive as productive, happy, and lifelong learners when their parents and educators work together to find and implement the appropriate and necessary supports.

In the next section, we look at the family circle, the educational arena, and the global community. We consider the roles and responsibilities of parents, the importance of teacher education and professional development, and approaches to gifted education around the world, as we examine optimal provisions for gifted children in the context of home, school, and the ever-changing social milieu.

Section V.

Being Smart about Families, Advocates, and Educators

Chapter 14

Parents

Throughout this book, we provide many ideas for optimizing learning experiences for high-ability learners in a variety of circumstances, including assessment situations, classrooms, extracurricular activities, social settings, and families. We revisit some of those ideas here, using a specific set of lenses: the parental perspective.

The Parental Perspective

> *"Teachers keep on telling us they're concerned about Sadie's social skills. However, Sadie has always been quite happy to spend time by herself. She doesn't particularly WANT to fit in with the other girls."*
>
> *"Dane is not doing particularly well in school, and everyone has been on his case about it. But his interests are all outside of school; there isn't really much for him to learn at school, and so long as he is passing, I'm happy—at least for now. He's teaching himself computer programming and how to speak Japanese. I think that's pretty good for a 10-year-old."*
>
> *"I appreciate your advice to seek a mix that keeps Christian happy and challenged, as opposed to maximizing his speed through the educational system."*

How can parents help their children stay appropriately challenged, happily engaged, and confidently secure? We begin this chapter with our "A" list of strategies for parents.

Activities:

- Collect a "bag of tricks" that you replenish on an ongoing basis so that it always contains a fresh surprise or two. It can include books, games, discussion starters, puzzles, puzzle books, art supplies, a writing journal, costumes and props, fun activities, special paints, crafts supplies, ideas for outings and experiments, and so forth for use when your child feels low, bored, anxious, discouraged, or needs time alone.

- Read for your own pleasure and learning. Read with your child. Read to your child.

- Explore sports, the arts, politics, business, whatever looks even a little bit interesting. Try to bring into your child's life activities and people that are as diverse as possible in every way.

- If you enjoy art galleries, libraries, bookstores, museums, concerts, and/or other cultural activities, share your pleasures with your child as often and as deeply as he is interested. Be careful not to overdo!

- Take virtual vacations with your child. Do the research and a plan a trip to a place your family might want to go. What makes travel beneficial is often the spirit of adventure in which it is done, which is very much influenced by parents' attitudes toward the possibilities for learning.

Augmented Learning:

- Cultivate your child's interests and areas of strength. Be creative in finding ways to use them as springboards to other learning.

- Provide ongoing guidance appropriate to your child's questions and interests. When you don't have the answer to a question, try to find the answer. Use whatever resources you can find—a newspaper, dictionary, thesaurus, atlas, or the Internet.

- Demonstrate the value of learning in your own life. In your home, discuss ideas that you hear about and current events, and include your child in the discussion to the extent that she is interested.

Accounting:

- Keep track of the kinds of learning activities that your child enjoys. Encourage his involvement. Take note of how he likes to learn, and share information with others who might benefit from knowing more about your child's learning profile. Keep a log, scrapbook, video, or written journal; any or all can be helpful.

- Encourage your child to keep a record of positive learning experiences and personal accomplishments, and/or create this kind of record together with him. This kind of "rainy day" portfolio encourages habits of self-reflection and can be good on down days, serving as a motivator and self-confidence boost.

Achievement:

- Encourage and help focus realistic expectations of success.

- Reinforce her feelings of accomplishment. Look for opportunities to praise and honor authentic achievements.

- Show faith in your child's ability to do well. A child who senses that her parents have confidence in her is more likely to be confident in herself, and she will be more motivated to take on challenges as a result.

Autonomy:

- Respect your child's need for autonomy. Kids thrive in relaxed settings where they are given a chance to explore, play, and create on their own terms, independently as well as with others.

- As much and as safely possible, respect his desires for independence and privacy.

- Don't work too hard to keep your child busy and engaged in activities that you think are worthwhile; make sure that there is plenty of room for his independence and individuality to grow.

Attitude:

- Listen to your child. *Really* listen. Work together to find ways to overcome problems and concerns.

- Lighten up. Maintain a sense of humor. Don't be overly serious or demanding or critical.

- Be enthusiastic about the things that you do.

- Model perseverance and an ongoing enjoyment of learning and challenge. Model sensible risk-taking.

- Ask questions that matter. (But prioritize first.)

- Advocate on behalf of your child.

Advocacy: Helping Schools Meet Children's Needs

Five ingredients for success…passion, preparation, inspiration, perseverance, and the ability to take advantage of serendipity.
(Delcourt, 2003, p. 27)

"Gifted children are easy targets for spending cutbacks. 'They have so much already, why give them additional perks?' is the position commonly taken by people who don't understand what giftedness is."

An advocate is a person who notices a problem and works to solve it, often on behalf of someone unable to advocate for him- or herself. Learners with special educational needs have always needed advocates. Concerned parents, teachers, and students themselves must be prepared to involve themselves in advocacy roles, especially in the face of changing educational policies, legislation such as the *No Child Left Behind Act*, and funding cutbacks in many schools and jurisdictions.

The Advocacy Process

Advocacy can be compared to bridge building…. Advocates look to the future, nurture relationships, design a new vision.
(Enerson, 2003, p. 38)

Successful advocacy can be thought of as a problem-finding and problem-solving process that is characterized by a commitment to actively listening to all stakeholders. Here are some steps:

1. A potential advocate identifies what she considers to be a problem. She becomes knowledgeable about processes, players, relationships, goals, and commitments.

2. She finds others who share her concerns and begins a discussion and networking process. She facilitates collaboration in identifying and clarifying the important issues, possible solutions, and optimal ways of proceeding.

3. Members of the advocacy group broaden the circle of awareness and fine-tune their perspectives and plans by discussing the issues with others. They gain momentum through recognition, commitment, and compromise. This part of the process works best when it includes all possible stakeholders (particularly those who seem to be opposed to the preferred solutions) and decision-makers. As with Step 2, this is an ongoing, interactive discourse characterized by open and active listening.

4. As concern widens and builds, it generates a growing momentum toward change. This part of the process is actively encouraged and strategically massaged by the advocate(s). They can sustain momentum by publicizing the positive aspects of their movement, saying thank you, and developing sound policies.

5. Action is taken to rectify the problem.

Advocacy can work on many levels, from an individual person providing a student with more appropriate educational programming, to a larger arena—improving the way an entire district or jurisdiction deals with gifted children. In order to be effective, advocacy requires patience, attention, and respect for all participants, including the realization that one can often learn a lot from those who seem to be adversaries.

The first step is information gathering. There will inevitably be many questions to answer. What are the school's or the system's governing rules, principles, and politics? What are the costs of current programs? What are the costs of the proposed changes, and how will they be funded? How will changes be implemented? Who will monitor events? What is the timeline? What are the possible unplanned implications of the change? Parents who are informed are the best advocates for their children.

We have consulted with families in many successful advocacy situations—working with parents to ensure that an individual child's learning needs are well met, with principals to help a school move toward better learning provisions for all gifted students, with gifted consultants to help a board move toward more inclusive giftedness policies and practices, and with parent groups to address needs for system-wide changes. In all successful cases, there was at least one keen, patient, and persistent advocate who had a flexible vision of the way things could be and who was willing and able to become informed, to actively listen to all stakeholders, and to see the advocacy process as a long-term collaborative endeavor.

We have also been involved with attempts at advocacy that have been unsuccessful or counterproductive, leading to a problem getting worse instead of better. Unsuccessful attempts are often characterized by an adversarial or self-righteous attitude on the part of the would-be advocate. One of the biggest challenges for an advocate is to find a way to respect the points of view of those who do not initially see things the way that the advocate sees them. This is important for many reasons. It is only by understanding others' points of view that one can develop a response or a way to present one's own views in a meaningful, targeted, and sophisticated way, and then to communicate this persuasively. If an advocate is successful, it is often those who initially appear to be adversaries who will be in charge of implementing the changes—and who will be able to sabotage them if they disagree. Sometimes those who appear to be enemies later turn out to be our most important friends.

Advocating for Your Child

> *"Sure, I think teachers should use different ways to enhance kids' understanding of concepts and to assess their learning. But how can I actually make this happen in my son's school?"*

The most common advocacy situation that a parent finds himself in is that of working toward change for his own child. We have a number of suggestions for parents who are thinking about advocating for their child:

1. *Become informed about gifted assessment and identification practices in your school or community.* Learn all you can. Parents have the right to know how students are selected for special programming, as well as the findings of any assessments that are done. What tests are used? What criteria determine gifted identification? Who administers the test? What do the results indicate? Were tests results explained to you? To your child? You need to be well informed in order to understand the implications, to explain things to your child, and to participate intelligently in decision-making and advocacy processes.

2. *Learn all you can about available educational opportunities.* Find out about the different possible learning opportunities within your community (as we discussed in Section III). Inquire about core and supplementary programs being offered at your school and in your district. What are the governing administrative policies, programs, and provisions for gifted learners? Is there a special education coordinator with whom you could speak, or a gifted resource specialist who can provide information about the various services available? Is there a parent advocacy group? If not, consider starting one.

3. *Arrange onsite visits.* Make an appointment to visit the targeted or most promising school and talk to the principal. Ask for a tour. Listen. Observe. Be respectfully inquisitive. Are the administrators and teachers at this school interested in and attuned to the needs of their most able learners? Do academic programs appear to be responsive to students' individual profiles of subject-specific abilities, learning styles, and interests? Although it may be difficult to draw conclusions from one or two visits, you can often get a feel for the kinds of learning and thinking activities going on in an educational setting just by being there, looking in the classrooms, and observing the hallways, resource center, gym, and playground. Do the children seem happily engaged and motivated? Does the learning environment seem like a positive place that supports children's emotional and social growth? Are children receiving individualized attention as needed? Do children seem supported? Do staff members look like they are enjoying their work with students?

4. *Investigate other avenues.* If the most promising school does not appear to respond well to gifted educational needs, or you want to see what other options might be available, investigate additional school settings, as identified when you were thinking about suggestion #2. You may be fortunate to find the perfect educational match for your child in the regular program at your neighborhood public school. Or you may discover something else that works for the time being. Or you may decide to become an advocate of more student learning opportunities in your child's current educational setting.

5. *Initiate change if necessary.* If you cannot find a situation that meets your child's learning needs, you may want to consider reviewing the advocacy steps enumerated here and becoming an advocate for some kind of change. Before doing so, think about this step very carefully, because determining what constitutes an educationally sound curriculum or placement for an exceptional learner requires consideration of many complex and dynamic interacting variables.

Parents may advocate for specific changes in different areas, such as programming options or instructional methods. A comprehensive plan is critical to prevent a change from becoming a jump-start to a dead-end. The following guidelines will help:

- Before setting out to advocate for any changes, ascertain that there are specific and recognizable needs to be met.

- Try to define a reasonable target, a sensible timeline, fair tasks and responsibilities, and workable parameters. Then show flexibility.

- Prioritize. You cannot change everything at once.

- Be practical and realistic about what can be coordinated or altered.

- Remember that change is frightening to some who have always done things another way. There will be resistance.

- Because a school community is a complex and interdependent workplace, strive to nurture collaboration, a climate of trust, and mutual respect. Work together with educators to consider ways to establish effective home and school processes and to maintain open communication channels among children, parents, and teachers. Aim for free-flowing dialogue.

- Remember that change is an emotion-laden process. Optimism, pessimism, stress, grandiosity, and confusion are some of the many feelings that may be experienced along the way by those involved; these can interfere with people's willingness to be reasonable, both on the part of those experiencing these feelings and by way of reaction from others. Try to monitor and regulate your own feelings and to be patient with the feelings of others.

● Maintain resolve, and keep working to encourage momentum.

Because change has the potential to upset the status quo, it is usually controversial. To bring about smooth and efficient change, try to ensure that, as much as possible, all people involved (teachers, administrators, parents, and students) feel a part of any proposed implementation process. Those likely to be affected by a change will be more accepting if they are kept informed and given a chance for input along the way. This includes teachers, administrators, other professionals, parents, and students.

A given change will mean different things for different people and thus will have variable impacts on people's responses, concerns, comfort level, and so on. The best change processes include dialogue, clarification of expectations, collaboration, and ongoing monitoring and reflection. Although there are always people ready to criticize unfamiliar approaches, change is likely to be viewed more favorably when all participants are engaged in the process.

Advocating for All Kids

Very often, a parent advocating for one child makes a much bigger difference than she knows. When a teacher becomes better able to meet the special learning needs of one gifted student (usually by being more flexible and responsive in teaching methods), she becomes better able to meet many other students' learning needs as well. If she is an enthusiastic or creative practitioner who happens to be a leader in her school environment, and if the school culture is ready for this kind of change, there can be a subtle or dramatic shift in the way student learning needs are met throughout the school.

Parents can advocate for increased professional development opportunities for teachers that will enable them to better recognize and address the diverse needs of all of their students. Parents can also help to promote and initiate a wider conception of talent development and giftedness within the community by questioning spending cutbacks that might threaten gifted special education options and by tapping into community resources in order to build rich, multi-dimensional, and collaborative learning environments. Many sectors of society, including business, industry, media, professionals, and seniors, can be helpful in extending the range of learning options for children. Parents who are involved with their children's schooling enhance the likelihood of their children's academic engagement and success; teachers who listen to and respect parents' views can find their teaching enriched and their professional satisfaction greatly increased; children who are involved in self-advocacy acquire important skills of reflection, co-operation, negotiation, self-respect, and independence. Administrators may find that they have a more all-encompassing school, one that is increasingly attuned to and respectful of the values of teaching for depth, breadth, and individual learning needs. When working together in a spirit of collaborative advocacy, parents, teachers, students, and administrators can create a better school culture.

We offer some final considerations for would-be-advocates:

- Change is almost always more complex than it appears to be. Successful change depends on the interaction of many variables (the educational setting, teacher commitment, administrative support, parent-teacher collaboration, and children's ability to cope).

- Take the time needed to do your homework. One expert suggests researching your child's learning style, abilities, and educational needs for up to two years before advocating for change (Rogers, 2002). It is not always necessary to spend that long, but do become as well-informed as necessary.

- Think very carefully about focus and relevance. Be sure that your driving principle is to find or create a better fit between your child and the schooling situation. There is nothing to be gained—and considerable time, energy, and goodwill lost—with pointless change.

- Be patient. Change almost always takes longer than anticipated.

- Be considerate and respectful of others, even those who appear to be impeding your well-informed advocacy efforts. Listen respectfully and thoughtfully to others' views and concerns.

From advocacy, we move now to a discussion of supportive parenting, including general caring principles and strategies, sibling relationships, talking to children about their giftedness, and seeking professional help.

Supportive Parenting

Kids who once had childhoods now have curriculums; kids who ought to move with the lunatic energy of youth now move with the high purpose of the worker bee.

(Kluger & Park, 2001, p. 32)

"Some children are handicapped by their giftedness."
"How do I support my daughter? Once your child is labeled gifted, you're walking a different path."

As with any other exceptionality, a child's giftedness affects the whole family. Whether the child's giftedness is celebrated, accepted, and/or resented, it needs to be recognized and reconciled by the whole family. This becomes even more important when the school labels a child as gifted. Responsibility for making good sense of the situation lies primarily with the parents. Over the next few pages, we discuss ways in which parents can support children's gifted development.

There is a common misconception that the best way to foster high-level development is to expose children to sophisticated learning tools, structured educational activities, and more and more lessons and schoolwork. However, a busy and highly structured agenda is not always the best goal. One of the most important supports parents can provide for gifted-level development is to encourage their child's social and emotional development, including a spontaneous enthusiasm for learning that is curiosity-driven. Kids are not learning automatons. People sometimes forget that gifted children are indeed *children* who will be happier and more successful as adults if they experience plentiful opportunities for play and exploration during childhood, and if they have easy, natural opportunities for interaction with adults they respect and trust and by whom they feel loved and respected.

Parents can fan that inner spark that motivates and sustains learning, but it must be done carefully and lovingly, not artificially. Parents should act to safeguard children who become caught up in a world that is too fast-paced, test-oriented, or overwhelming. Children need to be protected from excessive input where learning becomes a stress-filled duty rather than a joy.

Many parents wonder how to support their gifted children's needs to learn, to be stimulated, and to be appropriately challenged without being too demanding or controlling and without losing the easy acceptance that their children also need from them. Well-intentioned parents can become frustrated and disconnected from their children and caught up in a web of failed expectations and misunderstandings, or instead, they can take the same strands of challenges, strengths, and opportunities and weave with their children a facilitative circle of trust, appreciation, and understanding.

Top Ten Strategies

The following ideas echo approaches that we discuss elsewhere in this book, many of which pertain to specific issues or concerns, but all of which bear repeating in the context of thinking about supportive parenting:

1. **Listening.** Listen attentively and actively to your child. Respect your child's feelings.

2. **Perspective.** A sense of humor goes a long way in parenting, as in life. It is very important to maintain a healthy perspective on the ups and downs of daily life and our children's experiences, as well as our own.

3. **Attunement.** Stay attuned to your child's world. Pay attention to the various factors that might be affecting his emotional, social, behavioral and/or academic functioning.

4. **Clarification.** Clarify everyone's expectations—your own, your child's, the school's, and others,' such as extended family members.' Are the various demands being placed on the child well-defined, fair, and flexible? If not, think together about ways to improve matters.

5. **Information.** Seek information about high-level development. Pay close attention to sources that provide insight into the particular kinds of support that your child requires.

6. **Exploration.** Expose your child to a wide range of extracurricular opportunities for play, exploration, and learning in response to his individual abilities, interests, and needs.

7. **Consultation.** Consult with professionals and other parents to explore possibilities such as alternative learning opportunities in your child's school, within the community, and beyond.

8. **Advocacy.** When necessary, advocate for appropriate learning options that will suit your child's individual needs and levels of advancement in different areas.

9. **Co-operation.** Work with educators, other parents, and members of the community to create as rich and engaging a learning environment as possible for your child and others.

10. **Awareness of Special Needs.** Be aware of your child's special needs, whether these relate to gender, ethnicity, disability, or specific talents or abilities, and be prepared to offer support.

While all of these perspectives are important, parents should also realize that they can best strengthen a child's learning spirit and help sustain her drive to mastery by respecting her choices, nurturing her independence, and allowing that sometimes the most valuable learning of all is that which happens serendipitously through the many experiences of daily life with friends, neighbors, classmates, and family members.

More Strategies

> *"I found this website…. I just kept wandering through it. I found an article written by a mother of gifted children, and I was sitting there crying away, going 'I know! I know!'"*

Becoming well-informed is key. Although there are many possible sources of information about gifted development and education, it is not always easy to distinguish material that is good from material that might be inaccurate, overly simplified, or even misleading. There are probably more questionable or bad resources and websites than good ones. On our *Being Smart* site (www.beingsmart.ca), we list resources which we have found to be most useful, and we encourage interactive updating of our information by informed readers. We offer here a few suggestions for becoming discerning about resource access.

Whenever you visit a website where books are sold, look for titles and descriptions that are appealing, and see if it is possible to see "inside" the book or read excerpts from it. A table of contents can help you decide what it is that you really want to learn more about. Some online book-sellers assign ratings, offer reviews, or suggest other books on similar or parallel topics.

Sometimes you can find online lists of books recommended by organizations (for example, the Association for Bright Children [ABC] in Canada, or the National Association for Gifted Children [NAGC] in the United States). Lists that are organized in some way can be helpful, such as books written with parents of gifted students in mind, texts written for teachers and professionals, material dealing with specific aspects of giftedness and talent, and so on. You might find books that explore different aspects of giftedness; gender-, age-, or culture-specific material; and program ideas designed to supplement classroom instruction. Articles in journals and periodicals can be good sources of current information. Many publications run articles on a variety of gifted-related topics such as educational programming, gender issues, developmental phases, at-risk students, school reform, and so on. Sometimes an entire issue is devoted to one specific theme which is considered in depth. You can subscribe to these different publications or find them at university libraries, or you may be able to borrow them from the education office within your school district. They are not just for teachers! (We note some journals and how to access them on our website.)

Indexes and articles in gifted education journals can also be downloaded from the web. You can request individual back issues or mailings of specific articles (usually for a small fee), and you can sometimes order a trial subscription to a publication of choice. Although the publications we note deal specifically with giftedness, there are many other professional journals (educational, psychological, sociological, and others) which sometimes address gifted children or gifted education concerns. If you find an article worthwhile, you might also want to check into some of the sources it lists at the end.

The use of electronic mail to contact experts in the field can also be invaluable as a source of discourse, support, and stimulation. The addresses we provide on our website are only a small sampling, but they are starting points for surfing the Net in support of young and adolescent learners. Due to the dynamic immediacy of online communication networks, websites are frequently in a state of flux and revision. Keep checking for current information. You may find announcements about regional or national contests, updated booklists for avid readers, and so on.

In addition to the targeted gifted education sources, there are many novels and movies with gifted protagonists or about children with exceptional abilities. For example, a movie may highlight an approach to education that supports autonomy and encourages engagement. A library or bookstore with a well-planned and well-staffed children's department is often an ideal place to find these kinds of books and movie references. Librarians, counselors, and teachers may also have material to suggest.

It is time now to consider the family as a whole and to look at sibling relationships in families where there are one or more gifted learners.

Sibling Relationships

One Gifted, Another Not

> *"My brother was a math whiz. When we were growing up, my parents said they couldn't afford summer camp for me, but somehow they could always afford special trips and contests and all kinds of activities for him."*

> *"My dad was never too busy to do stuff with me. He used to love quizzing me, and we'd have long philosophical discussions. It made me feel sort of embarrassed, though, because it was obvious that he thought I was more interesting than my sister."*

> *"My sister is the smart one I guess, and I'm just average. She was identified as gifted, but when I took the gifted test, they said I didn't quite make it."*

When one child is identified as gifted and another is not, what are the implications for the family? Just as in families in which only one of the children is an accomplished athlete, the unlabeled siblings often resent the implication that they are less capable, and they may feel a need to prove their worth, sometimes by challenging the ability or worth of the designated gifted one(s) in the family, and sometimes by choosing another domain of achievement for themselves. An unlabeled sibling of a child designated as gifted can feel incompetent or stupid, even though he may be highly capable himself.

Some parents take giftedness far too seriously and give it more weight than it deserves. Although this is a problem regardless of the family makeup, it becomes a much bigger problem in a family where not all siblings are labeled gifted. *Yes*, it is important to recognize and address exceptionality where it occurs, but *no*, a child who scores above a certain IQ is not more deserving of parental time and other family resources than her lower-scoring siblings.

Emotional and behavioral problems can be expected when one sibling is given more recognition, special opportunities, or attention than another. This is true whether it is the child who has been labeled gifted or the non-labeled child. In some cases, parents work so hard to equalize the situation and make sure that the child who is not labeled as gifted feels good about himself that they inadvertently foster insecurities and self-doubts in the child who is labeled as gifted. In these instances, children who are identified as gifted may experience negative effects and may even wonder whether they are somehow imposters in their gifted designation.

Julie Stoyka, a teacher candidate in one of our preservice programs, studied the long-term effects of gifted labeling on a set of fraternal triplets, one of whom was not labeled as gifted. At the time of their interview, the sisters were 31 years old. In a short paper entitled "Triple Threat," Julie transcribes thoughts as conveyed independently by the triplets she calls "April, May, and June," and she shares her own reflections, as well.

Triple Threat

April: I remember that two out of three of us were told, "You are going into a special program." It was a big deal for my family. I was excited. I think was proud—I was one of those kids who liked to do well in school. But there was a torn feeling in my family of should we do it, should we not do it, because of what it would indicate to my other sister if we went into a gifted program and she didn't. In the end, I remember we had to do things right—treat the individual, rather than think of ourselves as a group. So I remember it being a pretty complicated decision at my house.

May: She always reveled in being different, so she took it as a positive—like "I'm different than you guys"—and purposely made sure she seemed different than us and tried to make us feel that she was better than us. And she tried to find other ways to be superior in school.

June: I was the only one who wasn't smart. Now I can say that I have a more positive view of it, but it was really hard. Especially because we all went to the same school, and we had a lot of the same friends. So I think, for me, it came up a lot more as an issue. It took me a lot longer to do my work, and I sometimes felt that everyone else was feeling sorry for me. So I started doing different things.

Julie writes: There are some important findings from these comments and others made by the sisters. First, June claims to now view the experience in a more positive light. Secondly, all three sisters make reference to being "different" or being individuals. Third, June managed the experience. Fourth, they all got along then, and cohesiveness has prevailed over the years. Although June did have some negative feelings, she chose to overcome them. When June was diagnosed with a learning disability in high school, everything seemed to fall into place. "I suddenly realized that it was my learning disability that was holding me back, not that I was stupid," she recalls. June then made what she feels was a tough decision: she chose to go to a different university than her sisters. Free of her gifted sisters and labels, she finally began to achieve academically.

Interestingly, April also speaks now from the perspective of having acquired teaching experience. As an educator, she believes that in gifted programs, "Too much recognition is placed on the fact that you're good at school. I don't know how to surpass that, but I think it's about getting involved in things that are bigger than school. I think it's true—a lot of people are good at school, but they're not good at putting it all together. So emphasis on life skills, communication skills, presentation skills, thinking skills, entrepreneurial skills is more important than the marks."

This is where parental encouragement and support is very important! Parents have a lot to do with reinforcing and maintaining a strong and healthy family dynamic.

All three of the sisters I interviewed are happy, stable women with at least one undergraduate degree, wonderful home lives, and fulfilling careers. They are close with each other and the other members of their families. Over all, they feel good about their past and current relationships with their triplet siblings.

Having known these women for nearly 25 years, I have watched each woman grow as an individual. Each has forged a separate identity for herself, and today, all three excel in different areas, regardless of whether they were labeled gifted or not. As adults, they all have independent interests and pursue different activities. And yet, while all three proudly proclaim their individuality, they are extremely proud of being part of a warm, loving, and supportive family group, and they refer to themselves as the "triple threat."

Parents who create a happy and healthy home environment where each child feels loved and valued will reduce the likelihood of short- or long-term problems from destructive sibling comparison and rivalry. There are many things to consider. Here are some sibling-related strategies for parents of gifted and non-identified gifted children:

- Look for ways to be explicit in valuing each child's strengths and abilities.

- Help children to know and appreciate their own unique strengths and areas of weakness.

- Avoid comparing children.

- Provide each child with opportunities for learning that are consistent with her interests and abilities.

- Look for activities for each child that will allow her to shine. Each child needs her own area of special competence.

- Don't allow the pursuits of one child to take precedence over another's or to consistently disrupt family leisure time.

- Try to disassociate the gifted label from the child.

- Be sensitive to the stressors that the gifted child and her non-labeled sibling(s) experience due to the gifted exceptionality.

- Be alert to signs of a child feeling inferior or superior relative to her siblings.

- Consider family counseling if necessary.

Environmental Response Differences

> *"When they were little, Josie needed me to be a traditional mother, making rules and enforcing them consistently and dependably. It was important for Diana, though, that I give her some leeway and bend the rules from time to time."*
>
> *"Maleke welcomes almost any change as an adventure, an opportunity for learning and exploration. My other two need lots of preparation and advance warning."*

With both adults and children, even when they are all members of the same family living in the same household, people respond very differently to the same environments. Siblings do not react in the same ways to parental pressures to perform or to other aspects of home life or parenting style. Factors influencing children's response include birth order, birth spacing, sex, identification with one parent or the other, perception of their parents' treatment of them relative to their siblings, personality, interests, ability, and temperament. Parenting approaches that work well with one child do not necessarily work well with another, and although it is important to try very hard to be fair, it is sometimes essential to treat children differently than each other independently of their intellectual ability.

The important factor that must be consistent for all children is that their parents provide support in the form of love, nurturing, respect, a variety of stimulating learning experiences, and encouragement for responsible independence. How all of this is provided may well vary across individual children in the same family. When parents manage to do a good enough job with each of these factors, their children tend to move in very different directions, each thriving in distinctly individual and self-fulfilling ways.

Differences of Opinion

How siblings relate to each other also varies from one family to the next, as well as among sibling pairs within the same family. Consider, for example, those children trying to keep pace with an older brother or sister, or kids who are not as confident of their abilities as their sibling might be, or youngsters who feel under-appreciated in light of the accomplishments of a brother or sister, regardless of gifted identification status. It can be very difficult to stand by while someone else receives accolades, special learning opportunities, or extra parental attention. Parents should try to ensure that *each* child has opportunities to extend her learning reach, regardless of how far that might extend.

Consider the following reflection, submitted by Laressa Rudyk, a gifted sibling.

On Being a Gifted Sister

I was identified as gifted in Grade 4, but my sister Taryn, who is exactly one year older than me, was not identified as gifted.

Upon reading a case study one day, I remembered with worry and guilt a conversation Taryn and I had three years ago, during which she said, "Nobody understands how hard it was to have a sister like you." I recalled my extreme sensitivity to Taryn's feelings when we were kids. I remember deliberately "dumbing down" my abilities as early as age five in front of our parents to protect her feelings. Our father was particularly insensitive and treated my sister and me differently. Our mother, a psychologist, was very aware that I was scared of hurting Taryn's feelings, and we discussed it in private regularly.

Taryn and I have the same birthday, exactly one year apart. On my fifth birthday and her sixth, our father gave each of us a book: hers was Cinderella and mine was a Mensa puzzle book. When Taryn saw my book, she started crying, dropped her book, and ran out of the room. I guiltily dropped my book, picked up her book, and went after her. Ever since, our father has given us exactly the same thing for our birthdays, probably at my mother's insistence.

On my tenth birthday and Taryn's eleventh, our father made us a birthday cake and put the numbers 10 and 11 on the cake. In binary. He put the cake down in front of us and told us to try to figure out what the candles represented. I recognized the numbers immediately but pretended that I didn't. He eventually said to me, "Come on. It's binary. You know that." Last week, I asked Taryn if she remembered the binary birthday cake incident. She most certainly did. "It was so mean to put the candles on our cake in binary when he knew that I didn't know binary. I asked him to explain it and he just waved me off, telling me not to worry about it. That was pretty awful because it was supposed to be my cake, too."

Of course, conflict happens from time to time within all families. Although it is difficult for many people to handle conflict happily and well, there is considerable research evidence suggesting that in fact, conflict is an important part of a healthy family dynamic (Steinberg, 2004). Children need to learn the skills involved in conflict resolution, and they need examples, guidance, and instruction in order to find ways to settle things constructively, responsibly, and creatively. Adults who can express their opinions honestly and well, and can disagree with others productively and respectfully, have assets that are valuable in personal and professional relationships. These skills are best acquired in a safe and loving environment, and the family circle is the best of all places to learn conflict resolution skills.

A good way to reduce unnecessary friction among siblings is for parents to help their children to offer support to and learn from one another. Each child can learn to contribute to the family dynamic, buoy up the others' weaknesses, demonstrate his own strengths, share in achievements, and celebrate each family member's successes as a shared success. Parents can model this behavior for their children. Although differences of opinion can be expected and should be considered healthy, the overall family climate should be one of fostering, not festering—one of warmth and generosity to each other, not one of ill-will. When there are giftedness-related issues or changes, or if there are emotional, social, or academic implications that demand attention, or if family dynamics become chronically strained, then supportive parenting strategies become particularly important. We discuss some specific areas of focus below.

Talking to Children

Life has a way of confusing us, blessing and bruising us....
(Lyrics from *L'Chaim, Fiddler on the Roof*)

Discussing a child's giftedness with the child is important and somewhat tricky. Such a conversation should be handled carefully and thoughtfully, with the emphasis on giftedness or high cognitive ability as a difference from others, but not a superiority to others. It helps if parents see giftedness as a different way of thinking and processing with associated differences in learning needs, just as with a child with a learning problem of one sort or another. It becomes a necessary conversation to have when the child herself is officially labeled gifted, is feeling different or odd somehow, or is having trouble with social interactions.

Rosa's Question

Parent:

> *Should we tell our child that he is gifted? I am sure that my son knows—he certainly feels different—but we don't know whether or not to talk about it. If so, how do you suggest we broach the topic?*

Our Response:

> *It sounds like it would be a good idea for you to discuss with your child how his mind works differently than most other kids' minds. You might say something like this: "You will find that there are lots of things that you learn more easily and more quickly than others. That doesn't mean you necessarily learn it better or that you don't have to work to learn things, but that you've got some advantages in some situations. Other kids have other kinds of strengths."*

If everything is going well and there is no need for any kind of official labeling process at school, there may be no need to have this kind of conversation, although it is still important that parents remain alert to the possibility that it may arise at some point.

Gifted Adolescents

> *"She knows just what buttons to push and is so bright conceptually. It's difficult to argue with her."*
> *"He pretends to listen, and then he goes and does what he wants."*
> *"I can't help but wonder if I was like that when I was a teenager."*

Parents of teenagers often experience a troubling conflict between providing enough support on the one hand, and enough independence and autonomy on the other. Highly capable teens can be particularly hard to parent because they are often able to argue unusually effectively for privileges that they are not emotionally ready to handle, and they can usually find their parents' hot buttons and guilt triggers, or use other effective parent-manipulation techniques. They can challenge all of the rules, including ones that parents learn from friends, family, and the commonly held beliefs of their culture. As we discussed in Chapter 12, it often helps parents if they remind themselves that many of those who go on to do the most interesting things with their lives do not have an adolescence in which they sail perfectly smoothly through the various academic and social passages.

Once a child becomes a teenager, grades are out of the parents' control. Very often, the best way for a parent to encourage a gifted adolescent's academic progress is (somewhat paradoxically) to let go of his emotional attachment to his child's academic success, realizing that a high level of education is not required in order to make a good life, and letting the child come to realize, deeply, that any decision to succeed is his own.

Although it is quite normal to have high educational and career ambitions for intellectually capable children and to want to enjoy children's successes vicariously, parents do their best adolescent parenting when they learn to focus instead on the teenager's human development and on the skills and interests that the teen considers important, whether in school or outside of school. For parents of highly capable learners, this means learning to let go of their own personal wishes for the child and their own investment in their children's academic and career ambitions. That step is necessary for the child to connect with her own ambitions and to find her own interests and motivation to succeed, so that she feels that her successes are her own. This "letting go" is very often a real challenge for parents of highly capable learners, who may have hopes that the child will become a doctor or scientist, while the child dreams of joining a rock band.

Sometimes gifted children experience problems that cannot be solved, even with the best parenting strategies and support mechanisms. In cases like this, it is wise for parents to consider seeking professional help, at the same time understanding that this does not mean that they are not good parents. On the contrary, seeking help when it is needed reflects their awareness that sometimes, just as with medical exceptionalities, an expert is required to help parents figure out the best way to proceed in supporting their children's development.

Seeking Professional Help

Grant me the serenity to accept the things I cannot change, the courage to change the things I can, and the wisdom to know the difference.

(Serenity prayer)

Wise professional guidance can help parents figure out the difference between those qualities in their children that they should accept or even cherish as assets and those that they should address and work to change. Parents may, at times, know what needs changing but require advice as to how to do it. Just as very few of us have the expertise required to set our child's broken bone, or even to know that a bone is actually broken, very few parents have the training in child development and exceptionality that is sometimes required to make it happily through a gifted child's growing up years without some professional help from time to time. Unfortunately, finding the right person at the right time can present a problem.

Who to Consult?

"Are there people who specialize in counseling gifted kids? If so, how does one find them?"

Yes, there are people who specialize in working with gifted children and their families and/or teachers. In fact, that is exactly what both of us, the authors of this book, do. The best way to find the required experts in the field is through the networking ideas we discuss elsewhere in this book. People have found us through contacts that they have made at organizations such as the Association for Bright Children and the National Association for Gifted Children, or by asking other parents, or by talking to educators and doctors. Sometimes they have found us through Internet searches and by tuning in to other parents' referrals in online chat rooms. Sometimes they have made a call to places where we work (for example, a school board or university) and have been referred to us. Usually they tell us that they have heard about us from two or more sources. Additional tips for selecting a counselor or therapist for a gifted child are provided by James Webb (2004) at www.giftedbooks.com.

There are many possible avenues of professional help, depending on the nature of the problem a family is experiencing. When fees are involved, they vary considerably with kinds of expertise. Coverage by health plans is also variable. Availability of professionals differs markedly from one community to another. In general, as one would expect, the more specialized and exceptional the situation (for example, the highly gifted child with emotional problems at adolescence), the more likely it is that appropriate specialists will be found only in larger urban areas.

If the problem is one of specialized tutoring or of educational advocacy, parents can contact an educational consultant who has experience working with gifted learners. This person might be an educator or a retired teacher with a master's degree in special education. Alternatively, it might be a psychoeducational consultant with a master's degree or doctorate in some aspect of educational psychology or special education, working either within or outside of the child's school system. Ideally, it is someone with training and advanced understanding of giftedness issues and a successful track record in dealing with them.

If the problem requires a psychoeducational assessment, the best consultant is usually a psychologist with training and experience in giftedness, or a psychoeducational consultant (someone with both educational and psychological training, as well as expertise in assessment). This kind of professional should have a doctorate in psychology or education. If it is simply a matter of having a test administered and the scores transferred to a report for the purpose of meeting gifted identification criteria, the services of a psychometrist may be sufficient. This is someone with a master's level certification in test administration, but not in interpretation or synthesis of findings.

In situations requiring counseling help for family dynamics or emotional issues, there are counselors with master's degrees or doctorates in counseling psychology or social work who have training and expertise in working with high-ability learners. When there are serious emotional or psychological problems, a psychiatrist with expertise working with giftedness may be the right professional to consult. Psychiatrists are medical doctors specializing in psychiatry and can prescribe medication if needed.

With such a wide range of possibilities, in combination with a real scarcity of gifted specialists in each category, it is no wonder that so many parents find it daunting to figure out whom to turn to. However, by finding one professional with some expertise in working with giftedness, you have a very good chance of tapping into a larger local network. At the very least, if you discuss your concerns with one of these professionals, you should be able to get a better sense of what kind of help you do need, and you can obtain ideas about where to look for a more appropriate referral, if necessary. In fact, about half of the parents who call us, after discussing their situation with us: (a) have a plan for proceeding without further help, (b) have decided to postpone action for the time being, or (c) have names of other professionals to consult. Parents who read this book and who increase their knowledge on giftedness issues and act upon some of the suggestions we provide here are in a good position to make sense of their child's exceptionality and thereby prevent some of the problems that parents of gifted learners often experience.

When to Consult?

Many of the parents who consult us about their gifted children are feeling a mixture of confusion and uncertainty. The parent who sent us this request in the vignette below is representative of some of those who get in touch with us.

A Parent's Request for Help

Luke's reading is coming along slowly; he is showing no great interest in the activity. This would not concern us very much at this point, except that the school has made it abundantly clear that acceleration is impossible unless Luke's reading and writing skills keep pace with his math and reasoning skills. I must admit that, at times, I wonder whether Luke's learning ability is as advanced as the assessment results seem to indicate. However, I'm concerned because most of the literature that I've read suggests that Luke is likely to encounter difficulties if the school does not respond more appropriately to his needs.

Also, we have sought the assistance of a psychiatrist because of Luke's argumentativeness. Things seem to be improving, but my husband and I wonder whether boredom at home and at school contribute, in part, to his acting out. Would it be helpful for Darren and me to meet with you once again before Luke's spring identification, placement, and review committee (IPRC) meeting? When we met with the principal, the special education resource teacher, and Luke's teacher last December, the school administration clearly stated that neither acceleration nor out-of-level instruction would be considered. I am concerned that Luke's academic needs will not be adequately addressed at the IPRC. Would it be possible for you to contribute your opinions and interpretation of his assessment results to the hearing? I fear that we'll need an advocate!

This message illustrates the confusion and concern that many parents feel as they try to navigate their way through the circumstances of a gifted child's childhood. In this case, one of us had previously done a psychoeducational assessment, in which Luke had scored exceptionally well on an intelligence test and extremely well on mathematics achievement tests, but had scored in the average range in both reading and writing. We responded to this parent's message by affirming the school's current position on full acceleration, pointing out that it is quite reasonable and sensible not to do a whole-grade acceleration at this time. We wrote, "If Luke isn't reading and writing at least at a moderately high level in the grade into which he would be going, we would not be helping him by accelerating him there."

We affirmed the concerns about Luke running into difficulties if his giftedness needs were not met, while at the same time cautioning a need for a balanced perspective, saying." Not all children whose learning needs are not well met at school have problems." We also agreed with the parents about the importance of working with the school to make sure that their son's gifted needs were addressed, and we set up a meeting to discuss ways to facilitate that.

Luke's vignette illustrates a situation when it is a good idea for parents to consult experts. His parents had some concerns about his development in a number of areas, including problems with boredom, anger management, and argumentativeness, as well as his exceptional educational needs. They understood that the social/emotional and giftedness needs might be interacting and reinforcing each other, and they had chosen to try to combat them both at the same time. They were seeing a counselor for the social/emotional needs, in this case a psychiatrist, and they were consulting us for help with educational planning. Other parents in similarly complex situations may choose to tackle one problem at a time (and in fact, this would be our usual recommendation), in the hope that as one problem area is solved, others will diminish. In many cases, once a child's learning needs are being well met, his argumentativeness (or boredom, or frustration, or other problematic behavior) does in fact diminish. In more serious cases, however, it can be a good idea to address several issues simultaneously, as this family was doing.

As with everything else we discuss here, giftedness is truly an individual developmental differences phenomenon. Each story is unique, and therefore each situation must be looked at in its own context. The simplest answer to the question of when or why to look for professional help is to try to pay attention to the child's development and to seek help when things aren't going as well as you would like.

When families have to deal with exceptional circumstances such as parenting a gifted child, they often find that "common sense" parenting approaches fail them. They discover that what they read about child development, what their friends and family tell them about parenting, and what educators recommend they do based on experiences with other children and adolescents do not apply very well to their particular situations. Often, they just need some help understanding the exceptional developmental needs of their children. Sometimes they really only require some reassurance that their sense of the situation is right and that they do know how to proceed with the current and the next stage of parenting.

Consulting with a giftedness expert can mean having one's parenting instincts confirmed and finding support, strategic approaches, and guidance for responding to the unique challenges a child presents. In some cases, families need targeted professional assistance in sorting things out, and a consideration of the various aspects that we address here can be helpful.

Being Pre-emptive

One of the problems with seeking professional help is that we risk pathologizing a situation that is not pathological; we risk making the child feel that there is something wrong with her when in reality, the problem is that everything is "exceptionally right." Depending on the circumstances, there are ways to provide counseling help that will not make the child feel that she is somehow deficient. Many experts on giftedness recommend that educators and parents pay routine pre-emptive attention to gifted learners' possible counseling needs. For example, small group and individual counseling mentorships and consultations can provide close attention to affective as well as cognitive development. Similarly, a focus on the arts can be used "as a therapeutic intervention as well as a creative and expressive outlet" (VanTassel-Baska, 2000, p. 358).

The routine provision of career counseling is another recommendation that is often made for gifted learners. This can provide a forum for self-discovery and the opening up of possibilities for an exceptional adolescent. If this is not offered at a child's school, parents might consider looking for outside assistance.

Parents might want to talk to a giftedness expert when they have concerns that their child is unhappy, may not be learning at the level he is capable of, is hiding his giftedness, is being singled out as a behavior problem for acts of mischief or boredom, or is not making good academic or career decisions. Just as there are medical specialists available to deal with specific physical problems, parents can take comfort in knowing that there are professionals who can help them sort things out if they run into trouble with parenting their exceptional children.

In the next chapter, we consider some broader educational applications of the many and varied concepts that we have explored thus far. In particular, we look at teacher training and development. We consider ways that teachers can be encouraged to engage in professional growth in support of high-level learners and to adopt an adaptive instruction approach consistent with the mastery model.

Chapter 15

Teacher Development

I've come to a frightening conclusion that I am the decisive element in the classroom. It's my personal approach that creates the climate. It's my daily mood that makes the weather.... I can humiliate or humor, hurt or heal. In all situations, it is my response that decides whether a crisis will be escalated or de-escalated and a child human-ized, or dehumanized.

(Haim Ginott, from a poster)

Without exception, there is a need for training of teachers globally which in turn will prepare them to recognize and meet the needs of children from all cultures who exhibit gifted attributes.

(Baldwin, Vialle, & Clarke, 2000, p. 571)

"I need more in the way of practical ideas and strategies to help these kids learn and enjoy the learning experience."

Because gifted learners are as diverse in their talents and abilities as are other learners, teachers of gifted students need access to a wide range of possible educational options. No one gifted option will serve all high-ability children within a given classroom, much less within a whole school.

If teachers are to facilitate both the challenge and support required to meet diversely exceptional gifted learning needs, they need support them-selves, as well as readily available diverse learning options.

Where teachers are provided with the necessary training and sup-port for this kind of individualized attention, they are able to create a climate of authentic inquiry-based learning for all students, including those who are gifted. Unfortunately, the vast majority of teachers have *not* received special training in gifted education. In this chapter, we discuss what is necessary in teacher education, teacher development formats, ways of sustaining teachers' interest in learning and teaching, and gifted consultancy (including our own dynamic scaffolding model).

Teacher Development

> *"Teachers are not properly prepared to teach the range of kids identified as gifted."*
>
> *"I feel that gifted children are all expected to be the same as normal children, only smarter, when clearly through my experience they aren't, and the sooner this is realized by teachers and school administrators, the better it will be for the children."*
>
> *"Children are languishing in programs that just don't work for them because there is nothing else available."*

Most teacher educators acknowledge that one of the weaknesses in teacher development programs is teachers' preparation for working with special needs learners, including those who are gifted. Teacher candidates are expected first to learn all of the tasks associated with teaching their "regular" students, including the basics of child development, basics of pedagogy, classroom management, and planning and implementing instruction. It is only as they move along in their careers that teachers are encouraged to acquire some additional qualifications, including training in special education.

When a new teacher arrives in her first classroom, the problem with this approach is immediately apparent. In most classrooms, there are several students who are different from the norm. In addition to confronting issues of classroom organization and management, a teacher without any special education training or support has to spend a lot of time dealing with curriculum adaptations for children who are unable to handle normal grade-level expectations. Addressing the diversity of learners in a classroom requires considerable know-how, even for experienced educators. Moreover, because the needs of students with learning difficulties are often so much more evident to the teacher, it is not surprising that in many cases, gifted students' special learning needs are not only not *met*, they are not even *recognized*.

Unfortunately, and contrary to most people's perceptions, the situation is not much different than this for teachers who teach in gifted programs. In most jurisdictions, teachers of gifted students have very little training other than one or two introductory courses on giftedness. There is little theoretical understanding of exceptional development and only very limited training for adapting curriculum to meet the exceptional learning needs of the students with whom they are working. There is a prevailing sense that it is possible to create a gifted curriculum that will work well for all gifted learners, an idea which wrongly assumes that gifted learners are alike in their learning needs. Most teachers in gifted programs find themselves working alone or perhaps with one or two colleagues to invent a curriculum, with little or no training or support. As a result, there are tremendous variations in what is offered to students in gifted programs. Programming varies from an extra burden of age-normal work, with no time or attention paid to divergent thinking or to students' abilities and interests, to a laissez-faire emphasis on "creativity," with little in the way of content mastery and higher-order thinking.

We've spoken with many teachers about what they need in order to feel more competent in their work with gifted learners, and their perceptions closely match our own observations. We have organized their ideas into four separate modules.

1. **Assessment Information and Support**

   - help with assessment report interpretation

   - help with application of assessment results to classroom practice

   - professional support in understanding children's individual learning profiles and their relationship to learning, achievement, and alternative evaluation techniques

2. **Curriculum Information and Support**

   - better understanding of the flexibility in official curriculum guidelines; for example, how much leeway from the mandated curriculum is a teacher allowed when working with gifted learners?

   - practical strategies for program design and implementation

- programming modifications for individual and developmental diversity
- diverse placement options
- community-based learning options

3. Areas of Specific Concern for Information and Training

- motivation to learn
- creativity
- higher-order thinking skills
- gender issues
- emotional, social, academic, cultural, and developmental implications of giftedness
- study skills and work habits
- classroom management techniques
- cognitive/developmental issues

4. Ongoing High-Level Professional Development

- opportunities for action research (that is, teacher-directed research that is embedded in classroom practice)
- ongoing training opportunities
- ready access to a gifted consultant or coordinator who can provide information and resources as needed
- leadership and networking possibilities within the district and beyond
- access to a gifted resource center for information, connections, and support
- advocacy networks

As with gifted students, teachers usually have good ideas about what it is they need to know, particularly as this reflects their changing classroom circumstances and demands. A large body of research evidence shows that the most effective learning happens for teachers (as with students) when they feel that they are an integral part of the consultation and planning process, and when they feel that their learning experiences are personally relevant. When teachers are directly involved in needs assessments and development planning, they are more likely to be engaged in their own learning. An additional benefit of teachers' involvement in this kind of authentic consultative process is that it provides them with an excellent model for facilitating the same kind of process with their gifted learners.

Teachers need to be given the tools and support necessary to adapt educational programming for exceptionally capable learners. They should also be encouraged to participate in creating their own professional development.

Formats

Preservice training provides the fuel and thrust necessary to become an effective teacher. *Inservice* training is what replenishes the source and sustains the momentum. We briefly discuss these two forms of teacher development.

Preservice Teacher Education Programs

Teachers need information that will broaden their understanding and appreciation of children with special needs—for example, information on how to identify learning problems, and on how to adapt the environment and their instruction to accommodate those problems. Their courses should include such things as dynamic assessment, individual education planning, adaptive instruction, differentiated learning, multicultural education, and holistic curriculum development. ... Teacher training should also include practical training in, and experience with consultative and collaborative practices in schools.

(Andrews & Lupart, 2000, p. 19)

Although there are some exceptions, special education is a highly problematic omission from most teachers' preservice (initial) training. There are many ways to provide the kind of education that teachers need if they are to work effectively with their gifted students. This includes incorporating the basic principles of special education, including giftedness, in initial teacher training programs. In order to be prepared to work with students with exceptional learning needs, aspiring teachers (sometimes referred to as teachers-in-training or teacher candidates) need a mix of appropriate resources and educational experiences, as well as solid grounding in research and developmental theory. We offer the following preservice programming recommendations, which we adapted from work by Andrews and Lupart (2000):

- facilitating communication skills, such as active listening
- working with paraprofessionals, specialists, volunteers, administrators, support staff, teacher aides, mentors, and other support personnel
- fostering students' self-regulatory abilities
- individualizing instruction, pacing and modifying instruction, and monitoring students' progress
- selecting and developing materials that address the diverse needs of students
- interacting with parents of special needs students, and determining how they can be effectively involved in their child's education
- assessing, managing, and preventing problem behavior
- balancing group and individual needs
- promoting social development of students, particularly those who are experiencing difficulty with their peers
- being aware of changing technology and potential benefits in meeting student needs
- developing a foundation of information pertaining to assessment practices, materials, curriculum approaches, and identification and placement procedures

Later in this chapter, we focus on ways of encouraging and sustaining engagement in learning and teaching among new teachers of gifted children, but for now, we would like to discuss some of the components of inservice teacher development for all teachers, both new practitioners and more seasoned professionals.

Inservice

> "*I've learned that teachers must learn to resist the temptation to make their students fit the curriculum. Rather, the curriculum must fit the students' needs. In this way students will be less frustrated and more fulfilled.*"
>
> "*The professional learning program on giftedness really opened my eyes to new teaching strategies and how to recognize the needs of the gifted student.*"
>
> "*After taking the course, I'm being more flexible and less afraid to try new things in the classroom. All of my ideas will take time to implement; however, I am patient and willing to see my strategies through.*"

Another good avenue for providing teachers with the necessary training for working well with gifted learners is to enhance the quality and range of courses available. It would be beneficial to see more and different kinds of graduate courses that address the nature of high-level learning and appropriately responsive teaching.

Along with special courses on high-level development, teachers need ongoing access to giftedness expertise so that they can consolidate and fine-tune their understandings, as well as learn about emerging possibilities and options for the students in their classrooms. The term inservice is often used to refer to such professional development (PD) opportunities. Given the challenging nature of their work, teachers cannot be expected to stay up to date on their own with everything that becomes available in their community and beyond with regard to gifted and other special learning needs. And as with anyone acquiring expertise in any area, teachers need support as they work to implement the appropriate strategies.

In our experience, inservice and professional development workshops provide potentially lively and dynamic opportunities for teachers to learn together about enhancing their ability to facilitate high-level learning. Such workshops can include interested teachers from within one school or from several schools, and they work best when delivered in a coherently organized series, with opportunities between workshops for ongoing interaction, support, and consultation among teachers and with experts.

Here are three different perspectives recently conveyed by teachers from different schools who participated in a professional learning program on giftedness.

Teachers' Perspectives on Professional Development (PD)

#1 Elisa: Remediation and Grade 3 Teacher

After hearing about project-based learning during the PD session, I decided to try it out in the classroom with one of my gifted students. I wanted the project to be challenging for Adam, yet have structure and relevance, so we met often to discuss what he needed to cover and what he wanted to include in his report.

After a few weeks, Adam presented his ideas creatively on display board and audio tape. His classmates enjoyed the presentation and learned interesting facts not covered in class. I asked Adam to self-evaluate his work and reflect on the outcomes. He said he learned a lot and had fun. We both were satisfied with the results. Thank you!

#2 Edison: Grade 5 Teacher

I learned to be flexible about who might be gifted. Perhaps a child will shine in new areas, and I'll have to be prepared to offer support.

The ideas we discussed made me think about various social, behavioral, and motivational issues. I'll try to promote learning experiences that will enable my students to be proud of their abilities. I'll be open and sensitive to their feelings, and I'll provide a positive emotional setting to support the gifted children in my class.

#3 Deidre: Remediation Specialist

This was the first time I attended a presentation on giftedness. I gained an understanding of this phenomenon and learned about identification. As a remediation specialist, and due to time constraints, I don't get to know my students in the same way as the classroom teacher. This presentation highlighted the fact that I have to make an extended effort to discover exactly what interests the gifted student, and where his/her talents lie.

I learned that a teacher who tries to provide an extension activity might be completely off target unless she has prior knowledge of the student's interests, hobbies, personality traits, abilities, concerns, and experiential background.

Knowledge is power. A teacher who has insight into how a student functions and what interests him/her is better able to implement meaningful and motivating programs.

Teachers who share and use their understandings of how to work effectively with gifted learners find that they become better able to meet other kinds of special learning needs as well. By understanding the principles of and practices involved in addressing individual learning needs, teachers get better at seeing and addressing them in a variety of students in their classrooms. As a result, the classroom culture evolves into a more engaging and inclusive place, where diversity is welcome and each child's abilities are respected and nurtured.

We have seen repeatedly that when teachers are provided with opportunities to think constructively about giftedness and acquire sound strategies for working with high-level learners, *and* when they are supported in their implementation of these understandings, the school and all children in the system benefit tremendously. Whether they are teaching exceptional students in regular or ability-grouped classrooms, teachers should be given both the training and the support they need in order to provide their students with an education commensurate with their abilities. Ideally, then, inservice programs for teachers should incorporate information on how to identify, understand, and plan for individual learning differences. We recommend that programs include:

- intelligent approaches to interpreting assessment information
- ways to recognize and address individual learning needs in a timely manner
- flexible instructional strategies
- well-targeted curriculum adaptation
- appropriate evaluation models
- ways to work cooperatively with the parents of special needs learners, other educators, and other professionals

This is not a comprehensive list. It cannot be comprehensive, because the best professional development is flexible and fluid, taking its shape from responding to the questions, concerns, and needs of the participants.

Consider, too, that teachers who work with high-ability students, whether identified as gifted or not, also need guidance in understanding high-level development and giftedness. They need to know how to create a classroom climate that addresses domain-specific giftedness, incorporates an emphasis on higher-order thinking, and provides opportunities to acquire solid work habits and study skills.

They also have to stay on top of their subject area. Gifted learners are usually on the leading edge in their knowledge of their chosen subject or domain of strength, and they can spot an out-of-date teacher quickly. Therefore, teachers have to be up on the technology, the terminology, the latest book trends, and so forth. Professional development should include a focus on understanding affective issues associated with giftedness, including strategies for fostering children's social and emotional development as well as their cognitive development. In the current political climate of increasing concern about educational outcomes for all learners, and with the perspective on giftedness changing from mystery model to mastery model, this is an ideal time for educators to do something constructive by ensuring that all teachers know how to support high-level development in their students.

Administrative Support

Professional learning is at the heart of teacher professionalism.
(Ontario College of Teachers, Ethical Standards, 1999)

Meaningful professional development does not occur in a vacuum. It requires involvement and support on the part of principals and other members of a school's administrative team. Principals can contribute to their own professional growth by participating in teacher inservice programs on giftedness and high-level development. By becoming familiar with the issues in gifted education alongside their teachers, they are better able to support them in planning and implementing well-designed programs.

The following vignette illustrates one middle school principal's blueprint for helping teachers meet gifted learning needs in his school. After attending one of our professional development programs on giftedness with many classroom teachers and other educators within his district,

Jerry Rosenfield wrote about the importance of collaborative effort and decided to implement a multi-grade program to support the gifted learners in his school. Here is the skeletal framework of his action plan.

A Principal's Initiative

Objective:

To facilitate peer collaboration among teachers for sharing ideas and materials for children who are advanced relative to their age or grade.

Target Subject Areas and Population:

Collaboration and sharing of materials and ideas will occur for core subjects in Grades 6, 7, and 8, with a focus on enrichment materials and extension activities for in-class use with individuals who warrant it. (We seldom accelerate to the next grade level of work.)

Approach:

We will conduct a workshop to increase appreciation of giftedness. We will then arrange for departmental meetings to formalize: (1) collecting age-appropriate and grade-appropriate enrichment materials and activities, (2) organizing these materials, and (3) open-sharing, where teachers will discuss how the materials might be best used.

Out-of-class opportunities for students will include enrichment and "special talent" groups, which will involve coaching for participation in regional, national, and international competitions.

Implementation Process:

1. *Meet with program leaders to have them "buy in."*

2. *Arrange departmental meetings facilitated by program leaders and staff resource teachers to establish a mechanism for sharing enrichment materials and for collaborative activities among teachers.*

3. *Invite the Board's gifted education consultant to work with separate groups of teachers by department to encourage dialogue and to help plan strategies for classroom use.*

4. *Facilitate inter-class teacher observations of classes, by invitation, so that teachers can see how individual students are involved in meaningful enrichment activities.*

5. *Maintain contact with the consultant for ongoing support as required.*

6. *After a few weeks, solicit evaluations from all participants.*

7. *Continue to build from there.*

This description from a middle school principal represents the early planning stage of what he hopes will ultimately be a comprehensive undertaking to support gifted learners in his school. After developing this plan, the principal put it into action. Since then, the district gifted education consultant has provided professional development to small staff groupings by subject area. Teachers are being encouraged to examine their own practice in relation to serving high-ability students and to adopt some suggested strategies for differentiating their instruction.

Administrators who understand gifted learning needs and who think creatively can find context-sensitive ways to support teachers in enhancing programs and learning options for the high-ability students in their schools.

What Can Parents Expect?

"What can I expect my child's regular classroom teacher to know about addressing his specific needs and levels of advancement in different subject areas?"

There are established standards of practice for the teaching profession, and some relate specifically to special needs children. In Ontario, for example, the standards are set forth by the Ontario College of Teachers, a self-regulatory body for the teaching profession in that province. The ethical standards and the standards of practice combine to serve as a foundational document for accredited preservice and inservice teacher education programs. They include the following commitments to students:

- *support for student learning*, such that teachers understand and use a range of teaching methods to address learning, cultural, spiritual, and language differences, and family situations

- *equitable and respectful treatment*, such that teachers accommodate the differences in students and respect their diversity, help students to connect learning to their own life experiences and spiritual and cultural understandings, and provide a range of ways for students to demonstrate aptitudes, abilities, and learning

- *knowledge of the student*, such that teachers recognize the strengths and weakness of students and know that teaching those with exceptionalities requires the use of specialized knowledge and skills

- *professional development*, such that teachers understand that teacher learning is directly related to student learning, and engage in a variety of learning opportunities, both individual and collaborative, that are integrated into practice for the benefit of student learning

- *knowledge of teaching practice*, such that teachers know ways to shape instruction so that it is helpful to students who learn in a variety of ways

- *planning for instruction*, such that teachers respond to learning exceptionalities and special needs, adapt teaching practice based on student achievement, and apply teaching strategies to meet student needs.

The National Association for Gifted Children (NAGC) in Washington, DC has established guidelines for professional development in gifted education. The document states, "Gifted learners are entitled to be served by professionals who have specialized preparation in gifted education, expertise in appropriate differentiated content and instructional methods, involvement in ongoing professional development, and who possess exemplary personal and professional traits" (National Association for Gifted Children, n.d.).

Although this may seem like a tall order, these guidelines provide a good starting point for thinking about appropriate standards. NAGC's lists of guiding principles, minimal standards, and exemplary standards can be seen currently at www.nagc.org/table6.htm. There are recommendations for comprehensive professional development programs that address the nature and needs of gifted learners, certification processes, and support mechanisms such as time, opportunity, and funding.

NAGC offers resources, conferences, programming models, and hands-on sessions for educators at all grade levels. This organization also provides resource information for parents who want to learn more about provisions for gifted education or who have gifted-related concerns. Canada has no such national organization at this time, but Canadians are welcome at NAGC conferences and can readily access their many resources.

There is much, much more to teaching than actual practice. Integral aspects of teaching involve commitment, integrity, and lifelong learning.

Teachers who grow professionally and who contribute meaningfully to the learning community in which they work become stronger, more effective teachers and raise the bar for others. At the same time, they reinforce the importance of ongoing and collaborative learning for their students.

Educators can participate in various kinds of learning experiences. They can enroll in academic courses offered at universities or colleges or through distance education programs; partner with professional networks (business, industry, committees); form study groups and network with colleagues; participate in conferences and workshops that focus on specific areas of interest (such as giftedness or high-ability learners); plan and implement action research or job embedded research activities; develop innovative curriculum materials; read and contribute to journals and educational publications that focus on aspects of teaching and learning; arrange opportunities to observe exemplary practice; increase their levels of competence in computer technology; and collaborate with consultants in areas in which they wish to gain expertise or acquire additional support. Professional opportunities like these not only help teachers remain current in their practice within an ever-changing educational environment, they also serve to enhance the teaching profession as a whole.

Andrews and Lupart (2000) write extensively about the inclusive classroom, and they share important insights about professional development that are in keeping with the mastery model perspective on gifted education. They emphasize that students should be offered learning experiences that are responsive to individual needs and competencies. They add that "whether a student has been identified as having exceptional needs is no longer a relevant issue—in a community of learners the needs of all students must be served" (p. 215). We agree with them that essential and enabling conditions for this are "professional training and development, pooling of resources, and administrative leadership and support" (p. 19). We have developed an approach to teacher training involving interested educators working with a gifted education consultant who acts as a catalyst for change. We describe it here.

A Dynamic Scaffolding Model (DSM) of Teacher Development

"I need some practical ideas for the classroom. But I also need some help figuring out how to put them in place for individual kids."
"It's important for me to be able to indicate what I would like to learn about in professional learning sessions."

In the dynamic scaffolding model of teacher development, the gifted education consultant acts as a catalyst for helping classroom teachers acquire knowledge about giftedness, learn to address special learning needs, and acquire ongoing access to peer collaboration and professional expertise. By providing ways for teachers to consolidate and build upon their understandings, the consultant helps teachers target learning for their students.

Based on current research about how learning happens (which applies to teachers as well as to their students) (Bransford, Brown, & Cocking, 2000; Shonkoff & Phillips, 2000), we have developed a three-tiered model of teacher support:

1. appropriate professional development in collegial settings

2. ongoing and targeted individual consultation opportunities

3. diverse kinds of liaisons and networking.

We have integrated into our model many consultation specifics that teachers have identified as being important to their work with gifted learners. We have found that a competent and readily accessible gifted education consultant can serve as a catalyst for a large number of schools, providing teachers with increased know-how, the tools necessary to support highly capable learners, and the ongoing help and encouragement required to ensure that it all comes together well. One such consultant can effectively help educators at all levels in many schools provide flexible, lively, and challenging learning environments designed to meet individual students' interests, needs, and domain-specific strengths. Although the planning of teacher development initiatives and new programming components for high-ability students requires some revisiting of beliefs and structures (Moon & Rosselli, 2000), a gifted education consultant in a position of responsibility within a board can act to oversee, steer, and champion a variety of exciting development efforts.

How the Model Evolved

> *"I'd like to have more specific hands-on information about exceptional learners—the ones who are having difficulty and the ones who are excelling."*

The dynamic scaffolding model of teacher development that we describe here and elsewhere (Matthews & Foster, 2005) reflects a number of principles and processes that have been developed in response to current realities in gifted education. We have successfully introduced this model, and variations of it are now being implemented in other places. We describe one school board's experience with the model.

One board of education which had been providing a very challenging education to all of its students for many years (without a formal system of identifying and programming for gifted learners) wanted to develop a system that would allow teachers to be better trained in meeting exceptionally capable students' learning needs in its approximately 80 affiliated schools. We suggested that a gifted education consultant with the necessary expertise working under the auspices of the board's Special Education Department would be ideally positioned to begin helping teachers become more knowledgeable about giftedness and guide them in finding good ways to program for their gifted students. The concept of a scaffolded approach for teacher training was adopted, and the initiative took off from there.

There are numerous ways to conceptualize scaffolding, but in general, its essential components include eight steps (Hogan & Pressley, 1997):

1. Engage the learner in the task.

2. Establish an individually-relevant shared goal.

3. Actively diagnose the learner's needs, including assessing and addressing misconceptions.

4. Provide tailored assistance.

5. Encourage goal-directed motivation.

6. Provide ongoing feedback that encourages self-monitoring.

7. Create an environment where the student feels free to take learning risks.

8. Assist internalization, independence, and generalization to other contexts.

Scaffolding can be a highly effective way of teaching. For a consultant in teacher development, it is useful for facilitating the learning of the teachers with whom he is working and for providing them with a model for later using the steps with their own students.

Meeting Gifted Learners' Educational Needs

> "I have lots of questions about gifted kids, but I'm not sure who to ask, or even what to ask."
>
> "I think a class' advancement can swing according to the individual teacher's strengths and interests. In other words, if you give exceptional math students to a teacher with an English degree, or vice versa, the enrichment won't be where the students need it."

Throughout this book, we have emphasized the importance of matching a student's education to her individual abilities. This is not always easy to do, and teachers need both training and support. They benefit from opportunities to learn more about engagement, relevance, and matching learning opportunities to individual students' levels of knowledge and understanding (Bransford, Brown, & Cocking, 2000). Generally speaking, the more exceptional a particular student, the more challenging it is for teachers to stimulate that student's engagement in the school-based learning process and to provide relevant learning opportunities that match specific ability levels. One difficulty is that the more exceptional a particular learner's profile is, the less likely it is that a teacher will have had experience working with such a profile. In addition, most teachers do not have the support and resources in place to assist them in developing the necessary expertise.

It is interesting to take a quick look at some of the ways teachers are currently helped to nurture giftedness in their students. In some jurisdictions, there are special education consultants who circulate among schools, offering support and addressing programming needs across the full spectrum of special education, from the very low-functioning students, through those with behavioral, sensory, and learning problems, to those who are gifted. These general specialists are often spread thinly, and their focus on gifted children is limited by constraints of time, available resources, and their own expertise. Some school boards offer self-contained gifted classes which function autonomously, require little by way of teacher training for working with gifted learners, and provide neither expertise nor resources to support the teacher's ongoing work with diversely exceptional students. In such systems, not only is the education provided in the specially grouped gifted class often problematic, but it is also frequently the case that no attention is paid to those high-ability children who for whatever reason do not participate in such programs.

When a school or board of education has a designated gifted program coordinator, that person typically handles administrative functions (such as chairing identification and placement committee meetings), responds to parents' queries, and checks curricular issues, but rarely has either the time to offer extensive professional development in giftedness, or ongoing consultation or assistance to regular classroom teachers. There are schools that provide special accommodations of one type or another to children formally identified as gifted but which pay little or no heed to those who have not acquired the requisite label. Other schools have neither special programs nor gifted education consultants, and they have few if any learning options designed to encourage gifted-level development in children or support for the teachers to help them develop and implement appropriate programming.

We know that some schools and boards of education provide their gifted students with excellent learning opportunities that are well targeted to their special educational needs. This occurs most frequently in situations modeled on adaptive instruction approaches, where there is an explicit commitment to respecting and attending to individual differences generally (Johnsen, Haensly, Ryser, & Ford, 2002). It also occurs in some special schools and programs that are designed for high-ability learners and that provide their teachers with the support necessary for matching their students' individual learning needs.

In order to provide this kind of appropriate programming, it is particularly important to target the attitudes of teachers and administrators regarding the needs of gifted students and to reinforce them in positive ways. Inservice provisions that facilitate information and idea sharing are an effective way of doing this (Gross, 1997).

Consultants' Responsibilities

Two key aspects of the Dynamic Scaffolding Model are as follows:

1. *A series of workshops:* When professional development workshops are offered by an expert in gifted development and education to interested teachers, opportunities are provided for teachers to share their understandings about the nature of gifted development, as well as to learn practical methods for facilitating high-level learning.

2. *Ongoing availability and support:* Following a teacher's participation in a professional learning program, and consistently from there on, the gifted education consultant is available to help teachers apply what they have learned in their classrooms and stay apprised of resources that are available in the community and beyond.

Learning how to meet the educational needs of their most exceptional students gives teachers the skills and understandings that help them to create a more dynamic classroom climate for all of their students. At the same time, they find that their own engagement in the teaching process is enhanced, and they become more enthusiastic supporters of students' optimal development. For those educators who work collaboratively in addressing the nature of high-level learning and appropriately responsive teaching, there is an added bonus of becoming part of a network that offers peer support and a rich sharing of resources over time.

In our workshop discussions and ongoing pre- and post-workshop communications, we have discussed this model with participating teachers. They tell us that the professional development support that they value most includes understanding and using assessment information, implementing curriculum adaptations, finding out more about high-level development, and learning how to support giftedness in students.

The consultant also has another role, that of liaison. This role involves promoting professional development opportunities that have an outreach component, and networking with education leaders and consultants elsewhere. The consultant can also address the concerns of parents within the system by offering them support and information about gifted development. There are many ways to do this, including providing open panel discussions or forums in which the focus is on specific issues, resources, educational practices, and other relevant concerns. These discussions give parents an outlet for their ideas, suggestions, and questions pertaining to giftedness. It also helps to strengthen sensitivity, collaboration, and understanding among those who live and work with gifted children, and those who seek to know more about this exceptionality. A particularly valuable way to encourage ongoing networking and liaison activities is for the consultant to create an interactive website where participants can discuss matters of interest, provide mutual support in problem-solving, and share resources and effective techniques.

Of course, the success of a consulting model is directly linked to the competence and commitment of the specialist who is responsible for making it happen (Moon & Rosselli, 2000). Ideally, the consultant will have a rich background of understanding and expertise in gifted development and education, be able to provide lively and meaningful inservice training activities, enjoy working with teachers, demonstrate leadership skills, and be approachable and encouraging in his attitude so that teachers feel comfortable about the process. The consultant needs to be enthusiastic about building a strong conceptual foundation for learning, as well as building bridges among stakeholders—parents, administrators, policy makers, teachers, and students—in the learning process.

The Dynamic Scaffolding Model in Review

We established the DSM in order to facilitate growth among teaching professionals, with positive outcomes for students.

The gifted education consultant offers interested teachers professional development opportunities; is readily accessible to consult with teachers individually and/or in groups to provide targeted expertise in the area of gifted education; and provides a range of networking opportunities, liaisons, and other services.

Because of the highly political nature of education in general and gifted education in particular, being responsive to both individual differences and to changing circumstances and contexts (the *dynamic* part of the scaffolding model's name) is essential for those who are interested in enacting any kind of change in gifted education. However, by taking a proactive leadership role in gifted education consultancy and by opening up a wide range of dynamically responsive and scaffolded support mechanisms to teachers, school boards can enhance their commitment to the learning needs of all of their students and increase opportunities for gifted-level development in as many of them as possible.

Next we describe how new teachers of gifted children can infuse an educational environment with knowledge and renewed vigor gained from well-designed preservice programs.

Engagement in Teaching and Learning

> *The conventional wisdom is that we can't find enough good teachers.... The truth is that we can't keep enough good teachers.*
> (Thomas Carroll, cited in Schouten, 2003)

> *"I'm thinking about how individual development actually is. A student who is advanced intellectually might not be so advanced morally or emotionally. We need to be tightly tuned to the progress of all aspects of the individual."*
> *"Should students be rewarded for learning? How do I know which is the right instructional strategy for gifted students?"*

New Teachers

One of the most overlooked resources in the teaching profession is the entry every year of new teachers who are trained in inquiry-based, reflective processes and in high-level development of children. What can experienced teachers learn from the kinds of questions and issues prospective teachers raise and hope (or fear) to address in their work with gifted learners? How can we best support new teachers?

We find that many teacher candidates who are enrolled in preservice education programs with a high-ability focus are deeply engaged by educational concerns and issues. They often ask important questions of the field, and they have fresh and valuable perspectives, insights, and action research ideas, showing a remarkable breadth and depth of inquiry and insight into the teaching process. Their concerns are profound and show the tremendous potential and dedication that these prospective educators have for meeting the needs of their future students.

We support prospective teachers' collaborative questioning and reflective processes by working hard to provide them with the resources they need to address their questions, and by guiding their learning on an ongoing basis as opportunities arise for doing that. It is important for the teaching profession and for us all that these educators-to-be sustain their spirit of inquiry and concern. Those of us already in the field can be good models of teaching and learning by helping to nest their inquiry within a supportive and responsive milieu—we can appreciate their views, allay their concerns, and engage them in collegial learning. We can also benefit from their enthusiasm and inquisitiveness if we use their questions as building blocks to stimulate our own thinking and exploration (Bereiter & Scardamalia, 1993; Matthews & Foster, in press).

Tapping preservice teachers' curious and engaged attitudes toward the learning process is an important way to enrich gifted education, and it can foster dynamic and lifelong professional development among new and experienced educators. One good way to extend and learn from what is offered in preservice gifted education programs is to encourage gifted consultants to stay attuned to what goes on in these programs, and then to harvest and share that wealth in the consultant's district and elsewhere through professional development and various consultation venues. Another approach is to help the new teachers who have participated in preservice gifted-related experiences: (a) to feel comfortable about sharing what they've learned, and (b) to feel empowered in their work.

Sustaining New Teachers' Engagement in Teaching and Learning
Encourage teachers to:

- continue to reflect on their practice

- enhance their professional growth through involvement in ongoing professional development dialogues, active learning, and job-embedded research initiatives

- motivate their colleagues' engagement in learning so as to create a more knowledgeable professional community

- plan and implement new ideas and innovative practice

- engage in action research (or job embedded research initiatives)

Guiding Principles

Schools are revolving doors that spit out teachers as fast as they are hired.... It seems that a third of new teachers quit after three years, and nearly half are gone after five years.

(Schouten, 2003)

"Teaching is wonderful, but it's draining!"

New teachers ought to be respected by colleagues, parents, and students, and their various contributions should be acknowledged and shared. Sadly, we are experiencing a time when many new teachers feel burnout and make the choice to leave the profession. We offer here two guiding principles for enhancing all new teachers' experience and for encouraging their engagement in their work.

Principle #1: Support Reflective, Ongoing Collaborative Learning

We can help new teachers feel empowered rather than overwhelmed and stay engaged in learning and knowing more (for example, about gifted education) if we solicit and use their ideas and perspectives, and if we facilitate collaborative endeavors with more experienced educators. A principal, subject coordinator, administrator, resource liaison, or gifted education consultant can act as a facilitator or help to coordinate professional development sessions or dialogues, and most certainly can offer support (for example, moral, logistical) for this kind of interactive learning process among educators of varying experience.

Principle #2: Embed Teachers' Learning within a Supportive Milieu

If new teachers are to have validating, empowering, and motivating experiences, they need to sustain their engagement in learning. And experienced teachers, administrators, consultants, and other educators have to create mechanisms to support new teachers' continued growth. This means helping new teachers use knowledge in productive and meaningful ways. Good teachers are too often overworked and underpaid. They can persist with ongoing focused engagement in learning only when it has meaningful application in practice and if there is a solid return on their investment of time and energy. By nurturing and showing appreciation for the kinds of professional growth we describe here, by broadening them and then translating them into best practice in schools, we empower new teachers to contribute more proactively to their educational environment

We have observed the importance and motivating effect of certain learning experiences that act as springboards to better gifted education. The curricular elements and techniques for learning in initial teacher training programs in a gifted or high-ability group are at once expansive and focused. We discuss the possibilities for broad-based use of such programming for inservice/professional development.

Using Preservice Initiatives More Extensively

Much can be culled and extended from the preservice gifted education experience and then reconfigured as valuable inservice for a larger audience. Many course components from initial training programs are worth harnessing for professional development purposes. Educators need to become more aware of the possibilities and then take the initiative to personalize or tailor them to use collaboratively for their professional growth.

Preservice Gifted Training

Preservice teacher training programs in gifted education can offer interesting learning activities including but not restricted to:

- engagement in individual and collaborative case study analyses, presented in problem-based learning format (and often focusing on domain specificity and optimal programming applications)

- ongoing opportunities for dialogue on topical issues pertaining to giftedness, such as assessment concerns; social, emotional and motivational implications of giftedness; and differentiated programming initiatives, resources, and support mechanisms

- web-forum discussions

- learning-based reading and group presentations relating to research studies, theoretical underpinnings, and models as they relate to past and present developmental, cognitive, and psychological perspectives

- practicum experience with associates who demonstrate expertise in adaptive instruction and differentiated programming techniques for children with exceptional learning needs

- collaborative problem-solving activities

- self-directed reflection on learning experiences

- individual action research learning investigations on self-selected topics of interest

Teacher candidates have indicated that each of the learning experiences listed above is effective for a number of reasons, including that it:

- engages them personally in authentic problem-solving activities (for example, pertaining to concerns or issues having to do with constraints, practicalities, or support systems as relating to gifted education)

- enables them to feel respected and valued as competent thinkers and professionals

- encourages them to recognize the expertise of their colleagues as essential to their own thinking, teaching, and learning

- helps them discover their own resourcefulness and the resources available to them (many of which are unrelated to gifted training but are very generic to all teacher training)

- allows them to experience the scaffolded and incremental nature of learning

- facilitates the modeling of learning for their own students

- promotes a shared mindset and curiosity, emphasizing the value of inquiry-based learning and enabling teachers to develop their own questions and answers about what really matters to them (within the classroom, school, and community)

- broadens individual and collective knowledge bases about teaching methods, programming options, issues, and concerns pertaining to gifted education

- allows for the paradigm shift from a mystery to a mastery model to be introduced, recognized, and discussed, and for the implications and attendant educational possibilities to become more widely acknowledged

One prospective teacher summed up the concern this way:

> *The ideas of extra support and collaborative efforts among teachers sound great, but will this actually occur in practice? Are teachers adequately prepared, supported, and equipped to handle all of the challenges?*

We owe it to our children to move the answer to this question to a definitive *yes*, rather than a tentative *maybe*, or even a disheartening (and all too frequent) *no*.

In our final chapter we look at other ways to share understandings and work toward optimal learning for all children.

Chapter 16

Optimal Learning for All Children

We begin this chapter by considering current gifted education trends in Canada, the United States of America, and worldwide. We conclude by discussing ways of sharing resources, establishing university-based resource centers for high-ability students, and staying up to date with current research in child development.

Trends and Directions in Canada

There are islands of exciting programs being developed and implemented through the efforts of outstanding teachers throughout the country…. [H]igh ability students are being challenged by teachers who are committed to excellence.
(Leroux, 2000, p. 701)

OPPORTUNITYISNOWHERE. There are two ways to read this road sign, which relates directly to our attitude about gifted education.
(Millar, 2000, p. 25)

Where gifted education thrives in Canada, we see a harmonious orchestration among administrators, teachers, and parents.
(Leroux, 2000, p. 701)

As Canadian authors, we devote this first segment to an overview of what's happening in gifted education in our country of approximately

30 million people. In Canada, each of the 10 provinces and the northern territories has its own legislated education system. Standards of practice, funding, and other education-related matters fall under the jurisdiction of the individual regional Ministries of Education. We provide an encapsulated synopsis of best practice in Canada, recognizing that there is much more that could be said about each region of the country. For those who wish to find out more, each of the Ministries of Education can be accessed online.

Education in Canada is currently experiencing a period of challenge and change on a number of fronts. Quite predictably, this is having an impact on the programs and provisions for high-ability students, as well as others. Based on a review of recently published articles on gifted education across Canada, it appears that the current trend is toward policies of inclusion, which means that increasingly, it is the regular classroom teacher who is responsible for addressing the needs of advanced learners. Inclusion is based on the concept of "restructuring and unifying the educational system for all students" and "it gives the regular classroom teacher primary responsibility, abandoning the traditional special education pull-out approach to service delivery for students with exceptional learning needs" (Andrews & Lupart, 2000, p. 47).

As we have discussed throughout this book, for any approach to work to meet gifted learners' needs, teachers must be provided with the knowledge and support they need to do it well. There is an ongoing and pressing need for more coordinated and targeted teacher training and development in gifted education, as well as support in this area of special education throughout the country. As we discuss elsewhere in this book, it appears that such provisions are much more the exception than the rule.

Although there are many valid criticisms of and problems with the current situation in regard to gifted education in many areas of Canada, there are also reasons for optimism about the future. In Alberta, for example, the Center for Gifted Education at the University of Calgary provides teacher specialization in gifted studies at the graduate level, with courses on conceptual issues, curricular and program planning, social and emotional development of gifted students, and practica in gifted education. Educators at the Center for Gifted Education in Calgary collaborate with colleagues from other centers around the globe, act as community liaisons, conduct research in gifted education, provide consultation services, develop teacher training programs, and provide teacher-oriented curriculum resource material and a range of library services. Such provisions strengthen the educational landscape in that province for all children, including but not limited to those who are exceptionally capable.

In Ontario, the provincial Association for Bright Children has been an active and effective lobbying force for the past 20 years and has influenced legislation mandating that gifted students' exceptional learning needs be met. More and more teachers are becoming involved in professional development opportunities related to giftedness and high-level curriculum. There is much to be gained from participation in these activities, as illustrated by the following evaluation of a full-day inservice workshop.

Professional Development: A Teacher's Perspective

I learned practical strategies that I can actually use in my classroom. The initial discussion enabled me to develop with other teachers a general understanding of giftedness. We were able to talk about the emotional, social, and behavioral aspects of giftedness, and I was reassured that other teachers also had concerns and frustrations about dealing with these issues within the confines of the school system.

Some of the strategies we considered are approaches that I already use, and I will continue to expand upon them now that I have additional ideas and suggestions. I learned that recognizing each child's strengths and weaknesses is an essential first step. I think I'd also like to work more collaboratively with my students. I will take time to listen to them and acknowledge their needs, and then match those needs with the curriculum in order to try and develop a more challenging and meaningful program.

In New Brunswick, the five-year Bachelor of Education program has been amended to emphasize pedagogy, incorporating the principle of individual developmental diversity and respect for each learner's abilities across many dimensions. Specifically, teachers in training there are learning about the uniqueness of the learner, inclusion, mastery learning, student participation and autonomy, as well as adaptive instruction. A focus on exceptional students, on individualizing instruction, and on differentiating curriculum is an integral part of the plan, all of which help teachers work effectively with gifted learners.

Manitoba's *Education Agenda for Student Success 2002-2006* (Manitoba Education, Citizenship, and Youth, 2002) outlines strategies for differentiated instruction and positive learning outcomes within that province's philosophy of inclusive education. Similarly, Nova Scotia's *Challenge for Excellence* (Nova Scotia Department of Education, 1999) provides a framework for developing and implementing programs for their gifted students. The momentum in Quebec appears to be moving toward "talent education" or extraordinary behaviors in any field of human endeavor, rather than exclusively academic giftedness. Françoys Gagné is a leader in that movement, both in his own province and internationally (Gagné, 2003; Masse, 2000).

In British Columbia, parental concerns voiced by the large membership of the Gifted Children's Association identified lapses in Ministry of Education leadership and the need for greater support for gifted learners in relation to various aspects of policy and programming (such as consistency, assessment practices, continuity, and funding) (Mendaglio & Pyryt, 2000). Such advocacy has had a considerable impact on the funding of gifted education in British Columbia and has also influenced practice, as well as setting the stage for positive future change. There are some wonderful programs operating in the Vancouver area. The following descriptions of programs in Vancouver are culled from framework documents and personal communication. It is interesting to see the many learning options already in place.

Gifted Education in Vancouver

The Gifted Education and Resource Specialist for the Vancouver School Board is enthusiastic about what is happening in her district. Within this board, schools offer gifted students several options: classroom enrichment, independent studies, advanced placement, and school-wide enrichment. In addition, there are area challenge centers housed in some schools for groups of identified-gifted learners. The board also offers city-wide initiatives such as future problem-solving activities, summer learning programs, multi-age cluster classes, and primary gifted student support. We learned that teachers are encouraged to merge gifted education with social responsibility; children are expected to contribute to the class and school community, value diversity and defend human rights, and solve problems in peaceful ways.

The school board has also established a transition program which offers early entrance to university for academically highly gifted students in partnership with the University of British Columbia and the provincial Ministry of Education. This two-year program is designed to promote academic excellence and social and emotional development of academically gifted adolescents who are committed to the goal of early entrance to university. On the day we visited, they were enthusiastic about their work in cellular biology and English literature (Dickens), some were collaboratively planning a rock climbing field trip, and others were involved in classes at the university (where the program is housed).

Although the current situation for gifted learners in most parts of Canada is far from ideal, we believe that because it is a time of educational and societal change, it is also a time of great possibility. There are many signs that concerned individuals who are willing to invest time and energy in advocacy have opportunities now to effect real and lasting change. As the paradigm shifts toward a mastery perspective, we look forward to seeing its increasing impact on education for high-ability learners from coast to coast.

American and International Perspectives

Gifted programs are too often patchwork collections of random practices and activities.... It is important to look critically at the nature of the process of identifying gifted and talented children and provide them with special provision and programs to meet their special needs.

(Persson, Joswig, & Balogh 2000. p. 745)

"I can't help but wonder what's going on in schools in other parts of the world. What kinds of learning provisions are available to gifted children elsewhere?"

"The world is becoming more and more of a global community. We should be borrowing educational ideas from other countries."

Each country has its own ideological, political, cultural, and economic values that inform its educational agenda, and so, quite predictably, approaches to gifted education and provisions for highly able students differ from one country to the next, as well as across regions within each country. What follows is a quick around-the-world tour of what is happening in gifted education outside of Canada. It is by no means comprehensive, but it does offer a glimpse into the global gifted community. (Additional references for various regions can be found by accessing the *Being Smart* website at www.beingsmart.ca.)

We have extracted much of the information we present here from the *International Handbook of Gifted and Talented* (2000), a comprehensive edited text that considers gifted-related practices and challenges around the globe. We have also spoken to a number of individuals over the course of visits to other countries and during education conferences when educators have had opportunities to share ideas and understandings.

In the United States, as in Canada, programs and policies differ greatly from state to state and from district to district. All of the various learning opportunities described in Section III of this book are offered in American schools, although certainly not in every school or at every grade level. Funding allocations, curriculum mandates, and programming pace, scope, and complexity vary across school districts, as do teacher training levels, methodology and commitment, emphasis on cognitive and affective domains, community advocacy and involvement, and many other factors

There are numerous gifted education resource centers, associations, and parent support organizations throughout the U.S. The best known of these is the National Association of Gifted Children, or NAGC, which has an informative website (www.nagc.org). Most states have a designated person within their state department of education to act as a resource and information link to schools and individuals, and most states have an active state association for parents and teachers (such as Kentucky Association for Gifted Education, Texas Association for Gifted Education, etc.). Many states have legal mandates which state that gifted children must be provided with academic challenge that is commensurate with their abilities and potentials, and in addition, some states mandate that teachers who work with gifted students must have a special endorsement or a certain number of hours of gifted education training. In response to such mandates, a number of universities across the U.S.

offer graduate training programs and advanced degrees in gifted education. A few universities in the U.S. also have centers for gifted education with services such as assessment, weekend enrichment and accelerated classes, consulting services, and guidance.

Taken all together, these various agencies, associations, and resource specialists provide an impetus for continued growth including standards review, improvements in teacher training, and resource development. We would like to see even more opportunities for teacher development and a more coordinated effort by those who see gifted education not as a privilege for a select few, but as a benefit that helps all children realize their abilities.

We now turn our attention to gifted education in Europe and beyond. In 1994, the European Council, a body for intergovernmental cooperation among 25 Eastern and Western European states, issued a policy paper regarding the education of gifted children (Persson, Joswig, & Balogh, 2000). Recommendations included:

1. research and debate among various professionals on defining the giftedness construct

2. research into identification practice, school success, and reasons for academic failure

3. inservice training for teachers

4. prevention of the negative consequences of gifted labeling

5. recognition of gifted learners' educational needs

6. provision for high-ability children within regular school settings

This sounds to us like a wish list for gifted education everywhere!

As might be expected, European countries have differed in their implementation of these recommendations. Many (mostly in Eastern Europe) have legislation in place for their high-ability students, whereas others (mostly in Western Europe) have incorporated inclusive strategies such as acceleration, in-class provisions, and enrichment. In some countries in both Eastern and Western Europe, there are specially designated learning environments or higher education in private or state-controlled facilities. Several of the European countries include gifted education in teacher development opportunities (Persson, Joswig, & Balogh, 2000).

Great Britain has an active National Association for Gifted Children, accessible online at www.nagcbritain.org.

In each of the Arabic countries in the Middle East, gifted children are generally identified as those who demonstrate high ability, intelligence, creativity, task commitment, and/or high achievement. As elsewhere, there is a broad spectrum of special provisions for gifted students, including acceleration, enrichment, special schools, special classes, extra courses, extracurricular activities, individual educational programs, supplementary classes, competitions, mentorships, and computer-based learning opportunities. And also as elsewhere, program offerings vary considerably from country to country within this region.

In Israel, gifted education has been a recognized part of the formal education system since the 1970s. From the advent of special classes, workshops, and programs, provisions have expanded to include after-school enrichment centers that offer learning opportunities in various subject areas. Other approaches include dual university/high school enrollment, weekly pull-out classes, and university-based enrichment programs for students who excel in mathematics and science. There are many nation-wide science activities (such as Olympiads, science institutes, summer mentorship programs, museum programs, clubs), and advanced level courses are available at enrichment centers after school and during holidays for Israel's more highly motivated students. In many cases, "the children are not labeled, but the courses are" (Subhi & Maoz, 2000, p. 752). The Israel Arts and Science Academy, the Weizmann Institute of Science, and the Society for Excellence through Education all promote and nurture excellence, leadership, and skill development in various subject areas.

In China, both individual identification and group screening processes have been used to identify gifted children. Special schools for artistically talented children have long been established, whereas special educational provisions for intellectually gifted children are relatively new. Program offerings across China include early enrollment, skipping grades, special classes, gifted schools, special courses in specific subjects, and extracurricular programs (Shi & Zha, 2000). Issues that have been identified as requiring attention at this time include generating funding and staffing for the study of gifted children, teacher training programs, increased understanding of developmental aspects of giftedness and talent, creativity, and the role of brain function in giftedness.

In other Asian countries, including India, Indonesia, Japan, Korea, the Philippines, Singapore, Taiwan, and Thailand, the educational philosophy tends to be one in which children are taught in accordance with and with respect for individual differences. Yet there are cultural issues, traditional barriers, and philosophical considerations that have direct bearing on how gifted education is characterized and practiced. Identification/assessment procedures tend to be somewhat rigid, and gifted programming initiatives are relatively new. As occurs in other areas of the world, there are very often gaps between official policy and actual implementation. Some countries provide gifted education support, while others do not. It has been noted that flexibility, the pooling of expertise and resources, and a greater responsivity to diversity will be critical to the development of this region's capacity to address the needs of its gifted children in the years to come.

Many educators in Asia are becoming interested in learning about Western approaches to gifted education. For example, in March of 2004, a delegation of about 15 educators came from Singapore to the United States to discuss gifted education internationally. They have been working for several years with Joyce VanTassel-Baska and the Center for Gifted Education, and they were interested in our work at Hunter College, as we are in their work in Singapore. We are making plans for ongoing interaction in international professional development for teachers of gifted learners. In May of 2004, more than 20 educators from Korea visited Toronto, Calgary, and Vancouver in order to learn more about gifted education initiatives, and we had the opportunity to facilitate discussion about Canadian programming and teacher training initiatives, as well as to learn something about their work in Korea. International exchanges like this are wonderful for opening up channels of communication among educators interested in gifted-related issues. Whenever we travel, we make a special point of finding out about educational systems in the countries we are visiting.

Educators in Australia have been doing innovative work in gifted education for some time now. There are several active organizations and institutions involved in considering the needs of gifted learners, such as Children of High Intellectual Potential (www.chip.edu.au). Australian gifted education provisions include enrichment and extension, special schools and classes, acceleration, supplementary programs involving broad-based community input, cluster groups, and networks whereby schools develop particular expertise and become models for others to emulate (Braggett & Moltzen, 2000). There are Special Interest Centers within secondary schools that offer high quality instruction in specialized disciplines, and Special Interest Secondary Schools wherein students obtain comprehensive instruction in such subjects as music, languages, agriculture, dramatic arts, information technology, visual arts, science, popular entertainment, or sports. These special schools often attract students from across the region. Enrichment is the most widely used strategy across Australia in providing for gifted and talented students (Braggett & Moltzen, 2000).

In New Zealand, gifted children are typically offered enrichment in the regular classroom setting, although some also have access to pull-out programs, acceleration, separate schools and classes, cluster grouping, and correspondence schooling (Braggett & Moltzen, 2000). Teachers are being given more training to assist them in the provision of appropriate programming. There is an established and active center for gifted education and a large association for gifted children (NZAGC) that plays an important role in its support of educators, parents, and children. Numerous research initiatives on a variety of gifted related themes are being undertaken in both Australia and New Zealand.

In Africa, traditional culture, political developments, apartheid, differing conceptions of giftedness, and different interpretations of what equal educational rights imply, as well as many other factors, have all had an impact on gifted education. In the sociocultural context of African society, identification procedures are often problematic. Little or no formal provision for gifted children is made in sub-Saharan countries. The National Association of Gifted and Talented Children in South Africa (NAGTCSA) was founded in 1997, and there is hope that its work on behalf of gifted children will result in sound policy decisions and better educational provisions. At the same time, the reality is that, for a number of reasons, "gifted education will probably not be a priority item on the education agenda of most African countries in the near future" (Taylor & Kokot, 2000, p. 813). It remains to be linked to national development needs and traditional culture, as well as to be better integrated into regular classroom teaching.

In Latin American countries, too, there is considerable diversity in attitudes toward and programming for gifted learners. It appears that Brazil is consolidating its special services in different levels of education, and other countries such as Peru, Cuba, Mexico, and Argentina have also shown significant progress. In Brazil, there is a special training program for gifted students at the college level, as well as programs serving relatively small numbers of students in the public school system in many regions, and some programs offered to gifted children attending private schools. One such program focuses on technology and the humanities. In 1993, Brazil founded a Center for the Development of Potential and Talent, which serves children by means of activities and interest groups. There is, however, little in the way of teacher training in gifted education.

Many other Latin American countries have little or no provision at all for their gifted and talented population (Soriano de Alencar, Blumen-Pardo, & Castellanos-Simons, 2000). There are large differences in the kinds of educational provisions for gifted children, and many services are dependent upon societal, financial, political, and other kinds of influences and have yet to find their way into the schools. Acceleration is being considered as one learning alternative, and enrichment activities and clubs are popular in some schools (in drama, science, music, and other subject areas). Cluster grouping is also fairly common. Schools operated by foreign communities (including American, Israeli, and European) are more likely to offer programs for their high-ability students. Mexico has a program underway that addresses many aspects of giftedness, including identification, thinking skills, research, and creativity, and aspires "to develop the creative and productive potential of all students as well as to promote their academic achievement" (Soriano de Alencar et al., 2000, p. 826).

The World Council for Gifted and Talented Children is an international gifted advocacy organization that organizes a world conference and publishes a newsletter with information about gifted-related happenings on a global scale. One issue featured articles about a summer workshop in Israel, a new book from Japan, a certificate course being offered in South Africa, recent developments in Brazil, a gifted conference in Thailand, workshops in Spain, and a description of trends and activities in Austria (World Gifted, 2003). Individuals can find interesting reading in gifted newsletters and journals from other countries by searching online and submitting a request for the article or newsletter.

Our very brief review of giftedness around the world suggests that there is a widespread and increasing awareness of the importance of: (a) encouraging high-level development in children, (b) embracing diversity and understanding giftedness across a wide range of individual differences, and (c) sharing expertise internationally. Leaders in education who foster international networks of real communication, listening, and learning on all sides can help to strengthen these awarenesses and so act as catalysts in a move to a global village where diverse kinds of gifts are encouraged, thereby enriching us all.

Sharing Resources in a Changing World

Positioning our efforts within the best possible education for all and acknowledging that we do not know the limits or scope of human potential gives us a conceptual framework for the future.

(Klapp & Porath, 2000, p. 34)

Schools need to develop ways to link classroom learning to other aspects of students' lives. Engendering parent support for the core learning principles and parent involvement in the learning process is of the utmost importance.

(Bransford, Brown, & Cocking, 1999, p. 23)

We are living through an unprecedented and accelerated change in the way that people live their lives, a situation that is understandably creating tremendous stress for people and for the communities in which they live. As individuals experience unpredictable changes, their health and prosperity depend increasingly on their having acquired the effective coping, communication, and decision-making skills that are provided by a good education (Keating & Hertzman, 1999). In many ways, we are reaching a time of crisis in education, a time when too many students have too many needs that teachers do not have sufficient resources to meet (Matthews & Menna, 2003).

This predicament within society and education may be even more problematic for gifted learners and their parents than for others. Although giftedness is generally perceived as a strength (and of course, in many ways, it is a strength), it can also be a liability for certain people at certain times in their lives. One factor that increases problems for gifted learners in times of overly stretched resources is the fact that teachers (and sometimes parents) perceive these children as being able to take care of their own needs. In a context of many urgent and competing needs, gifted students' special learning needs can be assigned a low priority and thereby be more or less ignored.

As we discuss elsewhere in this book, being exceptional is in itself a risk factor for some children and adolescents. When the exceptionality is not addressed meaningfully, it can lead to feelings of differentness, loneliness, boredom, frustration, and other developmental problems. Another factor which increases the risks associated with being gifted is the acute sensitivity of many gifted children and adolescents; they perceive more of what is happening around them and in the world than do their age-peers, but they frequently do not have the necessary psychological maturity to manage their heightened sensitivity well. For example, seeing graphic pictures of war or suffering may lead to feelings of hopelessness. It is important that they have adults they can relate to who can answer questions, respect their feelings, understand their concerns, and help them cope with troubling circumstances (Matthews & Foster, 2003).

One solution to educational resources that are stretched to (and sometimes past) the breaking point is to look beyond the school walls for other resources that can be tapped. There are some wonderful examples of situations in which educators and parents have worked together to enrich learning experiences in situations of great stress. An example that comes to mind is the remarkable successes chronicled in the book *The Power of Their Ideas: Lessons for America from a Small School in Harlem* (Meier, 2002). Research comes together in suggesting that there is a need for parents and educators to work collaboratively with students and to reach out to the community and beyond for learning opportunities—an approach that may be particularly appropriate for gifted learners.

Although science has made tremendous progress over the past several years in identifying how learning happens, too often, educators have had little or no access to the relevant findings. Concerned about this, a consortium of top international scientists recently synthesized the main findings about teaching and learning (Bransford, Brown, & Cocking, 1999). Along with several other points, their report emphasizes the needs for school-family partnerships, opportunities for relevant and authentic learning, and community involvement in the learning process. They recommend community-centered approaches to education that encourage communities of learners (both for students and for teachers) and that connect learning to students' lives and interests.

All of the participants in and beneficiaries of the learning process, including students, parents, teachers, and community members, have worthwhile ideas about how to make schooling more valuable and meaningful for gifted learners. We have found that many of the most intractable problems in gifted education are solved when the interested parties work to find ways to share their perspectives in collaborative problem-solving forums.

In order for this school-community partnership to succeed, everyone has to be listened to. Students' individual needs for relevant and authentic learning must be respected, and the student, school, and family all have to work cohesively. It is important that *students* feel engaged in and responsible for co-creating their own learning in ways that ensure that their teachers are not left with the burden of customizing the curriculum for each student. The *teacher's* role is that of a pedagogical and content expert—someone who can facilitate productive problem-finding and problem-solving; be knowledgeable about and responsive to individual, developmental, and cultural differences in learning needs; and guide students intelligently through the learning process. *Parents'* roles vary across situations but include investigating learning opportunities in the community and beyond, including such things as special classes, competitions, community service options, mentoring, apprenticeships, etc.—all of which could be considered for academic credit.

This sounds like an intensive investment of time and trouble for each student in the context of working to educate many students in large and growing classrooms—and it is. However, this kind of collaborative approach to solving gifted-related learning problems for one student is almost always worthwhile; it prevents further problems with that student and helps her realize her capabilities both at school and beyond. This, in turn, has obvious benefits for the school as a whole and for society at large.

We have seen this kind of effort in action, and we know that as soon as it happens for one student, that teacher's attitudes begin to change, and then, through a process of osmosis and infiltration, or through professional development and collaboration, the school climate can and does improve. Teachers begin to realize that, contrary to many people's expectations, they have some of the best curriculum development allies and resources in their students and parents, and that there are all kinds of opportunities available outside the school that can supplement the increasingly resource-stretched situation within its confines. Parents are relieved that their high-ability child can begin to be academically challenged and successful, and even the busiest parents are only too glad to help with figuring out how to make that happen within the context of the regular school system. They usually find that this is a relatively small investment of their time with a big payoff in the light of more expensive alternatives.

Here are three interactive principles that comprise a collaborative approach:

1. Facilitate the student's engagement in his own learning.

2. Facilitate partnerships between the school and the family.

3. Facilitate community involvement in the student's learning.

Advantages to the collaborative approach include shared resources and creative problem solving; mentorship, apprenticeship, and community service opportunities; and authentic and community-based learning opportunities.

There are many reasons to think that by encouraging and facilitating collaborations among families, schools, and communities, we will find and create the best educational responses to a rapidly changing world. By opening the door to collaborations, schools can gain access to the resources that they are lacking and reduce the burdens that they are experiencing. Educators find themselves reassured and sometimes even professionally reenergized when they realize that they do not have to do it alone anymore, and in fact, it is better if they do not. When parents and educators work together in educational problem-finding and problem-solving, everyone benefits.

A University-Based Resource Center

"I read with interest about the proposed center for gifted education. What I wouldn't give to have a place that would try to understand the special needs of my daughter! We struggle to make appropriate educational decisions for her. I wish you and your colleagues well in your endeavor to develop this center. I predict a 'line up out the door' for your services!"

"I feel that this is great progress toward better learning for all kids. There is hope of breaking down traditional structures. Please let me know if there is anything I can do to volunteer my time to help out with this center."

"We are so lucky to have the Gifted Center available! I don't know what I would have done without your help!"

The education faculties of some universities have developed excellent gifted education resource centers that are active, inclusive, vibrant places of learning, support, and interaction. Each center has its own focus and specialization, such as curriculum development, student programs, high-ability research, and teacher development, and we mention several of them throughout this book. For a list of university-based resource centers specializing in various dimensions of giftedness, you can go to the "Links" page of www.beingsmart.ca or directly to http://ericec.org/faq/gt-urls.html.

At best, a gifted resource center provides many kinds of activities and functions, including information and encouragement for parents, educators, and children; cutting edge research and dissemination; a laboratory to support teacher development; and an active outreach into diverse communities. We have been involved in initiatives to create such centers at our home institutions of the Ontario Institute for Studies in Education of the University of Toronto, and Hunter College, City University of New York, and we have spoken to people at many of the large gifted centers throughout North America. We include here a synthesis of their suggestions and our experiences.

Objectives of a Gifted Center

Objectives of a gifted center should include the following:

- provide information and support for parents, educators, and academics interested in meeting the needs of exceptionally capable learners

- foster gifted-level outcomes in diverse kinds of learners

- promote educational liaisons and collaborative networks at all levels and in a variety of ways

- enable interested individuals to engage in research on high-level development and education

Components of a Gifted Center

Teacher Development

- expertise and resources for teachers, from initial teacher training, through inservice workshops and ongoing professional development, to graduate courses and programs

- access to a network of resources and opportunities for learning about high-level learning

Teacher Support and Networking

- a means of connecting with others involved or interested in conferences, research initiatives, leadership seminars, and workshops on giftedness issues

- clarification of identification and assessment issues

- suggestions for instructional models based on assessment findings

- material at different grade levels and in various subject areas for use by those who work with children who are advanced in specific domains or who have multiple exceptionalities

Student Support and Networking

- a place where gifted learners themselves might receive information and support

- access to diverse extracurricular learning enrichments

- information on counseling and mentorships

- connections to other children and adolescents with similar interests and concerns

Family Support and Networking

- connections to other parents with giftedness concerns

- access to reliable information

- opportunities for networking with educators

- help for siblings of gifted learners who may have issues and special learning needs of their own

School Support

- support for administrators in developing school cultures where gifted learners are challenged and high-level ability is nurtured
- access to teacher development programs
- support for action research
- access to practical information and resources
- networking possibilities
- support for interschool collaboration

Intra-University Collaborations and Community Outreach

- coordination of applicable resources within the university across programs, departments, and disciplines
- collaborations with parent groups, business partners, government connections, and educational relationships of many kinds, from local to international in scope
- sharing of resources as applicable
- interschool mentorships, teacher seminars, parent awareness workshops
- proactive inclusion of at-risk students

Research, Publication, and Dissemination

- support for collaboration, design, and completion of research on high-level development and education
- a point of active and dynamic learning and dissemination

A well-planned and well-run university-based gifted center can work to bring together teacher development and support; student and family support; research and dissemination activities; and access to a wide range of local, regional, national, and international learning opportunities. It can create the productive and invigorating confluence of activities, energies, and expertise that form the foundation of authentic exploration and discovery.

A gifted center is a *real* place—where people can talk, have a cup of coffee, and put their hands on actual books. Another essential aspect of such a center is its virtual or Internet-based dimension. A comprehensive website enables parents, educators, and students to access current information on gifted development, educational options, and research findings.

Different places have different priorities, resources, funds, and tools with which to work. A gifted education and resource center has to be created for and adapted to the local context. If you live in a place that has such a center, use it and work with it to help it meet your needs. If you do not have a facility like this available, you might think about linking to one or becoming involved in advocacy for starting or supporting the establishment of such a resource in your community. A university-based center can provide a link among existing activities and programs related to gifted education, including coordinating resources for students, families, and teachers, stimulating real understanding of the nature of giftedness, and optimizing learning and life experiences for many people.

Keeping Up-to-Date

Societal circumstances beyond the control of the individual contribute considerably to the development of potential, and a major task confronting the gifted individual throughout the life-course is to cope effectively with the changing social reality.

(Schoon, 2000, p. 219)

Parents and educators who are interested in giftedness very often want to know and understand more about current findings on early child development, particularly as these apply to teaching and learning. There are many reasons why keeping up to date with the changing social reality is particularly important when living or working with exceptionally capable children and adolescents. One reason is the desire to encourage gifted learners to consider possible careers in cutting-edge fields. If gifted learners don't know about emerging opportunities in the neurosciences, for example, they are unlikely to think about preparing themselves for entering this specialty. Another reason to stay current is to ensure that children have access to the best learning opportunities.

It is very difficult for professionals to stay apprised of the latest research findings in their own fields. Understandably, then, it is considerably more difficult for the general public to know much about research findings that might affect them but that are being discovered and reported in fields in which they are not actively involved. Current findings concerning the brain, for example, have a direct and important impact on many aspects of teaching and learning, as well as on parenting, but few educators or parents have ways to access anything other than what is available in the popular press and on the Internet. And it is very difficult for laypeople to discern solid dependable findings from the confirmations of common sense (and often false) notions of the way children's brains develop. Symposia for shared learning are a good way to disseminate information on many topics that have a bearing on high-level development.

Millennium Dialogue on Early Child Development

In November of 2001, we were involved with a symposium that brought several top international scientists to the University of Toronto to have a dialogue across their diverse disciplines on the complexities of early child development. The Millennium Dialogue facilitated interconnections among professionals in different fields, as well as interested others, in order to cross-fertilize new research initiatives.

Charles Nelson, a renowned American neuroscientist, spoke about current knowledge of neurological development as applied to child development, emphasizing, among other things, the importance of neural plasticity—the fact that the brain is much more flexible and adaptable for a much longer time than many people realize. Alicia Lieberman, an American child psychologist and scientist widely recognized for her work with young children and their families, spoke about emotional development in early childhood. As with many of the other participants in the Millennium Dialogue on Early Child Development, she emphasized the importance of early emotional and social experiences in all subsequent development, certainly including cognitive development. Richard Tremblay, an internationally-respected Canadian research psychologist, discussed findings on aggression and the importance of working with high-risk children at a very young age, as well as with their parents, to help them feel accepted and supported in having their needs met. Megan Gunnar, Tom Boyce, Dan Keating, Michael Rutter, and Ron Barr, each of whom is working on the exciting frontier of his or her respective field of epidemiology, developmental psychology, and medicine, brought perspectives on their own disciplines into the discussion.

Emergent information technologies provide an unprecedented opportunity to create a conversation across fields and levels of expertise to include diverse geographic and cultural perspectives and, most importantly, to learn collaboratively about child development.

This electronically-mediated dialogue was planned as an ongoing discussion. It is accessible to anyone interested in the relationships between child development and society (see www.acscd.ca.). This is just one example of innovative ways being developed to help us all stay well-informed about rapidly changing knowledge and understandings in fields that affect our lives. As the worldwide web evolves, we can anticipate that it will provide increasingly sophisticated and useful possibilities for connectivity and access to information.

In the meantime, and perhaps always, there continue to be other, more traditional ways to keep up to date, including reading newsletters, journal articles, and books like this one, and attending education conferences where experts and practitioners share their research and ideas.

Conclusion

Although many challenges face us today, in our lives, in our communities, and globally, there are also many indicators that it is a time of unprecedented opportunity for making a difference. In this book, we provide evidence-based suggestions for supporting the development of those who are exceptionally capable in one or more domains and for fostering optimal development in all children. We emphasize that giftedness is a highly diverse phenomenon that is not easily measured or always recognized. We are excited about the paradigm shift that we are seeing in the field of gifted education and the ways in which a mastery perspective that will reach more children is gaining momentum. We hope that we have given you in these pages some tools for coping with the challenges and for being smart about the opportunities that you have in your own work with bright children.

Appendix

In this Appendix, we explain test interpretation, discuss assessments for young children, and provide some information on psychoeducational assessment reports. Although we have chosen to place this material in an appendix, it still matters a great deal. Testing and test documents are, in the words of one parent, "the nuts and bolts of assessment that parents have to deal with. Test results may be all they've got to advocate for their child, and they need to thoroughly understand them." Aspects of test interpretation may not be exciting, but understanding them is nevertheless useful for parents and educators alike.

Interpreting Test Scores

> *"We had the testing done, and the report came, and there weren't any scores. The psychologist said that she never includes the scores— that scores just confuse people."*

Test scores can be confusing to parents, as well as to teachers. Some psychologists respond to this problem by describing a child's functioning on an assessment and omitting the scores from the report. Much like a non-graded anecdotal approach to academic report card writing, this can leave parents, teachers, and children wondering about a child's actual ability, including the nature and degree of any exceptionality. Parents may find that, upon reading a number-free assessment report, they are even more confused about their child's ability than they were before doing the assessment.

Some psychologists' assessment reports include the scores but provide very little interpretive information other than classification labels such as "superior" or "average." This can be appropriate, as when an assessment is being used for labeling purposes only (that is, for a child to gain access to a gifted program). In such circumstances, the testing includes only those measures required for identification, and the report can be very short and succinct (1 to 3 pages). In addition to the basic scores, this kind of identification report includes only a few relevant observations and programming recommendations, unless there is some variability across subtest scores or test behaviors that the psychologist thinks should be noted.

However, when parents or educators want a more detailed understanding of a child's learning needs, a full psychoeducational assessment should usually be conducted. This typically includes the following components:

- an individually-administered intelligence test

- a battery of high-ceiling academic achievement tests, including various aspects of mathematical calculation and reasoning, reading decoding and comprehension, technical writing skills, and other skills as indicated

- an assessment of school functioning through an analysis of report cards and interviews with teachers as necessary

- measures of self-concept and attitudes to learning

- interviews with the child and parents

- observations of the child's response to different test situations, including areas of strength, errors, and learning challenges

The resulting assessment report is designed to be as informative as possible to parents and teachers about the child's learning profile, including strengths, challenges, and detailed recommendations for both home and school. Most parents and educators find that the most useful approach to understanding this kind of an assessment is to be able to see the scores and also to get some help in interpreting them. It is usually supplemented by an opportunity to discuss the findings with the educational psychologist responsible for the report.

In Table A.1 (*Standard Score Classifications*), we provide the categorical descriptors that are most frequently used to designate ranges of scores achieved in standardized tests. Although "very superior" is generally agreed upon as the appropriate classification for standardized test scores above 130, what constitutes giftedness is much more disputed. In some school districts, 120 is high enough for gifted consideration; in others, scores have to be 140 or more, or (in very rare cases) even higher than that in order to be eligible for a specific type of school or program.

Table A.1. Standard Score Classifications*

Test Score	Classification
130+	Very Superior
120-129	Superior
110-119	High Average
90-109	Average
80-89	Low Average
70-79	Below Average
69 and below	Mentally Retarded

for tests with a standard deviation of 15, which includes virtually all current editions of major standardized tests

Translating Standard Scores into Percentiles

> *"These numbers don't make any sense to me! Why can't psychologists just use English?!"*

For most people, the best way to understand test scores is in percentiles. Percentiles provide the clearest and simplest explanations of a person's actual functioning relative to other people. Knowing that a child has scored at the 50th percentile (that is, scoring at or higher than 50% of people his age) in some areas, and at the 99th percentile (at or higher than 99% of people his age) in other areas has some implications for his learning needs that would be less obvious if the same two scores were reported as simply the numbers "100" and "135."

A student who scores at the 50th percentile (a standard score equivalent of 100) is scoring exactly at average for her age, and her ability level will usually be well-matched by the regular curriculum. On the other hand, a student who scores above the 99th percentile is clearly exceptional in her abilities and learning needs, in a way that might not be as obvious if the corresponding score was reported as a standardized score (that is, 135). When parents or educators are provided with assessment information and the standard scores do not seem to make sense, they should ask for the percentile equivalents. It is a very reasonable request to make.

Table A.2. Translating Standard Scores into Percentiles*

Score	Percentile
155	99.99
150	99.96
145	99.87
140	99.62
135	99
130	98
125	95
120	91
115	84
110	75
105	63
100	50
95	37
90	25
85	16
80	9
75	5
70	2
65	1

* *for tests with a standard deviation of 15*

Score Conversion: One Test as Applied to Another

> "*I am trying to convert my daughter's WPPSI-R scores into an IQ score so that I can understand some of the material I've been reading. I have no idea when I am reading these articles if they apply to my child.*"

Standard scores such as those provided for the *Wechsler Preschool and Primary Scale of Intelligence* (WPPSI-R) are already IQ scores and do not need to be converted. Sometimes when people ask questions like these, what they really want to know is, "How well did my child really do on the test?" In these cases, knowing the score classification and how to convert a standard score into a percentile is often all that is needed. Tables A.1 and A.2 can be helpful in making sense of scores that you access.

The Composite Score

> *"What is a composite score actually made up of?"*

A composite score, as its name suggests, is a single score that summarizes several subtest scores. For example, an intelligence test's full scale score (often called an Intelligence Quotient or IQ) is a composite of several subscales, each of which is itself a composite of several subtests. Where scoring is relatively consistent across subtests, a composite score can provide reasonably good shorthand communication for understanding a child's abilities.

However, when there is a large discrepancy across scores, the composite score does not make sense on its own. Combining highly disparate ability scores to create a single score yields only *misinformation* rather than *useful* information. For example, a child who scores 140 (99.6th percentile, very superior range) on the verbal scale of the WISC-III, and 80 on the performance scale (9th percentile, bottom of the low average range) is a child who is probably best understood as being verbally gifted and as having significant problems with some aspect(s) of abstract/ visual processing. His overall IQ would be in the high average range (a full scale IQ of 110), which reflects neither his giftedness nor his learning problems. Obviously, in cases like this in which there are wide discrepancies across the component scores, a composite score is best omitted from consideration, as it is misleading rather than helpful in understanding how a child functions.

Interpreting Lower-than-Expected Scores

> *"We were surprised. Cindy's test scores were considerably lower than we thought they'd be."*

There is no way for a child to do exceptionally well on a test other than to know the information and have the skills being tested. High scores always reflect a high level of competence on whatever is being tested. However, when test scores are lower, that does not necessarily mean that a child does not have the knowledge and/or skills being tested. When scores do not seem to reflect a child's actual ability, there are many possible different reasons—in addition to the possibility that the child is not as competent as she otherwise appears to be. Some of the reasons for test scores underestimating a person's ability include illness, test anxiety, environmental conditions such as noise or heat, depression, and a lack of rapport with the tester.

Language is another important consideration. If a child's first language, parents' language, or language of schooling is not the language of testing, the child is at a serious disadvantage in an assessment for giftedness. He has not had the same opportunities as others his age to learn some of the facts being tested or how to communicate that knowledge effectively and succinctly in a test situation. Moreover, he has not had the same opportunities to think through, discuss, and work out complex problems in that language. In such cases, scores should be seen as a low estimate of the child's actual ability. This is most obviously true in linguistic areas of an assessment, although there is a second-language impact on quantitative and spatial reasoning areas, too.

Similarly, culture is an important factor in interpreting test scores. Some children grow up in families and cultures where learning and achievement are practical in their focus, or where creativity is not thought to be necessary for meaningful outcomes, or where time spent trying to solve abstract reasoning puzzles presented without context is considered wasted. Some children do not see the point of doing a puzzle for its own sake or just because a stranger has asked them to do so. These children will not function as well on standardized tests as they might in more applied settings, and they won't do as well as children who grow up being encouraged to participate in challenging intellectual games and puzzles.

Temperament is another reason for children to perform more poorly on tests than they do in their lives. Some highly capable children have very little interest in sitting through a test in which the examiner has all the fun figuring out the activities and giving the orders. Children who are independent, curious, individualistic, or creative and who have strong ideas about what they do and do not like to do are often very hard to test, particularly when they are young.

Test scores are not always accurate reflections of an individual's actual ability, and many circumstances can impair a child's ability to demonstrate her competence. When trying to make sense of test scores that appear not to make sense (usually scores that are lower than expected), or when trying to interpret test findings, there may be explanatory factors to consider.

Understanding Scoring Patterns

Each student has a unique developmental history and set of learning needs. There are, however, some scoring patterns that can help make sense of most children's assessment findings. We describe four of these patterns here.

1. Global Giftedness

Some students who achieve extremely high scores across almost all of the subtests of all of the measures administered might be understood as "globally gifted." The clearest example of such a case would be a student who scored consistently above the 99th percentile on all intelligence and academic subtests on an assessment, across all subject areas. This student would be a candidate for a range of acceleration and enrichment opportunities, supplemented by interest-based extracurricular learning options.

2. Domain-Specific Giftedness

There are students who show clear domain-specific trends across subtests—for instance those who can be considered mathematically gifted or linguistically gifted, but who function more closely to average in their other abilities. In such cases, educational adaptations are required in certain subject areas only and might not be needed or make sense in others.

3. Multiple Exceptionalities

Some students show different extremes across different tests, or across kinds of items on the same test, that come together in patterns indicating learning and/or attention problems along with gifted-level development. Some of these students are gifted and learning disabled, and they require accommodation for both of their learning exceptionalities. These are the students who tend to be most unhappy and frustrated with school and who very often have self-esteem problems.

4. Anomalous Scoring Patterns

Not all assessments yield consistent results that fit into a particular scoring pattern. Some students have very high scores in some subtests in a certain domain, but not in other subtests that appear to be measuring similar kinds of ability. This requires attention to the details of the items administered, including error analyses, especially on the lower-scoring subtests. Parents have the right to a clear interpretation of the test results in language that they can understand, as described in Standard 11.6 of the *Standards for Educational and Psychological Testing* (the standards in official use by registered psychologists in Canada and the U.S.) (American Educational Research Association, American Psychological Association, & National Council on Measurement in Education, 1999). Parents and educators who have been given an assessment report that does not make sense in relation to their understanding of the child in question should ask about any discrepancies between their sense of the child's ability and the scores obtained.

Looking for the Anomaly

Sam was nine years old, in Grade 4, in a regular classroom program when we met him. Although he loved math and was always looking for opportunities to develop new and related skills, he hated math at school. He had stopped doing his homework or complying with his teacher's requests to complete math activities. Naturally, his math grades started slipping badly. His parents brought him to our office for an assessment.

Sam participated enthusiastically in the assessment, enjoying the intellectual challenges, and in particular, the mathematical puzzles. He did very well generally, and there were no indications whatsoever of any cognitive processing or other kind of learning problem. He reported that math was his least favorite school subject. Although he scored well into the very superior category (above the 99th percentile) on the two mathematics achievement subtests administered and on one of the two quantitative subtests on the Stanford-Binet Intelligence Scale (Fourth Edition) (SB-IV), he scored in the average range on a second SB-IV quantitative subtest. This put his overall SB-IV quantitative area score in the high average range. It was clearly not representative of his exceptional mathematical ability as demonstrated elsewhere in the assessment, and it weakened the likelihood that a recommendation for gifted math programming would be followed up by the school.

Upon inspection of the SB-IV mathematical subtest where Sam scored in the average range, it became obvious that there had been an interaction between the test design and his knowledge base. The lower score on the problematic subtest reflected a lack of specific content knowledge rather than any lack of exceptionality in his mathematical reasoning ability—although the much broader assessment provided by the academic achievement tests demonstrated that his content mastery was exceptionally strong. By excluding the anomalous SB-IV subtest from consideration, programming recommendations could be made for Sam, including advanced work in mathematics that fit his learning needs.

Sam's teacher responded favorably to the recommendations. She received administrative support and implemented changes thoughtfully and creatively, which led to a much improved academic situation for Sam. After a few weeks, his parents reported that for the first time in years, he was looking forward to going to school and was actually enjoying doing his homework, because, as he said, "I'm learning stuff now!" Had the assessment scores been reported without considering the subtest scoring patterns, Sam would probably not have been identified as having special educational needs. Instead, it is likely that he would have continued the slide into the academic apathy and behavior problems which had brought him into the office for testing in the first place.

We have covered many of the basic concepts surrounding tests and assessments. Our intention with this material is to take some of the confusion and mystery out of assessment, so that both teachers and parents can understand why certain tests are used and how tests can be helpful when professionally administered and interpreted. We now discuss assessments of young children and how they can be used to make good programming and placement decisions.

Assessments and Young Children

As we explain in Chapter 3, standardized test results are generally not considered reliable until after age seven. However, sometimes program or school placement decisions must be made for children considerably younger than this. Circumstances will vary; however, it is important to identify useful educational strategies for the individual child, as well as to refine and target assessment practices appropriate to the school's particular needs.

Assessment tools to use with young children include:

1. Standardized tests
   - ○ intelligence/cognitive abilities
   - ○ academic aptitude (combination of cognitive and academic skills)
   - ○ academic ability (reading, mathematics)
2. Informal tests
   - ○ learning readiness and academic skills (colors, reading, numbers, other school-relevant knowledge and skills)
   - ○ self-regulation
   - ○ social development
3. Observations
   - ○ individual child interacting with a teacher
   - ○ individual child interacting with a parent
   - ○ individual child interacting with another child
   - ○ small group
   - ○ classroom group
4. Interviews
   - ○ parent(s)
   - ○ child
   - ○ parent(s) and child
5. Previous educators' reports
6. Parent questionnaires

There are some important issues to consider. The first is test reliability. There are individual differences in timing in children's cognitive, psychomotor, and social/emotional development. So, for example, a child's willingness to forego his own curiosity in playing with test manipulatives like blocks and beads for the sake of conforming to a strange adult's requests develops at different times in different children. An early capacity to do so does provide an early scoring advantage, but it does not always indicate exceptional ability. In addition, test validity (that is, does the test really test what it is supposed to be testing?) should be considered. Cost is also a factor. Standardized intelligence testing is very expensive (generally at least $500 per child). Setting up observations can also be very expensive in time and organizational resources for the school. Sometimes schools and/or parents invest tremendous resources in a program admissions process that might be better spent in other ways.

We get deeper understandings of a child's probable suitability for a particular school when we use a combination of several tools, including observations of the child in different circumstances, reports from previous teachers, and/or interviews with parents and the child. However, when dealing with questions about program eligibility and placement or admission decisions, it is a lot easier to defend numbers-based decision-making than to defend qualitative assessment data obtained from interviews and observations.

Different schools have different programs and different constraints, and they need to think about matching the selection process to their own needs and perspectives. For some schools, there is a pressing need to limit applicants and defend admissions decisions, and so a clearly-defined and defensible set of criteria must be established and held to; standardized test scores are often the simplest and most effective way to do this.

For schools which target exceptional children (for example, those who have learning problems or are gifted or deaf), the assessment measures must provide the relevant information on the nature and degree of the child's exceptionality, sometimes in addition to other school-relevant criteria such as cognitive, academic, and social/emotional skills. For other schools, the entrance concerns are more about being as inclusive as possible while minimizing behavioral issues. In this kind of circumstance, standardized intelligence or academic tests will not yield the most useful information, and observational and teacher-report data may be best.

Here are two questions for parents and educators to ask themselves when thinking about testing young children for program placement or admission purposes:

1. What information do we need in order to make a good decision?
2. What are the best tools for getting that information?

A Case Study with Excerpts from a Psychoeducational Report

In the following vignette, we present some excerpts from a psychoeducational report in order to illustrate the kinds of information contained in such documents.

Paul's Story

Paul, a Grade 7 student, was one of those kids you recognize immediately as a "computer nerd." His hair was lanky and unkempt, his glasses were always slipping down onto his nose, his posture and gait were ungainly, and he appeared oblivious to the world around him. He looked as if he had never seen the sun, and you couldn't imagine him playing any kind of sport. In class, he was lost in his own world. He often asked the teacher to repeat questions, and sometimes he laughed aloud at inappropriate moments.

Paul was not achieving particularly well at school, and he had certainly never been identified by a teacher as having special abilities in any area. Even in kindergarten, he found school a waste of time. He often asked his mother if perhaps he could stay home and do something useful, like teaching himself a new computer program. Paul's parents vacillated, seeing how miserable he was going to school, and recognizing that he seemed to be a misfit among his age-peers.

Paul's oddness never really troubled him. He was not interested in what most of the other kids did or said, and he did not appear to notice that he was not included in their activities. He never liked it when teachers tried to help him fit in better, and he truly hated the social skills group he was forced to attend in Grade 4.

Paul's mother wondered if he might be intellectually gifted, in spite of the fact that he had not been recommended even for the gifted screening tests in their school board. She had been an excellent student, her husband had a Ph.D. in philosophy, and there were several eminent scientists and musicians in the extended family. Given the family history, Paul's difficult and individualistic temperament, and his intense interests, she thought that his differentness might be a reflection of exceptional intelligence instead of the "weirdness" and "social problems" that people had been suggesting through the years. She felt that if Paul were in a more intellectually challenging milieu, he might find school more interesting.

Paul's mother arranged to have him tested on the IQ test that her school board recognized for gifted identification. The results follow:

Wechsler Intelligence Scale for Children - Third Edition (WISC-III)

Area	Standard Score	Percentile	Classification
Verbal Score	140	99.5	Very Superior
Performance Scale	106	66	Average
FULL SCALE ("IQ")	126*	96	SUPERIOR

A psychometric note to the mathematically observant or curious: The full scale IQ is not an average of the other scale scores, but rather a reflection of the deviation from the mean of the sum of all the subtest scores. The farther from the mean, the higher the score, and so if most or all subtests are above the mean, the full scale score will be higher than expected on the basis of an average taken across scale scores.

The psychologist's comments included these observations:

Paul was serious, focused, intense, and attentive throughout the testing session. He demonstrated excellent task commitment and an interest in working with abstract intellectual concepts. The WISC-III Verbal subtest and scale scores demonstrate his exceptionally well-developed verbal reasoning abilities and conceptual mastery of many areas. His very high scores on the information and comprehension subtests in particular illustrate his exceptional knowledge of a very broad range of areas. He answered in some depth and with considerable assurance and accuracy questions on science, history, geography, and politics. For example, when asked why it is important to have freedom of speech in a democracy, he replied, "If we didn't have, no one could ever say anything against the government. The government could then do what it wanted, and no one could stop it."

On the performance scale, Paul's scores were considerably lower than on the verbal scale. This was not because of any kind of cognitive processing problem that was observed (he did all subtest tasks very well, frequently getting all items correct), but only because of the timing factor. When he was asked about his lower performance on that kind of task, he said, "I prefer not to make mistakes and do it slowly, rather than to make mistakes and get it

*done really quickly." He then described his work with program-
ming computers, where if he makes an error, he only realizes it
later, and then it is very costly in time and effort to recover it. So he
has learned to work very carefully. Although this approach does
not lead to scoring exceptionally well on subtests like those on the
performance scale of the WISC-III, it is a very intelligent way to
approach many real-world tasks.*

Paul's story illustrates the need to be very careful when interpreting test scores. He had appeared to be a bright average (although not
gifted) kid at school, and his overall IQ score would not be considered
high enough to give him the gifted designation in most jurisdictions. In
the past, many people would have interpreted the discrepancy between
the verbal and performance scales as evidence of a learning disability.
However, some thoughtful observation and discussion with Paul, in combination with a careful analysis of the scores, leads one to the realization
that he is not learning disabled at all. Rather, he is a highly competent
learner who has learned to be very careful in certain kinds of tasks and
who requires gifted programming if he is to find much purpose in attending school.

By the way, Paul's story has a happy ending. His mother took the
report to her school principal. He became proactive in ensuring that
Paul was identified as gifted and offered a placement in a full-time gifted
class. Paul actually likes school now, at least most of the time. He has
found people he enjoys talking to, and he has won some academic contests and awards.

References

Aguirre, N. (2003). ESL students in gifted education. In J. A. Castellano (Ed.), *Special populations in gifted education: Working with diverse learners* (pp. 17-28). Boston: Allyn & Bacon.

Amabile, T. M. (1996). *Creativity in context: Update to the social psychology of creativity.* Boulder, CO: Westview.

American Association of University Women Educational Foundation (AAUWEF). (1998). *Separated by sex.* Washington, DC: AAUW Educational Foundation.

American Educational Research Association, American Psychological Association, & National Council on Measurement in Education. (1999). *Standards for educational and psychological testing.* Washington, DC: American Educational Research Association.

Andrews, J., & Lupart, J. (2000). *The inclusive classroom: Educating exceptional children* (2nd ed.) Toronto, ON: Nelson.

Armstrong, T. (1991). *Awakening your child's natural genius: Enhancing curiosity, creativity, and learning ability.* New York: Putnam.

Assouline, S. G., Colangelo, N., Lupkowski-Shoplik, A. E., Lipscomb, J., & Forstadt, L. (2003). *The Iowa acceleration scale* (2nd ed.). Scottsdale, AZ: Great Potential Press.

Baldwin, A., Vialle, W., & Clarke, C. (2000). Global professionalism and perceptions of teachers of the gifted. In K. A. Heller, F. J. Monks, R. J. Sternberg, & R. F. Subotnik (Eds.), *International handbook of giftedness and talent* (2nd ed., pp. 565-572). Oxford, UK: Elsevier Science.

Bennett, B., & Rolheiser, C. (2001). *Beyond Monet: The artful science of instructional integration.* Toronto, ON: Bookation.

Bereiter, C., & Scardamalia, M. (1993). *Surpassing ourselves: An inquiry into the nature and implications of expertise.* Chicago: Open Court.

Bloom, B. S. (Ed.). (1985). *Developing talent in young people.* New York: Ballantine.

Blumenfeld, P. C., Soloway, E., Marx, R. W., Krajcik, J. S., Guzdial, M., & Palincsar, A. (1991). Motivating project-based learning: Sustaining the doing, supporting the learning. *Educational Psychologist, 26,* 369-398.

Bolig, E. E., & Day, J. D. (1993). Dynamic assessment and giftedness: The promise of assessing training responsiveness. *Roeper Review, 16(2),* 110-113.

Borland, J. H. (1989). *Planning and implementing programs for the gifted.* New York: Teachers College Press.

Borland, J. H. (2003). *Rethinking gifted education.* New York: Teachers College Press.

Borowitz, S. (2003). *When we're out in public pretend you don't know me: Surviving your daughter's adolescence so you don't look like an idiot and she still talks to you.* New York: Warner Books.

Bowd, A., McDougall, D., & Yewchuk, C. (1998). *Educational psychology for Canadian teachers* (2nd ed.). Toronto, ON: Harcourt Brace.

Braggett, E. J., & Moltzen, R. I. (2000). Programs and practices for identifying and nurturing giftedness and talent in Australia and New Zealand. In K. A. Heller, F. J. Monks, R. J. Sternberg, & R. F. Subotnik (Eds.), *International handbook of giftedness and talent* (2nd ed., pp. 779-797). Oxford, UK: Elsevier Science.

Bransford, J. D., Brown, A. L., & Cocking, R. R. (Eds.). (1999). *How people learn: Bridging research and practice.* Washington, DC: National Academy Press.

Bransford, J. D., Brown, A. L., & Cocking, R. R. (Eds.). (2000). *How people learn: Brain, mind, experience, and school.* Washington, DC: National Academy Press.

Castellano, J. A. (2003). The "browning" of American schools. In J. A. Castellano (Ed.), *Special populations in gifted education: Working with diverse learners* (pp. 29-43). Boston: Allyn & Bacon.

Ceci, S. J. (1996). *On intelligence: A Bioecological treatise on intellectual development.* Boston: Harvard University Press.

Cloud, J., & Morse, J. (2001, August 27). Home sweet school. *Time Magazine* (Canadian edition), *158(8),* 45.

Colangelo, N., & Assouline, S. G. (2000). Counseling gifted students. In K. A. Heller, F. J. Monks, R. J. Sternberg, & R. F. Subotnik (Eds.), *International handbook of giftedness and talent* (2nd ed., pp. 595-607). Oxford, UK: Elsevier Science.

Colangelo, N. Assouline, S.G., & Gross, U.M. (2004). *A nation deceived: How schools hold back America's brightest students.* Volumes 1 and 2. Iowa City, IA: The Connie Belin & Jacqueline N. Blank International Center for Gifted Education and Talent Development.

Coleman, L. J., & Cross, T. L. (2000). In K. A. Heller, F. J. Monks, R. J. Sternberg, & R. F. Subotnik (Eds.), *International handbook of giftedness and talent* (2nd ed., pp. 203-212). Oxford, UK: Elsevier Science.

Coloroso, B. (2000). *Kids are worth it!* Toronto, ON: Penguin Books.

Coloroso, B. (2002). *The bully, the bullied, and the bystander.* New York: Harper Collins.

Council of State Directors of Gifted Programs. (2004). *The 2001-2002 state of the states gifted and talented education report.* Longmount, CO: Author.

Courtney, R. (1989). *Play, drama and thought: The intellectual background to drama education.* Toronto, ON: Simpon and Pierre.

Cox, J., Daniel, N., & Boston, B. (1985). *Educating able learners: Programs and promising practices.* Austin, TX: University of Texas Press.

Cropley, A. J., & Urban, K. K. (2000). Programs and strategies for nurturing creativity. In K. A. Heller, F. J. Monks, R. J. Sternberg, & R. F. Subotnik (Eds.), *International handbook of giftedness and talent* (2nd ed., pp. 485-498). Oxford, UK: Elsevier Science.

Csikszentmihalyi, M. (1991). *Flow: The psychology of optimal experience.* New York: Harper Collins.

Csikszentmihalyi, M. (1996). *Creativity: Flow and the psychology of discovery and invention.* New York: Harperperennial.

Csikszentmihalyi, M., & Wolfe, R. (2000). In K. A., F. J. Monks, R. J. Sternberg, & R. F. Subotnik (Eds.), *International handbook of giftedness and talent* (2nd ed., pp. 81-93). Oxford, UK: Elsevier Science.

Delcourt, M. A. B. (2003). Five ingredients for success: Two case studies of advocacy and the state level. *Gifted Child Quarterly, 47(1),* 27.

Deutsch Smith, D. (2004). *Introduction to special education: Teaching in an age of opportunity* (5th ed.). Boston: Pearson.

Dickson, K. (2003). Gifted education and African American learners: An equity perspective. In J. A. Castellano (Ed.), *Special populations in gifted education: Working with diverse learners* (pp. 45-63). Boston: Allyn & Bacon.

Dweck, C. S. (1998). The development of early self-conceptions: Their relevance for motivational processes. In J. Heckhausen & C. S. Dweck (Eds.), *Motivation and self-regulation across the life span.* New York: Cambridge University Press.

Enersen, D. (2003). The art of bridge building: Providing for gifted children. *Gifted Child Quarterly, 47(1),* 38-45

Feldhusen, J. F. (1995). Talent development: The new direction in gifted education. *Roeper Review, 18,* 92.

Feldhusen, J. F. (2003). Beyond general giftedness: New ways to identify and educate gifted, talented, and precocious youth. In J. H. Borland (Ed.), *Rethinking gifted education* (pp. 34-45). New York: Teachers College Press.

Feldhusen, J. F., & Jarwan, F. (2000). Identification of gifted and talented youth for educational programs. In K. A. Heller, F. J. Monks, R. J. Sternberg, & R. F. Subotnik (Eds.), *International handbook of giftedness and talent* (2nd ed., pp. 271-282). Oxford, UK: Elsevier Science.

Feldman, D. H. (1991). Why children can't be creative. *Exceptionality Education Canada, 1(1)*, 43-51.

Feldman, D. H. (2003). A developmental, evolutionary perspective on giftedness. In J. H. Borland (Ed.), *Rethinking gifted education* (pp. 9-33). New York: Teachers College Press.

Feldman, D. H., & Goldsmith, L. T. (1986). *Nature's gambit: Child prodigies and the development of human potential.* New York: Basic Books.

Ferguson, S. (2003, September 22). The ABCs of classroom fun. *Maclean's Magazine, 116(38)*, 17-22.

Ford, D. Y. (2003a). Desegregating gifted education: Seeking equity for culturally diverse students. In J. H. Borland (Ed.), *Rethinking gifted education* (pp. 143-158). New York: Teachers College Press.

Ford, D. Y. (2003b). Equity and excellence: Culturally diverse students in gifted education. In N. Colangelo & G. A. Davis (Eds.), *Handbook of gifted education* (pp. 506-520). Boston: Allyn & Bacon.

Foster, J. (2000). *A case study approach to understanding the gifted experience: Children's and parents' perceptions of labeling and placement.* Unpublished doctoral dissertation, Ontario Institute for Studies in Education of the University of Toronto, Toronto, ON.

Fullan, M. (1991). *The new meaning of educational change* (2nd ed.). New York: Teachers College Press.

Gallagher, J. J. (2000). Changing paradigms for gifted education in the United States. In K. A. Heller, F. J. Monks, R. J. Sternberg, & R. F. Subotnik (Eds.), *International handbook of giftedness and talent* (2nd ed., pp. 681-693). Oxford, UK: Elsevier Science.

Galton, F. (1869). *Hereditary genius.* London: Macmillan.

Gardner, H. (1983). *Frames of mind.* New York: Basic Books.

Gardner, H. (1991). *The unschooled mind: How children think and how schools should teach.* New York: Basic Books.

Gardner, H. (1998). A multiplicity of intelligences. *Scientific American, 9*, 18-23.

Goertzel, V., Goertzel, M., Goertzel, T. G., & Hansen, A. M. W. (2004). *Cradles of eminence* (2nd ed.). Scottsdale, AZ: Great Potential Press.

Goleman, D. (1995). *Emotional intelligence.* New York: Bantam.

Good, T. L., & Brophy, J. E. (1994). *Looking in classrooms* (6th ed.). New York: HarperCollins.

Gottfried, A. W., Gottfried, A. E., Bathurst, K., & Guerin, D. W. (1994). *Gifted IQ: Early developmental aspects.* New York: Plenum Press.

Gould, S. J. (1981). *The mismeasure of man.* New York: W.W. Norton.

Gross, M. U. M. (1993). *Exceptionally gifted children.* London: Routledge.

Gross, M. U. M. (1997). Changing teacher attitudes toward gifted children: An early and essential step. In J. Chan, R. Li, & J. Spinks (Eds.), *Maximizing potential: Lengthening and strengthening our stride.* Proceedings of the 11th World Conference on Gifted and Talented Children. Hong Kong, The University of Hong Kong Social Science Research Center.

Guilford, J. P. (1967). *The nature of human intelligence.* New York: McGraw-Hill.

Halsted, J. W. (2002). *Some of my best friends are books: Guiding gifted readers from pre-school to high school* (2nd ed.). Scottsdale, AZ: Great Potential Press.

Hannell, G. (1991). The complications of being gifted. *Gifted Education International, 7,* 126-128.

Hargreaves, A., & Earl, L. (1990). *Rights of passage: A review of selected research about schooling in the transition years.* Toronto, ON: Queen's Printer for Ontario.

Harter, S. (1982). The Perceived Competence Scale for Children. *Child Development, 49,* 788-789.

Harter, S. (1999). *The construction of the self: A developmental perspective.* New York: The Guilford Press.

Heward, W. L. (2002). *Exceptional children: An introduction to special education* (7th ed.). Upper Saddle River, NJ: Prentice Hall.

Higgins-Biss, K. (1995). *The importance of being humorous: The implications for social competence and self-concept in high level cognitive development.* Unpublished masters thesis, Ontario Institute for Studies in Education of the University of Toronto, Toronto, ON.

Hogan, K., & Pressley, M. (Eds.). (1997). *Scaffolding student learning: Instructional approaches and issues.* Cambridge, MA: Brookline Books.

Hollingworth, L. (1926). *Gifted children: Their nature and nurture.* New York: Macmillan.

Howe, M. J. A. (1990). *The origins of exceptional abilities.* Oxford, UK: Basil Blackwell.

Howe, M. J. A. (1999). *Genius explained.* Cambridge, MA: Cambridge University Press.

Johnsen, S. K., Haensly, P. A., Ryser, G. R., & Ford, R. F. (2002). Changing general education classroom practices to adapt for gifted students. *Gifted Child Quarterly, 46,* 1.

Juster, N. (1961). *The phantom tollbooth.* New York: Random House.

Kaufman, A. S. (1994). *Intelligent testing with the WISC-III.* New York: Wiley.

Kaufmann, F. A. (1981). The 1964-1968 Presidential Scholars: A follow-up study. *Exceptional Children, 48,* 2-10.

Keating, D. P. (1980). The four faces of creativity: The continuing plight of the underserved. *Gifted Child Quarterly, 24(2),* 56-61.

Keating, D. P. (1990). Adolescent thinking. In S. S. Feldman & G. R. Elliott (Eds.), *At the threshold: The developing adolescent* (pp. 54-89). Cambridge, MA: Harvard University Press.

Keating, D. P. (1991). Curriculum options for the developmentally advanced. *Exceptionality Education Canada, 1,* 53-83.

Keating, D. P. (1996). Habits of mind for a learning society: Educating for human development. In D. R. Olson & N. Torrance (Eds.), *Handbook of education and human development: New models of learning, teaching, and schooling* (pp. 461-481). Oxford: Blackwell.

Keating, D. P. (Ed.). (in press). *Nature and nurture.* London: Guilford Press.

Keating, D. P. & Hertzman, C. (Eds.). (1999). *Developmental health and the wealth of nations: Social, biological, and educational dynamics.* New York: Guilford Press.

Kerr, B. A. (2000). Guiding gifted girls and young women. In K. A. Heller, F. J. Monks, R. J. Sternberg, & R. F. Subotnik (Eds.), *International handbook of giftedness and talent* (2nd ed., pp. 649-657). Oxford, UK: Elsevier Science.

Kerr, B. A., & Cohn, S. J. (2001). *Smart boys: Talent, manhood, and the search for meaning.* Scottsdale, AZ: Great Potential Press.

Kerr, B. A., & Nicpon, M. F. (2003). Gender and giftedness. In N. Colangelo & G. A. Davis (Eds.), *Handbook of gifted education* (pp. 493-505). Boston: Allyn & Bacon.

Kitano, M. K. (2003). What's missing in gifted education reform. In J. H. Borland (Ed.), *Rethinking gifted education* (pp. 159-172). New York: Teachers College Press.

Kitchen J., & Matthews, D. J. (2004, April). *A gifted school-within-a-school: Examining perceptions of gifted programs in public secondary schools.* Paper presented at the meeting of the American Educational Research Association, San Diego, CA.

Klapp, J., & Porath, M. (2000). Past, present, and future of gifted education in British Columbia. *Alberta Gifted and Talented Education, 14(2),* 26-35.

Klein, A. G. (2002). *A forgotten voice: A biography of Leta Stetter Hollingworth.* Scottsdale, AZ: Great Potential Press.

Kluger, J., & Park, A. (2001, April 30). The quest for a super kid. *Time Magazine* (Canadian edition), 32.

Kornhaber, M., Krechevsky, M., & Gardner, H. (1990). Engaging intelligence. *Educational Psychologist, 25,* 177-199.

Leroux, J. A. (2000). A study of education of high ability students in Canada. In K. A. Heller, F. J. Monks, R. J. Sternberg, & R. F. Subotnik (Eds.), *International handbook of giftedness and talent* (2nd ed., pp. 695-702). Oxford, UK: Elsevier Science.

Lieberman, A. F. (1993). *The emotional life of the toddler.* New York: The Free Press.

Lubinski, D., Benbow, C. P., & Morelock, M. J. (2000). Gender differences in engineering and the physical sciences among the gifted: An inorganic-organic distinction. In K. A. Heller, F. J. Monks, R. J. Sternberg, & R. F. Subotnik (Eds.), *International handbook of giftedness and talent* (2nd ed., pp. 633-648). Oxford, UK: Elsevier Science.

Maclean's magazine. (2004, Feb. 2). *Editor,* 10.

Manitoba Education, Citizenship, and Youth. (2002). *Education agenda for student success (2002-2006).* Retrieved July 2, 2004, from www.edu.gov.mb.ca/ks4/agenda

Marland, S. P. (1972). *Education of the gifted and talented* (Vol. 1). Report of the Congress of the United States by the U.S. Commissioner of Education. Washington, DC: Government Printing Office.

Matthews, D. J. (1997). Diversity in domains of development: Research findings and their implications for gifted identification and programming. *Roeper Review, 19,* 172-177.

Matthews, D. J. (1998). Enhancing learning outcomes for diversely gifted adolescents: Education in the social/emotional domain. *The Journal of Secondary Gifted Education, 10,* 157-168.

Matthews, D. J., & Foster, J. F. (2003, April 10). Helping children cope with circumstances in difficult times. *Canadian Jewish News.* (reprinted with permission at www.beingsmart.ca).

Matthews, D. J., & Foster, J. F. (2005). A dynamic scaffolding model of teacher development: The gifted education consultant as a catalyst for change. *Gifted Child Quarterly, 49,* 3, 222-230.

Matthews, D. J., & Keating, D. P. (1995). Domain specificity and habits of mind: An investigation of patterns of high-level development. *Journal of Early Adolescence, 15,* 319-343.

Matthews, D. J., & Menna, R. (2003, Winter). Solving problems together: The importance of parent/school/community collaboration at a time of educational and social change. *Education Canada, 43(1),* 20-23.

Matthews, D. J., & Steinhauer, N. (1998). Giftedness, girls, others, and equity: Theory-based practical strategies for the regular classroom. *Exceptionality Education Canada, 8(2),* 41-56.

Meier, D. (2002). *The power of their ideas: Lessons for America from a small school in Harlem.* New York: Beacon Press.

Mendaglio, S., & Pyryt, M. C. (2000). Centre for Gifted Education: Yesterday, today, and tomorrow. *AGATE, 14(2),* 15-19.

Millar, G, (2000). Looking backward and forward at the millennium: An Alberta learning perspective. *AGATE, 14(2),* 20-25.

Mitchell, A. (2003, September 27). Slow schooling: It makes mainstream education look like fast food. *The Globe and Mail,* F1, F10.

Moon, S. M., & Rosselli, H. C. (2000). Developing gifted programs. In K. A. Heller, F. J. Monks, R. J. Sternberg, & R. F. Subotnik (Eds.), *International handbook of giftedness & talent* (2nd ed., pp. 499-521). Oxford, UK: Elsevier Science.

National Association for Gifted Children. (n.d.). *Gifted education programming criterion: Professional development.* Retrieved June 29, 2004, from www.nagc.org/table6.htm

Nelson, C. A. (1999). Neural plasticity and human development. *Current Directions in Psychological Science, 8,* 42-45.

Nelson, C. A. (in press). Neural development and life-long plasticity. In D. P. Keating (Ed.), *The nature and nurture of early child development: Beyond myth to science, policy, and practice.* Oxford: Blackwell.

New York State. (1982). *Education Law, Article 90, Section 4452.* Albany, NY: Author.

Noble, K. D., Subotnik, R. F., & Arnold, K. D. (1999). To thine own self be true: A new model of female talent development. *Gifted Child Quarterly, 43,* 140-149.

Nova Scotia Department of Education. (1999). *Challenge for excellence: Enrichment and gifted education.* Halifax: Author.

Oatley, K., & Jenkins, J. M. (1996). *Understanding emotions.* Cambridge, MA: Blackwell.

Ohio Department of Education. (2000). *Project Start ID: Statewide arts talent identification and development project.* Columbus, OH: Author.

Ontario College of Teachers. (1999). *The standards of practice for the teaching profession.* Retrieved June 29, 2004, from www.oct.ca/en/CollegePublications/PDF/standards.pdf

Ontario Ministry of Education. (1984). *Special education handbook.* Toronto, ON: Author.

Ontario Ministry of Education and Training. (1999). *Ontario secondary schools grades 9 to 12: Program and diploma requirements.* Toronto, ON: Author.

Ontario Ministry of Education and Training. (2000). *Individual education plans: Standards for development, program planning, and implementation.* Toronto, ON: Author.

Oreck, B. A., Owen, S. V., & Baum, S. M. (2003). Validity, reliability, and equity issues in an observational talent assessment process in the performing arts. (Article includes the *Talent Assessment Process.*) *Journal for the Education of the Gifted, 27(1),* 62-94.

Palloff, R. M., & Pratt, K. (2001). *Lessons form the cyberspace classroom: The realities of online teaching.* San Francisco: Jossey-Bass.

Perkins, D. N. (1981). *The mind's best work.* Cambridge, MA: Harvard University Press.

Persson, R. S., Joswig, H., & Balogh, L. (2000). Gifted education in Europe. In K. A. Heller, F. J. Monks, R. J. Sternberg, & R. F. Subotnik (Eds.), *International handbook of giftedness and talent* (2nd ed., pp. 703-734). Oxford, UK: Elsevier Science.

Piirto, J. (1999). *Talented children and adults: Their development and education* (2nd ed.). New York: Macmillan.

Piirto, J. (2004). *Understanding creativity.* Scottsdale, AZ: Great Potential Press.

Piper, W. (1930). *The little engine that could.* New York: Platt & Munk.

Pipher, M. (1994). *Reviving Ophelia: Saving the selves of adolescent girls.* New York: Ballantine.

Raven, J. C., Court, J. H., & Raven, J. (1998). *Standard Progressive Matrices.* London: Lewis.

Reilly, J. (1992). *Mentorship, the essential guide for schools and business.* Scottsdale, AZ: Great Potential Press, formerly Ohio Psychology Press.

Renzulli, J. S. (2003, November). *Senior scholars speak out.* Paper presented at annual meeting of National Association for Gifted Children, Indianapolis, IN.

Renzulli, J. S., & Reis, S. M. (1985). *The schoolwide enrichment model: A comprehensive plan for educational excellence.* Mansfield Center, CT: Creative Learning Press.

Renzulli, J. S., & Reis, S. M. (2000). The schoolwide enrichment model. In K. A. Heller, F. J. Monks, R. J. Sternberg, & R. F. Subotnik (Eds.), *International handbook of giftedness and talent* (2nd ed., pp. 367-382). Oxford, UK: Elsevier Science.

Richert, E. S. (2003). Excellence with justice in identification and programming. In N. Colangelo & G. A. Davis (Eds.), *Handbook of gifted education* (pp. 146-158). Boston: Allyn & Bacon.

Rivero, L. (2002). *Creative home schooling: A resource guide for smart families.* Scottsdale, AZ; Great Potential Press.

Robinson, N. M. (2003). Two wrongs do not make a right: Sacrificing the needs of gifted students does not solve society's unsolved problems. *Journal for the Education of the Gifted, 26(4),* 251-273.

Robinson, N. M., & Robinson, H. B. (1982). The optimal match: Devising the best compromise for the highly gifted student. In D. Feldman (Ed.), *New directions for child development: Developmental approaches to giftedness and creativity* (pp. 79-94). San Francisco: Jossey-Bass.

Rogers, K. B. (2002). *Re-forming gifted education: How parents and teachers can match the program to the child.* Scottsdale, AZ: Great Potential Press.

Rogers, K. B. (2003). A voice of reason in the wilderness. *Journal for the Education of the Gifted, 26(4),* 314-320.

Roid, G. H. (2003). *Stanford-Binet Intelligence Scales* (5th ed.). Itasca, IL: Riverside Publishing.

Ruf, D. (in press). *Losing our minds: Gifted children left behind.* Scottsdale, AZ: Great Potential Press.

Salmon, G. (2000). *E-Moderating: The key to teaching and learning online.* Sterling, VA: Stylus.

Santrock, J. W. (1994). *Child development* (6th ed.). Madison, WI: Brown & Benchmark.

Sattler, J. M. (2001). *Assessment of children: Cognitive applications* (4th ed.). San Diego, CA: Jerome Sattler Publishing.

Scardamalia, M. (n.d.). *Knowledge forum.* Retrieved June 29, 2004, from www.knowledgeforum.com

Schipper, B., & Rossi, J. (1997). *Portfolios in the classroom: Tools for learning and instruction.* York, MA: Stenhouse.

Schoon, I. (2000). A life span approach to talent development. In K. A. Heller, F. J. Monks, R. J. Sternberg, & R. F. Subotnik (Eds.), *International handbook of giftedness and talent* (2nd ed., pp. 213-225). Oxford, UK: Elsevier Science.

Schouten, F. (2003, January 30). *High turnover worsens teacher shortage.* Retrieved July 2, 2004, from www.detnews.com/2003/schools/0301/30/a01-72737.htm

Schultz, R. A. (2002). Understanding giftedness and underachievement: At the edge of possibility. *Gifted Child Quarterly, 46(3),* 193-205.

Shi, J., & Zha, Z. (2000). Psychological research on and education of gifted and talented children in China. In K. A. Heller, F. J. Monks, R. J. Sternberg, & R. F. Subotnik (Eds.), *International handbook of giftedness and talent* (2nd ed., pp. 757-764). Oxford, UK: Elsevier Science.

Shonkoff, J. P., & Phillips, D. A. (2000). *From neurons to neighborhoods: The science of early childhood development.* Washington, DC: National Academy Press.

Silverman, L. K. (2003). Gifted children with learning disabilities. In N. Colangelo & G. A. Davis (Eds.), *Handbook of gifted education* (pp. 533-544). Boston: Allyn & Bacon.

Silvertown, R. (n.d.). *Virtuoso: The Travel Network Corp.* Retrieved June 28, 2004, from www.virtuoso.com/ge/active_0404a.html

Simonton, D. K. (1994). *Greatness: Who makes history and why.* New York: Guilford Press.

Simonton, D. K. (1997). Creative productivity: A predictive and explanatory model of career trajectories and landmarks *Psychological Review, 104,* 66-89.

Simonton, D. K. (2000). *Genius and giftedness: Same or different?* In K. A. Heller, F. J. Monks, R. J. Sternberg, & R. F. Subotnik (Eds.), *International handbook of giftedness and talent* (2nd ed., pp. 111-121). Oxford, UK: Elsevier Science.

Soriano de Alencar, E. M. L., Blumen-Pardo, S., & Castellanos-Simons, D. (2000). Programs and practices for identifying and nurturing giftedness and talent in Latin American countries. In K. A. Heller, F. J. Monks, R. J. Sternberg, & R. F. Subotnik (Eds.), *International handbook of giftedness and talent* (2nd ed., pp. 817-828). Oxford, UK: Elsevier Science.

Spearman, C. (1927). *The abilities of man: Their nature and measurement.* New York: Macmillan.

Stanford Achievement Tests. (2003). *Stanford achievement tests, tenth edition.* San Antonio, TX: Harcourt Educational Measurement.

Stanley, J. C., & Benbow, C. P. (1983). Educating mathematically precocious youths: Twelve policy recommendations. *Educational Researcher, 11(5),* 4-9.

Stanley, J. C., Keating, D. P., & Fox, L. (1974). *Mathematical talent.* Baltimore: Johns Hopkins Press.

Steinberg, L. (2004). *Adolescence.* New York: McGraw-Hill.

Sternberg, R. J. (1998). Principles of teaching for successful intelligence. *Educational Psychologist, 33(2/3),* 65-72.

Sternberg, R. J., & Williams, W. M. (2002). *Educational psychology.* Boston: Allyn & Bacon.

Stipek, D. (2002). *Motivation to learn: Integrating theory and practice* (3rd ed.). Boston: Allyn & Bacon.

Subhi, T., & Maoz, N. (2000). Middle East region: Efforts, policies, programs, and issues. In K. A. Heller, F. J. Monks, R. J. Sternberg, & R. F. Subotnik (Eds.), *International handbook of giftedness and talent* (2nd ed., pp. 743-756). Oxford, UK: Elsevier Science.

Subotnik, R. F., Olszewski-Kubilius, P., & Arnold, K. D. (2003). Beyond Bloom: Revisiting environmental factors that enhance or impede talent development. In J. H. Borland (Ed.), *Rethinking gifted education* (227-238). New York: Teachers College Press.

Tannenbaum, A. J. (1983). *Gifted children: Psychological and educational perspectives*. New York: Macmillan.

Tannenbaum, A. J. (2000). A history of giftedness in school and society. In K. A. Heller, F. J. Monks, R. J. Sternberg, & R. F. Subotnik (Eds.), *International handbook of giftedness and talent* (2nd ed., pp. 23-53). Oxford, UK: Elsevier Science.

Taylor, C. A., & Kokot, S. J. (2000). The status of gifted child education in Africa. In K. A. Heller, F. J. Monks, R. J. Sternberg, & R. F. Subotnik (Eds.), *International handbook of giftedness and talent* (2nd ed., pp. 799-815). Oxford, UK: Elsevier Science.

Terman, L. M. (Ed.). (1925-1959). *Genetic studies of genius* (Vols. 1-5). Stanford, CA: Stanford University Press.

Thorndike, R. L., Hagen, E. P., Wright, E. N. (1988). *Canadian Cognitive Abilities Test, Form K*. Toronto, ON: Nelson.

Thurstone, L. L. (1938). *Primary mental abilities*. Chicago: University of Chicago Press.

Tieso, C. L. (2003). Ability grouping is not just tracking anymore. *Roeper Review, 6(1)*, 29-36.

Tomlinson, C. A. (2003a). *Differentiated instruction: The critical issue of quality*. Paper presented at the annual meeting of the National Association for Gifted Children, Indianapolis, IN.

Tomlinson, C. A. (2003b). Fulfilling the promise of the differentiated classroom: Strategies and tools for responsive teaching. Alexandria, VA: Association for Supervision and Curriculum Development.

Tomlinson, C. A., Kaplan, S. N., Renzulli, J., Purcell, J., Leppien, J., & Burns, D. (2001). *The parallel curriculum*. Thousand Oaks, CA: Corwin Press.

Tomlinson, C. A., & Reis, S. M. (2004). *Differentiation for gifted and talented students*. Thousand Oaks, CA: Corwin Press.

Toto, C. (2004, March 8). The burden of brilliance. *The Washington Times*. Retrieved from http://washingtontimes.com/metro/20040307-104351-9236r.htm

Toynbee, A. (1967). Is America neglecting her creative talents? In C. W. Taylor (Ed.), *Creativity across education* (pp. 23-29). Salt Lake City, UT: University of Utah Press.

Treffinger, D. J., & Feldhusen, J. F. (1996). Talent recognition and development: Successor to gifted education. *Journal for the Education of the Gifted, 16,* 181-193.

U.S. Department of Education. (2001). *No Child Left Behind Act of 2001.* Washington, DC: Author.

Van Pelt, D. A. (2003). *Home education 2003: A report on the pan-Canadian study on home education.* Medicine Hat, AB: Canadian Centre for Home Education.

VanTassel-Baska, J. (2000). Theory and practice in curriculum development for the gifted. In K. A. Heller, F. J. Monks, R. J. Sternberg, & R. F. Subotnik (Eds.), *International handbook of giftedness and talent* (2nd ed., pp. 345-366). Oxford, UK: Elsevier Science.

VanTassel-Baska, J., & Little, C. A. (2003). *Content-based curriculum for high-ability learners.* Waco, TX: Prufrock Press.

Vygotsky, L. S. (1978). *Mind in society.* Cambridge, MA: Harvard University Press. (Original work published 1930.)

Wahlsten, D. (1997). The malleability of intelligence is not constrained by heritability. In B. Devlin, S. E. Fienberg, & D. P Resnick (Eds.), *Intelligence, genes, and success.* New York: Springer-Verlag.

Webb, J. T. (2004). *Tips for selecting the right counselor or therapist for your gifted child.* Retrieved June 29, 2004, from www.giftedbooks.com/ aart_webb3.html

Webb, J. T., Amend, E. R., Webb, N. E., Goerss, J., Beljan, P., Olenchak, F. R., & Lind, S. (in press). *Misdiagnosis and dual diagnoses of gifted children and adults: ADHD, Bipolar, OCD, Asperger's, depression, and other disorders.* Scottsdale, AZ: Great Potential Press.

Webb, J. T., Meckstroth, E. A., Tolan, S. S. (1994). *Guiding the gifted child: A practical source for parents and teachers.* Scottsdale, AZ: Great Potential Press (formerly Gifted Psychology Press).

Wechsler, D. (1981). *Wechsler Adult Intelligence Scale-Revised.* San Antonio, TX: Psychological Corp.

Wechsler, D. (1989). *Wechsler Preschool and Primary Scale of Intelligence- Revised.* San Antonio, TX: Psychological Corp.

Wechsler, D. (2003). *Wechsler Intelligence Scale for Children* (4th ed.). San Antonio, TX: Psychological Corp.

Winner, E. (1996). *Gifted children: Myths and realities.* New York: Basic Books.

Woodcock, R. W., McGrew, K. S., & Mather, N. (2001). *Woodcock-Johnson III.* Itasca, IL: Riverside Publishing.

World Council for Gifted and Talented Children. (2003, November 3). *Newsletter of the World Council for Gifted and Talented Children.* Vol. 22(3).

Wright, L., & Borland, J. H. (1993). Using early childhood developmental portfolios in the identification and education of young, economically disadvantaged, potentially gifted students. *Roeper Review, 15,* 205-210.

Yalom, I. (1983). *Existential psychotherapy.* New York: Basic Books.

Zeller, C. W. (1993, December). *ABC Newsmagazine.* Retrieved June 29, 2004, from www.kanservu.ca/~abc/zeller.htm

Index

A

abstract reasoning 69, 268, 390
academic
  achievement 44, 47, 65-66, 69,
    73, 78, 83, 90
  overload 204, 214
acceleration
  early entrance 93, 333
  full-grade 136-138
  practices 137
  radical 136, 138, 294
  single-subject 93, 136
  subject-specific 45, 68, 82, 127
achievement
  academic mismatch 204, 209
  academic overload 204, 209,
    215-217, 231, 241
  tests 47, 64-68, 73, 83
  underachievers 206, 273
adaptive instruction 26, 109, 145,
    354, 365
ADHD 77
adolescence 17, 256, 267,
    269-270, 272, 282-283, 285,
    299, 329, 331, 375

advocacy 310-315, 318-319
  for all children 23, 315
  for gifted learners 62, 188,
    274-275, 312-315, 365
  process 8, 79, 91
Africa 372
age
  early identification 92
  for testing 50-52, 394-395
aggression 243
America
  homeschooling in 151
  programs in 187
anomalous scoring patterns 391
anxiety 55, 84, 216, 223, 230,
    249, 276
arrogance 91, 231-232
Asia 371
Asperger's Syndrome 240, 304
assessment
  classroom-based 63-65, 68, 79,
    83, 85
  concerns about 44, 101
  diagnostic 89
  dynamic 10, 61-64, 80

assessment *(cont.)*
  formal 14, 28, 47-49, 50, 57, 64,
    79-80, 82, 87, 114
  group 69
  informal 28, 76, 79, 114
  measures 47, 51, 61, 66, 74,
    79-80, 87
  parents and 102-103
  performing arts 74
  private 49, 56-57
  programs 181
  questions 43
  reports 80, 385-386, 395
  timing 8
  tools 394
  young children 64, 93, 179,
    266, 385, 393
Association for Bright Children 330
Australia 371-372
authenticity 202

B
bibliotherapy 166-167
book lists 165-167, 320
boredom 46, 114, 142, 171, 209,
    212-213, 241
boys 282-286
brain development 19, 29
bullies 243-246

C
Calgary 371
Canada 255, 363
Canadian Cognitive Abilities Test
    69
careers
  counseling 75, 275-276
  days 76, 164, 185
  exploration 13, 127, 164, 174,
    181

interest inventories 75, 274
  unconventional 127, 278
characteristics
  administrative 188, 313, 354
  classroom 38, 57, 59-60, 68, 79,
    82, 93, 108-111, 113-122
  school 80, 85, 135, 139,
    147-148, 157, 181, 186
  student 27, 57-58
  teacher 39, 57, 62, 64, 79, 83,
    98, 107, 337-339
checklists 10, 58, 87, 103, 118
China 370
cognitive ability 8, 16, 69, 327
collaboration
  classroom 10, 12, 79
  cross-panel 173
competition 159, 229, 370
conceptual mastery 67, 143, 397
confidence 18, 100-101, 128-129,
    152, 160, 195-196, 264
conflict resolution 242, 246-247,
    327
consultancy 338, 357-362
content mastery 33, 65, 80, 181,
    195, 293
counseling 218, 282-286, 324,
    330-335
creative 38
creativity 39
  testing 73
critical thinking 33
cross-grade expertise 173
cultural differences 286-290
curriculum
  compacting 114-115, 173
  modification 80, 100, 108-109,
    175, 340
  planning 9, 23, 49, 54, 68
cut-off scores 43, 70, 85, 89

cyber-learning 131

D

definitions
 creativity 31-35, 37, 39
 giftedness 3, 5-6, 10, 16-22, 25,
  27, 29, 31-32, 39
 intelligence 13-17, 22, 26, 48,
  70, 79-80, 253
depression 44, 52, 137, 227, 241,
 269, 298, 390
developmental advancement 6
divergent thinking 33-35, 37, 339
domain-specific giftedness 391
dual exceptionalities 297, 304
dual track programs 142
dynamic scaffolding model 338,
 351-352, 355-357

E

early entrance 93, 138, 367
educational options 107, 187,
 337, 381
elitism 9-10, 24, 26, 101, 113
eminence 14, 18
emotional
 intelligence 227
 issues 25, 331
 problems 56
empathy 243
environmental influences 10, 15,
 253
equity 287-289
Europe 168, 369
exceptional learning needs 49,
 189, 339, 342
exceptionally gifted 138, 141, 294
extracurricular enrichment 158,
 190, 379

F

failure 19
 academic 10
 fear of 216, 229-230
 responses to xvi, 266
 school 46, 80
family
 challenge 178, 181, 183, 185,
  231, 271
 excursions 168
 parenting 256, 271, 318, 325
 pressure 26
 siblings 47, 101, 124, 177, 179,
  232, 267, 290, 321-325, 327,
  379
 support 5, 55, 79, 92, 101
flexibility 47, 67, 99, 109, 122,
 146, 152, 339
flow 34-35
friends 47, 101, 176-179, 216,
 241, 257, 267, 312
funding 9, 26, 310, 349, 364, 366,
 370

G

gender stereotypes 282, 286, 290
genetic predisposition 10, 254
genius 3, 212, 256
gifted classes
 full-time 58-60, 135
 part-time 9, 59, 135, 142
Gifted Education Center 378
girls 117, 127-129, 163, 211, 226,
 243, 273, 282-286
global giftedness 391
grade skipping 93
grades 77-78, 88, 203, 205-206,
 208, 216, 220, 329

guidance
  academic 8, 10, 26
  career 75-76, 127, 129-131,
    164-165, 274, 276-277, 335
  mentors 76, 119, 159, 162
  parental 182, 271, 307, 323, 325

H

higher-order thinking 169, 293,
  339-340, 346
highly gifted 18, 75, 77, 124,
  145-146, 184-185, 293-294, 331
home schooling 135, 150-153
homework 77, 194, 202, 205,
  263-264, 272, 392
humor 51, 162, 181, 196, 217,
  256, 258-261, 310, 318
Hunter College Campus Schools
  140

I

idealism 277
identification
  criteria 17, 34, 58-59, 78, 85,
    89, 91, 182, 186-187, 266, 312,
    395
  cut-off scores 43, 70, 85, 89
  early identification 8, 51, 92
  evidence-based 88
  labeling 63, 81-82, 94, 99, 101,
    322, 328, 369
  measures 47, 51, 61, 66, 79-80,
    87
  procedures 43, 58-59, 83-84,
    98, 371-372
  process 28, 36, 44, 55, 64,
    74-75, 79, 81-82, 84, 86-91,
    97-98, 101, 174, 176, 178, 182,
    184, 186-189, 224, 312, 314,
    367, 370, 395

identification *(cont.)*
  recommendations 44, 49, 81,
    86, 91, 185, 189, 369, 393
  tests 8, 10, 28, 35, 43, 45, 47-49,
    55, 69, 79, 87
imposter syndrome 224, 230
inclusion 288, 364-365, 380
independence 285, 309, 316, 319,
  325, 328, 353
independent study 119, 173
individual developmental differences 21, 256-258, 334
individual education plans
  174-175
individuality 180, 238-239, 262,
  271, 284, 309
inservice programs 345-346
integrated curriculum model 15,
  110
intelligence
  domains 17-18, 28, 163, 175,
    187, 383
  global 7, 84, 201
  history 31, 47, 61
  multiple intelligences 14, 17
intelligence quotient (IQ) xv,
    xvii, 5, 10-11, 15, 17, 22, 27-28,
    38, 48, 53, 60, 68-69, 71, 90-91,
    118, 189, 203, 260, 281-282,
    298, 322, 339, 356, 388-389,
    396-398
intelligence tests 5, 69-70, 89
International Baccalaureate 147
interpersonal skills 69, 234
intrinsic motivation 35, 203-204
Iowa Acceleration Scale 93, 139
isolation 137, 166, 236, 285,
  291-292

J

Japan 371, 373
journals 63, 103

K

Keating's analysis of creativity 39
Knowledge Forum 201
Korea 371

L

labeling 81-82, 86, 94, 98-99,
 101, 113, 140, 206, 225, 322,
 328, 386
language immersion 135,
 143-144, 158-159, 174
Latin America 372
leadership 22, 69, 145, 159, 186,
 240, 294, 340, 356, 370, 379
learned helplessness 204,
 209-211, 217, 229, 241
learning (*see also* problems,
 learning)
 disabilities 6, 23, 109, 116, 294,
 296-298
 gaps 136, 138, 371
 pace 68, 131-132, 136-138, 187,
 219
 styles 28, 47, 63, 69, 76, 80, 132,
 201, 295
learning options
 extracurricular 107, 158-159,
 307
 school 5, 13-14, 19, 23, 25, 27,
 29, 45-46, 49, 54, 57, 61, 75,
 80, 83, 121, 124, 126, 138,
 147-150, 161, 174-187, 189-190,
 212, 264, 312-314, 319, 341,
 346, 348, 352, 354, 366,
 370-373, 375-377, 380, 398
legislative issues 151

library 117, 133, 151, 164, 183,
 301, 321, 365
linguistic giftedness 84, 254

M

marks 57, 77-78, 300, 323
Marland Report 13, 22
mastery model of giftedness
 5-10, 13-14, 21, 24, 39, 68,
 85-86, 88-89, 113, 177, 188,
 262, 289, 335, 346, 350, 362
mastery orientation 211
mathematical giftedness 10
mentors 76, 159-164, 174
minority 209, 287-290
motivation
 extrinsic 202-203
 intrinsic 35, 144, 148, 184,
 202-204, 237, 291
 learning 13, 18, 26, 28, 38,
 45-46, 50-52, 57, 60, 62, 68,
 157, 173, 193
 maximizing 218
multiple exceptionalities 391
multiple intelligences 14, 17
multipotentiality 75, 163, 165,
 275-276
music 8, 16-17, 20-21, 28, 31, 37,
 69, 74-75, 145-146, 158, 179,
 203, 207, 213, 225, 255, 258,
 261-262, 267, 270, 275,
 372-373, 396
mystery model of giftedness
 5-10, 13, 15, 25, 58, 87, 89,
 346, 362

N

National Association for Gifted
 Children (NAGC) 85, 110,
 320, 330, 349, 350, 368, 370

National Research Center on the
Gifted and Talented 111
nature and nurture 15-16, 253-254
networks 151, 240, 340, 350, 371,
378
neural plasticity 29, 382
New Zealand 372
No Child Left Behind 23, 310
nomination 91, 162
norming flexibility 67
norming population 49

O

Ontario legislation 126
options, programming
acceleration 93, 110, 127,
135-144,
career counseling 335
career exploration 130, 162,
274, 278
curriculum compacting
113-114, 121
cyber-learning 174
dual track 135, 142-145, 174
extracurricular xiv, 101, 107, 307
gifted center 378-380
gifted classes 140-141
guided independent study 113,
119
home schooling 150-153
independent schools 148-150
mentorships 159-164, 293, 370
second language immersion
135, 142
single-subject acceleration 93
single-subject enrichment 113
over-programming 158

P

paradigm shift xiv, 13-15, 25,
362, 367, 383
parallel curriculum model 110
parenting
adolescents 267-273, 375
advocacy 37, 102-103, 122,
189-190, 315-320
concerns 4, 27-29, 56, 92, 98,
176-178, 182, 184, 189-190,
205, 224, 235-236, 242,
270-271, 318-333
early childhood 271
strategies 173-175, 225,
302-303, 316-318, 327, 329
supportive 37, 102-103, 123,
178, 317-320, 324, 327
passion 75, 270
peers
age- 18, 58, 67, 136-137, 238-239,
257, 261, 270, 295, 375, 396
coaching 130-131, 174
grade- 67
intellectual 100, 139, 142, 181,
187, 396
percentiles 80, 387
perfectionism 217, 230-231
persistence 32, 91, 160, 199-200
personality 100-101, 125, 131,
162-163, 189-190, 298, 325,
345
perspective 228
policy xi, xiv, 23, 45, 85, 90, 98,
175, 366, 369, 371-372
politics 308, 311
portfolio 64, 103, 118
potential xvi, 5, 16, 24-26, 28-29,
36-37, 202, 206, 208, 288, 368,
373, 381

precocity 10, 20-21
preservice programs 341-342, 357-358, 360-362
private schools 90, 135
problems
  academic 141, 184-185, 206, 242
  behavioral 72, 153, 223, 241-242, 286, 297, 322, 344, 354, 395
  developmental 24, 88, 101, 180, 187, 190, 340, 375-376
  emotional 16, 27, 72, 141, 154, 223, 241-242, 266, 269, 297, 331
  learning 6, 9, 44-46, 212, 264, 294-304, 328, 341, 354, 389, 395, 398
  motivational 141, 208, 360
  social 27, 50, 137, 166-167, 176-178, 216, 223, 228, 242, 244, 269
procrastination 216
prodigies 20, 28, 261
professional help 57, 230, 242, 249, 316, 329-331, 334
professional journals 320
program options 95, 109, 314
project-based learning 115-119, 122, 170, 173, 293, 344, 400
psychologists 49, 56, 385, 392
public schools 90

R
Raven's Progressive Matrices 69
reading 7, 10, 13, 63, 67, 158, 165-167, 394
reasoning
  ability 53-54, 65, 69-70, 73, 80, 272, 282, 393
  tests 45, 87
relaxation 158, 166

relevance 37, 80, 115, 130, 195, 316, 344, 353
reliability 65, 394
report cards 59, 77-79, 205, 385-386
research 115-116, 119, 121-122, 128, 146, 149, 152, 158-159, 163, 170
resources
  contacts 330
  cross-grade 121
  libraries 214, 301, 320
  reading 165-167, 300-301
  school-based 45, 89, 179, 188-189, 353

S
scholarship 279
school
  choice 181, 184, 187, 190
  culture 247, 315-316, 380
  reform 320
schools
  alternative 135, 147-148, 174-175
  elementary 37, 59, 126, 161
  high 119, 126-128, 130, 132, 133, 143, 147, 161, 279, 370
  independent 148-150, 174
  magnet 147
  middle 122, 126, 346, 348
  Montessori 148-149
  primary 184, 286
  private 90, 135, 148, 182-186, 369, 373
  publicly-funded 180
screening
  measures 8, 47, 61, 66, 79-80, 87, 177, 386, 391, 395

processes 64, 74, 182, 189, 310, 312, 370

tests 5, 10, 28, 43, 45, 47-49, 55, 79, 312, 388, 394-396

second language

immersion programs 142-145

schooling 142-145

self-concept 226-227

self-directed learners 153

self-esteem 44, 55, 140, 194-195, 204, 227, 240, 269, 298, 391

self-regulation 199, 394

SENG—Supporting the Emotional Needs of the Gifted 249

sibling relationships 316, 321

Singapore 371

single-subject acceleration 93, 136, 174

skipping 93, 135-138, 370

social competence 101, 232, 259

social skills 130, 235, 238-240, 259-261, 285

South Africa 372-373

special education 6-7, 12-14, 16, 22, 26, 29, 46, 71, 86

specialty subject areas 146

standard deviation 21, 48-49, 71

standard scores 47-48, 80

standardized tests 50, 102, 387

Stanford Achievement Tests 66

Stanford-Binet Intelligence Scale 48, 59, 71, 392

strategies, classroom 107-133

stress 171, 177, 216-217, 231, 259-260, 269, 303, 314, 374

student portfolios 83

Study of Mathematically Precocious Youth 13, 127

study skills 213

Supporting the Emotional Needs of the Gifted 249

T

talent assessment process 37, 74

talent development 15, 21, 87, 284, 287, 315

talent search 23, 280

talented children 135, 262, 367, 370

task commitment 78, 163, 295, 370, 397

teacher development

initial 341, 360, 379

inservice 342-346, 348, 356, 360, 365, 379

preservice 322, 341, 348, 357-358, 360

professional development 112, 116, 122, 138, 150, 289, 315, 343, 345-356, 358-360, 365

teacher

action research 115, 340, 350, 358-359, 361, 380

collaboration 38, 147, 201, 377

new 177-178, 187, 202, 214, 338, 342, 357-360

qualifications 150, 338

teaching

classroom culture 236, 345

environment 38, 61, 80, 102, 109-110, 133, 140, 149, 163, 186, 190, 241, 254

strategies 108, 343, 345, 347

temperament 28, 93, 264, 295, 325

tests

above-level 45

academic achievement 47, 65-67, 83

administration 47-48, 176

tests *(cont.)*
  advance preparation 50
  anxiety 55, 71, 84, 390
  aptitude 22, 73, 394
  career inventories 74-75
  ceiling 66, 292
  classroom-based 64, 79, 85
  cognitive ability 8, 69
  creativity 10, 33, 35-37, 73-74, 87
  diagnostic 68
  group 49, 65, 67
  high-ceiling 8, 45, 67-68
  individual 45, 47-48, 50, 53-54,
    70, 72, 80, 173-178, 180, 183,
    188, 292
  informal 28, 179, 188
  intelligence 8, 17, 47-48, 54-55,
    60, 68-71, 79-80, 89, 292, 333,
    386, 389, 391, 394-395
  interpretation 28, 48, 70, 80,
    298, 331, 385, 392
  learning styles 76, 190
  mean 21
  norm-referenced 87
  preparation 50, 55
  problems 56, 181, 183-187,
    190, 216, 389
  reliability 37, 51, 80, 394
  retesting 87
  scoring 47, 65, 73, 80, 387
  scoring patterns 80, 391
  self-concept 47, 386
  standard deviation 21, 48-49,
    71, 292, 387-388
  standard scores 47-48, 80
  standardized 47-50, 68, 83, 102,
    292, 387-388, 390, 397
  teacher-made 64-65
  validity 70, 73-74, 394
thinking skills 37, 323, 340, 373

Toronto 371
  University of Toronto 378, 382
travel 127, 142, 168-170, 176, 308

U
underachievement 80, 205, 207,
  209
uneven profile of abilities 295
United States 255, 288, 363, 371
University of Toronto Schools 140
university-based resource centers
  363, 378

V
Vancouver 371
victims 243

W
web-based information 320
Wechsler Adult Intelligence Scale,
  Revised 71
Wechsler Intelligence Scale for
  Children 47-48, 71, 396
Wechsler Preschool and Primary
  Scale of Intelligence 71, 388
well-being xiv, 34, 152, 177, 223,
  226, 231, 249, 271
whole-grade acceleration
  136-138, 174, 333
work habits 59, 78, 80, 204, 213,
  264, 340, 346
World Council for Gifted and
  Talented Children 373

Y
young gifted children 256, 285

Z
zone of proximal development 82

About the Authors

Dona Matthews has been teaching, writing, counseling, consulting, and conducting research on giftedness-related issues since 1985. She holds an M.Ed. in Counseling Psychology and a Ph.D. in Special Education (Gifted), both from the Ontario Institute for Studies in Education of the University of Toronto (OISE/UT). She has worked in many capacities to support high-level development in diverse populations, including doing academic research and publishing; consulting to parent, education, and government organizations; teaching at the University of Toronto, Ryerson Polytechnic University, the University of British Columbia, and Hunter College; initiating and directing an extracurricular program for academically gifted children at the University of Toronto Schools; and conducting a busy private practice doing psychoeducational assessment and counseling. In September of 2003, she moved to New York City, where she is Director of the Center for Gifted Studies and Education at Hunter College of the City University of New York.

Joanne Foster holds an M.Ed. in Special Education and Adaptive Instruction, and an Ed.D in Human Development and Applied Psychology, both from the Ontario Institute for Studies in Education of the University of Toronto (OISE/UT). She has worked in the field of education since 1975 and has taken on various responsibilities, including classroom teacher at different grade levels, gifted education program coordinator, resource consultant, professional development leader, community liaison in giftedness issues, and university lecturer. Currently, Dr. Foster teaches Educational Psychology as well as Gifted Studies at OISE/UT to teacher candidates interested in working with high-ability students, and she is the Gifted Education Consultant for the

Toronto Board of Jewish Education. She also consults to other schools, helping teachers fine-tune their programming for special-needs learners. She is a frequent guest lecturer across Ontario for the Association for Bright Children (ABC), serves on a number of educational committees within the Toronto area, and addresses educators across North America on topics pertaining to high-level development.

Other Books from Great Potential Press, Inc.

Helping Gifted Children Soar: A Practical Guide for Parents and Teachers
by Carol A. Strip, Ph.D., with Gretchen Hirsch
Glyph Award Winner!
This user-friendly guidebook educates parents and teachers about gifted issues such as working together, designing curriculum, meeting social and emotional needs, and finding support. Establishes a solid foundation for gifted education.
ISBN# 0-910707-41-3 / 288 pp./ paperback / $17.95 US/ $27.95 CAN

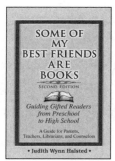

Some of My Best Friends Are Books, 2nd Edition: Guiding Gifted Readers from Preschool to High School
by Judith Halsted
Are you looking for a good, updated reading list for advanced readers? In this new edition, author Judith Halsted shows how books have the power to affect the lives of bright children by allowing them to identify with the characters, situations, and themes they find. Reading books is one way for gifted children to find comfort, support, and understanding.
ISBN# 0-910707-51-0/ 430 pp./ paperback/ $26.95 US/ $41.95 CAN

Re-Forming Gifted Education: How Parents and Teachers Can Match the Program to the Child
by Karen Rogers, Ph.D.
Foreword Book of the Year Award Winner!
Parents may need to negotiate with their child's school for an education plan. The author describes several models for acceleration and enrichment, as well as grouping. For each option, she reports what research says about that option and its benefit to gifted children.
ISBN# 0-910707-46-4/ 512 pp./ paperback / $29.95 US

To order or request a free catalog, contact:

Great Potential Press, Inc.
Toll-free 1.877.954.4200 Fax 602.954.4200
www.giftedbooks.com

In Canada, contact Monarch Books of Canada
Toll-free 1.800.404.7404

Other books published by Great Potential Press, Inc.

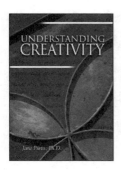

Understanding Creativity
by Jane Piirto, Ph.D.
Dr. Piirto offers many suggestions for enhancing creativity in this comprehensive book. Learn to discover talent through a child's behaviors; and learn how to encourage creativity by valuing work without "evaluation." Talent in a domain, environmental factors, motivation, discipline and practice are all explained as elements of creativity. Well-known creative individuals are used as examples.
ISBN# 0-910707-58-8/ 544 pp./ hardcover/ $49.95 US
      0-910707-59-6/ 544 pp./ paperback/ $29.95 US

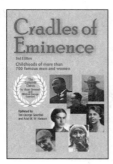

Cradles of Eminence: Childhoods of More than 700 Famous Men and Women
by Victor Goertzel, Mildred Goertzel, Ted Goertzel, and Ariel Hansen
This updated edition of the 1962 classic describes the common childhood experiences of famous people, and includes a chapter with eminent individuals from the last half of the 20th century. The majority of these famous people had strong mothers, felt "different" from others, disliked school, and came from families with very strong opinions. Nearly all showed characteristics that are used today to identify children as gifted.
ISBN# 0-910707-56-1/ 488 pp./ hardcover/ $39.95 US/ $59.95 CAN
      0-910707-57-X/ 488 pp./ paperback/ $24.95 US

Grandparents' Guide to Gifted Children
by James T. Webb, Ph.D., Janet L. Gore, M.Ed., A. Frances Karnes, Ph.D., and A. Stephen McDaniel, J.D., A.E.P., E.P.L.S.
Grandparents, due to greater life experience, may often be the ones to realize, even before parents, that a child is gifted, and that the child will need additional emotional and intellectual support. The authors offer many suggestions for building a bond with a grandchild and for leaving a legacy of memories.
ISBN# 0-910707-65-0/ 314 pp./ paperback/ $19.95 US
      0-910707-68-5/ 544 pp./ large print paperback/ $24.95 US

To order or request a free catalog, contact:
Great Potential Press, Inc.
Toll-free 1.877.954.4200 Fax 602.954.4200
www.giftedbooks.com

In Canada, contact Monarch Books of Canada
Toll-free 1.800.404.7404

Other books published by Great Potential Press, Inc.

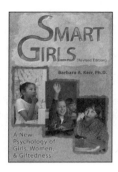
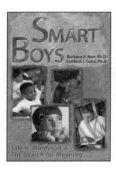

Videos from Great Potential Press, Inc.

Available in DVD or VHS

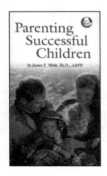